LEARNING CIVIL PROCEDURE

LEARNING CIVIL PROCEDURE

David Dittfurth
St. Mary's University

CAROLINA ACADEMIC PRESS
Durham, North Carolina

Library of Congress Cataloging-in-Publication Data

Dittfurth, David A.
  Learning civil procedure / by David Dittfurth.
      p. cm.
  ISBN-13: 978-0-89089-554-2 (alk. paper)
  ISBN-10: 0-89089-554-6 (alk. paper)
  1. Civil procedure--Study and teaching--United States. I. Title.

KF277.P7D58 2007
347.73'5--dc22

                                                        2007008946

CAROLINA ACADEMIC PRESS
700 Kent Street
Durham, North Carolina 27701
Tel: (919) 489-7468
Fax: (919) 493-5668
www.cap-press.com

Printed in the United States of America.

to Amirra, in appreciation

for my happiness

CONTENTS

Part II
Forum Choice

Part III
Preparing the Case

PART IV

ADJUDICATION

TABLE OF CASES

PREFACE

Learning civil procedure is not an easy task, and the materials may lack the glamour or the emotion of, say, a course in constitutional law. Nevertheless, the rules, laws, and practices of civil procedure provide vitally important information for lawyers.

Civil procedure is about litigation, and lawyers are all about litigation. Some may brag that they never go to court, but even they must study what the courts do. They must, because the law is molded in courts, in litigation. The raw material of the Constitution, or of federal statutes, must be refined and given human-sized meaning. That's what courts do, and do on a daily basis.

In order to better learn about courts, one needs to watch how the procedural machinery guides their operations. And one of the best ways of understanding that machinery is to watch it while it works with the substantive law that is its fuel. In this book, I talk much about causes of action and their elements, and about how one goes about presenting or defeating them. It is this interplay between substance and procedure that gives shadow and depth to a course in Civil Procedure.

It's empowering when you realize that you're beginning to understand how the basic judicial machinery works, and that you know how to use it. As you read more cases in Civil Procedure, you will begin to notice the moves and countermoves of lawyers attempting to gain leverage through procedural devices or through just plain tricks. In the adversarial system of our courts, most of the work of litigation is left to the advocate, and your job is to become one of those advocates. You are also learning how to be a competent lawyer because competence, supplemented by diligence, is your first ethical obligation to a client.

The Civil Procedure course is a good place to begin your journey to professional competence. Good luck with that, and I hope this book helps you along.

David Dittfurth
November 1, 2006

ACKNOWLEDGMENTS

I wish to thank my research assistant, Todd Simons, for his tireless work in helping me in this endeavor and in doing research for the book.

My thanks and my love go to Amirra K. Dittfurth for reading the manuscript, for making extremely helpful suggestions, and for keeping me sane during the writing process.

LEARNING CIVIL PROCEDURE

PART I

INTRODUCTION AND BACKGROUND

CHAPTER 1

INTRODUCTION TO LAW

A. TERMINOLOGY

Civil action—This is a lawsuit brought most frequently, but not always, by private parties who seek the major civil judicial remedies of damages, injunctive relief, or restitution. Unlike a criminal prosecution, courts do not impose the punishment of jail time for violation of the civil law.

Common law—This is a term that has various meanings. It refers to the law created by the courts at common law in England and in the United States. It also refers to the nature of that law as judge-made, and one might still distinguish the common law from the positive law of statutes. State, but not federal, courts have a general power to create or alter the common law.

Constitution—This is the document that contains the basic framework for our system of governance. In its original form, it created and empowered the federal government. In the amendments to it, we have established the constitutional protections for individual liberties in respect to government.

Criminal action—The criminal law is almost exclusively statutory, and is characterized by its remedy of incarceration (jail time) and by the fact that the government always initiates and prosecutes a criminal case.

Federal—This adjective most frequently will be used to characterize our national government. The word can also be used to characterize our overall government structure, which features distinct and independent roles for national and local governments.

Procedural law (civil)—This phrase refers to the rules that govern the manner or means by which a civil action must be adjudicated. The primary procedural guides for litigation in federal district courts would be the Federal Rules of Civil Procedure and the Federal Rules of Evidence.

Statute—Legislatures consist of elected representatives of the people, and these bodies enact laws that usually must be presented to the chief executive for approval. Once approved, these laws will be included in the body of statutes that bind those within the authority of that legislature.

Substantive law—This phrase refers to the law that regulates our behavior or conduct. Law has a substantive effect in its primary stage when it prohibits certain conduct, such as reckless activity, and a further substantive effect when it creates a mechanism, such as a suit for damages in tort, by which the prohibition can be enforced.

B. Substantive Law

1. The Constitution of the United States

The Constitution of the United States was drafted at the Constitutional Convention in Philadelphia in 1787. That document contained seven articles. It was presented for ratification in conventions held in the states, and was ratified by the requisite number of states in 1788.

We tend to think of the Constitution, depending on one's metaphoric preference, as either our legal foundation or our highest law. In particular ways, the Constitution is the supreme law of the land; it even says so in the Supremacy Clause of Article VI. However, the Constitution has two primary functions: it enumerates the powers that can be exercised by the three branches of the Federal Government, and it restrains all government from acting in certain ways. The primary function of the Constitution, as it was originally ratified in 1788, was to create a new central government. It did so by dividing that government's powers among the legislative, executive, and judicial branches (Articles I, II, and III), and by enumerating relatively specific powers for each.

Article I creates the two Houses of Congress and confers on this legislative body powers to:

- pay the Debts and provide for the common Defence and general Welfare of the United States;
- define and punish Piracies and Felonies committed on the high Seas, and Offenses against the Law of Nations;
- declare War, grant Letters of marque and Reprisal, and make Rules concerning Captures on Land and Water;
- raise and support Armies;
- provide and maintain a Navy;
- make Rules for the Government and Regulation of the land and naval Forces;
- provide for calling forth the Militia to execute the Laws of the Union, suppress Insurrections and repel Invasions;
- provide for organizing, arming, and disciplining, the Militia, and for governing such Part of them as may be employed in the Service of the United States.

By this listing of specific powers, the Constitution limited federal governmental power. The Congress, unlike a state legislature, can legislate only where it has been given authority in one of these enumerated areas.

Article II of the Constitution creates the federal executive branch and declares that "[t]he executive Power shall be vested in a President of the United States of America," and that the "President shall be Commander in Chief of the Army and Navy of the United States, and of the militia of the several States." Article III of the Constitution creates, or authorizes the creation, of the judicial branch of the federal government. It confers the judicial power on "one supreme Court, and in such inferior Courts as the Congress may from time to time ordain and establish." That judicial power includes, for example, authority over controversies between citizens of different states and cases arising under the Constitution and laws of the United States.

The Supreme Court has, at different times, interpreted several of the enumerated legislative powers so broadly that congressional power seemed almost limitless. We currently live in a time of emergency that has been used to enhance the power of the President over both our relations with foreign governments and over our domestic affairs. The Supreme Court has even exercised its own power rather liberally in recent times. Nevertheless, the basic principle of constitutional law holds that the national government is a government of limited powers—limited in its exercise to those specific powers delegated to its branches in the Constitution. To make this implicit principle explicit, the Tenth Amendment states that "[t]he powers not delegated to the United States by the Constitution, nor prohibited by it to the States, are reserved to the States respectively, or to the people." If one can disregard the clumsiness of the prose, it merely says that those powers not delegated to the national government are reserved to the states.

The separation of government power among three branches was designed to prevent any one branch from gathering to itself too much power. Furthermore, the reservation of power for the states preserves the benefits of our federal system. In that system, governance of the day-to-day affairs of the ordinary citizen has been left to state and local governments. The ordinary citizen thus has more contact with the government over which he is likely to have more influence. In this light, the separation of powers and the federal system both have been designed to retard the momentum toward tyranny and to protect the ability of voters to control their governors.

During the ratification debates in the state conventions, those who opposed ratification of the Constitution argued that the document gave too much power to the central government. In response to these concerns, the first Congress proposed 12 additions to the Constitution, and 10 of those were ratified and made amendments in 1791. These first 10 amendments to the Constitution are known as the Bill of Rights. The amendments created significant limitations on the power of the new federal government. Originally, however, the provisions of the Bill of Rights restricted only the federal government and did not limit the power of states. Until the Civil War, the states were free to engage in government action that was not permitted to the federal government.

The Thirteenth Amendment, Fourteenth Amendment, and Fifteenth Amendment were ratified after the Civil War, and these amendments included major constitutional limitations on the power of state and local governments. In addition, through judicial interpretation, the Supreme Court has made many of the important individual liberties contained in the Bill of Rights applicable to state and local governments. The Court accomplished this expansion through the still-controversial process of selective incorporation into the Fourteenth Amendment. The Court has thus incorporated most of the important rights in the first eight amendments into the concept of liberty protected by the Due Process Clause of the Fourteenth Amendment. Because the Fourteenth Amendment protects individuals from state action, incorporation of the Bill of Rights provisions includes them in the list of rights that states cannot abridge. As a result, the major constitutional rights that we think of as personal can be asserted against any government official, state or federal.

The amendments to the Constitution, particularly the first eight and the fourteenth, limit the power of government to affect individuals. These provisions, for example, prevent government from restricting free speech; from engaging in unreasonable searches and seizures; from denying life, liberty, or property except through due process; or from denying persons the equal protection of the laws. We derive constitutional rights or liberties from the particular limitations on the power of government over us. Those limitations on government power and the rights they create must be enforced, and that enforcement in law has been primarily through the courts. Oddly enough, we enforce limitations on all of government through courts, another branch of government.

2. Statutory Law

The Congress of the United States enacts federal statutes, subject to the limiting power of the executive to veto. A proposed law must pass both Houses of Congress in order to be presented to the President. Once signed by the President, or passed over a veto, that bill becomes law. Assuming the law was within the power of Congress granted in the Constitution, it becomes the supreme law of the land, preempting any inconsistent law except a limiting provision of the Constitution.

A large body of federal statutes concerns itself with criminal law, all purportedly in areas within the constitutional power of Congress. These laws are enforced by federal prosecutors who bring criminal prosecutions in federal courts. Federal statutes also create administrative agencies, and these agencies, acting within their statutory authority, enforce statutory mandates. Agencies frequently have power to promulgate rules and regulations which add specific prohibitions to the broader statutory mandates, and they have power to take action against those who violate their rules and regulations.

Some federal laws provide rights to sue for violations of federal law. Section 1983 of Title 42 of the United States Code authorizes one who has been deprived of constitutional rights through state action to sue for injunctive or damages relief in court. Other federal statutes, such as the patent or copyright laws, describe the rights established and provide the judicial remedies that may be obtained by one injured through a violation of those rights. Whenever you hear of a new federal statute purporting to protect individuals from harm, learn whether it makes provision for those individuals to seek judicial redress for their injuries.

3. Judicial Law (the "Common Law")

In addition to statutory law, courts also create substantive law. These laws are known as common law and set the precedents that guide subsequent decisions in the courts. The common law courts of England enjoyed one significant power—the power to create judicial remedies for recognized wrongs. These courts are distinguished from the equity courts, which were said to have jurisdiction only when no adequate remedy existed in the common law courts. However, both types of courts created the authority for judicial remedies by formulating judicially acceptable causes of action for litigants. Common law courts are remembered for their primary remedy of damages, and the equity courts are known for their powerful injunctive remedy. In the federal and most state systems today, the common law and law of equity have been merged into one procedural system, and a lawsuit typically is referred to as a civil action, rather than as an action at common law or in equity.

While state courts enjoy power to create private causes of action, the federal courts do not have a general power to create causes of action. The enumerated powers conferred on the judicial branch in Article III of the Constitution have not been construed to give federal courts this general power, and the presumption is that such lawmaking, when within federal power at all, is vested in Congress. Therefore, the federal courts will ordinarily not adjudicate a federal claim for relief, which is the federal name for a cause of action, in the absence of congressional authority.

It should be made clear that, though federal courts do not possess the constitutional power to make or limit causes of action as a general matter, they do enjoy special constitutional authority to create causes of action or defenses to other causes of action. In Texas Industries Inc. v. Radcliff Materials, Inc., 451 U.S. 630 (1981), the Supreme Court listed areas in which federal courts have specialized power to create legal rules. This special federal common law comes from two sources, either directly from the Constitution or by statutory delegation from Congress.

Although commentators differ about the number of categories, the Supreme Court has found direct constitutional authority for federal common law in five types of cases. (1) Federal law may be used to protect the federal government when its operations are threatened by state law or when the lack of a uniform rule would seriously endanger federal programs or interests. See Clearfield Trust Co. v. U.S., 318 U.S. 363 (1943). One can also include in this category the Supreme Court's determination that federal common law establishes the res judicata rules applicable to the enforcement of federal court judgments. See Semtek International Inc. v. Lockheed Martin Corp., 531 U.S. 497 (2001). The Court has also held that, in order to protect the purse of the federal government, contractors who supply products to the federal government according to its specifications cannot be sued under state law for design defects. See Boyle v. United Technologies Corp., 487 U.S. 500 (1988).

(2) In suits between states, the law of one state should not control the dispute. In the absence of federal statutory law, federal common law governs disputes between states when adjudicated in federal court. See, e.g., Kansas v. Colorado, 206 U.S. 46 (1907). The Constitution provides a special forum for such conflicts by conferring original jurisdiction on the Supreme Court in cases in which a state is a party. Congress has given the Supreme Court original and exclusive jurisdiction when states appear on both sides of the litigation. See 28 U.S.C. § 1251(a).

(3) Federal common law also controls disputes implicating the nation's relations with foreign nations because in this area the federal interests are dominant, and state law would make impossible a uniform approach to such matters. See Banco Nacional de Cuba v. Sabbatino, 376 U.S. 398 (1964). (4) Federal courts make the law that governs actions within admiralty jurisdiction. No special body of state admiralty law ever existed. Furthermore, state law would not be appropriate because the events that justify admiralty and maritime jurisdiction routinely arise outside a state's borders. See, e.g., Kossick v. United Fruit Co., 365 U.S. 731 (1961). (5) The Supreme Court has, in addition, established a constitutional damage claim against federal officials to protect individual rights and the federal system from unconstitutional federal action. See Bivens v. Six Unknown Named Agents of Federal Bureau of Narcotics, 403 U.S. 388 (1971). Although a federal statute authorizes constitutional claims for damages against state officials, 42 U.S.C. § 1983, no statute provides this remedy when federal officials cause such harm. The Supreme Court concluded, in effect, that the special obligation of the courts to provide remedies to make effective constitutional limits on government authorized the creation of a constitutional claim for damages.

Special federal common law power can also be exercised within areas of Congress's constitutional authority, with Congress's permission. Here, Congress must have the constitutional power to legislate and must have delegated some of that power to the federal courts. This delegation can be found when

Congress authorizes, either expressly or by necessary implication, federal courts to create federal common law to make effective the congressional plan reflected in the statute. See, e.g., Textile Workers Union of America v. Lincoln Mills of Alabama, 353 U.S. 448 (1957).

C. Law Enforcement

1. Overview

In its primary effect, the substantive law prohibits behavior and thus represents the governing policy in regard to the ordering of individuals' conduct in society. Many people think of the law as a body of written rules that informs the public of what conduct society prohibits. Laws tell us that we may not steal, rob, or kill. We recognize these particular laws as criminal because they proscribe seriously harmful activity for which violators will be prosecuted. We know the police will arrest and incarcerate violators, and that a criminal prosecution can be initiated and maintained by the government's prosecuting attorneys. In a real sense, criminal laws are significant because this powerful enforcement mechanism exists.

In addition to the laws concerning crimes are ones that warn citizens against acting fraudulently in their business activities, negligently in driving their automobiles, abusing their neighbor's property, or breaching their formal agreements. These laws are civil in that they are not enforceable through a criminal prosecution brought by the government. Violators of civil laws therefore do not face the threat of incarceration, which is the primary criminal punishment.

Instead of the incarceration that protects society from criminals and provides its victims with a rough sense of retribution, civil law enforcement provides remedies that seek to repair the harm caused by a defendant's wrongful action. In most instances, the court will award monetary compensation for the plaintiff's injuries or an injunctive order commanding the defendant to cease his wrongful activities. In a civil case, however, the person harmed by a violation of the law must bring her own action in court to remedy the harm. In civil actions, therefore, substantive law not only tells us what actions are prohibited but it also creates, defines, and regulate the rights and liabilities of parties in regard to a violation of that prohibition.

Thus, laws appear to us against a background of their assumed enforcement either through criminal prosecution or civil lawsuits. However, that enforcement can become a reality only through the appropriate legal process in a court. Laws have distinctive significance, therefore, because government enforces them. Moral standards describe a society that can nurture our best qualities, and they inform our thoughts about law. But they are not law unless government threatens enforcement or offers its enforcement mechanisms for their protection.

The connection between law and law enforcement has great significance for one learning the practice of law. A written civil law provides only the first level of information for the lawyer. From this law, one must discover the legal rights that it provides. Legal rights are often thought of as one's right to be free from violations of laws, and that right necessarily depends upon one's ability to respond effectively to that violation. Lawyers see this right to respond in terms of a claim for relief—that is, a right of action in court. Only one who has been harmed by a legal wrong has a right, or standing, to assert a claim. If a legally recognized claim for relief exists, one can legitimately prompt a court to grant a remedy for the harm resulting from the wrong.

2. Private Right of Action (The Cause of Action)

With limited exceptions, one seeking an individualized civil remedy for a violation of legal rights does so in a court. Once asserted in court, these rights and the defenses to them can be played out as a case before a judge and a jury. When the jurisdiction of a court, representing the power of government, has been invoked, the Constitution's requirement of due process protects the opposing party's right to defend himself. These disputants may and most often do resolve their conflict through negotiation and settlement, and courts may provide facilities for mediating conflicts to reach settlements. By contract, some conflicts may be subjected to binding arbitration before entities other than courts, and administrative agencies also play a role in resolving civil disputes in their areas of authority. However, courts stand as the primary mechanism for enforcing civil law rights when the parties cannot settle their differences.

In commentaries, one learns important lessons about the philosophical, political, social, economic, and institutional underpinnings or origins of law. One who is educated in the law must contemplate such matters in order to have a sophisticated stance on the correctness of law and on how laws and legal processes can better serve the general welfare. This is not such a commentary. In this book, we will discuss current procedural rules and their application. However, one might remember that the prevailing details of the legal process are not written in stone; procedural rules are designed by fallible human beings attempting to bring about a fair resolution of legal conflicts. When applied, they may not always succeed.

a. Federal and State Courts

Because ours is a federal system of government, two court systems co-exist: one for each state and one for the federal government. Although significant differences exist between the two systems, both state and federal courts have a number of common characteristics and rules. For example, each system requires a civil litigant to begin by invoking the original jurisdiction of a trial court. That court's jurisdiction (or power) is original in the sense that it is the starting place for a lawsuit. If a party loses in the trial court, she has a right to appeal to an intermediate appellate court. Whoever loses in that appellate court can seek review in the system's supreme court, but parties typically have fewer rights to review in a supreme court.

In the federal system, the trial court is known as a district court. The intermediate federal appellate court is called a court of appeals, and the highest court is the Supreme Court of the United States. Most states have similar names for the courts at these levels although there are some notable exceptions. Subsequent chapters discuss in more detail the federal court system and the limits on the judicial power of federal courts.

b. Jurisdiction in Trial Courts

A trial court's power is dependent on two major elements—its jurisdiction and a claim for relief. The party who invokes a trial court's power, the plaintiff, must include allegations in her complaint showing that a federal court has subject matter jurisdiction and that she complains of a wrong for which the law allows judicial relief. In addition, the party being sued, the defendant, may challenge the court's power over him by raising an issue of the court's personal jurisdiction. If the court finds that it lacks either subject matter or personal jurisdiction, it must dismiss the plaintiff's complaint. If it concludes that the plaintiff has failed to state or prove a claim for relief, it must decide the case on its merits in favor of the defendant.

Before courts can act, however, they must have authority to decide cases on their merits. In legal terms, courts must have jurisdiction (authority to dictate the law). Two types of jurisdiction exist: subject matter jurisdiction and personal jurisdiction. A court must have subject matter jurisdiction to decide the type of case that has been brought before it. Federal courts have judicial power over only certain types of cases and over no others. Article III of the Constitution contains a description of these cases. The Constitution of the

United States does not restrict the cases state trial courts can decide, but state courts may be limited by state law according to the amount of damages sought or to the specialized nature of the litigation, such as domestic relations.

A court must also have personal jurisdiction—that is, authority over the defending party—in order to adjudicate a case. The Due Process Clause of the Fourteenth Amendment to the Constitution allows a court located in one state to adjudicate the obligations of resident defendants, but restricts that court's power over nonresidents. Under certain conditions, however, the Due Process Clause allows extraterritorial assertions of power. It allows jurisdiction over a nonresident when, for example, that defendant did business in the forum state and thus caused the plaintiff's claim to arise there.

In federal court, the defendant brings a jurisdictional issue to the court's attention by filing a motion to dismiss the case. If the court denies the motion, the case will go forward, but the defendant can reassert his objection to the trial court's jurisdiction upon appeal of any adverse decision. It should be noted that if a trial court has personal jurisdiction over the defendant, that jurisdiction continues throughout any appeals of the case. In the federal system, a district court's original subject matter jurisdiction establishes the overall authority of federal courts over the case, but other statutes determine when and how the appellate jurisdiction of a court of appeals or of the Supreme Court of the United States can be invoked.

c. Claims for Relief

In addition to threshold questions about jurisdiction, a court cannot give the plaintiff relief unless she can plead and satisfy the requirements of a recognized claim for relief. A claim for relief consists of what, in many states, would be called a cause of action plus the request for an appropriate civil remedy. As approved in 1938, Federal Rule of Civil Procedure 8 adopted the phrase "claim for relief" in order to avoid the various pleading requirements that had been applied in state court practice to the concept of a cause of action. Nevertheless, the substantive features of a claim are the same as those of a cause of action. Both a claim and a cause of action have to be legally accepted by the appropriate jurisdiction, both provide enforcement for those harmed by violations of the civil law, and both require the plaintiff to satisfy specific requirements—called "elements"—before being entitled to a judicial remedy.

Claims for relief thus provide the legal justification for a court to grant the remedy requested by the plaintiff. For example, allegations that show the defendant negligently drove his automobile onto a sidewalk and there injured the plaintiff state a legally recognized negligence cause of action for which courts are authorized to give a remedy. On the other hand, a plaintiff who asserts that she has been emotionally devastated by her fiancé's refusal to show up on their wedding day will not have stated a valid claim for relief in most jurisdictions. On the face of such a pleading, therefore, the jilted plaintiff cannot prevail, and should have her complaint dismissed. The difference between the two complaints comes from the substantive law of claims. Courts must have previously decided that one should be allowed to receive damages for the negligent infliction of personal injury. That legal authority creates the negligence claim for relief. Other precedents will have established the prevailing opinion that one jilted at the altar should not be given a judicial remedy.

The plaintiff must always allege and prove that the defendant's actions violated the law. By definition, a claim for relief will not lie for injuries caused by lawful action. The existence of the claim therefore provides proof that either judge-made, statutory, or constitutional law denounces the alleged actions of the defendant. The law may, however, prohibit certain behavior but choose to enforce that prohibition through the criminal law or by administrative agency action, rather than through a private right of action.

Courts define a claim for relief by insisting that the plaintiff plead and prove certain elements to establish her claim. For example, a breach of contract claim for relief must satisfy the following allegations:

- that a valid contract existed;
- that the plaintiff and defendant are in privity;
- that the plaintiff performed her contractual obligations;
- that the defendant breached the contract; and
- that this breach caused the plaintiff injury.

If the plaintiff's lawyer drafts her complaint, it will likely include allegations that provide some factual basis for concluding that each of these elements can be satisfied in this case. In preparing for trial, the plaintiff's lawyer will seek out evidence to prove the facts that support each conclusion reflected in these elements. The defendant, on the other hand, will seek evidence to disprove, for example, that a valid contract existed. If the defendant's evidence convinces the jury that the so-called material facts do not support each and every element of the breach of contract cause of action, the plaintiff cannot recover a judicial remedy. The plaintiff bears the burden of pleading and the burden of proof in supporting her case in every element. Failure to satisfy any one element of a cause of action means that the plaintiff loses her suit as a matter of law—the law that authorizes the cause of action so long as all elements are satisfied.

Courts and legislatures create claims for relief to compensate those who have been injured and not to provide a forum for scholars and other busybodies who are interested in debating legal questions. For related reasons, difficult-to-prove injuries, such as mental anguish, may convince courts that a claim for remedying that harm should not be created. Even proof that a defendant caused the plaintiff's injury may fail the requirement of proximate causation when, for policy reasons, the harm is too indirect.

To give relief for a claim, courts use a variety of remedial orders to punish a defendant or compensate a plaintiff, or to prevent the continuation of the wrongful action. Court-ordered remedies include damages, injunctive relief, declaratory judgments, or less common variations. The common law courts of England created the notion that plaintiffs could be compensated for all sorts of injuries by making the defendant pay money damages. The courts of equity came into being, in part, because the damage remedy was not adequate to relieve certain forms of injury. For example, a plaintiff who is threatened with an irreparable injury (or one not adequately remedied by damages) could have a court of equity issue an order demanding that the defendant not engage in the harmful action. Much later, the states and the federal government enacted declaratory judgment statutes providing courts with power to issue non-coercive judgments in which they declared the rights and obligations of the parties. These judgments do not order the payment of damages or enjoin the defendant's actions, but a subsequent violation of the declaration can be enforced by those remedies.

d. Affirmative Defenses

After the plaintiff pleads a claim for relief, the defendant gets an opportunity in the answer to respond. He might plead that the plaintiff has failed to state a valid claim or deny the facts alleged to prove an element of the claim. A defendant may also plead affirmative defenses which show that the plaintiff cannot prevail because of something beyond the elements of the claim. For example, statutes of limitations set a time limit—in years from the time the claim arose—within which a claim for damages must be commenced in court. These statutes reflect the dual notion that, after some period of years, a defendant should be free of any worry about a lawsuit and also that, because of delay, he may have lost witnesses and other valuable evidence. If the plaintiff has not brought suit in time, this defense can defeat the claim even though it is otherwise valid.

D. "Thinking Like a Lawyer"

1. Stare Decisis

An appellate court's opinion has legal authority beyond the parties to the instant case because its rulings bind the lower courts within its jurisdiction and influence other courts. An appellate court's published opinion influences the resolution of subsequent cases, and we describe this effect as the doctrine of stare decisis. This doctrine, simply stated, means that courts follow the law announced in previous cases, even their own previous decisions. Therefore, in current cases, a court will look for the precedents—that is, the decisions of appellate court cases involving similar issues.

Taken on its face, the doctrine of stare decisis describes a legal universe in which no change is possible. If only past decisions had legitimacy, the law would be wholly static and would offer no avenue for the creation of new rules. And, under the influence of this doctrine, courts often cling to a precedent long after the rule it announced has become dysfunctional. Even more frustrating is the judicial tendency to explain new results by reference to a rule that is, in reality, being abandoned. At some point, however, courts abandon these fictions and construct a new rule when the old one no longer works. Rules no longer work when the conditions that justified their creation have changed substantially or ceased to exist. Thus, changing conditions or attitudes change judicial opinions which, in turn, change the law.

At the end of the Nineteenth Century, the Supreme Court held in Plessy v. Ferguson, 163 U.S. 537 (1896), that separation of the races in public facilities did not violate the Equal Protection Clause when equal facilities were provided. By 1954, the Court had realized that even if equal facilities were provided (and they never were), separation of the races was inherently unequal. In its decision in Brown v. Board of Education, 347 U.S. 483 (1954), the Court therefore rejected the old perception of reality (and the attitudes it supported) and reinterpreted the Equal Protection Clause to include a powerful concept of social justice.

Although precedents guide the decision of current cases, a single precedent cannot tell us the time for change. Furthermore, the changing of rules does not occur according to the dictates of some meta-rule. Unless Congress changes the law through a statute, law changes when and to the extent judges believe that reason demands a change. Their reasoning takes account of related legal principles, public policy, or concepts of the public interest. Judges do not (or would not admit that they) decide based on unadorned personal preferences or prejudices. Judges, though, are not neutral beings able to decide cases free of subjective influences. For this reason, procedures, ritual, and protocol are installed to retard their ability to rely solely on personal whim. Therefore, the requirements of adversarial presentation based on precedent and of explanation of judicial decisions by reference to precedents maintain the doctrine of stare decisis.

2. Translating a Conflict into a Claim

A cynic might say that lawyers always look backwards as they move forward. Lawyers must take care to consider the authoritative judicial statements of the past because these will influence the resolution of their clients' problems. In this sense, a lawyer becomes adept at predicting judicial decisions in her cases by comparing those cases with ones the courts have already decided. This exercise is founded on the assumption that courts will follow the precedents. In obtaining this skill, however, one must also recognize that the doctrine of stare decisis has a great deal of play in its joints. In reality, a lawyer's prediction of an outcome is always based on her belief that she can formulate legal arguments and prove the facts necessary to achieve that outcome.

In the beginning, a lawyer listens to people tell their stories of need or woe. Listening constitutes an important beginning of the legal process. A lawyer listens in order to draw out those facts which illuminate legal possibilities, and clients consult lawyers primarily to gain information about, or protection from, these possibilities. The stories that people tell their lawyers vary in character according their needs. Many people approach lawyers without a concern for imminent legal trouble but only to arrange their affairs in contemplation of their own debility or demise. Others visit law offices as they would a dentist—only when existing problems drive them there. These are the people whose stories are of primary concern here.

The stories of people with imminent problems might well be characterized as laments, as opposed to the calmer and less emotional stories of those who wish to have a trust created or a will drafted. Laments might further be divided according to their dominant themes. One theme is that of accusation and another of justification. The accuser laments the wrong done her by another and seeks protection, compensation, or retribution through the law. In listening, a lawyer might unconsciously abstract this person by thinking of her as a potential plaintiff. The other side would be a story dominated by justification indicating that its author has done something to someone else and that this someone else refuses to forgive and forget. This unforgiving other person may now threaten to play the role of plaintiff, and the person before our hypothetical lawyer fears being forced to play the role of defendant.

Regardless of the story's theme, those who present their lament seek from the lawyer information about their rights or wrongs, advice about further action, representation in regard to potential litigation, and sympathy. (Although sympathy is not a concern of this book, the lawyer who does not recognize and respond to this need will inevitably be less client-friendly in serving those who seek his or her assistance.)

Assume a client complains of a wrong done her by another and wants compensation. Also assume that the person who caused her injury refuses to compensate her with a large sum of money. If a settlement cannot be reached, the injured person might consider using judicial coercion. A lawyer consulted by this client must predict whether she has a legal right to recover damages under the circumstances of the case. In order to make this prediction, the lawyer consults pertinent legal authority. This authority may be found in a body of statutes or in other legislative forms, such as in a constitution, but these authorities, though helpful, will ordinarily be too generalized in form to answer the particular questions of the client's case. In most instances, therefore, the lawyer must find decided cases in which a court gave a remedy to one harmed in the same manner as the client.

First, the lawyer needs to know whether the law allows the client to obtain a court order or judgment for compensation. The potential for obtaining that relief exists only when the available court system recognizes the client's problem as one which can fit an established pattern. One must begin with the assumption that a person cannot obtain relief in court for every wrong. Only when the facts fit a pattern recognized by courts in previous cases as stating a claim for relief can the client, as a plaintiff, hope to prevail in court. If the allegations made in a complaint—the formal document a plaintiff must file to begin a lawsuit—have been accepted as sufficient for judicial relief in the past, the plaintiff has established at least a right to invoke the court's power.

3. Learning to Think as a Lawyer Would

Law professors often begin first-year courses by teaching a basic form of legal reasoning. This form of reasoning consists largely of the application of precedents to hypothetical cases or problems. Students learn to "think like a lawyer" by being asked to predict how a court would decide the issues raised in a hypothetical or by being asked to make an argument for one side based on those precedents. We presume that lawyers—or at least well-prepared lawyers—go through a similar intellectual process before advising clients or when preparing for litigation.

Once students understand how to predict outcomes or to make legal arguments in easy cases, professors tend to make the hypotheticals more difficult. In fact, professors rarely spend time asking a student to handle easy cases—that is, those which include only the relevant facts found in a precedent. Instead, they prefer to formulate perverse hypotheticals which incompletely compare with the precedents. Most entertaining are those which have facts in common with precedents that reach contrary results. By mixing the facts in a hypothetical, the professor can torment the uninitiated by asking whether the rule of one or of the other should control. In some instances, this exercise highlights the relative significance of particular facts, thereby pointing the way to the dominant conceptual justification in that area of the law. Such an exercise can also show that no clear answer can be given. At this point, students are being asked to create legal arguments rather than to give simple answers.

A lawyer begins by researching the law to clarify the requirements of available claims and of the defenses to them. She also gathers information which she must transform into evidence sufficient to prove her side of the disputed issues. Beginning law school courses concentrate on appellate court opinions that deal only with legal issues that arise in respect to an established set of facts. In this sense, law students begin by learning only one part, the reasoning part, of a lawyer's job. Trial advocacy, research and writing, and other practice-skills courses teach students about the second part—the creation of facts. If the law school offers live-client clinical programs, a student can obtain actual training in dealing with clients, in negotiating with opposing lawyers, in gathering and presenting evidence, and in seeking to persuade judges.

a. Identifying the Problem

One begins legal analysis by discovering the specific issue that presents a critical problem. We generally define "the issue" as that legal question for which the law offers no easy resolution and whose answer determines the outcome of the case, or at least gives one side a significant advantage. Divining the issue often is more than half of the battle in resolving it. The second step is, of course, analysis of the issue one discovers. In the law, that analysis is most effectively presented in the argument and counter-argument form explained in the following section.

To discover an issue hidden in a mass of facts, start with the pertinent general rule of law. General rules are just that—general—and legal problems tend to arrive encased in a tangle of specific facts. As you learn general rules, you also learn more specific rules that deal with the various aspects of the same problem or which define elements of the general rule. For example, one might state a general rule for personal jurisdiction as follows: *A court cannot consti-*

tutionally assert jurisdiction over a defendant found outside the forum state un-less that defendant has had minimum contacts with that state. This rule tells you to be alert to a court's extraterritorial assertion of personal jurisdiction. There-fore, if you notice that a nonresident defendant has been served outside the forum state, you know that a valid assertion of jurisdiction depends on find-ing that he has had legally sufficient minimum contacts with the state.

Next, however, you need a statement of the rules defining minimum con-tacts. You will have learned that minimum contacts can exist when the de-fendant has had *continuous and systematic, though unrelated, contacts with the forum state* (general jurisdiction) or *less numerous, but purposeful, contacts with the forum state that give rise to the cause of action* (specific jurisdiction). Upon reviewing the facts of your case, you might dispose of general jurisdiction as a possibility because the defendant had too few contacts. By elimination, therefore, you have discovered that minimum contacts must be shown and that the only likely form would be specific jurisdiction.

At this point, you have narrowed the problem to one about the particular requirements for proving specific jurisdiction. Suppose the facts seem insuf-ficient to prove that the defendant's contacts were "purposeful." If you have a vague unease about purposefulness, you should turn to the pertinent cases to find a reason for that unease. Assume you find a Supreme Court case which resembles your problem, and the Court decided that its defendant had not acted purposefully. You now know that the purposefulness of the defendant's contacts is the issue, or at least one of them.

b. Making a Legal Argument

In the second stage of analysis, you shift from a neutral to an adversarial stance. This adversarial stance does not, however, allow you to become a blind partisan. You must imaginatively take one side of the issue and try to present that side's argument on the issue. For example, begin by taking the precedent you have found and compare its facts and reasoning to your case. Ask why the Court concluded that the facts in its case disproved purposefulness. Why did those facts prove the opposite of purposefulness? By going through this exer-cise, you will be discovering the legal significance of those facts to the Court. Now, return to your own case and look for any difference between the facts of your case and the precedent. One can always distinguish cases, but you must look for significant differences—that is, differences which, if present in the precedent, might have altered the outcome.

As you discover legally significant factual differences, you will be preparing an argument to distinguish this precedent. If you make a persuasive distinction, you avoid the decisive authority of that precedent. To complete your argument, find a favorable precedent which, if applied, would support personal jurisdiction in your case. Argue that this favorable case is a precedent because its significant facts, which proved the existence of purposefulness, are essentially identical to the facts in your case. If that court's line of reasoning would be undisturbed by inserting your facts, you can argue that the case supports jurisdiction in your case.

In summary, you discover the issue largely through application of rules, and you resolve it by comparing and distinguishing the cases in that area of the law. This use of the precedents supplements your application of the general rules and appears in the form of opposing legal arguments. To construct a legal argument, one shows how the facts relevant to the issue are similar to those of a favorable precedent. If an unfavorable precedent exists, that precedent must be distinguished by showing that its significant facts are different. As a further benefit of this argument and counter-argument form of analysis, you assume a perspective that allows you to weigh the persuasiveness of the opposing arguments, and to make a knowledgeable prediction about a future court's decision on that issue.

Because issues arise out of the clash of adversarial presentations, this form of analysis mimics the intellectual work of lawyers. In addition, courts make decisions on troublesome issues in the context of these conflicting interpretations of the precedents. By assuming that perspective, you benefit by making your prediction with the same information a court would use.

E. Outlining Cases and Rules

One cannot hope either to understand or to use well the decisions of appellate courts or the Federal Rules of Civil Procedure without first outlining them. Briefing is the technique used to outline appellate court opinions. Only through briefing can one break into understandable pieces what may appear incomprehensible, or at least less memorable, as a whole. The creation of a written brief also provides practice in the analysis of cases. This essential intellectual skill is one that should be acquired early and honed frequently. A lawyer cannot well serve his clients if has graduated from law school without mastering the basic skill of quickly pulling the essential value from a precedent.

As samples, I have included a brief of the Supreme Court's decision in *Pennoyer v. Neff* and an outline of Rule 11 of the Federal Rules of Civil Procedure.

1. Sample Brief of *Pennoyer*

Pennoyer v. Neff
Supreme Court, 1878

FACTS:
1. J.H. Mitchell sued Marcus Neff for unpaid legal fees in Oregon state court. Neff was not a resident of Oregon, and Mitchell provided him notice of this suit only through publication of information about the suit in a newspaper in Oregon. For this reason, Neff apparently failed to learn of the suit in time to appear and defend himself. As a result, the state court granted Mitchell a default judgment for $300 against Neff **in February 1866.**
2. Neff obtained title to land in Oregon from the federal government during **March 1866.** After learning that Neff had obtained title to this land, Mitchell "executed" his judgment by having the land sold in a "sheriff's sale" to Sylvester Pennoyer. Mitchell recovered the $300 from the sale's proceeds.
3. Neff later learned of this sale and sought to clear his title by suing Pennoyer in the <u>United States Circuit Court</u> in Oregon. [The circuit courts were the primary *federal* trial courts at the time.] The circuit court held for Neff, finding that the affidavit filed by Mitchell to satisfy the state law requirement for using newspaper publication as a means of service was deficient under Oregon law.
4. Pennoyer obtained review in the Supreme Court through a writ of error; he is therefore listed as "plaintiff in error." [No intermediate federal appellate court then existed.]
ISSUE: Whether Mitchell's judgment was invalid for lack of personal jurisdiction? [If so, Pennoyer's title, which depended on Mitchell's judgment, would be invalid.]
HELD: Mitchell's judgment was invalid because the Oregon state court failed to satisfy the Due Process Clause of the Fourteenth Amendment to the U.S. Constitution. The Oregon state court did not have *in personam* jurisdiction because Neff was not personally served within the territorial jurisdiction of that state, and it did not have *in rem* jurisdiction because judicial authority was not asserted over the land at the beginning of the litigation through seizure. Without jurisdiction, the Oregon court had no constitutional power to issue a valid judgment against Neff.

REASONING:
1. The courts had established two (territorial) principles of jurisdictional power, which are: (a) A state has exclusive power over persons or property within its borders, but (b) no state may exercise direct authority over persons

or property outside its borders. These principles can be best understood in the context of co-equal states, and they provide a means by which the conflicting claims of power by these states can be accommodated.

2. These jurisdictional principles had been used to condition the constitutional requirement that each state give full faith and credit to the judgments of other states. The courts of one state need give full faith and credit only to sister-state judgments founded on proper jurisdiction. However, the full-faith-and-credit requirement didn't apply here because the Oregon judgment was being challenged in Oregon.

3. In 1868, however, the Fourteenth Amendment was ratified, and it contains a Due Process Clause, which prohibits a state from depriving "any person of life, liberty, or property, without due process of law." The Court held in this case that the requirement of due process incorporates the two established principles by which a state court's jurisdiction is to be judged, and, unlike the Full Faith and Credit Clause, the Due Process Clause can restrict enforcement of a judgment even within the state that issued it.

4. The Supreme Court then reasoned in the following manner:

- Pennoyer's title exists solely because of Mitchell's Oregon judgment. Therefore, his title can prevail only if Mitchell's judgment was issued with proper jurisdiction, as required by the Due Process Clause.
- Constitutionally acceptable jurisdiction can exist only in one of two forms: (1) *in personam* jurisdiction, through power over the defendant's person; or (2) *in rem* jurisdiction, through power over the defendant's property.
- The Oregon state court did not have *in personam* jurisdiction over Neff because it did not formally assert its power by serving him with process while he was physically located within the borders of that state. Without this symbolic assertion of power over the defendant while found inside the state, the Oregon court appears to be exercising direct authority over an outsider in violation of the second principle.
- The Oregon court did not have *in rem* jurisdiction because it can assert that jurisdiction only by the formal seizure of local property at the commencement of litigation. In order to satisfy the first principle, a court's authority depends on its proper assertion of power at the outset of litigation.

5. The decision in this case does not affect three exceptional sets of circumstances.

- State courts have long asserted jurisdiction over suits for the termination of marital status brought by domiciliaries of that state and against spouses who cannot be served locally with personal service. Alternative

methods of service have been deemed sufficient to support divorce jurisdiction. [That jurisdiction does not, however, support a money judgment against the absent spouse for child support or alimony.]
- A corporation is *deemed* to be "present" only in the state of its incorporation, but it has no right to do business in other states free of reasonable restrictions. Other states may, therefore, condition the grant of the right to do business upon a corporation's consent to suit in those states.
- A state in which a corporation is incorporated can, arguably, specifically authorize its courts to assert jurisdiction to enforce its corporate law against that corporation's officers and shareholders even though they reside in other states. [*But see Shaffer v. Heitner.*]

2. A Sample Outline of Rule 11

One should ordinarily copy the language of a Rule into an outline because that language may be organized or chosen to create a special meaning. However, when following that language closely does not seem necessary, it may help to change the Rule's wording or organization to make its demands more understandable. Making sense of a Rule is the first purpose of an outline, and therefore your outline must make sense to you. To further accomplish that purpose, I have included comments made by the Advisory Committee, which drafted and proposed the Rule, to answer questions I had about the variety of sanctions available.

The second purpose of an outline is to put the Rule in a form that will be usable when you have to study for an exam. In making your outline, begin by recognizing that the professor covered only certain parts of the Rule. Unless he's a bigger jerk than you thought, he will not make the exam depend on material he did not cover in the course. Trust that assumption and outline only those parts of the Rule covered in class. When you come to the few days that you will be able to set aside for exam preparation, your time should not be wasted by reading the Rules. If your outline has been designed to make sense to you and to explain only that which was covered in class, you can spend much less time learning the Rule.

A more subtle value of the outline comes from the thought process you go through while going through the outlining process. After making an outline, you will have gained a better understanding of the Rule because the outlining process forces you to think about its function.

RULE 11. SIGNING OF PLEADINGS,
MOTIONS, AND OTHER PAPERS;

REPRESENTATIONS TO COURT;
SANCTIONS

(a) **Signature:** Each pleading, motion, or other paper must be signed by one attorney of record, who must include his or her address and telephone number. An unrepresented party must sign such papers.

(b) **Representations to Court:** By filing such papers, the signer certifies that

- to the best of his or her knowledge, information, and belief
- formed after an inquiry reasonable under the circumstances

   (1) the paper is not filed for an **improper purpose;**

   (2) the **legal contentions** contained therein **are warranted** by existing law or by a nonfrivolous argument for the extension, modification, or reversal of existing law;

   (3) the **factual contentions have evidentiary support** or are likely to have such after further discovery;

   (4) and the **denials of factual contentions are warranted** on the evidence or are reasonably based on a lack of information or belief.

(c) **Sanctions:** After providing notice and an opportunity to be heard, the court may impose a sanction for violation of subdivision (b) upon:

- **attorneys,**
- **law firms,** *[Rule 11(c)(1)(A): Absent exceptional circumstances, a law firm shall be held jointly liable for violations committed by its partners, associates, and employees.]*
- **parties** *that are responsible for a violation. [Rule 11(c)(2)(A): Monetary sanctions may not be awarded against a represented party for violation of subdivision (b)(2)—making an unwarranted legal contention.]*

(1) How a Complaint is Initiated.

   (A) By Motion: A motion for sanctions must concern only Rule 11 and describe the specific conduct that violates subdivision (b). Such motion shall not be filed unless, within **21 days after service** of the motion, the challenged paper is **not withdrawn or appropriately corrected.**

   (B) On Court's Initiative: The court may order a person to show cause why he or she should not be found to have violated subdivision (b). *[Rule 11(c)(2)(B): Monetary sanctions may **not** be awarded on the court's initiative unless the show cause order is issued before a settlement or a voluntary dismissal by the offending party.]*

(2) Nature of Sanctions: Limitations. A sanction is limited to that which is sufficient to deter repetition of the conduct that violates this Rule. Sanctions may include:

- directives of a nonmonetary nature;
  [The Advisory Committee's Notes to the 1993 Amendments suggest a "variety of possible sanctions" to include: striking the offending paper; issuing an admonition, reprimand, or censure; requiring participation in seminars or other educational programs; or referring the matter to disciplinary authorities.]
- an order to pay a penalty to the court;
- or an order for payment to the movant of some or all of the **reasonable attorneys' fees and other expenses** incurred as a direct result of the violation, if (a) imposed on motion and (b) warranted for deterrence. [*Rule 11(c)(1)(A): If warranted, the court may award to the party prevailing on the motion for sanctions the reasonable expenses and attorney's fees incurred in presenting or opposing the motion.*]

(3) **Order.** In its order the court shall describe the conduct determined to violate this Rule and explain the basis for the sanction imposed.
(d) Inapplicability to Discovery. Every subdivision of this Rule (except this one) is inapplicable to discovery matters subject to Rules 26 through 37.

[If you want to practice outlining, try Rule 19(a) and (b). My outline is on the following page, but you might try your hand before looking.]

Rule 19. Joinder of Persons Needed for Just Adjudication

(a) Persons to be Joined if Feasible. A person who is subject to service of process and whose joinder will not deprive the court of jurisdiction over the subject matter of the action shall be joined as a party in the action if (1) in the person's absence complete relief cannot be accorded among those already parties, or (2) the person claims an interest relating to the subject of the action and is so situated that the disposition of the action in the person's absence may (i) as a practical matter impair or impede the person's ability to protect that interest or (ii) leave any of the persons already parties subject to a substantial risk of incurring double, multiple, or otherwise inconsistent obligations by reason of the claimed interest. If the person has not been so joined, the court shall order that the person be made a party. If the person should join as a plaintiff but refuses to do so, the person may be made a defendant, or, in a proper case, an involuntary plaintiff. If the joined party objects to venue and joinder of that party would render the venue of the action improper, that party shall be dismissed from the action.

(b) Determination by Court Whenever Joinder not Feasible. If a person as described in subdivision (a)(1)–(2) hereof cannot be made a party, the court shall determine whether in equity and good conscience the action should proceed among the parties before it, or should be dismissed, the absent person being thus regarded as indispensable. The factors to be considered by the court include: first, to what extent a judgment rendered in the person's absence might be prejudicial to the person or those already parties; second, the extent to which, by protective provisions in the judgment, by the shaping of relief, or other measures, the prejudice can be lessened or avoided; third, whether a judgment rendered in the person's absence will be adequate; fourth, whether the plaintiff will have an adequate remedy if the action is dismissed for nonjoinder.

[Your outline goes here.]

RULE 19—OUTLINE

JOINDER OF PERSONS NEEDED FOR JUST ADJUDICATION

(a) Persons to Be Joined *if* **Feasible.** (*Should a person be joined?*)

A person whose joinder will not destroy subject matter jurisdiction and who is within the court's personal jurisdiction,

shall be joined as a party if —

> (1) in that person's absence complete relief cannot be accorded the parties (*inadequate judgment*), **or**
>
> (2) the person claims an interest relating to the subject of the action and is so situated that disposition in that person's absence may,
>
> > (i) as a practical matter, impair or impede the person's ability to protect that interest (*absent person's interest*), or
> >
> > (ii) leave any of the parties subject to a substantial risk of multiple or otherwise inconsistent obligations because of the claimed interest (*defendant's interest*).

[If joinder makes **venue improper** and the joined **party objects**, that party shall be dismissed from the action.]

(b) Dismissal When Joinder *Not* **Feasible.** (*Should the action be dismissed because the person cannot be joined?*)

If the person cannot be joined, the court shall determine whether in equity and good conscience the action should proceed in his absence or be dismissed.

The factors to be considered by the court are:

(1) whether a judgment rendered in the person's absence might be prejudicial to that person or to those already parties (*interests of absent person and of the defendant*);

(2) whether that judgment will be adequate (*interest of court and of the public*);

(3) whether the plaintiff will have an adequate remedy if the action is dismissed (*interest of the plaintiff*); and

(4) whether, by using protective provisions in the judgment, the shaping of relief, or other measures, the prejudice can be lessened or avoided (*avoid dismissal if possible?*)

CHAPTER 2

OVERVIEW OF FEDERAL TRIAL PROCEDURE

A. Overview

1. Litigation in Trial Court

The problem with an overview is that it is supposed to give you a quick view of the whole when you don't yet understand the parts. Too much explanation of the parts, however, requires the reader to invest time that might be better spent studying the chapter that provides more detailed coverage of the topic. The reader should therefore avoid trying to learn the parts in full and, instead, seek to gain a sense of the process of litigation. To aid in that endeavor, the following stands as a shortened version of the chapter's overview.

After the plaintiff decides to sue, she must decide where she wishes to sue. In finding a location for her case, she will consider the subject matter jurisdiction of federal courts in order to decide whether to file suit in federal court or to keep the suit in state court. She must also choose a court in which venue and personal jurisdiction would be proper. The defendant can forum shop by removing a case to federal court from the state court in which plaintiff files. If he objects to the forum choices of the plaintiff, he can file a motion to dismiss the suit or to change venue within the federal court system.

In order to start her suit, the plaintiff has to tell the court and the defendant what she's complaining about, and she does so in a pleading called a complaint. After receiving a copy of the complaint and the summons (process), the defendant has the option of responding with a preanswer motion seeking to dismiss for a variety of reasons, including lack of subject matter or personal jurisdiction. If that doesn't work, the defendant must serve the plaintiff with a pleading called an answer in which he makes his denials and asserts any affirmative defenses or counterclaims he may have. He may also implead someone whom the plaintiff didn't join in the complaint, but who is liable to him for the payment of his damages to the plaintiff.

After the pleadings stage, the parties have a better idea of what issues will be disputed in the case. They then begin the process of discovering information that can be used as evidence in support of their opposing sides of those issues. The importance of the discovery rules arises from the fact that they allow one party to force the other party and unfriendly witnesses to divulge information that may be helpful to that party.

If the plaintiff cannot find sufficient evidence to support the elements of her cause of action, the law prevents her from winning her case. Because she bears the burden of proving her case, a motion by the defendant showing that she cannot win justifies entry by the court of a judgment as a matter of law. The judge can enter such a judgment before trial in response to a motion for summary judgment or during trial in response to a motion for judgment (or directed verdict).

Only if the court finds that material facts are in dispute under the available evidence, does the case go to trial. The purpose of a trial therefore is to determine factual disputes about the material facts. This fact-finding can be done by a jury or, in the absence of a jury, by the judge. The Federal Rules of Evidence govern the presentation of the evidence, and the jury must consider only the evidence that is properly admitted by the judge under these Rules.

The party who loses in federal trial court has the right to one appeal to the appropriate court of appeals. That court does not take evidence; it looks only at the legal errors that might have been made by the trial court. If this appeal fails, the losing party has the opportunity to ask the Supreme Court of the United States to review the case, but that Court for the most part has complete discretion over its appellate docket and need not hear the case. Some losing parties try another route; they try to start the case going again in another trial court. However, this effort challenges the finality of judgments and is prohibited by the doctrine of res judicata. That doctrine seeks to make certain that every litigant who has had a full opportunity to litigate a case does not get a second chance.

2. Hypothetical

In reading the overview, try at various points to relate the procedural requirements to the following simple hypothetical.

> Jane Doe is a citizen of Texas and the owner of a small business. She approaches you and tells you that she had agreed with Acme, Inc., to deliver 10,000 widgets of a prescribed description on March 1, 2006. She complied with this agreement, but Acme failed to pay her. Acme has been using your client's widgets in its business.

> Further facts are that Acme is incorporated and has its principal and only place of business in Oklahoma. In 2005, Tom Smith, a local agent of Acme, who lives in Dallas, Texas, visited Jane in San Antonio, Texas, at Acme's insistence to urge her to enter a contract with it. Relying on Smith's representations about Acme's good qualities, she flew to Oklahoma to negotiate and sign her contract with Acme.

In negotiation, you have demanded the full payment of $100,000, plus interest, from Acme. Acme's lawyer contends, however, that Jane delivered low-quality widgets even though the parties had agreed she would deliver high quality widgets. Jane admits the parties agreed the widgets should be high-quality, but insists that the widgets she delivered were of that quality.

Assume that under Texas law the plaintiff suing for breach of contract must prove the following elements:

- A valid, enforceable contract exists.
- The plaintiff and the defendant are in privity.
- The plaintiff performed her contractual obligations.
- The defendant breached the contract.
- The defendant's breach caused the plaintiff injury.

See *O'Connor's Texas Causes of Action* 58 (2006). However, assume that Oklahoma law requires a defendant, who contends that the plaintiff did not perform her contractual obligations, to plead and prove this matter as an affirmative defense.

B. Forum Choice

Courts and commentators often speak ill of those who engage in forum shopping. Parties engage in forum shopping in order to find the most favorable judge and jury, to place the suit in a forum that is most convenient to them and most inconvenient to the opposing parties, or to gain the advantage of more favorable substantive or procedural law. More than a few defendants remove cases to federal court largely because they assume that these courts favor corporate interests, or at least carry a bias against the wealth-redistributing characteristics of tort law. The complications inherent in federal litigation favor those who have large law firms on retainer because those firms can afford to maintain specialists in federal practice.

Whatever one may say about the evils inherent in allowing lawyers leeway to seek favorable courts for their clients, the facts of a case and the law often make several forum choices available. If a lawyer represents her client competently, she will consider those choices. If one possible forum gives her client an advantage, she is very likely to choose that forum. Posed in this simple context, the failure to forum shop appears to be legal malpractice. As in every area of discretion, of course, some lawyer will push the envelope too far. However, the law also provides limits on these efforts and, in some instances, corrective devices, such as a motion for change of venue.

The topics considered in this section include some of the more difficult in the book. Questions about jurisdiction, either subject matter or personal, are difficult in the sense that they are not subject to bright-line rules that are easy to apply and that allow confident predictions about outcomes. Another reason for the difficulty comes from the fact that these rules must be applied to constrain the ingenuity of creative legal minds seeking the most favorable forum.

1. Jurisdiction

The word "jurisdiction" typically refers to a court's power to declare the law for a particular case or, more simply, to its legal authority to enter an enforceable judgment. First-year law students encounter two types of jurisdictional problems. Beginning civil procedure courses frequently use federal courts and federal procedure as their models. Therefore, students must learn first about the limited *subject matter jurisdiction* of federal courts. They then discuss the Constitution's limitation on any court's *personal jurisdiction* over defendants. In addition, courts may more generally use the term as a shorthand reference to governmental authority—for example, in speaking of the laws of *each jurisdiction*.

2. Subject Matter Jurisdiction

The United States Constitution created the judicial branch of the federal government. Article III of the Constitution expressly establishes a Supreme Court and authorizes Congress to create lower federal courts. Article III also lists the types of conflicts over which federal courts can constitutionally exercise judicial power—that is, it describes the subject matter of the nine categories of cases over which federal courts can have jurisdiction. For example, it allows federal courts to adjudicate cases arising under the Constitution and other federal laws (federal question jurisdiction), and controversies between citizens of different states (diversity jurisdiction).

Both Article I and Article III state that Congress has power to create federal courts other than the Supreme Court. This power has been interpreted to include a power to regulate the subject matter jurisdiction of those lower federal courts. Because Article III establishes the maximum judicial power of all federal courts, Congress cannot give the federal courts more power than is there allowed. Congress can, however, confer on the lower federal courts less than what Article III allows. In fact, Congress has never conferred on the lower federal courts the maximum judicial power allowed in Article III.

As a result of Congress's power over the lower federal courts, one seeking to sue in federal court must show that a statute authorizes the court to adjudicate her claim for relief. Congress has enacted general jurisdictional grants—over cases arising under federal law (28 U.S.C § 1331) and over controversies between citizens of different states (§ 1332). In these statutes, Congress confers original jurisdiction over the described cases to the United States District Court. The district court is the trial court in the Article III system of courts and is where private civil actions must begin—hence, the use of the term original jurisdiction.

In the hypothetical, the plaintiff has only a state cause of action for breach of contract. All common law causes of action should be presumed to be state created. Federal causes of action generally are creations of federal statutes. This state cause of action could well be brought in a state or federal court because Ms. Doe, as a citizen of Texas, could satisfy the requirements of § 1332(a) and bring a diversity action against Acme, as a citizen of Oklahoma, in federal court.

a. Supplemental Jurisdiction

Title 28 of the United States Code creates in § 1367 the authority for the exercise by federal courts of supplemental jurisdiction. Supplemental jurisdiction supports a court's jurisdiction over joined or subsequent claims that are sufficiently related to a claim over which the court has federal question or diversity jurisdiction. Once an independent ground of jurisdiction exists, other claims may be supported by that original jurisdiction. Supplemental jurisdiction can support claims added by the plaintiff or those asserted by parties other than the plaintiff.

b. Removal

Under 28 U.S.C. § 1441, a defendant has the power generally to remove a case from state to federal court if the plaintiff's case could have been brought originally in federal court. In brief, this means that the case can be removed if it appears from the plaintiff's original pleading in state court that it was based on a federal cause of action or that the requirements of diversity of citizenship jurisdiction can be satisfied.

For example, in the hypothetical, Ms. Doe might wish to bring suit in a Texas state court. If she files her breach of contract action solely against Acme, however, the defendant would be able to remove the case to federal court in Texas. Because Acme could have been sued in federal court on the basis of diversity, it can remove the case to federal court on that basis under these circumstances. As you consider the material on removal in a later chapter, you will discover that removal could be frustrated if Ms. Doe sued Acme in an Oklahoma state court. Ms Doe might also attempt to frustrate Acme's effort to remove to federal court by joining its agent, Mr. Smith, in a Texas state court, if she has a nonfrivolous claim against him.

3. Personal Jurisdiction

A court must have jurisdiction over a defendant before it can exercise power over him. As a general rule, either a state or a federal court can constitutionally exercise power over an individual defendant who is served with process (a copy of the complaint and the summons) while within the state in which the court is located (the forum state). At the other extreme, a state court violates the Due Process Clause of the Fourteenth Amendment if it exercises power over a defendant who was not residing in, not served with process in, and had no related contacts with the forum state. A nonresident can be forced to defend himself in the forum state however if his actions in that state created the cause of action. For instance, Acme sent its local agent to solicit business from Ms. Doe in Texas. That action would seem to show that Acme had purposeful contacts with Texas.

Due process provides a right that is personal to the defendant. If he fails to assert that right, he loses it. A court can thus gain power over a defendant who fails to make a timely or proper objection to an apparently unconstitutional assertion of extraterritorial jurisdiction. In this respect, the constitutional limit on personal jurisdiction differs from an objection to federal subject matter jurisdiction. The latter cannot be lost or waived, and the parties cannot confer subject matter jurisdiction by agreement.

4. Venue

Section 1391 of Title 28, U.S.C., restricts the plaintiff's choice among the available federal district courts. While the Due Process Clause prevents a plaintiff from choosing a court in a distant state, §1391 prevents the plaintiff from bringing suit in an inconvenient federal district in a large, multidistrict state. For example, Texas includes four federal judicial districts and encompasses a vast geographical area. If Ms. Doe decides to bring suit in federal court in Texas, she cannot chose the Southern District of Texas because venue would not be proper in that district. Even though any federal court in Texas has personal jurisdiction over Acme under the facts of the hypothetical, §1391 prohibits suit in a judicial district that would unnecessarily inconvenience the defendant.

However, even if the venue was proper in the United States District Court for the Western District of Texas, Acme could move for a change of venue under 28 U.S.C. § 1404(a) to federal court in Oklahoma. If the convenience of the witnesses and parties, and the interests of justice, favor transfer, a federal court can transfer a case even if the transferee district lies in another state.

C. Pleading and Motions

1. Pleadings

Rule 7(a) establishes only three forms of pleadings: the complaint, the answer, and the reply to an answer that includes a counterclaim. The two most frequently seen are the complaint and the answer. Even when a defendant impleads a third party, he does so through a third-party complaint, and the third-party defendant responds with a third-party answer. The only other pleading required by Rule 7(a) is an answer to a cross-claim. No other pleadings are allowed.

If a party is required to respond to a pleading with his own pleading, Rule 8(d) states that the allegations of the first pleading are admitted unless denied in the responsive pleading. This means that the defendant must file an answer in which he denies any objectionable allegations in the plaintiff's complaint. If he fails to answer or to include in his answer a denial of some objectionable allegation in the complaint, he admits that allegation. On the other hand, the Rules do not allow the plaintiff to file a pleading in response to an answer that does not contain a counterclaim. Therefore, the allegations in such an answer are deemed to have been denied, even though the plaintiff has not formally done so.

2. The Complaint

A plaintiff commences a civil action in federal court by filing a complaint with, and by paying the requisite filing fee to, the clerk of the district court. The local rules of the district should be consulted to discover whether other papers must accompany the complaint. Many districts require the plaintiff to attach a completed cover sheet that summarizes the nature of the claim.

Because the adversary system of presentation predominates in federal and state court systems in the United States, courts presume their role is a passive one. The parties, rather than the court, have the obligation to initiate and present matters needing judicial resolution. Therefore, plaintiffs must affirmatively invoke the jurisdiction of a federal district court and explain the nature of the case. The complaint must contain a statement showing that the court has subject matter jurisdiction, a short and plain statement of the plaintiff's claim, and a request for the relief that the plaintiff seeks. The statement of the claim for relief informs the court about the case and will serve to inform the defendant once service is effected.

In the hypothetical outlined above, Ms. Doe wishes to assert a claim for damages arising because of the defendant's breach of contract. The first element of a breach of contract claim, for example, is that the parties entered a valid contract. However, a conclusory allegation that "a contract was entered" does not provide the other party or the court very much information. A better allegation would be "On January 17, 2006, the plaintiff and the defendant met at the defendant's office in Tulsa, Oklahoma, to sign the contract attached hereto." After allegations showing the specifics of an apparently valid agreement, the plaintiff can allege how the defendant failed to abide by that agreement.

In the hypothetical, the primary issue seems to be whether the widgets she delivered were of the quality required in the contract. Under Texas law, Ms. Doe has the burden of pleading and proving that they were. However, under Oklahoma law, Acme has the burden of pleading and proving that they were not. This allocation of that burden might be one reason to file this suit in an Oklahoma court. The evidence in regard to quality of the widgets may be evenly balanced. If so, the holding on that issue must be against the party who has the burden of proof.

3. Service of Process

Before the defendant can be bound by any adjudication, he must have been given notice of the claim through service of process. The plaintiff typically files an original signed copy of the complaint with the clerk of the district court along with a completed summons form. Once the clerk signs and attaches the court's seal to the summons (the court's order to appear in court), the plaintiff must serve—that is, deliver—a copy of the complaint and the summons to the defendant in accordance with the provisions of Rule 4 of the Federal Rules of Civil Procedure.

Service of process (complaint and summons) fulfills two functions: it acts as the formal assertion of the court's jurisdiction over the defendant, and it notifies the defendant of the suit. Rule 4 allows delivery of process through various methods, including those permitted under the law of the forum state or by the state in which the defendant is served. In addition, Rule 4 allows the plaintiff to mail a notice of the suit to the defendant asking him if he will waive his right to insist on formal service. The mailing of notice does not operate as service of process, but if the defendant signs and returns the waiver-of-service form sent to him by the plaintiff, the plaintiff need not obtain formal service. If the defendant fails to waive service, the costs of formal service can be imposed on him.

4. Preanswer Motion

After service of process, the defendant might wish to object to the court's jurisdiction, to the venue of the suit, to the nature of service, because the claim is legally insufficient, or because the plaintiff failed to join a party who must be included. All of these objections can be included in a Rule 12(b) motion to dismiss filed before the answer. Although these objections can also be included in the answer, a defendant might wish to assert them in a motion to avoid the burden of drafting an answer.

Rule 12(b) allows, but does not require, a preanswer motion. If the defendant responds initially with a preanswer motion, he must do so within the time prescribed for serving an answer. If he does so, he need not serve an answer until the court rules on the motion or orders him to serve an answer.

The filing of a preanswer motion carries one significant danger—that is, the waiver of any waivable objection not included. Four of the objections that can be included in a preanswer motion are waivable. These are the objections to the court's personal jurisdiction, to the venue of the suit, to the service of process, or to the process itself. These objections can be waived—that is, lost—if not included in the first responsive paper served by the defendant.

5. Answer (Defenses and Claims)

The defendant can satisfy his initial requirement of a response by serving the plaintiff with a preanswer motion or with an answer. If the defendant responded first with a preanswer motion to dismiss, he need not answer until the court denies his motion. If his motion is denied, the defendant must file an answer in which he either admits or denies the allegations contained in the plaintiff's complaint. He can also assert affirmative defenses or counterclaims and cross-claims. Regardless of the form of his first response (answer or preanswer motion), it must be filed and served in accordance with Rule 12(a). Once the defendant receives a copy of the complaint and the summons, he typically has 20 days within which to serve the plaintiff with his formal response. The punishment for failure to make a timely response is the entry of a default judgment.

The defendant must *serve* his response (whether an answer or preanswer motion) on the plaintiff's lawyer within the time prescribed and must file it with the court within a reasonable time thereafter. By filing the complaint seeking redress from the court, a plaintiff submits herself to that court's personal jurisdiction. Therefore, the defendant need not follow Rule 4's more burdensome procedures for service. Instead, Rule 5 allows informal delivery of papers filed after the complaint by first-class mail unless those papers extend the court's jurisdiction over someone not currently in the suit. Rule 5 requires this service on a party's attorney, rather than on the party herself, if she is represented by a lawyer.

6. Amendments

For various reasons, a lawyer may conclude that her pleading is deficient. She may have failed to allege facts necessary to satisfy one of the elements of a claim, failed to add a party, or responded ineffectively or inaccurately to a previous pleading. If a lawyer notices such an error, she may cure it by drafting and filing an amendment to the pleading. She must be careful, however, to include all necessary allegations because an amended pleading completely replaces the original. One cannot, therefore, include only the additions in an amendment.

The Federal Rules of Civil Procedure place less importance on pleadings than some state systems, but one still must have a basis in the pleadings for the evidence submitted at trial. If the court's permission is required for an amendment, the defendant might object to the amendment on the ground that it asserts a new claim which is barred by a statute of limitations. Rule 15(c) allows an escape from the application of a limitations bar to an amendment through the concept of "relation back." If the original pleading was filed within the limitations period, the amendment relates back to that time if the claim in the amendment arose from the same transaction as the original claim.

7. Motions to Dismiss

Aside from pleadings, requests for action by the court must be made by written motions. All motions must be served on all parties and filed with the court. Local federal court rules often require that motions raising difficult issues be accompanied by a memorandum of law (a brief) supporting the movant's position. After receiving a copy of a motion, opposing parties may file a response accompanied by their own memorandum of law.

Judges determine many cases prior to trial. A judge can, for example, dismiss a case because the court lacks jurisdiction over the subject matter or the parties. Such dismissals end the case in that court but do not end the plaintiff's claim; they have no direct effect on—are without prejudice to—the plaintiff's right to refile her case in a different court. Involuntary dismissals because of improper venue, defective service, or failure to join a party under Rule 19 also operate without prejudice against refiling. A voluntary dismissal by the plaintiff ordinarily will have no effect on her refiling unless stated otherwise or unless the plaintiff has abused the privilege of early dismissal.

In contrast, a judge may make a summary adjudication of the merits. A summary judgment is an adjudication upon the merits of the case and therefore operates with prejudice against refiling. The plaintiff thus loses the ability to begin again in a trial court unless she successfully overturns the judgment on appeal. A dismissal with prejudice can have the same effect as a summary judgment. For example, the dismissal for failure to state a claim upon which relief can be granted [Rule 12(b)(6)] ends a plaintiff's claim. In order to grant this motion, the court must conclude that the facts alleged by the plaintiff, even if proved, do not support any legal right to recover. Other dismissals also may be given with prejudice as punishment for the plaintiff's failure to abide by court rules or to proceed in a fair and expeditious manner.

D. Parties and Claims

1. Joinder of Parties

Rule 20 of the Federal Rules of Civil Procedure permits joinder of multiple parties if the claims they assert, or the claims asserted against them, arise from the same transaction and have a common question of law or fact. Misjoined parties may be dropped from the case, or they may proceed, or be proceeded against, in a separate action. Rule 20 pertains only to the joining of multiple parties on either side of the civil action in a complaint; it does not control such matters as the addition of a new party, such as a third-party defendant.

Rule 19 deals with persons who have not been joined as a party by the plaintiff but who should be joined before the lawsuit can proceed. The court must be wary of allowing the adjudication of a claim that seriously affects the interests of an absent person or places the defendant at risk of double liability. Because compliance with the procedural conditions for joinder under Rule 19(a) does not supply subject matter jurisdiction, a court may have to consider whether a case can proceed in the absence of a nondiverse defendant.

2. Subsequent Claims

The Federal Rules of Civil Procedure generally permit but do not require defending parties to assert claims they may have which arise from the transaction that gives rise to the plaintiff's claim. An important exception to this general rule appears in Rule 13. That Rule *requires* the assertion by the defendant of a related counterclaim against the plaintiff and *permits* the defendant to assert even unrelated counterclaims. Rule 13 defines as a counterclaim one asserted back against an opposing party. A defendant must assert as a compulsory counterclaim any claim against the plaintiff that arises from the same factual base (transaction or occurrence) that gives rise to the plaintiff's claim. Such a counterclaim is compulsory in that the defendant will lose the claim if it is not asserted in the suit.

In addition to counterclaims against the plaintiff, Rule 13 allows a defendant to include in his answer a cross-claim against a co-defendant. Rule 13(g) permits the assertion only of cross-claims that arise from the same transaction that gives rise to the plaintiff's claim or which represent one defendant's claim that another owes him for some part of his liability to the plaintiff.

A lawsuit can become more complicated if a defendant chooses to file a third-party complaint, making a claim for relief against a new party. Rule 14 allows the impleading of new parties only when the defendant asserts a claim showing that the third-party defendant is or may be liable to the defendant (third-party plaintiff) for all or part of what the defendant may be liable to the plaintiff. Rule 14 implicitly recognizes the need to have such liability adjudicated in the plaintiff's suit even though the plaintiff may have no interest in doing so.

3. Joinder of Claims

With the exception of a Rule 13 permissive counterclaim, Rules 13 and 14 prevent defending parties from introducing claims that have little to do with the facts on which the plaintiff's claim is based. However, if a defendant asserts a claim that is sufficient under either Rule 13 or 14, he can join (or add) any other claim he may have without regard to the relationship of that added claim to the transaction that gives rise to the plaintiff's claim. In this way, Rule 18 (Joinder of Claims and Remedies) permits, without restriction, the joinder of claims—that is, the addition of any claim to one which is procedurally proper. However, if the presence of the joined claim is likely to prejudice the plaintiff or confuse the jury, the court can sever it for a separate trial.

E. DISCOVERY

If a case survives the first flurry of motions, the parties must set out to gather evidence to prove or disprove the claim and the defenses to it. The Federal Rules of Civil Procedure provide a number of discovery devices which force unfriendly witnesses and even other parties to surrender information relevant to the disputed issues in the case. In this manner, the parties gather information about the witnesses and documents that they can use to prove their side of the case.

Although a lawyer will begin gathering information about her case long before litigation begins, this investigation depends on the cooperation of those she questions. Once a civil action has commenced, however, the discovery rules—Rules 26 through 37—provide a means whereby she can force recalcitrant witnesses and the opposing parties to disgorge information about the case. Rule 26(a) requires the disclosure of information that parties would routinely seek, such as the names of witnesses and copies of documents that the other plans to use. The other discovery rules describe different devices that, for example, allow a party to take the oral deposition of witnesses and of the other party, and to demand answers from the other party to specific written questions.

To be discoverable, information need not be admissible under the rules of evidence but need only appear reasonably calculated to lead to the discovery of admissible evidence. Even if relevant, privileged information is protected from discovery. The attorney-client privilege, the privilege against self-incrimination, and other privileges must be asserted as objections to intrusive discovery requests. In addition, Rule 26 establishes two forms of the work product privilege. The qualified work product privilege protects documents and tangible things that are prepared in anticipation of litigation or in preparation for trial by the party or her agent. Also, an attorney's mental impressions, opinions, and theories concerning the litigation (opinion work product) cannot be obtained during discovery.

F. Judgment

1. Pretrial Orders

After discovery ends, Rule 16 requires the attorneys for the parties to meet and to draft a proposed pretrial order outlining the case as it will be presented at trial. The parties should determine which issues remain disputed, disclose their witness lists, and generally discuss the need for further actions or motions. Upon reviewing their product, the judge enters a pretrial order which will control the action thereafter. The pretrial order may clean up the loose ends and restrict the evidence to that which is relevant to the issues listed. Thereafter, the parties make their final preparations for trial based on this order.

2. Jury Trial

The Seventh Amendment to the Constitution of the United States requires federal courts to preserve the right to jury trial only as to claims for relief which would have been adjudicated in the courts of common law. Even when the right exists, one of the parties must demand a jury trial in order to enjoy that benefit. The Seventh Amendment preserves the right to jury trial only in civil cases being tried in a federal court and does not require state courts to grant a jury trial in civil cases.

The Federal Rules of Evidence regulate the introduction of evidence at trial and are designed to maintain the relevance and quality of evidence used by the jury to find the facts. Once the case has been presented to the jury, it will retire to answer the disputed factual questions based on the evidence admitted at trial. Once the jury makes its decision and answers the factual questions put to it, that verdict is returned to the court. The decision on these factual questions decides the case because the court has already determined what facts must be found to grant the plaintiff a remedy. Therefore, upon receiving the verdict the judge can enter a judgment for the plaintiff or for the defendant without further ado.

3. Judicial Determination of Facts

Only a small percentage of the civil cases filed in federal court end in a jury trial. In most cases, therefore, the parties settle their differences, or the case is terminated by dismissal or summary judgment before trial. If the case goes to trial before a judge without a jury, the presentation of evidence is less formal because the judge will himself consider only the evidence that is credible. Without the need to empanel and control a jury, a bench trial (trial to the judge) moves more rapidly toward decision. Judges also determine both the facts and the law in claims seeking only injunctive relief because a claim seeking only this equitable remedy would not be a common law claim.

G. Direct Challenge to the Judgment

If the defendant appeals the judgment, he will have to take further action in the district court to stay (halt) the enforcement of that money judgment during the appeal. Courts typically require the defendant to post a bond (a special form of insurance) by which a third party—the surety—guarantees payment of the judgment if the appeal fails. The bond thus protects the plaintiff during the appeal from losing the ability to collect on the judgment.

The party who loses in the trial court can appeal the judgment to a court of appeals with appellate jurisdiction over the case. Typically, appellate courts are assigned jurisdiction over cases decided in those trial courts which are located within a designated geographical area. For example, the United States Court of Appeals for the Eleventh Circuit hears cases decided by federal district courts located in Alabama, Florida, and Georgia. The other numbered circuits (First through Tenth) and the District of Columbia Circuit hear cases from the districts located within their respective circuits. When a case comes before a court of appeals, it will ordinarily be decided by a panel of three circuit judges. In very important cases, all of the circuit judges assigned to that circuit will sit to decide the issues. This court is said to be sitting en banc.

In the federal system, the loser in a court of appeals has only one further step. She can petition the Supreme Court of the United States for the issuance of a writ of certiorari. In doing so, the petitioner must explain why her case deserves the attention of the Court. The party who prevailed below—the respondent—can file a response to the petition. If, after reviewing the petition and the response, four members of the Court wish to consider the case, the writ will be granted. In most instances, however, petitions are denied without opinion, thereby ending the case. A few federal statutes grant a right of appeal to the Supreme Court. If an appeal lies, a party has a right to review. However, in the vast majority of cases, the Court exercises complete discretion in choosing the cases it will review.

If the writ is granted, the petitioner and respondent must file written briefs which focus on the alleged errors that could require reversal of the court below. Briefs filed before appellate courts are formal legal presentations by the advocates which discuss the facts and law in a form required by the court's rules. Once the briefs have been filed in the Supreme Court, the Court will set the case for oral argument. If the petitioner loses before the Supreme Court, no further judicial review is available. If the petitioner prevails, the Court will issue its mandate to implement its decision.

H. Precluding Relitigation

Once a party loses in the trial court, appeal allows him to challenge the errors made in reaching the judgment. If an appeal is unsuccessful or is not taken, that party may not relitigate the case in another trial court. Res judicata (the thing adjudicated) is the Latin phrase that refers to the body of rules which prevents this sort of relitigation.

1. Claim Preclusion

In a more particular sense, res judicata refers to one branch of the doctrine which goes by the more prosaic name of claim preclusion. Under the rule of claim preclusion, the losing party is prevented from retrying a claim previously litigated to judgment or any claim arising from the transaction on which the previous litigation was based. As a result of the preclusion of claims whether litigated or not, parties are forced to bring forward all possible claims or litigation in one suit.

2. Issue Preclusion

The rule of claim preclusion applies only after a judgment on the merits, and it applies only to subsequent suits between the same parties. The related rule of collateral estoppel (or issue preclusion) may apply even though the requirements for claim preclusion have not been satisfied, but it precludes the relitigation only of those issues that were actually litigated and decided in the first case. The parties need not be the same, but the issue of fact or law must be. The party against whom issue preclusion is asserted must have had a full and fair opportunity to litigate the issue in her first time in court.

CHAPTER 3

Judicial Power

A. Terminology

Jus tertii—This Latin phrase refers to the rights of third parties, and as a category of justiciability it generally prohibits a plaintiff from asserting the constitutional rights of someone else.

Justiciability—Courts adjudicate only justiciable controversies, and not hypothetical or academic issues. Justiciability, however, refers to the discretionary, rather than constitutional, limits that courts place on the cases that they will adjudicate.

Mootness—A claim that begins as a live controversy may become moot—that is, no longer a justiciable controversy—when, for example, the parties settle their differences, when a state repeals the law that was challenged, or when the plaintiff challenging his incarceration is set free. As a general rule, a case must remain a live controversy at every level from trial through appeal, or it must be dismissed.

Political question—A political question will not be adjudicated by a federal court when it is uniquely unsuitable for adjudication and uniquely suitable for final determination by another branch of the federal government. During the Vietnam War, many individuals sued to challenge various aspects of the war effort by claiming that this military action was contrary to the Constitution. The federal courts invariably dismissed these suits, even when brought by parties with standing to sue, because the case required decision of issues that were not appropriate for courts.

Standing to sue—Standing is the one category that the Supreme Court has described as a constitutional limit on the power of federal courts. The plaintiff must be someone who either has been harmed, or will be harmed, by the action that she challenges. A plaintiff, for example, cannot invoke federal jurisdiction to challenge a law that does not affect her personally, even if that law may be unconstitutional. This restriction prevents the courts from expanding their jurisdiction into areas better left to the political process.

B. Federal Judicial Power

1. The Judicial Branch

Federal courts are referred to as courts of limited subject matter jurisdiction because their power is limited to that which is written in Article III. In contrast, state courts exercise subject matter jurisdiction which is neither derived from nor limited by Article III. The tradition of each state having its own judicial system predates the Constitution, and state judicial power therefore derives from the sovereign power of the states. State courts also can and, indeed, must adjudicate cases that fall within the federal judicial power. State courts, for example, adjudicate constitutional tort claims brought pursuant to Title 42 U.S.C. § 1983 against state and local government officials. In some instances, Congress has granted jurisdiction to federal courts exclusive of the jurisdiction of state courts. For example, federal courts have such exclusive jurisdiction over patent and copyright cases. See 28 U.S.C. § 1338(a).

Prior to the ratification of the Constitution in 1788, the states possessed the governmental power which could be legitimately exercised in the territory of the United States. The states had created the Continental Congress to operate as the central government, but the founding document of that Congress, the Articles of Confederation, gave it little power independent of the states. Left free of centralized control, the states engaged in trade wars and other activities that threatened the cohesion of the new nation.

Aware of these problems and its own impotence, the Continental Congress authorized a convention for the purpose of proposing amendments to the Articles of Confederation. That convention met in Philadelphia in 1787 and, instead of amendments, proposed the replacement of the Articles with its newly drafted Constitution. Although the framers of the Constitution sought to replace the weak central government that then existed, they did not propose the creation of a central government with general power. To do so would have been a threat to the existence of state governments. Instead, the design of the Constitution was to create a government divided into three branches, each assigned a list of specific powers.

Shortly after the ratification of the Constitution, the first Congress proposed amendments that would become the Bill of Rights. The Bill of Rights consists of the first 10 amendments to the Constitution and was a response to the fear that the new government would be too powerful. The Tenth Amendment makes clear what was implicit in the Constitution's listing of specific powers — that is, the federal government can exercise only those powers enumerated in the Constitution. All powers not listed are reserved to the states or to the people.

In addition, the enumerated powers are not conferred on the federal government as a whole but instead are expressly assigned to a particular branch. Article I of the Constitution contains the enumerated powers of Congress, Article II describes the powers of the executive branch, and Article III lists the matters over which the judicial power of the federal courts extends. This separation of powers operates to restrain the overall power of the federal government because each branch is thereby dependent to some degree on the cooperation of the other branches. Therefore, the enumeration of each branch's powers in the Constitution operates, on the one hand, to protect the sovereign function of the states and, on the other, to give meaning to the balance of powers among the branches of the federal government.

Article III establishes the Supreme Court and provides for the creation of the lower federal courts. It states, in section 1, "The judicial Power of the United States, shall be vested in one supreme Court, and in such inferior Courts as the Congress may from time to time ordain and establish." This language represents a compromise reached by the framers between those who wished to write a lower federal court system into the Constitution and those who wanted no lower federal court system at all.

Congress's power to create the lower federal courts has been construed to include the power to confer all or less than all of the judicial power listed in §2 of Article III. Only the Supreme Court is expressly mentioned in Article III, and Article III expressly confers only limited original jurisdiction on the Supreme Court. Congress therefore regulates both the appellate jurisdiction of the Supreme Court and the jurisdiction that may be exercised by lower federal courts. As a result, one can invoke a federal court's jurisdiction only when that jurisdiction has been granted in a federal statute.

Usually, Congress confers jurisdiction on federal trial courts without denying jurisdiction over similar cases to state courts. On some occasions, Congress has conferred jurisdiction on federal courts while excluding state courts from exercising that jurisdiction. As noted above, §1338(a) of Title 28 confers jurisdiction in the following terms:

> The district courts shall have original jurisdiction of any civil action arising under any Act of Congress relating to patents, plant variety protection, copyrights and trademarks. Such jurisdiction shall be exclusive of the courts of the states in patent, plant variety protection and copyright cases.

Congress believed federal courts should have exclusive jurisdiction because of a special need for uniform treatment and for a forum sympathetic to the policies underlying the law in these areas.

2. Effects of Limited Jurisdiction

Section 2 of Article III lists the nine "subject matter" categories of cases or controversies over which the federal judicial power can extend. No significance has been attached to the difference in terminology: the limitations that restrict cases apply as well to controversies. Section 2 states:

The judicial Power shall extend to all [1] Cases, in Law and Equity, arising under this Constitution, the Laws of the United States, and Treaties made, or which shall be made, under their Authority;—to all [2] Cases affecting Ambassadors, other public Ministers and Consuls;—to all [3] Cases of admiralty and maritime Jurisdiction;—to [4] Controversies to which the United States shall be a Party;— to [5] Controversies between two or more States;—[6] between a State and Citizens of another State;—[7] between Citizens of different States;—[8] between Citizens of the same State claiming Lands under Grants of different States, and [9] between a State or the Citizens thereof, and foreign States, Citizens or Subjects.

To invoke federal jurisdiction, a plaintiff must affirmatively plead and, if challenged by any party or the court, prove that her case satisfies the requirements of a jurisdictional statute. A rebuttable presumption against the existence of jurisdiction has the effect of keeping the issue open until a final judgment has been entered. The issue of a federal court's subject matter jurisdiction cannot be avoided or ignored by the parties' waiver of any objection, by the parties' stipulation or consent to litigation in federal court, or by applying the doctrine of estoppel to a party who fails to make a timely objection.

A judge can and should raise a subject matter jurisdictional issue on his own without the urging of the parties, and a federal appellate court can raise the issue of a federal trial court's jurisdiction even though the issue was never raised in the lower court. This stringent rule is required because subject matter jurisdiction relates not to a right conferred on any party; instead, it arises from the need to preserve the Constitution's allocation of governing power among the branches of the federal government, and between the federal government and the states.

Until a judgment has become final, therefore, the plaintiff's claim remains vulnerable to a jurisdictional dismissal. Although jurisdictional dismissals are entered without prejudice against the plaintiff's refiling of the suit, statutes of limitations typically require the commencement of an action in a *competent* court within a specified period. When a dismissed case is refiled in state court, the plaintiff can find that this filing came too late to satisfy the state limitations period. Thus, a jurisdictional dismissal can effectively end an otherwise meritorious case unless a state savings statute suspends the running of the limitations period during its stay in federal court.

Even though subject matter jurisdiction plays such a fundamental role, federal courts retain power to issue the orders necessary for an orderly determination of their own subject matter jurisdiction. For example, one cannot ignore the preliminary injunctive orders of a federal court because of the assumption that it lacks subject matter jurisdiction. In order to adjudicate the issue of its jurisdiction, a federal court may, even prior to its initial determination of jurisdiction, enter restraining orders to maintain the status quo. A violation of such an order can be grounds for punishment through contempt even when the court is later determined to lack jurisdiction. A court cannot provide an orderly adjudication of rights under the law if parties can disregard its rulings based on their view of its jurisdiction. The need for order thus can outweigh the need for strict enforcement of jurisdictional limits.

3. The Passive Nature of Judicial Power

Article III grants judicial power to federal courts over only those "Cases" or "Controversies" that fall within one of the subject matter categories. The case or controversy language thus qualifies the particular grants of judicial power, and imposes an additional set of requirements that a federal court must satisfy before it can resolve a conflict. Therefore, every dispute brought to a federal court must satisfy the requirements of a case or controversy and, in addition, fit within one of the nine subject matter categories.

In order to present a case or controversy, a dispute must appear in a form historically viewed as making it susceptible to adjudication. In short, the dispute must look like the disputes that courts traditionally accepted for judicial determination. In delegating judicial power to federal courts over cases and controversies, the Framers of the Constitution could only have had in mind the conflicts that the courts of their day heard and adjudicated. They were familiar with common law or equity causes of action that had to be initiated by a person complaining of an actual harm caused him by the wrongful action of another individual. Courts did not (and do not) decide hypothetical cases. Furthermore, the complaining party had to prove the wrongfulness of the defending party's action by reference to existing law, created either by courts or by a legislature, and courts did not provide opinions to litigants about the lawfulness of future action.

Personalized harm provides some assurance that the plaintiff will be a vigorous advocate. The harm must, for the most part, have predated the lawsuit or at least be so imminent that a court runs no risk that it will not come about. A case must arise from a live and current controversy to avoid unnecessary litigation or the adjudication of hypothetical rather than real issues. In the absence of these characteristics, the conflict must be resolved either by one of the other branches of the federal government or by the states.

Traditionally, the judicial power over a case extended only to the issues necessary for the final resolution of the dispute. Courts should not provide opinions on matters beyond the actual dispute or about issues that are unnecessary to the remedy sought in the case. These unnecessary judicial opinions are viewed as dicta—extraneous pronouncements unsupported by the needs of a case—and, if included, exert diminished precedential authority.

The model for this tradition of restrained, pragmatic judicial power are the courts of the common law that operated in England and then in the United States before the ratification of the Constitution. Courts of the common law were characterized as forums to which the aggrieved brought their legal causes. A common law court did not initiate the exercise of its powers or choose the particular issues that it would resolve. A plaintiff filed her complaint with the court, and if it was in proper order and properly stated a recognized cause of action, the court would hear the conflict. This passivity, though not absolute by any means, is an important limiting characteristic of the judicial power.

The Supreme Court concluded, in the famous case of Marbury v. Madison, 5 U.S. 137 (1803), that courts have power to interpret and apply the Constitution, as the supreme law, to invalidate federal statutes. That power of judicial review has been extended to authorize invalidation of state statutes or of any other law or official action. The authority to interpret the Constitution, and then to apply that interpretation to defeat other governmental action, makes the courts a formidable force in government. Moreover, in federal courts, life-tenured, appointed judges wield that power. Because these judges exercise the often unpopular power of judicial review, they have reason to operate within the judicial tradition and to exercise power only over actual cases or controversies.

C. Standing to Sue

1. General Rules

The Constitution in Article III imposes standing requirements as an essential restriction on the federal judicial power over cases and controversies. Although Congress can expand that power by creating new rights, it cannot authorize the exercise of jurisdiction in the absence of standing. In Lujan v. Defenders of Wildlife, 504 U.S. 555 (1992), the Supreme Court held that Congress could not convert a generalized grievance about the invalidity of federal administrative action into standing to sue. Congress had enacted a provision that allowed suit to enforce the Endangered Species Act by "any person." The plaintiffs had not been individually harmed by the action they challenged and therefore were asserting a grievance they shared with the public at large. The Court held that Congress could not enhance federal judicial power by abrogating the constitutional limitation of standing.

As a general rule, a plaintiff seeking to establish standing sufficient to invoke the jurisdiction of a federal court must be prepared to prove:

- that she has suffered, or is imminently in danger of suffering, an injury in fact;
- that this injury is fairly traceable to the defendant's conduct; and
- that a favorable decision is likely to redress the injury.

A very limited, and questionable, exception to the general rule of standing applies when a taxpayer sues in federal court to challenge the expenditure of tax money. Under these circumstances, the taxpayer can prove standing by satisfying a two-pronged nexus test, which requires a showing that the taxpayer:

- has challenged an exercise by Congress of its taxing and spending power (that means the expenditure must be for a specific program rather than in discharge of the general costs of operating the government); and
- bases her challenge on a constitutional provision that is known as a specific limit on the taxing and spending power of Congress (to date, the Supreme Court has found such a limit only in the Establishment Clause of the First Amendment).

2. The Injury-in-Fact Requirement

The standing requirement allows suit only by a plaintiff who has suffered a personalized injury by the allegedly wrongful action of the defendant and which can be remedied by the court. The requirement prevents federal litigation by those who have nothing more than an academic or philosophical objection to a particular government action or to a particular law. With rare exceptions, federal courts cannot decide a case unless the plaintiff has suffered or is imminently in danger of suffering such an injury in fact (not simply an injury to alleged legal rights) because of the defendant's action.

The requirement of an injury is recognized implicitly in Rule 17, which states that only a real party in interest may bring a suit in federal court. A real party in interest might be seen as one who owns the claim. In the common law actions of tort or contract, for example, the plaintiff obtains the right of action because she has been harmed physically or economically by the defendant's wrongful action. It is helpful to note that common law harms have an objective quality in that all would agree that they constitute a personal loss.

Standing is a constitutional requirement derived from the case-or-controversy language of Article III. The concept derives largely from the judicial form created for common law litigation known to the Framers when they drafted the language of Article III. Since the ratification of the Constitution, however, very different forms of litigation have been developed. Modern constitutional law claims against government were unknown to the common law and, therefore, may not fit easily into that mold. For example, government interference with the freedom of speech imposed through a ban on signs posted to telephone poles will frustrate a potential speaker while not causing him any physical or economic harm. Because of these changes in the legal landscape, a close adherence to common law forms predating the Constitution would impose an intensely conservative restraint on judicial power. Therefore, a focus on plaintiff's injury cannot depend solely on his ability to assert a recognized legal right. Instead, the court asks whether the plaintiff was injured personally by the challenged action. More significantly, the legitimacy of the injury, for standing purposes, turns not on the seriousness of the harm but on the personalization of the effect caused by the allegedly wrongful action.

The standing requirement *also* promotes values which serve the adversarial method of adjudication. By requiring assurance that the parties have more at stake than philosophical differences, standing restricts adjudication to those conflicts which involve intensely personal interests. A court can presume that a plaintiff who complains of an objectively discernible personal injury, and who stands to gain significant compensation, will vigorously present her own legal rights. Furthermore, if the plaintiff aggressively pursues a judgment, the defendant has a comparable incentive to defend his position. Vigorous advocacy by the parties, in turn, insures that a court's decision will benefit from a comprehensive presentation of the case.

Because it is a matter going to any federal court's subject matter jurisdiction, the issue of standing remains open throughout litigation. It can arise when a plaintiff, having standing at the outset, loses that status because of events occurring during litigation. If intervening events make the case moot—that is, effectively remove the injury which created the controversy—the case must be dismissed. A simple example of a mooting event would be the out-of-court settlement of all claims.

The injury-in-fact requirements for standing were described earlier. In summary, one can say that the plaintiff must prove she suffered a sufficient injury and that the defendant caused that injury. The plaintiff must show that a final judgment will resolve the dispute and remove the effects of the injury.

The last two steps however—causation and redressability—appear to be different formulations of the same question.

a. Injury in Fact

An injury in fact need not be economic or physical. It can include injuries to one's aesthetic or environmental well-being so long as the effect is personalized. For example, a man who habitually fishes in a Montana river would have standing to challenge a defendant's pollution of that river, but a Sierra Club member residing in New York who has never visited Montana would not. Courts do not demand that an injury meet some theoretical minimum of intensity. Instead, standing turns on the personalized nature of the challenged action—in this example, on the interference with the plaintiff's pleasure in fishing. By focusing on the personalized effect, courts need not depend on proof that the fisherman has caught fewer or less edible fish. Evidence of such personalized effects proves that the fisherman does not complain merely because of a philosophical, political, or academic motive. On the other hand, if the effect on the plaintiff cannot be objectively differentiated from the effect on the public at large, the assumption is that the plaintiff merely has a subjective motive to prove the wrongfulness of the defendant's action. If the plaintiff seeks only to use the court as a forum for such an abstract legal debate, his suit must be dismissed for lack of standing.

To show sufficient personalized effect, the plaintiff must, in some manner, allege and prove that the challenged action affects her in some way differently from the public at large. In other words, by its own operation, the allegedly wrongful action must have a spotlight effect on the plaintiff. If so, a court is assured that the case arose because of something more than merely the passionate reaction of one who believes the challenged action should be prohibited. It can be assured, instead, that the passionate reaction arises because of a reason that distinguishes this plaintiff from everyone else in the general public.

As a further example, assume Congress has enacted two laws. One provides an annual appropriation of $100 million in tax money for support of the arts. The second imposes what amounts to a $100 million annual tax on the importation of sports utility vehicles (SUVs) imported from Japan. The owner of a Toyota dealership decides to challenge the constitutionality of both laws in separate suits in federal court. The appropriation for the arts affects the plaintiff in the same way it affects all citizens. Even if she paid more federal income taxes than most, that tax burden would not differentiate her from the public at large. In effect, courts assume that the $100 million would have been spent on some other program if not on this one. Therefore, invalidation of the appropriation would not reduce anyone's tax burden. The effect of this law thus is not financial. Besides, ordinary taxpayers might become fractious if the federal courts were open only to the rich. If the plaintiff's personal tax burden does not supply a sufficient injury, that injury could only arise because of the benefit given the arts. The plaintiff may passionately oppose government's support of the arts, but nothing other than the severity of her dyspepsia distinguishes her from all other members of the public.

The plaintiff does have standing to challenge the import tax on SUVs from Japan. She has suffered a sufficiently personalized injury because she owns a Toyota dealership. The tax on imports will directly affect her business, unlike its immediate effect on other members of the public—at least on those who do not annually purchase Japan-made SUVs. Her standing does not suffer even if the dealership will pass on the increased costs or even if no competitive disadvantage was likely to result. The plaintiff has standing because the tax has a personalized effect on her that does not originate with her idiosyncratic reaction to the law.

By requiring a personalized effect, the courts avoid serving as a forum for anyone who wishes to vent anger against the government or against a violator of the law. We can assume that in our litigious society someone would challenge just about every law or arguably illegal action if access to the federal courts was unlimited. Such unlimited access would allow courts to hear any issue that interested them, and their power to wield the Constitution would give them pervasive control over both legislative and executive actions. By using standing requirements as a self-imposed limit on their power, courts resist being drawn into confrontations with the other branches of the federal government which would prove dangerous to the balance of powers.

b. Causation

Standing requirements would be meaningless if the defendant's actions did not have to cause the plaintiff's injury. For example, the owner of the Toyota dealership might have recently suffered a loss of business, but she cannot use that injury to challenge the federal law appropriating money for the arts. Ordinarily a court, in concluding that the challenged action had a personalized effect on the plaintiff, answers the causation question as well. The import tax, in the hypothetical given above, has a spotlight effect on a limited group within the public at large—Toyota dealers being part of that group. In reaching this conclusion, a court would have already determined that the allegedly unconstitutional tax caused the injury.

However, a plaintiff need not show that the law being challenged itself caused his injury. In Duke Power Co. v. Carolina Environmental Study Group, 438 U.S. 59 (1978), the plaintiffs challenged, as a denial of due process, the federal law that capped a plant's liability in case of a nuclear accident. They contended that such a cap threatened to deny them full recovery in case of an accident. The underlying purpose of the federal law, however, was to facilitate and encourage construction of such plants.

The plaintiffs lived near the site of a planned nuclear plant, and they proved that its construction and operation would necessarily have detrimental esthetic and environmental effects on their neighborhood. However, the alleged violation of due process did not directly cause these effects because that violation depended on a nuclear accident which might never occur. Nevertheless, the Supreme Court held that the plaintiffs had standing to sue because their injury was caused, albeit indirectly, by the challenged law. Two points explain the Court's conclusion. First, standing does not require a past or existing harm; one which is reasonably imminent will do. Second, to the extent the federal law achieved its purpose by encouraging the construction of nuclear plants it would cause the construction of the plant that would have esthetic and environmental effects on these plaintiffs.

If the Court had been unwilling to accept this line of causation, the plaintiff's argument for standing would have failed. A showing of causation succeeds, therefore, only when a substantial likelihood exists that, but for the challenged action, the plaintiff's alleged injury would not have occurred.

c. Redressability

The redressability requirement prevents courts from engaging in litigation which cannot be effectively resolved by a judicial decree. If the injury cannot be remedied by a court, the case, for that reason alone, is not judicial in nature. The redressability step therefore requires a showing that the exercise of the court's remedial powers would redress the claimed injuries. For example, suppose an indigent person challenged a government ruling that allowed tax exempt status to hospitals that failed to provide her free medical services (the injury). Even if she obtained a favorable change in the law, hospitals could refuse to provide free services because the cost of that care was greater than the benefits from tax exempt status. Because the requested judicial remedy did not have a substantial likelihood of removing the plaintiff's injury, she would not have standing to sue.

3. Organizational Standing

An organization, like an individual, has standing to sue on its own right when some action has impaired its ability to provide services or when the challenged action would diminish the organization's membership or financial support. The organization thus has standing because it has itself suffered a personalized injury. For instance, if the Toyota dealership were a corporation, the import tax would cause it an injury in the same way it caused injury to the owner of an unincorporated dealership. Or, the Sierra Club would have standing if the Internal Revenue Service began imposing special disadvantages on the organization because of its environmental message. One must be careful to recognize that an organization, such as the Sierra Club does not have standing to enforce its social or philosophical values merely because of its long-standing special interest in the environment.

However, the Sierra Club can bring suit to represent or to join particular members of the organization suing to protect the environment if those members have standing to sue in their own right. The organization cannot exercise this representational standing unless the interests involved in the claim for relief relate to its primary purpose. An organization also cannot represent its members' interests when they seek damages relief based on proof of their personalized harm. The Sierra Club's presence is not appropriate, for example, in a suit brought by one of its members against a polluter for compensation to remedy damage to his land.

4. Taxpayer Standing

The one exception to the injury-in-fact requirement for standing was established in Flast v. Cohen, 392 U.S. 83 (1968). In that case an exception, described through a nexus test, was formulated to allow taxpayers to challenge the constitutionality of a federal law appropriating money that would, in part, benefit religious schools. As discussed in the Toyota hypothetical, a taxpayer cannot prove that government's *expenditure* of money increases her personal tax burden. When the Toyota dealer sought to challenge a congressional appropriation to support the arts, she could rest only on her objection to arts funding by government.

Under very limited circumstances, however, a taxpayer may challenge an expenditure of tax money by satisfying the *Flast* test. In *Flast*, the Court held that seven persons who claimed to have been harmed as federal taxpayers by the expenditure of federal funds to implement the Elementary and Secondary Education Act of 1965 had standing to challenge those expenditures as being an establishment of religion in violation of the First Amendment. The Act authorized the spending of federal money by local governments to aid in purchasing textbooks and in financing instruction in reading, arithmetic, and other secular courses in religious schools.

Even though the Act could not have harmed these seven plaintiffs in any way differently from the way it affected all other federal taxpayers, the Court upheld their standing to sue. The Court concluded that a taxpayer has standing to challenge an exercise by Congress of its taxing and spending power when she satisfies a two-pronged nexus test. The first prong requires the plaintiff to show a logical connection (nexus) between her status as a taxpayer and the type of statute challenged. A taxpayer can establish this connection only when challenging an exercise by Congress of its power under the Taxing and Spending Clause of Article I, §8, of the Constitution.

However, the nexus can exist only when a taxpayer challenges a congressional appropriation that expressly authorizes the expenditures of which the challengers complain. A taxpayer cannot satisfy this nexus by challenging an expenditure made according to the discretion of an executive official. See Hein v. Freedom From Religion Foundation, 2007 WL 1803960 (2007). The first prong cannot be satisfied by challenges to spending needed for the routine operation of government. If that were otherwise, a taxpayer could challenge any federal action by seeking to cut off funds necessary for its accomplishment. In addition, the Court has subsequently held that this first prong cannot be satisfied by a challenge to the action of an administrative agency or when the authority exercised is not based directly on the taxing and spending power. For example, a federal agency that distributes excess government property to a religious college acts under the property power, not under the taxing and spending power.

The second nexus requires the plaintiff to show a logical connection between her taxpayer status and the constitutional infringement alleged. The Court determined in *Flast* that a plaintiff may not simply show that Congress acted generally beyond its constitutional power or in violation of any constitutional restriction. She must allege that the challenged congressional expenditure violates a constitutional provision specifically intended to operate as a restriction on the taxing and spending power. In *Flast*, the Court concluded that the Establishment Clause of the First Amendment was intended to be such a specific bulwark against the use of federal tax money to establish religion.

As Justice Harlan pointed out in his *Flast* dissent, the two-pronged nexus test has nothing to do with the personal stake of the plaintiffs before the court. Any taxpayer in the United States could have satisfied the nexus test as a plaintiff in *Flast*. The most significant nexus appears to be, contrary to the reasoning of the Court, between the challenged action and the constitutional provision used for the challenge, that is, the Establishment Clause.

It is important to keep in mind that a plaintiff does not need the *Flast* test to establish standing to challenge a *tax*—that is, a law imposing the obligation on her to pay money to the government. A tax always has a direct economic effect on the taxpayer who has to pay it. The Toyota dealer, for example, has a personalized interest in challenging the special tax on imported Toyotas because she imports Toyotas and will now have to pay more for the privilege. That personalized effect establishes an injury in fact. However, the manner by which tax money is *spent* does not ordinarily have a personalized effect on someone solely because she pays taxes. Hence, to challenge spending, a taxpayer must use the *Flast* test.

D. JUSTICIABILITY

1. Rights of Third Parties—*Jus Tertii*

Federal courts tend to avoid the unnecessary adjudication of constitutional issues. They, for example, decide cases on statutory grounds if such an alternative allows them to avoid a constitutional issue. Constitutional decisions, especially those made by the Supreme Court, have broad-reaching and profound effects, and it behooves a court to use caution in causing such fundamental effects. Also, as a general rule, courts limit constitutional challenges to a law as applied to the plaintiff instead of deciding that it may have unconstitutional effects on others. This preference for as-applied constitutional challenges directly supports what is known as *jus tertii* or the rule against the assertion of rights of third parties.

The rule generally prevents a litigant from asserting the constitutional rights of others. When a constitutional provision is designed to protect one group, members of another group should not be allowed to use that right for their own challenges. This prohibition is misleadingly referred to as third-party standing. That phrase misleads to the extent it induces one to think a litigant can avoid the injury-in-fact test. The plaintiff must have standing in order to bring any case before a federal court and, in addition, must generally assert only her own legal rights.

In order for a plaintiff to avoid the rule and assert the constitutional rights of a third party, she must show: (1) that she has standing, (2) that the challenged law regulates a close relationship between the plaintiff and the third party, and (3) that there exists some hindrance to the third party's assertion of his own rights. A plaintiff will assert the rights of another when the rights of that other person are more compelling than those of the plaintiff. For example, a physician who regularly provides abortion services has standing to challenge a criminal abortion law because it directly regulates her professional conduct. However, she may have only a weak constitutional argument based on an alleged right to practice medicine without interference. On the other hand, a pregnant patient possesses a constitutional right to be free of undue legal burdens on her decisions about her pregnancy. The patient's constitutional right is more likely to overturn an abortion law than the physician's right to an unhindered medical practice.

Consider this hypothetical. A federal statute prohibits racial discrimination but is written with such ambiguous terms that it might arguably allow prosecution against violators who are private citizens. The Fourteenth Amendment has been interpreted to limit only state action, and, therefore, it provides Congress no power to directly regulate the activities of private citizens. Suppose further that the federal government brings a prosecution under that statute against a state official. In defense of the suit, the official contends that the statute as written would be unconstitutional if it were ever applied to private citizens.

A federal court will not adjudicate this defense because the state official has asserted the rights of a hypothetical private citizen who is not before the court. Allowing the official to raise this issue would force the court to decide a constitutional question that might never need adjudication. Furthermore, in order to decide such an issue, the court would have to guess that the government might bring such a prosecution and then speculate about the factual circumstances that might be presented in such a case. If that case ever arose, the constitutional issue might be presented in a very different light from the present case. And, because that prosecution may never occur, the court would be deciding a constitutional question that might have never been raised in a proper case.

Unlike the case of the state official, fewer objections to the physician's assertion of her patient's rights exist. Private individuals may have no reason to fear enforcement of the civil rights statute. However, the abortion law has a current effect on pregnant women's rights. This existing harm to the physician's pregnant patients relieves the court of any need to speculate about the probability of a future application of the law. Furthermore, pregnant women may be hindered in asserting their rights in court by difficulties caused by the cost and burden of litigation or by the possible loss of privacy. At the very least, the absence of a pregnant woman as a party does not suggest a lack of interest. The existing relationship also provides an objective reason to assume that the physician would protect her patients' interests and be a competent advocate for their rights.

Therefore, when the plaintiff challenges a law that regulates an existing relationship between her and the third party and which causes a present injury to that third party, the Supreme Court has created an exception allowing her to assert that person's rights. The doctor can assert her patient's rights because they spring from an existing controversy, but the state official cannot assert rights of a hypothetical person who may never be involved in a controversy.

2. Ripeness

To be ripe, a case or controversy must be live and current in the sense that a real conflict between the parties exists at the time of suit. The case will not be ripe for adjudication if, before the conflict can exist, some future and speculative event must occur. If the controversy does require further action, a court may adjudicate the case if it finds that adjudication is necessary because of (1) the hardship caused the parties by withholding decision, and because of (2) the fitness of the issues for judicial decision (state of the record).

A plaintiff can satisfy standing requirements by showing that, in the future, she will suffer an injury in fact. For example, a tax on imports from Japan may not go into effect until six months after its enactment. If a Toyota dealer files suit before the law's effective date, she has no existing injury. However, the law will inevitably cause her an injury in fact sufficient for standing. Nothing is gained by waiting for the effective date or for enforcement against the dealer.

To put it another way, the case is ripe for immediate decision even though no actual injury has yet occurred. A court can legitimately assume that the import tax will be enforced, and the plaintiff's established pattern of behavior—her Toyota dealership—commits her to a path which assures a court that the law will be enforced against her. The plaintiff and the government seem inalterably committed to action that will bring about conflict. Its actual existence awaits nothing more than the passage of time. Therefore, the factual record needed for determination of the legal challenge to that tax will not be changed or enhanced by awaiting the effective date of the statute.

Ripeness becomes a more troublesome issue when the conflict is not inevitable. Under those circumstances, a federal court must decide whether to proceed by considering two opposing considerations: the harm which might be caused the plaintiff by delay and the current fitness of the issues for adjudication. If, for example, the plaintiff will be forced to forgo allegedly lawful conduct or risk a serious criminal prosecution by the court's refusal to adjudicate, the case is more likely to be deemed ripe. On the other side of the ledger, a court must consider whether delay will allow the development of a better factual context for the legal issues.

The ripeness issue has become more complicated since the enactment of the federal Declaratory Judgment Act in 1934. The Act, in part, gives federal courts power to decide issues before the traditional remedies of damages or injunctive relief would be available, and to enter a judicial opinion on the legal rights and obligations of the parties. The exercise of this power can therefore create a question of ripeness. Normally, when the plaintiff seeks a damages remedy, she must prove an existing injury caused by past events. This requirement for the damages remedy thus prevents a plaintiff from coming too early into court, and forces her to wait until the conflict has ripened into an live controversy. Ripeness is also less of a problem when a party seeks injunctive relief. The standard test for preliminary injunctive relief requires the plaintiff to show that in the absence of an injunctive order she will immediately suffer an irreparable injury—that is an injury that cannot be remedied with a damages judgment or a permanent injunction. The irreparable-injury requirement depends on proof of imminent personal harm, and thus limits a plaintiff to those claims that are ripe for adjudication.

The Declaratory Judgment Act's remedy has another effect; it permits suit by one who could not have sued prior to 1934 for either injunctive or damages relief. For example, an inventor who has already invested in the necessary production equipment may hesitate to begin marketing a new product because of patent infringement threats made by a competitor. That competitor might choose not to initiate the infringement suit, finding that a threat alone was sufficient to deter competition. Under these circumstances, the inventor can file suit seeking a declaratory judgment in order to obtain a determination whether the competitor's patent is either valid or infringed.

The inventor appears to be seeking an advisory opinion at a point before either party could obtain either a damages or an injunctive remedy. However, the court need not speculate that the conflict will never ripen because the parties already have taken adverse positions. Furthermore, the plaintiff currently suffers a financial loss by being unable to use his investments to produce marketable goods. Finally, the issues in the case currently are fit for judicial resolution, and the court needs no further factual development. The case appears premature solely because the inventor has not started selling his allegedly infringing product.

3. Political Questions

As a matter of judicial self-restraint, a federal court may find a legal claim nonjusticiable under the "political question" doctrine. Under this prudential doctrine, federal courts refuse to adjudicate any claim that both requires them (1) to engage in a conflict of authority with another branch of the federal government and (2) to decide an issue that is peculiarly unsuited for adjudication but well suited for decision by that other federal branch.

The political question doctrine addresses cases which bring the federal courts into conflict with one of the other branches of the federal government. When this conflict appears, a federal court will refuse to decide an issue which is unsuited for adjudication. For example, the Constitution appears to assign to Congress exclusive authority over impeachment and removal of federal officers. For that reason, federal courts will not review Congress's impeachment decisions.

The Supreme Court noted in *Baker v. Carr* that a case may be justiciable even though it involves the assertion of a political right and has political implications. In *Baker*, the Court held that an equal protection challenge to a state law apportioning the Tennessee legislature did not give rise to a nonjusticiable political question. The Court concluded that the political question doctrine arose from restrictions emanating from the separation of powers, and did not restrain a federal court's questioning of state law. Since the Tennessee law could bring the federal courts in conflict only with a state rather than with a co-equal branch of the federal government, the political question doctrine did not apply.

In determining which issues are nonjusticiable, the Court reasoned, a case-by-case analysis must be applied in light of six independent considerations. These considerations are: (1) a constitutional assignment of exclusive authority over the issue to another branch of the federal government, (2) a lack of judicially manageable standards, (3) the need to make a policy determination requiring nonjudicial discretion, (4) the likelihood that a judicial decision would express a lack of the respect due that other branch, (5) an unusual need for adhering to a political decision already made; and (6) the potential for causing serious problems because of conflicting pronouncements by branches of the federal government. See Baker v. Carr, 369 U.S. 186, 217. (1962). These are independent considerations in that only one need apply in order to compel dismissal of a case, and they are probably listed in descending order of importance. See Vieth v. Jubelirer, 541 U.S. 267, 277-78 (2004).

Unless the Constitution excludes judicial review, these considerations suggest no bright-line rule. They do, however, suggest the nonjusticiability of questions touching foreign policy or international relations, especially those matters that affect the use of our troops by the President as commander-in-chief. For example, the lower federal courts rather uniformly refused, on political question grounds, to decide questions about the validity of the Vietnam conflict. Such legal challenges would have forced courts to consider remedies which would have unforeseeable effects. In addition, the judicial system's adversarial process is not well designed to produce judgments about the likelihood of future events or which can accommodate rapid change. Furthermore, these matters can be better managed by an executive having access to advisers with varied areas of expertise. Similar challenges to troop deployments in Iraq or Afghanistan would be inappropriate for judicial decision and would be dismissed. It is important to realize, however, that at some point the courts must exercise their power to interfere with executive power that treads too directly on individual constitutional rights.

4. Mootness

A controversy must remain live at every stage of litigation or be dismissed because of mootness. A case is moot when the requested judgment cannot have any practical effect on the controversy or when the issues have become academic because they have been resolved by intervening events. For example, the parties may moot a claim for damages by reaching a negotiated settlement. If a challenged statute is repealed during the appellate process, a court normally will dismiss those claims that seek only injunctive or declaratory (prospective) relief. However, the court cannot dismiss as moot a claim alleging that, while in effect, the statute caused the plaintiff financial injury for which compensation has not been paid.

A suit obviously lacks an actual controversy when the parties have settled a claim brought solely for damages. The injury which provided the plaintiff standing to sue has been erased by the settlement. Greater difficulty is encountered when suits solely for injunctive or declaratory relief appear to have been mooted by events which occur after the beginning of the suit. For example, repeal of the challenged statute, suspension of the program being challenged, or the passage of time may all end a conflict. As the law has developed, however, apparent mootness can be overcome in some situations.

a. Collateral Consequences

Mootness has a constitutional basis in that Article III requires a live case or controversy, but a significant degree of flexibility exists in its application. In some cases, mootness can be overcome by showing that, though the challenged action has been discontinued or the primary harm of that action has ended, certain consequences of that action still exist to cause harm to the plaintiff for which relief can be granted. The repeal of a challenged law ends the controversy for injunctive or declaratory relief from a future harm, but does not erase the past harm for which the plaintiff may seek damages. A person who claims to have been convicted of the crime of violating an unconstitutional law retains standing, even after his sentence has been served, to challenge the harm caused his record by the conviction. In these instances, one can say that the harm has not been completely erased by the event claimed to cause mootness.

b. Voluntary Cessation

Assume a prosecuting attorney has threatened the owners of adult theaters with criminal action for showing "adult" movies. In reaction, the owners have brought suit solely for an injunction to prevent future harassment. Were the prosecutor to be replaced by another elected official who declares that he does not intend to prosecute owners of adult movie theaters, a court would find that the owners' claim for prospective relief was moot. However, suppose the original prosecutor stayed in office but had decided during litigation that he is unlikely to prevail. He might declare to the court that he has changed his policy and will no longer engage in this program of harassment. Under these circumstances, a federal court would be hesitant to assume that the case had been mooted. Before dismissing, the court would demand that the prosecutor prove that there was no substantial likelihood that he would resume his offensive conduct in the near future.

c. Capable of Repetition yet Evading Review

In some cases, the nature of the harm is such that it will expire before litigation can be completed. This may occur when the action being challenged is of short duration, such as a 10-day temporary restraining order or when the condition regulated by the challenged law cannot last long enough for full litigation. For example, a criminal abortion law directly affects a woman during her nine-month pregnancy, but a challenge by her could never be completed before the end of that pregnancy. Under such circumstances, federal courts will not strictly enforce the mootness doctrine if the complaining party might suffer the same harm again. If this exception were not made, such litigants would be denied a forum.

d. Class Actions

In a class action, certain named parties may be deemed representatives of a numerous class of persons. Before the district court can certify the class, it must find that the named representatives have standing to sue. In some instances, the claims of all representatives may be mooted by intervening events. For example, a state law permitting women to purchase alcoholic beverages at 18 but prohibiting men from doing so until they reach 21 raises a serious question under the Equal Protection Clause. Men between 18 and 21 would have standing to bring that challenge, but their case would be mooted if they were unable to obtain a final adjudication before reaching 21 (when they were no longer affected by the law). A small number of these individuals could, however, bring a class action on behalf of all other similarly affected men. As one representative of the class reached 21, he could be replaced by a new representative who was below 21. In this fashion, a class action can provide a mechanism to avoid what might otherwise be a mooting event.

E. FEDERAL COURTS

Article III of the Constitution begins by vesting the judicial power of the United States in "one supreme Court, and in such inferior Courts as the Congress may from time to time ordain and establish." Among the other specific powers assigned to Congress, Article I expressly grants it power to "constitute Tribunals inferior to the supreme Court." The Constitution thus expressly creates only one federal court—the Supreme Court—leaving to Congress the creation of all other federal courts.

After the ratification of the Constitution, the first Congress established lower federal courts through a comprehensive statute known as the First Judiciary Act of 1789. The first section of the Act provided that the Supreme Court should consist of a chief justice and five associate justices. It also provided for a two-tier system of federal trial courts. The Act divided the existing states into thirteen districts and established a trial court—the district court—in each. In addition, the Act created three federal circuits and in each established a second, more important trial court—the circuit court. A circuit court held sessions twice a year in each district within its circuit and was initially presided over by the district judge of that district and two justices of the Supreme Court. A circuit court exercised important original jurisdiction, including diversity jurisdiction, and also had limited jurisdiction to review certain final decisions of the district courts.

The modern structure of the federal judicial system began to appear in 1891 when Congress created an intermediate appellate court—the circuit court of appeals—for each then-existing circuit. Congress retained the circuit court as a trial court but abolished its appellate jurisdiction. Therefore, between 1891 and 1911 (when the circuit courts were abolished), there existed two trial courts (the district and circuit courts), an intermediate appellate court (the circuit courts of appeals), and the Supreme Court. In 1948, Congress renamed the intermediate appellate courts as the United States Courts of Appeals for the [First] Circuit.

1. District Courts

Statutory provisions found in Title 28 of the United States Code (the Judicial Code) create 94 federal judicial districts for the United States and its Territories. A separate district court presides in each district. As a general rule, each judicial district is contained within the borders of a state. Some states have only one district, such as Delaware, but some of the larger states have more than one district. Texas, for example, has four districts—the Northern, Eastern, Southern, and Western. Florida, because of its shape, has a Middle District, and California has a Central District. In larger states, the districts themselves may be divided into smaller areas known as divisions. The formal title of a district court refers to the district and division in which it is located. For example, the federal court located in San Antonio, Texas, is the United States District Court for the Western District of Texas, San Antonio Division.

Except in the few instances in which Congress has mandated a three-judge panel, a single district judge sits to hear a case tried before the district court. However, in especially important cases, all judges assigned to a district may sit en banc to decide the issues.

2. Courts of Appeals

The Judicial Code assigns each of these districts to a judicial circuit. A court of appeals has appellate jurisdiction over the cases decided by district courts located within the geographical area of its circuit. Currently, 12 courts of appeals exercise general appellate jurisdiction bounded by the geographic area of their circuits. These include the 11 numbered circuits and the United States Court of Appeals for the District of Columbia. The United States Court of Appeals for the Federal Circuit has its headquarters in the District of Columbia but exercises appellate jurisdiction over all district courts in particular cases. For example, the Federal Circuit hears patent infringement appeals, but that jurisdiction extends throughout the United States. The Judicial Code also determines the number of circuit judges assigned to each circuit. The following statistics are taken largely from the website of the Administrative Office of the United States Courts at <uscourts.gov>, and they are accurate through September 30, 2005. Other information was taken from the website for the United States Court of Appeals for the Federal Circuit <fedcir.gov>.

CIRCUIT	ACTIVE JUDGES (SENIOR)	JURISDICTION
District of Columbia	12(2)	District of Columbia
Federal	12(5)	Nationwide but limited subject matter jurisdiction [patents, trademarks, for example]
First	6(4)	Maine, Massachusetts, New Hampshire, Puerto Rico, Rhode Island
Second	13(11)	Connecticut, New York, Vermont

Third	14(9)	Delaware, New Jersey, Pennsylvania, Virgin Islands
Fourth	15(1)	Maryland, North Carolina, South Carolina, Virginia, West Virginia
Fifth	17(3)	Canal Zone, Louisiana, Mississippi, Texas
Sixth	16(10)	Kentucky, Michigan, Ohio, Tennessee
Seventh	11(4)	Illinois, Indiana, Wisconsin
Eighth	11(10)	Arkansas, Iowa, Minnesota, Missouri, Nebraska, North Dakota, South Dakota
Ninth	28(22)	Alabama, Arizona, California, Idaho, Montana, Nevada, Oregon, Washington, Guam, Hawaii
Tenth	12(8)	Colorado, Kansas, New Mexico, Oklahoma, Utah, Wyoming
Eleventh	12(6)	Alabama, Florida, Georgia

A panel of three judges hears cases appealed to a court of appeals, and the panel can include a district judge from within that circuit. On rare occasions, all circuit judges of a circuit who are in regular active service can be called to sit en banc to decide an important case. In an especially large circuit, such as the Ninth, the court can use fewer than all of the judges for an en banc hearing or rehearing.

3. Supreme Court

The Supreme Court of the United States sits only in Washington D.C., and all justices, able and not disqualified, sit to hear each case. A quorum of six is required. The Court currently consists of a chief justice and eight associate justices. The number of justices has varied from a low of six to a high of ten. Although the number of justices is set by statute and not by the Constitution, Congress is not likely to increase or decrease that number. In 1937, President Roosevelt proposed his "court packing" plan which, if passed, would have allowed him to nominate new justices for each sitting justice who was over 70 years old until the total number reached 15. Although Roosevelt's proposal was rebuffed by Congress, his audacious challenge to the Court's independence has probably tainted any subsequent attempt to alter the number of justices.

The Court's term commences on the first Monday in October and normally ends in June of the following year. The Supreme Court can exercise original jurisdiction—that is, trial jurisdiction—under the Constitution over cases affecting ambassadors or other ministers of foreign countries and over cases in which a state is a party. Because the Court is not designed to act as a trial court, Congress has limited the Court's exclusive original jurisdiction to controversies between two states. As a practical matter, the bulk of the Court's caseload consists of cases within its appellate jurisdiction.

The Supreme Court exercises a largely discretionary power to review cases decided in the federal courts and by the highest court of a state. A request for review is made to the Court through a petition for a writ of certiorari. The petition consists of an explanation of the need for decision by the Supreme Court. The decision to hear a case can be made by as few as four of the justices (the "rule of four"). If fewer than four justices vote to hear a case, the petition will be denied. Although the Court has appellate jurisdiction over all cases decided in federal courts, it can hear only those decisions by state courts based on a question of federal law.

In rare cases, federal statutes provide for the initial decision of an especially important case by a three-judge district court. Cases decided from such courts can be appealed directly to the Supreme Court. An appeal from these decisions is a matter of right, and, therefore, the Court is obligated to decide such cases in some manner.

F. Federal Judges

1. Appointment

a. Article III Judges

The President of the United States nominates all federal judges who then must be approved for office by the Senate. Article III states that federal judges of the "supreme and inferior Courts, shall hold their Offices during good Behaviour." Good behavior has long been understood to mean life tenure. With such protection, federal judges can make difficult decisions without fearing removal by the voters. Article III provides further protection for federal judges by stating that their compensation may not be reduced during the time they are in office. In this way they are protected against a vindictive Congress which holds the power over the federal purse.

Although federal judges enjoy extraordinary protection from political retaliation, the appointment power operates as an indirect control. A President can choose nominees for the Supreme Court and other federal courts based on their legal philosophy in order to counterbalance a trend in the law which he deems inappropriate. The voters of the United States, as a whole, elect the President, and they can register their discontent with federal courts by electing someone who pledges to reverse particular judicial trends. The Senate also exercises political control by supporting or opposing (or, perhaps, not taking action on) the President's nominations for federal judgeships.

The President nominates individuals to be either the Chief Justice or an Associate Justice of the Supreme Court. He also nominates individuals to sit as circuit judges in a particular circuit, and others to sit as district judges in a particular district. Section 251 of Title 28 authorizes the President to appoint, with the consent of the Senate, nine judges to constitute an Article III court known as the United States Court of International Trade. Section 252 declares that these judges shall hold office during good behavior. The court has special jurisdiction over cases arising under the customs laws.

b. Other Federal Judges

Only those judges appointed to the Supreme Court (justices), to the courts of appeals (circuit judges), to the district courts (district judges), or to the Court of International Trade are appointed by the President with the consent of the Senate. Congress has, however, recognized the need for other judges to assist Article III judges in their work. Section 631 of Title 28 authorizes the appointment of United States magistrates by the judges of a district. Full-time magistrates do not enjoy the Article III protection of life tenure, but are, instead, appointed for a term of eight years. A part-time magistrate may be appointed to serve in a district for four years.

Within the territorial jurisdiction prescribed in that appointment, a magistrate has power to try minor criminal offenses, to hear certain pretrial matters in civil cases, and, if the parties consent, to try civil cases. Although no party may waive a defect in subject matter jurisdiction, a party may constitutionally waive his right to trial by an Article III judge and consent to trial by a magistrate.

Section 151 of Title 28 creates a unit in each district court known as the bankruptcy court. Section 152 authorizes the number of bankruptcy judges sitting in each district, and gives to each court of appeals power to appoint individuals to serve as bankruptcy judges in that circuit. A bankruptcy judge is appointed for a term of 14 years and exercises jurisdiction in accordance with Title 11 of the United States Code and § 157 of Title 28. A district court has appellate jurisdiction to hear decisions in its bankruptcy court, and § 158 also provides for the appointment by each court of appeals of a bankruptcy appellate panel of bankruptcy judges from the circuit to hear these appeals, with the consent of the parties. Therefore, an appeal from a bankruptcy court can be heard by either a district court or the bankruptcy appellate panel.

Section 171 of Title 28 creates the United States Court of Federal Claims. Although the 16 judges sitting on this court must be appointed by the President with the consent of the Senate, they hold office for a term of 15 years. In other words, they do not have the full protection provided in Article III. This court exercises jurisdiction over claims made against the United States which are based on federal law or on contracts with the United States.

Special federal courts exercise jurisdiction in geographical areas under federal control, and judges in these courts do not exercise Article III jurisdiction or enjoy Article III protection. The Superior Court in the District of Columbia, for example, along with the appellate court for local cases, the District of Columbia Court of Appeals, are federal courts but function as state courts.

2. Removal

The only method by which an Article III federal judge can be deprived of life tenure and removed from office is through the impeachment process. The Constitution declares that all civil officers may be impeached and removed for "Treason, Bribery, or other high Crimes and Misdemeanors." A majority of the House of Representatives must vote in favor of articles of impeachment, thereby acting as the rough equivalent of a grand jury issuing an indictment. The Senate then has a trial on those articles, and must find the judge guilty by a two-thirds vote. Although the total number of impeachments is low, judges have been the most frequent targets of the process, and some have been removed from office through conviction on articles of impeachment.

Congress has also provided methods by which federal judges may be substantially divested of their powers but not of their office. Under §372(b) of Title 28, any Article III federal judge who, though eligible, has failed to retire may be certified as unable to discharge his duties because of permanent mental or physical disability. The only remedy, however, is the appointment of an additional judge for the dispatch of the disabled judge's caseload.

A federal judge is required to disqualify himself in an individual case if he is found to be personally interested or if there exists an appearance of bias. The specific grounds are set out in 28 U.S.C. §455(b), which applies to justices, circuit judges, district judges, and magistrates. If a judge does not disqualify himself, §144 of Title 28 expressly provides the procedure for raising a question about the impartiality of the judge. In addition, §47 of Title 28 provides that a judge shall not "hear or determine an appeal from the decision of a case or issue tried by him." This narrow rule is significant because district judges may be assigned to sit on panels for the court of appeals of their circuit.

G. Hypotheticals and Explanations

1. The Internal Revenue Code established tax-exempt status for non-profit charitable corporations, and the Internal Revenue Service (IRS) promulgated regulations that define "charitable." In 2005, the IRS promulgated a new regulation that defined as charitable any non-profit hospital that provided emergency medical care to those unable to pay for medical services. The prior IRS regulation classified as charitable only those hospitals that provided free emergency care plus a substantial degree of non-emergency medical care to the poor. Several poor persons who had been receiving free non-emergency medical care from charitable hospitals under the old regulation were denied that service after the new IRS regulation went into effect. Grace Jones is the leader of a private organization that supports a national health care program for the poor. She has joined with several of those poor people who no longer receive free non-emergency health care in a suit against officials of the IRS, claiming the new regulation is invalid because it conflicts with the Internal Revenue Code. **Do these plaintiffs have standing?**

Explanation

None of the plaintiffs have standing. Ms. Jones has not suffered an injury in fact in that she personally has lost nothing because of the new IRS regulation. The other plaintiffs have suffered an injury in fact, but they cannot satisfy the causation requirement for standing.

Rules

(1) Standing to sue requires the plaintiff to prove that she has suffered, or is imminently in danger of suffering, an injury in fact; that this injury is fairly traceable to the defendant's conduct; and that a favorable decision is likely to redress the injury. (2) To show sufficient personalized effect for an injury in fact, the plaintiff must allege and prove that the challenged action affects her in some way differently from the public at large. (3) A showing of causation succeeds only when a substantial likelihood exists that, but for the challenged action, the plaintiff's alleged injury would not have occurred. (4) Redress-

ability requires a showing to a substantial likelihood that the exercise of the court's remedial powers will redress the claimed injuries.

Application:

The federal courts cannot exercise their power to strike down invalid laws except upon presentation of a case that raises that issue by someone harmed by that law. Ms. Jones cannot allege and prove that she was denied any personal benefit or personally caused harm by the promulgation of the IRS regulation. She therefore cannot have suffered an injury in fact.

The other individuals can satisfy the injury in fact requirement because they can allege that the IRS regulation affected them personally in that the regulation has an effect on a narrow class to which they belong. However, their injury cannot be fairly traced to the challenged action of the defendant. It would be purely speculative to conclude that current charitable hospitals halted the provision of free non-emergency medical care because of the tax benefits of the new regulation. Those hospitals were more likely to have made that decision because of the costs of such free medical care and other financial demands. See Simon v. Eastern Kentucky Welfare Rights Org., 426 U.S. 26 (1976).

2. **Would your answer to the standing question change if the Internal Revenue Code included the following provision: "Any person may commence a civil suit in federal court against the Internal Revenue Service to enforce the provisions of this Code"?**

Explanation

No, Congress has no power to confer standing on plaintiffs who do not satisfy the constitutional requirements.

Rule

The requirement of standing is a constitutional limitation on the judicial power of federal courts, and that limitation cannot be removed by Congress.

Application

Unless the plaintiffs can satisfy the injury in fact test for standing, they cannot invoke federal jurisdiction. Because these plaintiffs cannot satisfy the test for standing, the statutory provision cannot supply standing. To allow Congress to create jurisdiction without regard for the constitutional requirement of standing would be an unconstitutional expansion of the judicial power at the expense of the executive power.

3. Oklahoma prohibits men from drinking intoxicating beverages before the age of 21. However, the state allows women to drink such beverages from the age of 18. Weary of losing such a potential market for her products, a bar owner from Oklahoma has brought suit in federal court against the state officials responsible for enforcing the drinking-age laws. The plaintiff contends that Oklahoma laws violate the Equal Protection Clause because they discriminate on the basis of gender. **Should the court adjudicate the equal protection claim?**

Explanation

Yes, the bar owner can assert the rights of her customers.

Rule

In order for a plaintiff to assert the constitutional rights of a third party, she must show: (1) that she has standing, (2) that the challenged law regulates a close relationship between the plaintiff and the third party, and (3) that there exists some hindrance to the third party's assertion of his own rights.

Application

The bar owner has suffered and continues to suffer an economic harm in that the Oklahoma law limits her customer base. She does not have a legal right to insist on an unhindered ability to sell her wares, but her male customers do have a constitutional challenge to laws that treat them differently solely because of their sex. And she can be trusted to vigorously pursue the challenge to a regulation of the relationship between her as vendor and her customers. If the law prevents her from asserting their rights, underage male residents of Oklahoma will find their rights adversely affected or diluted. Under similar facts, the Supreme Court held that the bar owner did fit the exception to the rule prohibiting a plaintiff from asserting the constitutional rights of a third party. See Craig v. Boren, 429 U.S. 190 (1976).

4. Assume that three 19-year-old plaintiffs joined the bar owner's suit in federal court as individuals (not as representatives of a class), and personally asserted the equal protection claim in federal district court. After several years of litigation and appeal, the Supreme Court issued a writ of certiorari to hear the constitutional issue. However, these three young men

turned 21 before the case could be heard by the Court. **Would they be allowed to remain as plaintiffs?**

Explanation

No, the claims by these plaintiffs are moot.

Rule

Mootness occurs whenever a party ceases to have a real dispute against the defendant, other than the naked desire for abstract vindication, and when a judgment would have no practical effect on their disagreement. A case is moot when the personalized conflict has been resolved and any remaining legal issues have become academic.

Application

As individuals, these three young men no longer suffer a harm because of the challenged statute. A plaintiff's claim has to present a live controversy at all levels of litigation, and their claims are therefore moot. They do not present a situation that would satisfy any of the exceptions to mootness. They could have avoided this problem by seeking to certify their suit as a class action on behalf of all underage males in Oklahoma, but they did not do so.

5. ABC, a Texas corporation, recently produced a robotic cat that it plans to market as a toy or novelty at $2,500 each. After preparing over 10,000 of these robots for market, ABC received a letter from the attorney for XYZ, also a Texas corporation. The attorney claimed that ABC's robotic toys infringed XYZ's patent. ABC halted the sale of its robots, and XYZ has not sued. However, ABC is losing large sums of money on its investment. **Can ABC seek declaratory judgment in federal court?**

Explanation

Yes, this case is ripe for adjudication.

Rule

A court may issue the declaratory judgment if it finds that adjudication is necessary because of (1) the hardship caused the parties by withholding decision, and because of (2) the fitness of the issues for judicial decision (state of the record).

Application

Although this conflict appears not to have ripened into a live controversy, the parties already have taken adverse positions. The plaintiff currently suffers a financial hardship by being unable to use its investments to produce marketable goods. Finally, the issues in the case currently are fit for judicial resolution, and the court needs no further factual development. ABC's product exists, and the infringement contention of XYZ's needs nothing further. This case appears premature solely because the inventor has not begun selling his allegedly infringing product, and no reason requires the court to await that action.

6. Harold Robbins, a citizen of Iowa, is a member of the National Guard whose active duty obligation supposedly ended in September 2006. His unit has been ordered back to Iraq for its third tour of duty in that war-torn country, and the U.S. Defense Department has extended the service obligations of all members of the unit. Mr. Robbins responded by filing suit in federal court against the Department of Defense. In his suit, he contends that under federal statutes his service obligation cannot be extended and that ordering his unit for a third tour of duty is in violation of the Constitution of the United States. **Should the federal court adjudicate these claims?**

Explanation

No, these claims present a nonjusticiable political question.

Rule

As a matter of judicial self-restraint, a federal court may find a legal claim nonjusticiable under the "political question" doctrine. Under this prudential doctrine, federal courts refuse to adjudicate any claim that both requires them (1) to engage in a conflict of authority with another branch of the federal government and (2) to decide an issue that is peculiarly unsuited for adjudication but well suited for decision by that other federal branch.

Application

Such legal challenges force courts to consider remedies that would have unforeseeable effects. In addition, the judicial system's adversarial process is not well designed to produce judgments about the likelihood of future events, and these matters can be far better managed by an executive branch that has access to advisers with varied areas of expertise. We do not want our war policy being made by federal court.

PART II

FORUM CHOICE

CHAPTER 4

SUBJECT MATTER JURISDICTION

A. Terminology

Aggregation—In seeking to satisfy the amount requirement of § 1332(a) for diversity or alienage jurisdiction, the plaintiff may seek to add the amounts requested in several small claims to show that, in the aggregate, the lawsuit is worth more than $75,000.

Alienage jurisdiction—Controversies between citizens of a state and citizens or subjects of a foreign country come within federal jurisdiction.

Complete diversity—Section 1332(a) authorizes original federal jurisdiction, subject to the amount requirement, when no citizenship of any plaintiff matches a citizenship of any defendant named in the complaint.

Creation test—A plaintiff's claim for relief arises under federal law, and therefore satisfies federal question jurisdiction, if a federal statute directly establishes that remedy.

Minimal diversity—Section 1335 allows federal jurisdiction in interpleader cases, subject to a special amount requirement, when any defendant has a citizenship different from any other defendant. Section 1332(d) allows jurisdiction over a class action when any member of the plaintiff class has a citizenship different from any defendant.

Nucleus of operative fact—This refers to an event or logically related series of events that give rise to several causes of action. It is the equivalent of asking whether a subsequent or joined claim arose from the same transaction or occurrence that gave rise to the original claim.

Remand—If a case has been erroneously removed to federal court, the plaintiff can seek a remand order from the federal court sending the case back to the state court from whence it came.

Removal—A defendant can remove a case filed in state court to the federal court for the judicial district in which the state court was located if the plaintiff could have filed in federal court.

Supplemental jurisdiction—Section 1367(a) authorizes a federal court to adjudicate a state-law claims that arise from the same nucleus of operative fact that gave rise to the claim over which the court has original jurisdiction.

Well-pleaded complaint rule—As a general rule, a court will find the existence of federal question jurisdiction only when the plaintiff's complaint shows that her claim for relief was created by federal law.

B. Limited Federal Subject Matter Jurisdiction

Parties cannot litigate every case in federal court because the Constitution limits the federal judicial power. Therefore, in order to invoke or avoid the jurisdiction of a federal court, parties must be aware of those conditions that satisfy federal subject matter jurisdiction. ["Personal jurisdiction" refers to any court's power over a nonresident, nonconsenting defendant; "subject matter jurisdiction," as used here, refers to a federal court's power over the claim or over the mix of parties.]

State court systems often have several levels of trial courts, but state courts can adjudicate almost any type of case. State courts therefore are said to have general and unlimited jurisdiction. The Constitution allows federal courts to adjudicate only specific types of cases, and thus prevents them from exercising power over any other type of case. Furthermore, Congress must confer jurisdiction over any case that the Constitution assigns as part of the federal judicial power, and most of the problems with federal subject matter jurisdiction arise from the interpretation and application of those jurisdictional statutes.

Article III of the Constitution creates the judicial branch of the federal government and expressly authorizes it to exercise judicial power over specific types of cases or controversies. Section 2 of Article III lists these cases and controversies and, in conjunction with the Tenth Amendment, limits federal judicial power to these alone. Section 2 describes the subject matter of cases over which this judicial power can extend. In total, it lists nine categories:

- (1) cases arising under federal law,
- (2) cases affecting the representatives of foreign countries,
- (3) admiralty cases,
- (4) controversies to which the United States is a party,
- (5) controversies between two or more states,
- (6) controversies between a state and a citizen of another state,

- (7) controversies between citizens of different states,
- (8) controversies between citizens of the same state claiming lands under grants from different states, or
- (9) controversies between a state or its citizens and a foreign country or citizens of a foreign country.

In this book, these are often referred to as "independent categories of subject matter jurisdiction." Each category is independent of the others in that satisfaction of the conditions of one category is sufficient for federal subject matter jurisdiction. For instance, a federal court can adjudicate a controversy between citizens of different states even though the claim asserted in that controversy does not arise under federal law. Most civil procedure professors concentrate their attention on only two of these categories: cases arising under federal law (federal question jurisdiction) and controversies between citizens of different states (diversity jurisdiction). These categories provide the jurisdictional base for much of the civil litigation that enters the federal court system.

The listing of categories in §2 does not confer jurisdiction on federal courts; it merely authorizes congressional delegation of such jurisdiction. Article III is therefore not self-executing; none of these powers can be exercised unless Congress first enacts a statute delegating that power to the lower federal courts. Congress has delegated much of this judicial power through statutes, most of which are found in Title 28 of the United States Code.

1. Diversity Jurisdiction

28 U.S.C §1332(a): The district courts shall have original jurisdiction of all civil actions where the matter in controversy exceeds the sum or value of $75,000, exclusive of interest and costs, and is between … citizens of different States.

Article III of the Constitution extends the judicial power of federal courts to controversies "between Citizens of different States." In the statute granting this diversity of citizenship jurisdiction, Congress currently limits jurisdiction to those cases in which the amount in controversy is in excess of $75,000. The current general diversity statute, §1332(a), also has been interpreted to require complete diversity of citizenship between plaintiffs and defendants. The statute also confers alienage jurisdiction, subject to the same amount in controversy requirement.

The purpose for including diversity jurisdiction in Article III is generally assumed to be the protection of nonresidents from local hostility in state courts. By allowing federal jurisdiction, nonresidents can seek refuge in a federal forum presided over by a judge who is not subject to removal by the local electorate. This purpose is not, however, perfectly reflected in the statutes which allow either original or removal jurisdiction on the basis of diversity. A plaintiff may, for instance, invoke diversity jurisdiction even though she is a citizen of the forum state. However, a local defendant may not remove a case from state court to federal district court on the basis of diversity.

The federal courts will not exercise jurisdiction over cases requiring the determination of marital status (divorce or annulment), the determination of child custody or support, the determination of alimony rights, or the probate of an estate. They will, however, take diversity jurisdiction to enforce money judgments based on state court orders in regard to these matters. These restrictions are derived from the diversity statute, and Congress could theoretically confer jurisdiction over these cases. However, the federal courts are not well designed or supported for divorce and child custody issues, and the state courts have developed expertise and support systems for these matters.

a. Concept of Complete Diversity

In Strawbridge v. Curtiss, 7 U.S. 267 (1806), the Supreme Court held that the then-existing diversity statute required complete diversity of citizenship between parties opposed in interest. This requirement has been carried forward through subsequent reenactments and therefore remains a requirement of the current statute, §1332. As a result, no state of citizenship assigned to any plaintiff may be the same as a state of citizenship assigned to any defendant. For example, if one plaintiff is a citizen of New York and another plaintiff is a citizen of Indiana, diversity of citizenship does not exist if even one of the defendants has either New York or Indiana citizenship.

To determine the existence of complete diversity, one first places each party named in the complaint on his proper side of the litigation and assigns each his, her, or its state of citizenship. If any state of citizenship on one side matches a state of citizenship on the other side, §1332(a)'s requirement of complete diversity cannot be satisfied. Prior to suit, of course, the plaintiff may choose the parties to be named in the complaint and thereby protect the ability to invoke federal diversity jurisdiction. This choice is limited by the need to join parties who are liable on the claim and who can satisfy a judgment. Also, Rule 19 of the Federal Rules of Civil Procedure provides the defendant a tool to force the joinder of parties needed for just adjudication. If the plaintiff has failed to join a nondiverse party who must be joined under

Rule 19(b), the inability to satisfy the complete diversity requirement will cause dismissal of the suit.

b. Citizenship Determined at Commencement

In order to determine the existence of complete diversity of citizenship, the law must set a time at which citizenship is to be frozen for this determination. The filing of plaintiff's complaint commences a federal civil action, and the citizenship of the parties named in the complaint is determined as of that time. A change in the citizenship of the parties that occurs after the suit is commenced will not be considered. If a plaintiff changes her residence to another state after the claim arose but prior to the commencement of suit and thereby creates diversity, the court might suspect that she did not change his domicile. However, if the plaintiff has actually acquired a new domicile, her new state of citizenship will determine the existence of diversity. If the court is not satisfied that the plaintiff had the intent to make the new state her home, diversity jurisdiction fails and the case must be dismissed.

Once complete diversity has been determined to exist, it will not be destroyed by the defendant's assertion of subsequent claims. For example, a defendant might assert a counterclaim against the named plaintiff and against another person added in the counterclaim. If this new party is a citizen of the same state as the defendant, complete diversity appears to be destroyed because the new party is on the plaintiff's side of the litigation in opposition to that defendant. Whether the court has jurisdiction over the defendant's counterclaim is, however, a question separate from the question of whether it has jurisdiction over the plaintiff's claim. If the court lacks jurisdiction over the counterclaim, it will dismiss that claim but leave the plaintiff's claims in place. If the court has supplemental jurisdiction over the counterclaim, it will retain that jurisdiction even though complete diversity does not exist.

c. Alienage Jurisdiction

Section 1332 authorizes the exercise of original jurisdiction in district courts over civil actions between "citizens of a State and citizens or subjects of a foreign state." It also allows jurisdiction when the civil action is between "citizens of different States and in which citizens or subjects of a foreign state are additional parties," so long as the matter in controversy exceeds $75,000. This "alienage jurisdiction" protects citizens of foreign countries from state court bias in favor of local residents. In addition, alienage jurisdiction gives federal courts control over litigation which could have adverse effects on our relations with foreign countries. Alienage jurisdiction is limited by the provision which requires courts to deem a permanent resident alien to be a citizen of the state in which he has his domicile.

d. General Rules Applicable to § 1332(a)

In order to invoke jurisdiction under § 1332(a) complete diversity must exist between parties opposed in interest. One determines the existence of complete diversity in the following manner:

- Establish the citizenship of all parties included in the complaint at the time of commencement (time of complaint's filing).
- Complete diversity does not exist (and diversity jurisdiction fails) if any plaintiff has a state of citizenship that is the same as any defendant.

A natural person, who is a U.S. citizen or a permanently resident alien, has citizenship in the state in which he or she is *domiciled* at the time of commencement. A child has his domicile in the state in which his parents or custodians reside. A person who has capacity can change her domicile to another state by satisfying two requirements: (1) by voluntarily acquiring physical residence in the new state (2) with the present intent to make that state her home for an indefinite period of time.

A corporate party is deemed to have citizenship both (1) in the state of its *incorporation* and (2) in the one state in which is located its *principal place of business*. A corporation's principal place of business is located either in the one state in which the corporation does the bulk of its business or in the state where its headquarters are located.

The party invoking federal jurisdiction must affirmatively plead and, if challenged, prove the existence of facts from which the court can conclude that the matter in controversy is for a sum or value in excess of $75,000. Ordinarily, the amount the plaintiff claims in the complaint will control if made in good faith. To overcome the plaintiff's allegations, the defendant must show to a legal certainty that the claim is really for less than the required amount.

e. Natural Persons

A United States citizen is a citizen, for diversity purposes, of the state in which he is domiciled at the time the action is commenced. Domicile differs from residence in that one may have several residences but only one domicile. For example, a wealthy person may own houses in different states, but that person is deemed to have only one domicile. An individual's domicile is what is usually thought of as his home—that place which would be considered his principal place of residence.

There are two ways in which domicile may be determined. First, domicile may be determined by operation of law for those deemed incapable in law to establish their own. For instance, under the common law a minor is deemed to have the same domicile as his parents even though he resides in a different state. At one time, the common law deemed a wife always to have the same domicile as her husband, but that (probably unconstitutional) rule has been replaced by a rebuttable presumption that spouses have the same domicile.

An adult may change his domicile instantly if he complies with two requirements: (1) he must voluntarily move (as opposed to being assigned by the military, for example) to a different state, and do so (2) with the present intent to make that state home for an indefinite period of time. One might suspect the requisite intent is absent when a party changes his physical residence shortly before commencing suit. In order to determine whether that change in residence amounts to a change in domicile, the court considers circumstantial evidence relevant to proving or disproving that the requisite intent existed. Evidence showing that the party bought a home, obtained a new job, registered to vote, enrolled his children in school, or established other connections to that state prove intent. On the other hand, evidence that the party entered a short-term rental agreement, failed to move his family, and maintains primary contacts with his previous residence tends to prove that he lacks the requisite intent.

f. Corporations

Section 1332(c) states that a corporation is deemed a citizen of "any State by which it has been incorporated" *and* of the one state in which it has its principal place of business. Until the enactment of § 1332(c) in 1958, a corporation was deemed a citizen only of the state of its incorporation. In 1958, Congress decided to limit the ability of a corporation to invoke diversity jurisdiction by adding, as another state of citizenship, the state in which its principal place of business is located. This addition limits jurisdiction because by increasing the chances that a corporation will have two states of citizenship § 1332(c) reduces the likelihood of complete diversity.

A problem arises when the corporate activities have been rather evenly spread among several states. In general, federal courts name as a corporation's principal place of business either (1) the state in which the corporation carries on the major portion or bulk of its corporate activities, or, if no such state exists, (2) the state in which its "nerve center" or executive headquarters is located. If the corporation has clearly established its major operations in one state, even though doing business in several, that state will be deemed its principal place of business even though its executive offices are located in another state. When a corporation has its major operations in one state, its local connections are analogous to an individual's domicile. As a result, the corporation generally should have fewer reasons to fear judicial or juror hostility in that state's courts. If a corporation's activities are spread evenly among several states, Congress's direction to find a principal place of business requires the courts to choose among those states. The logical candidate is that state in which the company has established its headquarters.

g. Unincorporated Associations

Unincorporated associations such as partnerships, or unions, are generally not given entity treatment for purposes of determining their citizenship. For diversity purposes under § 1332(a), an unincorporated association is treated as an aggregation of individuals, and the citizenship of each individual member must be considered in determining the existence of complete diversity. A large labor union thus may not be able to invoke diversity of citizenship jurisdiction in its own name because its members are domiciled in every state. However, if the membership of an association is sufficiently large, the members might be able to satisfy Rule 23 and sue, or be sued, as a class. If a class action is certified, only the citizenships of a limited number of named class representatives will be considered in determining the existence of jurisdiction.

Section 1332(d)(10) creates a statutory exception to the usual rule by assigning an unincorporated association citizenship both in the state in which it was organized and in the state in which it has its principal place of business. This exception applies, however, only in regard to the minimal diversity jurisdiction conferred in § 1332(d) over civil class actions.

h. Realignment of Parties

If a Texas plaintiff in state court named, as defendants, one Iowan and one Texan, realignment, or repositioning, of the Texas defendant to the plaintiff's side would establish complete diversity. If the Iowa defendant learned, for example, that the plaintiff and the Texas defendant had completely settled their dispute, leaving only a claim by the Texas defendant against him, he could argue that a true alignment of the parties would allow him to remove the case from state to federal court. On the other hand, if the Texas plaintiff brought a diversity suit in federal court against two Iowa defendants, proof that one of the defendants should be on the plaintiff's side would destroy jurisdiction and cause dismissal.

In determining the existence of complete diversity, one asks whether a citizenship on the plaintiff's side matches a citizenship on the defendants' side. To answer this question, a judge begins by viewing the parties as aligned in the plaintiff's complaint. However, a plaintiff might misalign the parties in order to invoke diversity jurisdiction or, when filing in state court, to destroy diversity. To prevent this abuse, a federal judge has power to consider the correct alignment of the parties according to their interests in the primary dispute. If the judge concludes that the plaintiff's alignment is incorrect, he may place the parties in their proper positions and thereafter determine whether complete diversity exists.

As a general rule, a court will align parties according to their ultimate interest in relation to the primary and controlling matter in dispute. In simple cases, the court need only discover the primary point of dispute and then align the parties as they stand in relation to that dispute. Modern litigation is, however, rarely that simple. A court may often be faced with complex litigation in which the interests of parties can be both common and opposing, depending on which of the various facets of that litigation is considered. Under the general rule, a court is required to discover which of these various facets is to be identified as the primary and controlling matter in dispute. For example, if a plaintiff sues two insurance companies seeking to have them cover a business loss, the insurance companies may cross-claim each contending that the other is primarily liable. Under these circumstances, one of the companies might appear to have more in common with the plaintiff than with the other defendant. The court will probably find, however, that the primary matter in dispute is that of insurance liability and, in respect to that issue, the plaintiff is opposed to both companies.

A special alignment rule applies in stockholders' derivative actions. In these suits, a minority stockholder sues the officers or directors of the corporation claiming that they have wasted the corporation's assets. In order to qualify as a derivative action, the remedy must flow to the corporation, and the corporation must be a party. Although a corporation would appear to have the same interest as the plaintiff-shareholder, the officers and directors, as defendants, will often have their domicile in the same state in which the corporation either is incorporated or has its principal place of business. To avoid what would otherwise be a frequent barrier to diversity jurisdiction, the Supreme Court has aligned the corporation with the defendants whenever those who control the corporation (the officers and directors) are alleged to be "antagonistic" to the plaintiff. Antagonism can be shown whenever the parties who control the corporation have refused to rescind the action about which the plaintiff-shareholder complains.

i. The Jurisdictional Amount

Section 1332(a) requires that before a district court may exercise general diversity jurisdiction the matter in controversy must be of a sum or value in excess of $75,000, not including interest or costs. This limit is not found in Article III, but is purely the creation of Congress. Congress, in the Judiciary Act of 1789, established a jurisdictional amount of $500. It was changed in 1887 to $2,000, in 1911 to $3,000, in 1958 to $10,000, in 1988 to $50,000, and in 1996 to $75,000. The purpose of the jurisdictional amount is to prevent the federal courts from becoming small claims or collections courts required to expend their time on minor financial disputes.

Other statutes establish special jurisdictional amounts in particular cases. As noted above, § 1335 requires a stake of $500 or more in order to invoke the minimal diversity allowed for statutory interpleader. In the Class Action Fairness Act of 2005, Congress provided in § 1332(d) for minimal diversity over class actions. Congress also imposed the jurisdictional requirement that, in addition to minimal diversity, the matter in controversy exceed the sum or value of $5 million. Section 1332(d)(6) expressly allows the aggregation of the claims of all named and unnamed members of the class in order to satisfy this special jurisdictional amount requirement.

A court looks only to the plaintiff's complaint to determine whether the jurisdictional amount exists. It will not, therefore, consider counterclaims or cross-claims in determining whether the jurisdictional amount has been satisfied. In order to determine whether a claim has satisfied the jurisdictional amount, federal courts apply the "legal certainty" test. The Supreme Court described this test in St. Paul Mercury Indemnity Co. v. Red Cab Co., 303 U.S. 283, 288–89 (1938) (*citations omitted*) as follows:

> [T]he sum claimed by the plaintiff controls if the claim is apparently made in good faith. It must appear to a legal certainty that the claim is really for less than the jurisdictional amount to justify dismissal. The inability of plaintiff to recover an amount adequate to give the court jurisdiction does not show his bad faith or oust the jurisdiction.... But if, from the face of the pleadings, it is apparent, to a legal certainty, that the plaintiff cannot recover the amount claimed or if, from the proofs, the court is satisfied to a like certainty that the plaintiff never was en-

titled to recover that amount, and that his claim was therefore colorable for the purpose of conferring jurisdiction, the suit will be dismissed. Events occurring subsequent to the institution of suit which reduce the amount recoverable below the statutory limit do not oust jurisdiction.

This test causes dismissal in two situations. First, dismissal is called for if satisfaction of the jurisdictional amount depends on the availability of a particular type of damages which the controlling law does not allow. The plaintiff may, for example, allege damages of only $50,000 caused by the defendant's breach of contract. In addition, however, the plaintiff seeks an additional $30,000 in damages for pain and suffering. Plaintiff's total damages would therefore appear to satisfy the amount in controversy requirement of $75,000. However, the underlying claim for relief derives from contract law, and contract law uniformly prohibits the recovery of damages for pain and suffering. Since the applicable law bars the element of damage the plaintiff must allege in order to satisfy the amount requirement, he cannot, to a *legal* certainty, recover a sufficient amount.

Second, in a tort case in which the applicable law allows damages for pain and suffering, the evidence developed early in the case may show the plaintiff could not have in good faith expected to recover the amount required. Suppose the plaintiff must demand at least $25,000 for pain and suffering in order to satisfy the amount requirement. If, after discovery, the plaintiff's injury was shown to be only a fractured thumb, for which he took two aspirins before returning to his job as a carpenter the next day, no reasonable jury could award any amount close to the needed $25,000—that is, any such jury determination would be reversed by the judge. Although jurisdiction is determined as of the time the complaint is filed, the court *may* consider facts developed through discovery to conclude that the plaintiff did not made a good faith allegation in the complaint. If the plaintiff has not made a good faith allegation of damages, as shown by the discovered evidence, the court will dismiss the case.

A court does not lose jurisdiction if the defendant's actions reduce the amount in controversy. For example, jurisdiction does not fail simply because the defendant has a valid defense which reduces the claim to an amount less than $75,000. The matter in controversy, as well as the existence of complete diversity, is to be determined on the date the suit was commenced. Actions of the defendant that follow that date cannot alter the jurisdiction established at the time of commencement.

Jurisdiction also is not lost when the plaintiff recovers less than the jurisdictional amount at trial or when the defendant prevails at trial. If these were jurisdictional defects, the defendant would be robbed of the benefits of obtaining a final judgment in his favor. For similar reasons, the court does not lose jurisdiction if the plaintiff reduces his demand after the defendant removes the case from state to federal court.

j. Aggregation of Multiple Damage Claims

Suppose the plaintiff asserts two claims, one with a value of $50,000 and another with a value of $30,000. Neither claim satisfies the amount in controversy requirement alone, but the total value of both claims, in the aggregate, does satisfy the amount requirement. Courts allow aggregation to satisfy § 1332(a)'s amount requirement when one plaintiff asserts two claims (say, one for $50,000 and one for $30,000) against one defendant. This ability to aggregate, and thereby to satisfy the amount requirement, exists even when the plaintiff's multiple claims do not arise from the same transaction.

If the plaintiff had asserted the $50,000 claim against one defendant and the $30,000 against another defendant (claims *against multiple parties*), the values of the claims cannot be aggregated in order to satisfy the amount requirement. Likewise, if one plaintiff had asserted the $50,000 claim against the defendant, and a second plaintiff joined to assert the $30,000 claim against the same defendant (claims *by multiple parties*), the plaintiffs cannot aggregate the claims for jurisdictional purposes.

However, one exception exists to the nonaggregation rule that applies to claims by or against multiple parties. When multiple parties make claims which arise from a common and undivided interest in a single right or title, the claims can be aggregated. "Common and undivided interests" fit more easily within the conceptions of property law. For example, two persons who claim equal, undivided interests in land worth $80,000 have individual claims of only $40,000 in value. However, their claims are indistinguishable, and their adversary has no interest in how a judgment would be distributed. In addition, neither of the co-owners could bring suit without directly affecting the rights of the other. Once the two bring suit, their claims must both either prevail or fail; their interests are so intricately tied that no differentiation in outcome can occur. Under such circumstances, aggregation is allowed, largely because these two claims are really one claim, for $80,000, asserted by two owners.

k. Supplemental Jurisdiction over Insufficient Claims

If two or more plaintiffs seek to invoke the general diversity jurisdiction provided by § 1332(a), they must satisfy its complete diversity requirement and its amount requirement. If complete diversity exists but one of the claims asserted by a plaintiff does not have a value of more than $75,000, the court would seemingly be forced to dismiss that claim.

The general rule that applies when multiple plaintiffs assert insufficient claims prevents aggregation. When the claims by multiple plaintiffs are all insufficient in amount, the nonaggregation rule controls unless, in the rare case, all claims arise from a common and undivided right or title. However, when one plaintiff asserts a claim for more than $75,000 and another plaintiff asserts a closely related claim for $75,000 or less, supplemental jurisdiction supports federal adjudication of the insufficient claim. Section 1367(a) allows a federal court to exercise supplemental jurisdiction under these circumstances if the plaintiffs have been permissively joined under Federal Rule 20 or joined as members of a class pursuant to Federal Rule 23.

The Supreme Court in Exxon Mobil Corporation v. Allapattah Services, Inc., 125 S.Ct. 2611 (2005) (discussed more fully in the section on supplemental jurisdiction) held that insufficient claims by additional plaintiffs were supported by supplemental jurisdiction if they arose from the same nucleus of operative fact that gave rise to the plaintiff's claim that satisfied the amount requirement. More precisely, the Court held that § 1367(b) did not deprive a federal court of supplemental jurisdiction under these circumstances.

l. Minimal Diversity

Section 1335 of Title 28 grants district courts original jurisdiction over interpleader actions in which the stake is in the amount or value of $500 or more if: (1) two or more of the adverse claimants are of diverse citizenship (as defined in § 1332); and (2) the stakeholder has deposited the stake or a sufficient bond with the court. An interpleader action allows a stakeholder, such as an insurance company, which holds a sum of money it does not claim, to require a court to determine the rightful owner. If a number of individuals claim the benefits of that insurance policy, the company might fear that it could be liable for double the amount if it erroneously surrenders the stake to the wrong claimant. An interpleader action protects the company from this danger.

When a stakeholder brings an interpleader action, it appears as the plaintiff. If it has the same state of citizenship as one or more of the claimants-defendants, it could not invoke diversity jurisdiction under § 1332. To remedy this problem, § 1335 allows the stakeholder to bring the case in federal court if diversity of citizenship exists between two or more of the adverse claimants who appear, initially, as defendants. The lack of diversity between plaintiff and defendants does not cause the failure of subject matter jurisdiction because the Supreme Court has determined that this "minimal diversity" is within the constitutional grant of diversity jurisdiction allowed by Article III. Complete diversity thus is a requirement only of the general diversity provisions (subsections a through c) of § 1332, not of the constitutional allowance of diversity jurisdiction.

In 2002, Congress enacted the Multiparty, Multiforum Trial Jurisdiction Act, which added § 1369 to Title 28 of the United States Code. That section allows jurisdiction where there exists minimal diversity between opposing parties arising from a mass tort—that is, a multiparty civil action that arises from an accident in a discrete location in which at least 75 persons died—an airplane crash for instance. Jurisdiction under § 1369 also requires, in addition to minimal diversity and the fact of 75 deaths, one of the following:

- that a defendant resides in a state other than where the accident occurred,
- that any two defendants reside in different states, or
- that substantial parts of the accident took place in different states.

These provisions provide federal courts with diversity jurisdiction over cases that are primarily interstate in character. Section 1369(b) therefore limits jurisdiction when a "substantial majority" of the plaintiffs and the "primary defendants" are citizens of the same state, and the laws of that state will govern the merits of the case.

In 2005, Congress enacted the Class Action Fairness Act to regulate interstate class actions. The most significant jurisdictional change caused by this Act was the addition of subsection (d) to § 1332. Section 1332(d) confers federal jurisdiction over certain class actions brought in accordance with either Federal Rule 23 or state rules and over so-called "mass actions" when only minimal diversity exists between adverse parties. A class action under § 1332(d) falls within the original jurisdiction of federal district courts if the matter in controversy—that is, the aggregate of all claims by named and unnamed members of the class [see § 1332(d)(6)]—exceeds $5 million, and one of the following conditions is met:

- any member of the class of plaintiffs is a citizen of a state different from any defendant,
- any member of the class of plaintiffs is a citizen of a foreign state or is a foreign state and any defendant is a citizen of a state, or
- any member of the class of plaintiffs is a citizen of a state and any defendant is a foreign state or a citizen or subject of a foreign state.

However, minimal diversity jurisdiction does not extend to a class action that otherwise fits these requirements if (1) the plaintiff class consists of fewer than 100 named and unnamed members or (2) the primary defendants are state or governmental entities or officials protected from a federal damages judgment by the concept of sovereign immunity. See § 1332(d)(5).

A class action is defined in § 1332(d)(2)(B) as a civil action brought by at least one party as the representative of other unnamed members of the class. In some states, state procedural rules allow a large number of named plaintiffs to join as parties even though their claims share only a few common issues. Section 1332(d)(11)(B) treats these large-group "mass action" claims as if they were class actions, and they thus fall within the minimal diversity jurisdiction provided in § 1332(d) if:

- the monetary claims of 100 or more persons are to be tried together,
- on the ground that the claims share common issues of law or fact.

However, this provision of minimal diversity jurisdiction allows federal courts to adjudicate only the claims of plaintiffs that satisfy the jurisdictional amount requirement of § 1332(a), which currently requires each claim to be of a sum or value in excess of $75,000.

2. Federal Question Jurisdiction

28 U.S.C. § 1331: "The district courts shall have original jurisdiction of all civil actions arising under the Constitution, law, or treaties of the United States."

Article III of the Constitution contains the following subject-matter category of jurisdiction:

> The judicial Power shall extend to all Cases, in Law and Equity, arising under this Constitution, the Laws of the United States, and Treaties made, or which shall be made, under their Authority.

The Framers created this judicial power because they recognized the need for a forum that would be sympathetic to federal laws and programs. Furthermore, allowing federal courts at both the trial and appellate level to exercise "arising under" (or federal question) jurisdiction enhanced their ability to maintain uniformity in the interpretation of federal law.

Although federal question cases are normally litigated in federal court, Congress has not generally conferred this jurisdiction in a manner which excludes jurisdiction by state courts. In some instances, Congress has made the decision that particular federal rights require uniform treatment in federal court and has, therefore, granted the federal courts exclusive jurisdiction. For example, Title 28 U.S.C. § 1338(a) grants federal district court original jurisdiction over any civil action arising under federal laws relating to patents and copyrights, and this jurisdiction is made exclusive of state courts. Although most federal claims can be filed in state court, these can be removed under §1441 to federal district court.

Section 1257 of Title 28 grants the Supreme Court appellate jurisdiction to review federal questions in cases decided in state courts. The Court does not declare state law through this jurisdiction, and has no power to override a state's highest court in determining the nature of state law. It only has power to invalidate state law that conflicts with federal law. By adding jurisdiction over state cases to that which the Court exercises over lower federal courts, Congress has effectively made the Court the final judicial forum for federal issues. Furthermore, when the Supreme Court makes constitutional decisions, it acts as the final authority.

a. General Rules Applicable to §1331

The Supreme Court has interpreted this statute to require, as a general rule, satisfaction of the well-pleaded complaint rule and the creation test. A rare exception to this rule applies when a state law cause of action directly raises an "important federal issue" sufficient to justify federal question jurisdiction.

(a) Well-Pleaded Complaint Rule

In determining whether the plaintiff's complaint states a claim arising under federal law, the court will:

- look only at the plaintiff's complaint and not consider the defendant's answer,
- consider only those of the plaintiff's allegations that establish a prima facie right to relief, and
- not consider any of plaintiff's allegations that anticipate a defense.

(b) The Creation Test

Federal question jurisdiction exists when the well-pleaded allegations of the complaint show that federal, not state, law directly establishes the right to sue alleged by the plaintiff.

(c) Important Federal Issues

- Federal question jurisdiction does not (generally) exist when state rather than federal law creates the right to sue asserted by the plaintiff.
- On two occasions, the Supreme Court has held that federal question jurisdiction existed even though the plaintiff had alleged only a state cause of action. In these decisions, the state cause of action required a chal-

lenge to the constitutional authority of the U.S. Government, even though the Government was not a party.

b. The Well-Pleaded Complaint Rule

Section 1331 of Title 28 confers original jurisdiction on district courts over any civil action arising under federal law. The statute confers jurisdiction in essentially the same words as are used in Article III. The statute has, however, been interpreted by the Supreme Court to confer less jurisdiction than is authorized by the constitutional language, and the restrictions on the statute appear largely in procedural rules adopted by the Court. For example, the well-pleaded complaint rule limits federal courts in that it prevents them from hearing every case in which a decisive federal issue might appear.

The Supreme Court has interpreted § 1331 (but *not* the "arising under" language of Article III) to include a significant limiting rule—the well-pleaded complaint rule. The rule requires a court, in deciding whether federal question jurisdiction exists, to ignore any federal law allegations which merely anticipate or avoid a defense. Instead, the court can consider only those allegations of the complaint which state the elements of the plaintiff's claim.

The rule has two effects. First, it limits a court's jurisdictional inquiry to the plaintiff's complaint and prevents consideration of any defenses. By ignoring the defendant's pleading, the rule allows an early decision and one not subject to the defendant's whim in choosing whether to assert federal defenses. One of the rule's major advantages is that it allows the court to determine jurisdiction without expending substantial judicial resources and without imposing unnecessary costs on the parties. It also places the burden of alleging and proving jurisdiction on the party who invokes that jurisdiction in an original action. Therefore, if a federal question is not raised in the plaintiff's complaint, the case must be dismissed.

Second, the rule restricts a court's inquiry to those allegations in the complaint which are necessary to establish the plaintiff's prima facie entitlement to relief. The well-pleaded portion of the rule thus allows consideration only of those allegations which satisfy the minimum requirements of the plaintiff's claim for relief. Courts must ignore all other federal law references, including those made in anticipation of a possible defense. As a consequence, the rule reduces the possibilities for creating jurisdiction through artful pleading.

c. Declaratory Relief

The federal Declaratory Judgment Act of 1934, 28 U.S.C. § 2201, created an exception to the well-pleaded complaint rule. The Act allows a court to decide a case without entering either a damages or injunctive remedy, but simply by declaring what the law is when applied to the controversy before it. This declaration determines each party's rights or liabilities, and it can only be entered in an actual controversy. For example, a person threatened with a patent infringement suit by a patent holder who fails to file the action, can now invoke federal question jurisdiction by seeking a declaration that the patent is invalid or that it has not been infringed. In this manner, the Act allows one whose business may be endangered by a threatened suit to gain an early judicial determination. The Act's most important innovation has been the creation of a claim for relief for someone—such as the person threatened with an infringement suit—who previously could not have invoked federal question jurisdiction. Before the passage of the Act in 1934, allegations of the patent's invalidity could only be heard in federal court as a defense to the patent infringement suit.

Federal question jurisdiction over declaratory judgment claims is complicated by the Supreme Court's determination that the Act was not intended to expand federal subject matter jurisdiction. If the well-pleaded complaint rule prevents consideration of defensive matters from creating federal question jurisdiction, how can a former defense become a federal claim without enhancing jurisdiction? On the other hand, the remedial purposes of the Act would be undermined if it did not relieve parties from being held hostage by lawsuit threats.

To resolve the apparent conflict—that is, the Act on one hand creates new federal question claims, but on the other hand was not intended to enlarge federal question jurisdiction—the courts use what is known as a historical approach. (1) *Is the claim requesting only declaratory relief?* If the answer is no, the well-pleaded complaint rule should apply. If the answer is yes, proceed. (2) *Would the plaintiff's contentions, absent the declaratory judgment process, have arisen as a defense to a federal claim rather than a state one?* If the answer to this question is yes, jurisdiction will exist over the declaratory relief claim. If the answer is no, federal question jurisdiction over the declaratory relief claim is lacking.

Consider the case of the person threatened by a patent infringement suit. Assume she filed suit in federal court seeking a declaratory judgment that the patent was either invalid or that it had not been infringed; this relief would free her business from the threat of a lawsuit by the patent holder. The court would ask whether either party could have brought a federal question suit under these circumstances before 1934. The answer is yes, because the patent holder possesses a claim for infringement under the federal laws protecting patents. Because the answer to both questions is yes, the declaratory relief claimant can successfully invoke federal question jurisdiction as well.

The analysis is historical in that it requires one to look back to a time before the Declaratory Judgment Act's enactment in 1934. And a rather convoluted logic maintains the fiction that the Act does not enhance federal jurisdiction by allowing into federal court only those controversies which could have been there anyway, albeit because of a different sort of claim.

d. The Creation Test

In applying the well-pleaded complaint rule, a court must ignore nonessential allegations which merely respond to potential defenses. In order to disregard nonessential allegations, the court must first identify those key allegations upon which the plaintiff's claim is truly founded. The court then decides whether these allegations "arise under" federal law or, more precisely, whether federal law "created" the claim. The creation test provides the standard for making that determination.

To apply the creation test, one begins with the recognition that some law, either federal or state, must authorize the private right of action—the claim for relief—asserted by the plaintiff. Federal law creates the plaintiff's claim if federal law authorizes him to bring the private action he alleges. In general, only federal statutes create a private right of action to enforce federal law. For example, the federal patent statutes expressly permit anyone holding rights to a patent to sue an infringer for damages. Therefore, a patent holder who complains in federal court of an infringement is stating a claim for relief created by that federal law. Because the patent holder asserts a federal claim, she can invoke federal question jurisdiction.

Ordinarily, federal statutes do not authorize private rights of action for such matters as a breach of contract or for negligent infliction of personal injury. Those claims can be sued upon by private parties because the states uniformly authorize such suits. In most instances, these claims find authority in state judicial decisions rather than in state statutes. For this reason, they often are referred to as "common law" claims or causes of action. Therefore, if the allegations of a plaintiff's well-pleaded complaint show that he complains of a breach of contract, that claim exists because of (was created by) state law. As a result, the claim as alleged cannot be a federal claim and thus does not justify federal question jurisdiction.

e. Jurisdiction over Important Federal Issues

Although federal question jurisdiction generally requires the assertion of a cause of action created by Congress, the Supreme Court has long recognized an exception, though a rarely used one. Under this exception, a case based on a state law cause of action can be used successfully to invoke federal question jurisdiction when that cause of action depends on the decision of an important federal issue. As a result, satisfaction of the creation test will always be sufficient to justify federal question jurisdiction, but failure to assert a federal cause of action does not always demand the denial of that branch of jurisdiction. This exception, however, depends on a rather difficult determination — that is, what federal issues are sufficiently important to demand federal question jurisdiction.

In Smith v. Kansas City Title & Trust Co., 255 U.S. 180 (1921), the Supreme Court held that federal question jurisdiction could exist when the relief sought through a state cause of action necessarily depended on the decision of a substantial federal issue. In *Smith*, that question required decision of whether U.S. Government bonds were unconstitutionally issued and therefore invalid. However, the Court in Merrell Dow Pharmaceuticals, Inc. v. Thompson, 478 U.S. 804 (1986), held that Congress's refusal to create a private right of action to enforce federal drug labeling requirements supported the conclusion that plaintiff's use of those requirements to prove negligence in a state tort case did not create federal question jurisdiction.

In Grable & Sons Metal Products, Inc. v. Darue Engineering, 545 U.S. 308 (2005), the Supreme Court, in an unanimous decision, held that a question concerning the enforcement powers of the IRS sustained federal question jurisdiction even though that issue arose in the context of a state quiet-title cause of action between private parties. The issue was sufficient to justify federal question jurisdiction because:

- decision of the issue affects the U.S. Government's ability to enforce its tax laws;
- the issue was essential to the claim (it was the only contested issue);
- the issue was actually contested; and
- allowing jurisdiction will not lead to a flood of new cases coming into federal court, thereby depriving state courts of jurisdiction.

The Court placed special emphasis on the Government's direct interest in having a federal forum to vindicate the validity of its own administrative action even though it was not a party. The need for a clear rule for the enforcement of the Government's tax authority strengthens the need for uniform treatment in this case.

Had the Court accepted federal question jurisdiction over the state tort claim at issue in the *Merrell Dow* decision, that ruling would have drawn a flood of litigation into federal courts and out of state courts. This expansion of federal question jurisdiction at the expense of state court jurisdiction supported the Court's decision in *Merrell Dow* to deny federal question jurisdiction. The Court in *Grable* noted that few state quiet-title actions were likely to depend so clearly on an issue of such importance to the United States Government.

Although the Court's decision in *Grable* failed to provide a bright-line rule, it does provide a set of factors one can consider in determining whether a federal issue that appears in a state cause of action is sufficient to justify federal question jurisdiction. One key characteristic of a sufficiently important federal issue seems to lie in the effect of its decision on the operations of the federal government. That characteristic appears in *Smith* and *Grable*, but not in *Merrell Dow*.

f. Claims Arising under Federal Statutes

Some federal statutes expressly establish a particular right and also expressly provide that this right can be enforced in a private civil action. A plaintiff who complains that his patent right has been infringed and seeks remedies provided by this statute, thereby states a claim for relief that has been created by that federal law. The statute's express language proves that Congress *intended* both to prohibit particular activities and to use private lawsuits to enforce that prohibition. In this way, the patent laws create both a right (to be free of patent infringement) and a claim for relief (to sue the infringer).

To put into perspective the decision to create a claim for relief, one must recognize that procedures other than private lawsuits could be used to enforce the patent laws. For example, Congress could have, instead, created an administrative agency to enforce patent rights. Congress could have chosen to use the agency to enforce these laws and have denied patent holders the right to sue on their own. Federal statutes thus can create what appears to be a right without creating a private right of action (claim for relief). Because Congress has this choice, a federal statute that merely prohibits certain activities does not for that reason alone create a claim for relief. The statute must contain further language which authorizes a private lawsuit for the enforcement of the prohibition.

If a federal statute does not expressly provide for such a lawsuit, a court must find that it implicitly authorizes one before that statute can be deemed to have created a claim for relief. To find authority for a claim for relief, a federal court inspects the statute's language and structure, its legislative history, and other factors to determine Congress's intent. In other words, federal courts may infer that Congress intended to create a claim for relief even when Congress failed to say so. For example, a federal statute that prohibits water pollution implicitly protects those residing near navigable waters. If pollution harms such lands, an owner has standing to sue and can bring a federal claim against the polluter if the anti-pollution statute authorizes private suits to enforce the ban on pollution through lawsuits. If Congress banned pollution, one can assume that it also intended for its prohibition to be enforced. However, if the federal statute expressly authorizes enforcement of its pollution bar only by an administrative agency or through the criminal law, a court can only conclude that Congress considered its remedial options, consciously chose the remedies expressed in the statute, and refused to create a claim for relief.

g. Claims Arising under the Constitution

Although the Constitution has long been allowed as a defense against government action, its availability as an offensive weapon developed later. When the power of judicial review was established, the Constitution became a legal force that could invalidate other laws. A defendant could therefore assert a defense to his criminal prosecution based on the alleged unconstitutionality of the government's action. However, a plaintiff could not use the Constitution as a basis for a civil suit for damages or injunctive relief until other laws created constitutional claims for relief.

A private claim for relief alleging the unconstitutionality of action by state or local government officials is authorized by a statute, 42 U.S.C. § 1983. No statute creates a private claim for relief for violations of the Constitution by officials of the *federal* government. However, in Ex Parte Young, 209 U.S. 123 (1908), the Supreme Court accepted the power of federal courts to hear, without statutory authority, private claims founded on the Constitution which seek only injunctive relief. Without explanation, the Court approved such a claim even though in doing so it was exercising a common law power that federal courts ordinarily do not possess. Although the case involved a suit against a state official, the Court did not expressly limit its common law claim for injunctive relief to suits against state officials. The special importance of constitutional rights may be seen as the Court's justification for exercising this extraordinary power. And these rights cannot be fully protected if claims for their violation cannot be heard.

A claim for injunctive relief (as allowed by *Ex Parte Young*) does not provide a remedy for everyone whose constitutional rights have been violated. For example, assume that federal law enforcement officials erroneously enter an innocent person's home and subject him to a humiliating search, followed by detention in jail. The authorities recognize their error and do not institute a prosecution against the victim. He would, therefore, be unable to assert his constitutional rights as a defense. If the victim has no real fear that he will suffer from the same unconstitutional action in the future, he will not have standing to assert his constitutional claim in a civil action seeking injunctive relief. His only redress for violation of his constitutional rights would come through a civil claim for damages against the governmental officials.

In Bivens v. Six Unknown Named Agents of the Federal Bureau of Narcotics, 403 U.S. 388 (1971), the Court held that a plaintiff could recover damages against federal officials for a violation of the Fourth Amendment's prohibition against unreasonable searches and seizures. Therefore, a plaintiff asserting a claim for damages against a federal official for violation of the Constitution finds authority for that (federal) claim in this court-made law. In later cases, however, the Court has limited this claim by refusing to allow damages when special circumstances indicate that the remedy would be too intrusive—allowing enlisted personnel to sue their military officers, for example—or when Congress has already provided a sufficient remedy for the violation—by establishing federal civil service protections, for example.

h. Alternate State and Federal Claims

The plaintiff is master of her civil action and can choose to assert only a state law claim for relief even though an alternate federal claim exists. If the plaintiff files the state claim in state court, the defendant cannot remove the case to federal court based on federal question jurisdiction. If the plaintiff asserts both a federal and a state claim in state court, the defendant can remove both to federal court. If the plaintiff's two claims arise from the same factual background, a federal court would have supplemental jurisdiction over the state claim and federal question jurisdiction over the federal claim.

In rare cases, Congress may create a federal claim for relief and, in addition, declare that no other claim can be used to enforce that right. For example, the Employment Retirement Income Security Act of 1974 (ERISA) preempts all state common law claims seeking benefits under retirement plans regulated by ERISA. ERISA provides the exclusive claim for that relief. In such a case, assertion of a state law claim would be nothing more than artful pleading because no such claim can exist. If such is the case, a plaintiff who asserts only a preempted state claim cannot prevent the defendant from removing the case to federal court. Since no state claim can exist under these circumstances, the courts conclude that the action necessarily arises under federal law and thus can be removed on federal question grounds.

A recent Supreme Court decision applying this rule is Beneficial National Bank v. Anderson, 539 U.S. 1 (2003). In Anderson, the Court allowed removal of an action against a federal bank brought under state common law and statutory usury provisions. The plaintiffs brought their action based solely on state law, but the Court upheld the district court's refusal to remand the case, notwithstanding the absence of any well-pleaded federal claim. The Court held that § 86 of the National Bank Act completely preempted all state claims of usury against national banks. This complete preemption left the plaintiffs with no state claim, and therefore their pleading must be deemed to assert a federal action because they had no other. In order to find that a federal cause of action so thoroughly erases inconsistent state claims, three requirements must be satisfied: (1) the federal statute expressly created a federal cause of action; (2) Congress intended its cause of action to preempt all state remedies; and (3) the plaintiffs alleged state causes of action preempted by federal law.

3. Supplemental Jurisdiction

Supplemental jurisdiction finds its constitutional authority in the language of Article III which allows judicial power over cases or controversies. A case or controversy can include more than one claim for relief and, for this reason, provides sufficient support for supplemental jurisdiction. In 1990, Congress enacted § 1367 of Title 28, United States Code, which states that if "the district courts have original jurisdiction, [they] shall have supplemental jurisdiction over all other claims that are so related to claims in the action within such original jurisdiction that they form part of the same case or controversy under Article III." Courts have construed the "same case or controversy" language to include all claims arising from a common nucleus of operative fact. This statutory power supplants the court-made concepts of pendent and ancillary jurisdiction. Pendent jurisdiction was previously used primarily to support added claims by plaintiffs in federal question cases, and ancillary jurisdiction supported claims by defending parties in either diversity or federal question cases.

a. Application to the Complaint

The option of using either an independent ground or supplemental jurisdiction does not exist in regard to the plaintiff's original complaint. In its opening paragraph, the complaint must state the ground for the court's subject matter jurisdiction. The plaintiff's case must first fully satisfy one of the independent grounds as a jurisdictional foundation. In order to invoke federal question jurisdiction, for instance, a plaintiff must assert a federal claim for relief in the complaint. If the plaintiff does assert such a federal claim, she may add a state law claim that arises from the same case or controversy, and the federal court will have supplemental jurisdiction over it.

If the plaintiff asserts multiple claims in a complaint founded on diversity jurisdiction, he must satisfy the complete diversity requirement for all claims and parties. Section 1367(b) prevents a plaintiff in a case founded solely on diversity from using supplemental jurisdiction to circumvent § 1332(a)'s complete diversity requirement. In a diversity case, the plaintiff must show that no state of citizenship appears both on the plaintiff and on the defendant side of the litigation, as the litigation is structured in the original complaint. If the plaintiff could amend the original complaint in order to assert a claim against a new but nondiverse party, the complete diversity requirement would be violated. Even though the claim against this new party is part of the same case or controversy between the plaintiff and the diverse defendants, the supplemental jurisdiction conferred in subsection (a) of § 1367 is withdrawn by subsection (b).

b. Subsequent Claims

In federal question and diversity cases, defendants can assert counterclaims, cross-claims, or third-party claims. Such claims may have an independent jurisdictional ground. For example, a California defendant might assert a $100,000 counterclaim against a New York plaintiff. The defendant could have brought this claim as a separate suit in federal court pursuant to § 1332. On the other hand, a Texas defendant might respond to the Texas plaintiff's federal claim with a state law claim arising from the same factual base. Neither diversity nor federal question jurisdiction would support the Texas defendant's claim in a separate suit. As a compulsory counterclaim, however, supplemental jurisdiction supports its adjudication.

The concept of supplemental jurisdiction becomes less obscure when one recognizes that the factual events which cause a conflict often provide the basis for multiple claims for relief. Assume that three cars are involved in an accident on the freeway. The first car knocks the second car across the median into a third, and the injuries of the three parties result from these two collisions. Assume further that the driver of the third car sues the other two in federal court. The driver of the second car, now a defendant, wishes to assert a claim against the driver of the first car, named originally as his co-defendant. If the two defendants are not of diverse citizenship, no independent ground of jurisdiction would support the cross-claim because it is a state-created claim. However, supplemental jurisdiction allows the federal court to determine this claim because it arose from the same nucleus of operative fact. In effect, the two collisions, though distinct collisions, have a close causative relationship. The two events constitute one logically related series of events and, thus, a common nucleus of operative fact.

Assume that corporation-1 has been contacting those who do business with its competitor, corporation-2, to threaten them with economic retaliation if they continue dealing with corporation-2. Upon learning of these activities, corporation-2 first publishes a press release making very uncomplimentary remarks about corporation-1 and then sues corporation-1 in federal court. Corporation-2's basic claim is one founded on federal antitrust laws, but it adds a state law claim for unfair competition. In response, corporation-1 includes a counterclaim against corporation-2 for libel of its business, another state law claim. If diversity does not exist between the two, neither the unfair competition claim nor the libel counterclaim has an independent ground of jurisdiction. However, they both would be supported by supplemental jurisdiction even though, unlike the negligence claims in the automobile accident hypothetical, these state claims are not based on the same legal theory as the claim they supplement—the antitrust claim. Regardless of their legal nature, all three claims arise from a logically related series of events and would, therefore, be part of the same case or controversy.

In both hypotheticals, the supplemental claims would present a number of factual issues common to the claims supported by independent jurisdiction. The parties would therefore need to prove only slightly varying facts to establish the elements of all claims. Adjudication of the state claims thus adds little to the judicial power which would have been exercised by the court anyway. If federal courts were not allowed such supplemental jurisdiction, these supplemental claims might have to be adjudicated in additional suits in state court. In addition to avoiding these unnecessary costs, the exercise of supplemental jurisdiction enhances judicial efficiency. Because the legal issues arise from a common factual base, little additional effort is required for their determination, and juries are not likely to become confused in deciding the factual questions.

c. Discretion to Dismiss Supplemental Claims

Subsection (c) of § 1367 allows a federal court to dismiss supplemental claims whenever compelling reasons exist for not adjudicating the state claims. If, for example, the federal claim which establishes federal question jurisdiction lacks substance and the state claims seem far more important or pose novel issues of state law, a federal court may choose to dismiss the state claims. One would assume that the plaintiff would then bring the federal claim, as well as the state claims, in state court. Also, if the federal claim was dismissed for a non-jurisdictional reason before extensive preparation had occurred, the court has less reason to exercise its supplemental jurisdiction over the remaining state law claims.

C. Removal

Section 1441(a) of Title 28 of the United States Code reads, in part, as follows:

> [A]ny civil action brought in a State court of which the district courts of the United States have original jurisdiction, may be removed by the defendant or the defendants, to the district court of the United States for the district and division embracing the place where such action is pending.

1. Defendant's Choice of Forum

Section 1441(a) provides the general authority for the removal of cases to federal court. Several points can be drawn from the words of the statute. (1) The provision speaks only to civil cases. Special removal statutes allow the removal of state criminal prosecutions. (2) Section 1441(a) allows removal of a case only by "the defendant or the defendants." Neither plaintiffs nor third-party defendants have power to remove. (3) It permits removal only from state to federal court; it does not authorize defendants to take a case out of federal court and send it to state court. (4) Defendants can remove a state case to federal court only when that case is one of which the district courts of the United States have original jurisdiction. In simple terms, defendants can remove only those cases that the plaintiff could have filed originally in federal court. (5) The defendant must remove the case to the district court of the federal judicial district and division in which the state court is located. This requirement, rather than that of the venue statutes, determines the federal court to which a case is removed.

In most respects, forum-shopping is a plaintiff's gambit. A plaintiff often, if not always, chooses a court with an eye toward the practical advantages of that choice. She might bring suit in one state rather than another because of her convenience and/or because that choice inconveniences the defendant. She might have hopes of bringing the case to trial before a preferred judge or in a community in which prospective jurors are likely to view the plaintiff more favorably than the defendant. In addition to choosing among different states in which to sue, the plaintiff might have the ability to choose between a state court and a federal court. The plaintiff cannot sue in federal court unless the strict requirements for subject matter jurisdiction can be met. If those requirements can be met, the plaintiff might decide between a federal and state court largely because of the procedural advantages gained by that choice. For instance, most state courts routinely use twelve-person juries, but federal courts often use six jurors in civil cases. The juror pool from which the court draws these juries may differ significantly. A geographically extensive federal district may encompass large rural areas. Lawyers for plaintiffs in tort cases may fear the conservative tendencies of rural jurors and prefer the urban jurors who would dominate a state court's pool. Federal courts tend to follow more formal procedures, encourage more extensive cooperation between opposing lawyers, and require greater legal research. These complications make federal litigation more difficult and more costly. A lawyer might, therefore, choose or avoid federal court because of these complications.

Through removal, the defendant can trump the plaintiff's decision to file in state court if the plaintiff's claim could have been filed in federal court. By removing a case, the defendant gains whatever advantages a federal court offers over a state court and, perhaps, throws the plaintiff's lawyer into a forum in which she is uncomfortable. The defendant gains a further advantage by removal to federal court: once in the federal system, he might obtain transfer (a change of venue) to a federal court in a state more convenient to him. The transfer statute, 28 U.S.C. § 1404, applies only between federal courts; a state court cannot transfer a case to another state. Removal thus allows the defendant to escape a state court and, perhaps, even to escape the courts of a distant state.

2. Diversity Removal under § 1332(a)

As noted above, defendants can remove a case from a state trial court to a federal trial court only when the plaintiff could have successfully filed suit in federal court originally. However, a defendant seeking to remove based on general diversity jurisdiction under § 1332(a), must satisfy four requirements:

- The parties named in the plaintiff's pleading in state court must be of diverse citizenship.
- The defendants must be citizens of a state other than the state in which suit has been brought.
- The matter in controversy stated in the plaintiff's complaint must be of a sum or value in excess of $75,000.
- And, diversity removal must occur less than a year after the suit was commenced in state court.

Section 1441(b) limits removal on diversity grounds by prohibiting removal whenever one of the defendants is a citizen of the forum state. More precisely, § 1441(b) prohibits removal when any of the "parties in interest properly joined and served as defendants" is a citizen of the forum state unless removal is based on federal question jurisdiction. Congress must have believed that a citizen of the forum state needed no protection through § 1332(a) because that jurisdiction was conferred to protect nonresidents from bias in state courts. Moreover, under these circumstances, nonresident co-defendants are protected by the presence of a local defendant.

Because removal jurisdiction under § 1441(b) extends no further than the general diversity jurisdiction authorized by § 1332(a), the defendant can consider only the plaintiff's claim in showing that the amount in controversy requirement has been satisfied. He cannot, therefore, satisfy that requirement by asserting counterclaims or cross-claims. These claims do not count toward the jurisdictional amount in an original action and, therefore, cannot count in a removed action.

If the plaintiff's original pleading in state court shows a lack of diversity, the defendant cannot remove the case. On occasion, however, a plaintiff may add a nondiverse defendant in state court in order to prevent removal. If the plaintiff amends her complaint to dismiss the claim against that nondiverse defendant, thus making the case removable for the first time, the defendant has 30 days from the date he receives that amendment to remove, unless one year has passed since filing in state court. It is often said that a defendant cannot remove unless complete diversity exists both at the time the suit was filed in state court and at the time removal is effected. However, the purpose of this restriction is to prevent a defendant from taking action to create diversity, not to prevent a plaintiff from making diversity removal possible.

Section 1446(b) states that a case cannot be removed on the basis of jurisdiction conferred by § 1332(a) of this title more than one year after commencement of the action. This provision allows a plaintiff to prevent diversity removal if she fails to drop any nondiverse parties from the state court action until one year has passed since filing. By this late date, the parties and the state court will have invested considerable time and effort in the suit. Removal would force both parties to start anew in federal court in many respects. The plaintiff would start at the end of the queue waiting for a trial date in federal court, and she might well have to engage in further trial preparation.

3. Special Removal Provisions for Mass Accident Cases and Class Actions

Section 1369 grants federal courts jurisdiction over any civil action that involves minimal diversity between opposing parties and that arises from a single accident in which at least 75 persons have died. Special conditions restrict these actions to ones that are largely interstate in nature. See § 1369(a) and (b). Section 1441(e) authorizes the removal by any defendant of any action that, in whole or in part, could have been filed in federal court under § 1369. Unlike removal based on general diversity, a defendant who is a citizen of the state in which the action has been brought can remove under § 1441(e).

Section 1453 authorizes removal of class actions to federal court. Unfortunately, § 1453(a) and (b) seem to allow removal of all class actions to federal court. If accepted on its face, that statement would include class actions that had no constitutionally acceptable ground of subject matter jurisdiction. Since federal courts cannot exercise jurisdiction beyond that which Article III of the Constitution delegates to the judicial power, a statute that allowed removal jurisdiction without regard to that judicial power would be unconstitutional. The legislative history strongly indicates that the Multiparty, Multiforum Trial Jurisdiction Act of 2002 intended to confer removal jurisdiction through § 1453 only over those class actions within the minimal jurisdiction of § 1332(d).

Therefore, § 1453 presumably authorizes removal only of those class actions that would be within the original federal jurisdiction conferred by § 1332(d). These class actions are ones in which minimal diversity exists between a member of the plaintiff class and one defendant, which concern a matter in controversy of a sum or value in excess of $5 million, and which involve a class consisting of at least 100 class members. A defendant who removes pursuant to § 1453 can do so without obtaining the consent of other defendants and even if he is a citizen of the forum state. In addition, the defendant is not bound by the one-year limitation on diversity removal. Furthermore, a special rule allows appeal from a district court ruling on a motion to remand a case removed pursuant to § 1453. Although § 1453(c)(1) states that the appellant must make application to the court of appeals "not less than 7 days after entry of the order" to remand, that probably means "within 7 days after entry of the order."

4. Federal Question Removal

Unlike diversity removal, federal question removal does not have a one-year limitation. If the plaintiff at any time adds a federal claim, the defendant can remove if he does so within 30 days after receiving the pleading which makes the case removable. In order to remove successfully, the defendant must show that the well-pleaded allegations of the plaintiff's pleading establish federal question jurisdiction. As would be the case with original federal question jurisdiction, neither the defenses included in the answer nor the plaintiff's allegations which seek to avoid or anticipate a defense can create jurisdiction. In essence, the plaintiff must state a federal claim for relief in her original or amended pleading.

If a federal claim is joined in state court with state law claims, the entire case may be removed so long as the federal and state claims share a common nucleus of operative fact. Original jurisdiction over the whole case would exist because § 1331 allows original jurisdiction over the federal claim and § 1367 confers supplemental jurisdiction over the state claims. Because the plaintiff could bring all of these claims in federal court, removal jurisdiction exists over the whole case as well.

Section 1441(c) grants defendants an additional right to remove "[w]henever a separate and independent claim or cause of action within the jurisdiction conferred by section 1331 of this title is joined with one or more otherwise non-removable claims or causes of action." Under these circumstances, the entire case may be removed, but the federal court has the discretion to remand all matters dominated by state law. This provision protects defendants from being trapped in state court due to the deliberate joinder by the plaintiff of state claims which would be beyond a federal court's supplemental jurisdiction.

Section 1441(c) differs from § 1441(a) in that the latter allows removal of federal claims and any related state claims which would be supported by supplemental jurisdiction. The nonremovable claims mentioned in § 1441(c) would be state law claims that do not share a common nucleus of operative fact with the federal claim and are, therefore, not within the supplemental jurisdiction allowed by § 1367(a). If the plaintiff's federal and state law claims are unrelated, he could not have filed the *whole case* in federal court originally. Upon removal under § 1441(c), however, the plaintiff's federal claim can be removed and the district court can remand the unrelated state claims.

Section 1441(c) would be relatively unremarkable if it allowed removal only of the federal claim. However, it purports to allow removal of the entire case. Because of this scope, its conferral of jurisdiction over the state claims raises a troubling constitutional question. It should be remembered that § 1367(a) provides supplemental jurisdiction only over state claims which arise from the same factual base as plaintiff's federal claim. Because of that close relationship, the state claims form part of the same case or controversy represented by the federal claim. In this manner, § 1367 avoids conferring greater jurisdiction than is allowed by Article III. It thus merely recognizes that the case over which Article III grants judicial power includes all claims for relief springing from the same factually described conflict. If § 1441(c) confers jurisdiction over state claims which are not part of the case or controversy represented by the federal claim (or supported by diversity jurisdiction), it would seem thereby to confer judicial power not authorized in Article III.

Congress cannot confer judicial power on federal courts beyond that allowed in Article III, whether the attempt is to grant original or removal jurisdiction. Therefore, § 1441(c) cannot confer removal jurisdiction over unrelated state law claims that the federal courts cannot constitutionally exercise. Although this constitutional dilemma could occur, state procedural rules tend to restrict the joinder of unrelated claims, and a federal court can exercise its discretion to remand the state claims and thereby avoid the constitutional question.

5. Removal Procedure under § 1446

A defendant must remove a case within 30 days after receiving a copy, by service or otherwise, of the plaintiff's pleading showing that the case is removable. Service on a person who is designated in law as the agent for the defendant, such as a Secretary of State under a long-arm statute, delays the running of the 30-day removal period because the defendant could not know at the time of that service of the possibility of removal. However, service on a person actually designated as an agent by the defendant does constitute receipt by the defendant so as to begin the running of the 30-day period.

Section 1446(b) allows removal of a case that was not removable upon the filing of the plaintiff's original pleading but becomes so during state court litigation. This provision permits removal within 30 days after the time the defendant receives "an amended pleading, motion, order or other paper from which it may first be ascertained that the case is one which is or has become removable." Courts have held that removal can occur when the plaintiff settles his claims against the nondiverse defendant. Thus, a diverse defendant has power to remove even when the nondiverse defendant's name has not been formally removed from the plaintiff's pleading. However, as noted above, this last-minute form of diversity removal cannot occur more than one year after the state suit was commenced.

The language of § 1446(b) would also appear to allow removal if an order of the state court removed the nondiverse party. The federal courts have, however, refused to allow removal under these circumstances because federal jurisdiction might depend on possibly erroneous orders. Ignoring the removability of a case for this reason, however, gives plaintiffs power to frustrate the removal right of a diverse defendant even though state law recognizes the invalidity of the nondiverse defendant's joinder.

a. Procedure Applicable to a Removed Case

Removal procedure was greatly simplified in 1948, and further refinements were added in 1988. Today, a defendant may remove a civil case, pursuant to

§ 1446(a), by filing a notice of removal with the federal court along with a copy of all process, pleadings, and orders served upon him in state court. By attaching all papers filed in state court, the defendant provides the federal court with a complete file of the case. The notice of removal must contain a statement which explains the subject matter jurisdictional basis for removal. The defendant supplies these jurisdictional allegations because a plaintiff, having filed in state court, will have had no reason to plead facts showing federal subject matter jurisdiction.

In removing a case, the defendant does not ask permission of the state court or of the plaintiff. Instead, the defendant need only serve copies of the removal papers on the adverse parties and on the clerk of the state court from which the case was removed. Once service has been delivered to the state court, that court loses power to proceed further in the case. When the defendant provides notification to the state court and the parties, he effectively lifts the case from state to federal court. If the plaintiff wishes to complain about the removal, she must file a motion to remand in the federal court because it alone has power to determine the propriety of removal.

The Federal Rules of Civil Procedure control the management of a case after removal. Even though the plaintiff and, perhaps, the defendant may have filed pleadings in state court according to that state's procedural rules, re-pleading is not necessary. Rule 81(c) states that if the defendant has not answered prior to removal, he must do so (1) within 20 days after receipt, through service or otherwise of plaintiff's original pleading; (2) within 20 days after the service of summons (if a copy of the plaintiff's original pleading is not required to accompany the summons by state law); or (3) within five days after the filing of the notice of removal, whichever period is longest. Also, the defendant need not demand a jury trial in federal court if an express demand was made in state court or if the applicable state law does not require an express demand for jury trial. A defendant would always be safer, though, to make an express demand in federal court to avoid questions about waiver of his right to jury trial.

Although the state court loses power to affect a removed case, orders in effect at the time of removal are not automatically vacated by removal. All bonds, undertakings, or security given remain valid after removal; and all injunctions, orders, and other proceedings taken prior to removal remain in full force until dissolved or modified by the federal court. Particular problems can arise if the state court entered a temporary restraining order (TRO) before removal. A TRO is an injunctive order of very short duration which provides protection for a plaintiff who needs an immediate halt to the defendant's actions at the outset of litigation. These orders typically last only for 10 days, at which point a hearing will be held to allow the court to consider issuing a preliminary injunction to maintain the status quo during the pendency of the litigation.

If a state court TRO has been issued shortly before removal, it cannot remain in effect after removal beyond the time it would have ended under state law. As an added restriction, Rule 65(b)'s 10-day limit on a TRO creates a barrier against a state order which might otherwise last longer. For example, if a 10-day TRO is entered in state court on the morning of day 1, it will expire in 10 days from the date of its entry even if the case is removed to federal court in the interim. However, if the state court entered a 15-day TRO on day 1 and the case was removed to federal court on day 2, that order would expire on day 12—that is, 10 days after the case reached federal court.

In some instances, the transition can cause practical difficulties for the party depending on a state court TRO. Assume the plaintiff obtains a 10-day TRO in state court which should have protected her until the hearing in state court on his application for a preliminary injunction which was set to occur at the end of the 10-day period. But, on the day before the restraining order was to expire, the defendants filed their notice of removal in federal court. The next day, prior to the hearing on the preliminary injunction in state court, the defendants provide notice of removal to all parties and to the state court. This notification effectively removes the case, depriving the state court of any power to enter a preliminary injunction. In theory, the plaintiff need only seek an extension of the restraining order or the grant of a preliminary injunction in federal court. In practice, the plaintiff's attorney may find the shift in forum at this critical point very troublesome, especially if she is not familiar with federal procedure. However, when the 10-day state TRO expires, the defendant is free to act unless the federal court has issued a further order.

b. Remand

If the plaintiff contends that removal was procedurally defective or was done without jurisdiction, she must make that challenge in federal court by filing a motion for remand. If the federal court grants the motion, the case is sent back to the state court from which it was removed, and the federal court thereby surrenders its power over the case. The plaintiff can use as grounds for remand either a procedural defect in the removal, such as a failure to remove within 30 days, or a deficiency in jurisdiction.

If the removal was defective because of a lack of federal subject matter jurisdiction, the plaintiff can seek remand at any time because such defects cannot be waived. Even if the parties fail to notice such a jurisdictional defect, the court can, on its own motion, raise and decide the issue. On the other hand, if the plaintiff seeks remand because the defendant failed to comply with non-jurisdictional requirements, he must do so promptly. Section 1447(c) requires the plaintiff to complain of a procedural defect in removal by making a motion to remand within 30 days of the date on which the notice of removal was filed.

c. Appeal of Remand Decision

If the federal district judge denies the plaintiff's motion to remand, she cannot immediately appeal that order because, as general rule, only final judgments can be appealed immediately. Orders that do not end a case are referred to as interlocutory and normally cannot be appealed. In exceptional cases, § 1292 allows interlocutory orders, such as preliminary injunctions, to be immediately appealed. However, the law generally prevents interlocutory appeals because allowing appeal of each order entered in a case would produce interminable delays. Furthermore, the errors committed in the entry of interlocutory orders are often mooted by the final judgment. For example, a plaintiff has no reason to complain about the denial of her remand motion if she receives a favorable federal court judgment. On the other hand, an interlocutory order can provide a ground for reversal when the final judgment is entered. If the plaintiff loses in the federal court trial, for example, she might appeal and use, as a ground for reversal, the trial court's erroneous denial of the motion to remand.

If a federal judge grants the motion to remand, she ends that case's stay in federal court. Section 1291 gives the courts of appeals jurisdiction to hear all final decisions of the district courts. Therefore, because the grant of remand is final insofar as the federal court is concerned, the defendant ordinarily could appeal. However, Congress enacted § 1447(d) to prevent the appeal of remand orders (grants of motions to remand) even though these orders otherwise satisfy the final-decision requirement for appeal. Section 1447(d) provides that an order remanding a case is not reviewable "on appeal or otherwise." The "otherwise" refers to applications for the extraordinary writ of mandamus, which can be used as an alternative to appeal in some instances

Congress intended by this bar on appeals to bring an end to litigation which has as its sole purpose the choice of a court in which the merits of a suit would be adjudicated. At some point, it is better to stop fights about the choice of forum and allow the plaintiff to pursue her claim. The damage of an error in remand is, after all, only that the defendant will be forced to litigate in state court. Congress evidently assumed that neither the number of these errors nor the harm caused defendants by erroneous remands outweighs the delay that such appeals would cause to the progress of a case.

6. Devices to Frustrate Removal

If a plaintiff asserts a federal claim in state court, the defendant can remove the case on the basis of federal question jurisdiction. However, if the plaintiff possesses both a federal and a state claim arising from the same wrong, she might choose to assert only the state claim in state court to prevent removal by the defendant. A plaintiff should be wary of this tactic, however, because the value of staying in state court may not outweigh the benefits lost by omitting the federal claim. The plaintiff might find, as litigation wears on, that she would have a better chance of winning with the federal claim. If the plaintiff's resolve falters during litigation in state court and she amends to add the federal claim, the defendant can then remove if he does so within 30 days. No time limit, such as the one-year limit on diversity removal, restricts federal question removal.

In order to prevent removal, a plaintiff might initially join a nondiverse defendant in her state court pleading whom she intends to drop shortly before trial. Assume, for example, that a New York plaintiff sues a Delaware corporation which has its principal place of business in a state other than New York and joins, as an additional defendant, the corporation's New York employee. Prior to trial, the plaintiff amends to drop the employee as a party and proceeds to trial solely against the corporation. The plaintiff hopes, of course, for a more generous verdict if the jury does not worry that a working person would be burdened by it. If the plaintiff voluntarily dropped the nondiverse defendant within one year of commencement, the defendant can still remove if it does so within 30 days after receiving the amendment. A defendant might also remove a case where diversity exists but for the plaintiff's "fraudulent" joinder of this nondiverse defendant. State law must, however, clearly show that the plaintiff has no legitimate claim against the nondiverse party.

Another tactic plaintiffs use to prevent diversity removal is to assign part of the claim to a nondiverse party. If a nondiverse plaintiff has gained her interest through an assignment which is valid under state law, she would ordinarily be a real party in interest. If the defendant removed the case anyway, he could contest the motion to remand by arguing that this assignment was either unenforceable under state law—in which case the plaintiff would not be a real party in interest—or was a blatant attempt to render meaningless the congressional grant of removal jurisdiction. Section 1359, of Title 28 U.S.C., prohibits the use of partial assignments to *create* diversity jurisdiction but does not expressly prohibit their use to *defeat* removal jurisdiction. However, the right to remove should not be left at the mercy of such manipulable devices.

A plaintiff might also misalign the parties in her state court pleading to make the case appear to be one between non-diverse parties. To counter this ploy, a defendant can remove and then show, in opposing the plaintiff's motion to remand, that complete diversity does exist when the parties are properly aligned.

D. Hypotheticals and Explanations

1. Suit is commenced in federal court on March 15, 2006, by two plaintiffs (one is domiciled in Texas and the other in New Jersey). They complain about a breach of contract by the three defendants in November 2005. Two of the defendants are domiciled in Vermont, but one (D-3) changed his domicile from New York to New Jersey in February 2006. All parties are citizens of the United States. **Complete diversity?**

Explanation

No, complete diversity does not exist.

Rules

(1) For diversity purposes, a U.S. citizen is deemed a citizen of the state in which he is domiciled. (2) The primary requirement for diversity jurisdiction under § 1332(a) is complete diversity between opposing parties. Complete diversity cannot exist if any state of citizenship appears on both sides of the litigation. (3) A court determines complete diversity by considering only the states of citizenship that exist on the date suit was filed.

Application

P-1 (Texas)	D-1 (Vermont)
P-2 (New Jersey)	D-2 (Vermont)
	D-3 (New Jersey)

Since New Jersey appears on both sides of this suit, complete diversity has not been satisfied. Although a court considers D-3's citizenship only as it exists on the date suit was commenced, one might question the legitimacy of an alleged change of domicile that occurs after the cause of action arises but before suit is filed in federal court. See the next question.

2. Suppose D-3 in the case described above continued to own an apartment and to work in New York after March 15, 2006. His family lives with him in New York, and his children attend New York schools. He and his family spend their weekends in their New Jersey house, and he contends that his true domicile, and therefore his citizenship, is in New Jersey because he intends to remain there indefinitely. **How do the plaintiffs prove D-3's citizenship?**

Explanation

Rules

(1) A person with capacity can voluntarily change his domicile to another state by (a) establishing a residence in the new state (b) with the present intent to make that state his home for the indefinite future. [He need not intend to remain permanently, but he must not have a present intent to move at a certain date.] (2) Domicile, as a legal concept, resembles our more ordinary concept of a home. [To prove or disprove an alleged change of domicile, look at the connections one ordinarily maintains with the place he considers his home.]

Application

D-3 has not shown the requisite intent to change his domicile (and his citizenship). He "lives" in New York with his family. They treat New Jersey not as a home but as a weekend getaway. [One might counter D-3's claim of changed domicile by proving he has a New York driver's license, pays taxes in New York, and has declared New York his home at his place of employment. What else?]

3. A Texas citizen sued Nash, Inc., in a Texas state court alleging that Nash defectively designed the car that caused the plaintiff $2 million in damages. Nash is incorporated in Delaware, but has its executive offices in New York City. Six of Nash's 10 manufacturing plants are located in Michigan, but it has one plant located in Texas. Nash wishes to remove the case to federal court on the grounds of diversity. **Does diversity exist?**

Explanation

Yes, the parties have diverse citizenship, and the jurisdictional amount is satisfied.

Rules

(1) Under § 1332(c)(1), a corporation is deemed to have citizenship (a) in the state(s) of its incorporation and (b) in the one state in which is located its

principal place of business. (2) A corporation's principal place of business ordinarily will be in (a) the state in which it does the bulk of its business. If its business activities are evenly spread over a number a states, (b) courts tend to find that the location of its headquarters determines the location of its principal place of business.

Application

Because Texas is not one of Nash's states of citizenship, complete diversity exists between the adverse parties. Nash has citizenship in Delaware because it was incorporated in that state, and neither of the tests ("bulk of corporate activities" or "nerve center") suggests that Nash's principal place of business is in Texas.

4. **Why have I used state-created causes of action (breach of contract and tort) in these problems? Answer:** Diversity jurisdiction is required when only state causes of action are alleged.

5. Plaintiff (citizen of Utah) sues the defendant (citizen of Nevada) in a federal court in Utah alleging diversity jurisdiction. The plaintiff alleges a state breach of contract cause of action against the defendant and requests $50,000 as the profit she expected from completion of the contract and $130,000 in punitive damages because the defendant intentionally breached the contract. Utah common law of contract allows a plaintiff to recover only expectation damages. **What motion to dismiss should the defendant file? Will it succeed?**

Explanation

The defendant should file a motion to dismiss for lack of subject matter jurisdiction. The plaintiff can satisfy the requirements of diversity, but she cannot show that the matter in controversy is for a sum or value in excess of $75,000.

Rules

The Supreme Court, in St. Paul Mercury Indemnity Co. v. Red. Cab Co., 303 U.S. 283, 288–290 (1938), established the current test for deciding whether a plaintiff had satisfied the amount requirement.

> [T]he sum claimed by the plaintiff controls if the claim is apparently made in good faith. It must appear to a legal certainty that the claim is really for less than the jurisdictional amount to justify dismissal. The inability of plaintiff to recover an amount adequate to give the

court jurisdiction does not show his bad faith or oust the jurisdiction.... But if, from the face of the pleadings, it is apparent, to a legal certainty, that the plaintiff cannot recover the amount claimed or if, from the proofs, the court is satisfied to a like certainty that the plaintiff never was entitled to recover that amount ... the suit will be dismissed. Events occurring subsequent to the institution of suit which reduce the amount recoverable below the statutory limit do not oust jurisdiction.

Application

The defendant should file a motion to dismiss for lack of subject matter jurisdiction because, to a legal certainty, the plaintiff's claim is really for less than the jurisdictional amount of $75,000+. Under the law of Utah, the plaintiff cannot recover punitive damages as a remedy for a breach of contract. After subtracting the possibility of punitive damages, the plaintiff's breach of contract claim justifies a remedy of only $50,000. Once the court applies the remedial law of Utah, therefore, the plaintiff has been shown to a legal certainty to have asserted a civil action where the matter in controversy cannot exceed the sum or value of $75,000. The motion will succeed. If the defendant does not move for dismissal, the court can notice this defect in diversity jurisdiction on its own (*sua sponte*) and dismiss. A defect in subject matter jurisdiction suggests an absence of federal power and is therefore not a personal right. Because of the fundamental nature of this defect, it cannot be ignored by waiver, estoppel, or consent.

6. Plaintiff (citizen of Utah) sues the defendant (citizen of Nevada) in a federal court in Utah alleging diversity jurisdiction. The plaintiff alleges a tort cause of action against the defendant and sues the defendant for medical expenses of $150 in addition to pain and suffering damages of $75,000. Although the defendant is probably liable for the accident on which the suit is based, plaintiff's only injury was a bruised elbow. His medical expenses consist of an X-ray and one bottle of aspirin, and the plaintiff returned to work as a carpenter the day after the accident. **What motion to dismiss should the defendant file? Will it succeed?**

Explanation

The defendant will move to dismiss for lack of subject matter jurisdiction and will prevail because no reasonable jury could award the plaintiff more than $75,000 for a bruised elbow.

Rules

As noted in the quotation from *St. Paul Mercury Indemnity Co.*

[I]f, from the proofs, the court is satisfied to a like certainty that the plaintiff never was entitled to recover that amount … the suit will be dismissed.

In this instance, evidence gained after suit may be necessary to show that the plaintiff could never have hoped to receive an award that would satisfy the jurisdictional amount.

Application

In this case, no reasonable jury could award $75,000 for the inconsequential pain suffered by this plaintiff. As a matter of law, a court would overturn any jury award of that size. This judgment as a matter of law satisfies the "legal certainty" requirement and counters the good faith presumption that attaches to the plaintiff's allegation of damages. The defendant's motion to dismiss for lack of subject matter jurisdiction would, therefore, succeed under these facts.

7. Plaintiff (citizen of Utah) sued the defendant (citizen of Nevada) in state court in Utah alleging a state cause of action for trespass. The defendant constructed a five-story office building in a manner that encroaches on the unimproved property of the plaintiff in Utah. The defendant's office building unlawfully takes up a strip of the plaintiff's land that measures 43-feet by 3 and ½ inches. According to an appraiser, this encroachment has damaged the market value of the plaintiff's property by no more than $4000. The plaintiff, however, does not seek damages; she instead seeks an injunctive order commanding the defendant to remove the encroachment. The defendant's expert can testify that removing the encroaching part of the office building will cost the defendant several million dollars. **Can the defendant remove this case to federal court?**

Explanation

Yes, the defendant can show that from the defendant's perspective this claim is worth more than $75,000.

Rules

(1) The defendant can remove this case to federal court if the plaintiff could have filed it in federal court originally. The answer to that question depends on the satisfaction of the amount requirement for diversity jurisdiction. (2)

A request only for injunctive relief can satisfy the amount requirement because that requirement demands that the matter in controversy exceeds the sum or "value" of $75,000. A court must, therefore, attach a value to an injunctive remedy. (3) As a general rule, the value of a claim for injunctive relief will equal the benefit gained by the plaintiff by the issuance of the decree. This "plaintiff-viewpoint" approach causes a problem when the value to the plaintiff of the decree is different from the cost that the decree will impose on the defendant. (4) Courts have generally allowed jurisdiction under these circumstances by asking whether either the benefit to the plaintiff or the cost to the defendant exceeds $75,000. That "plaintiff—or defendant—viewpoint approach" seems to be a more reasonable method of determining the value of nonmonetary remedies.

Application

The defendant should be able to successfully remove this case to federal court and satisfy both the diversity and amount requirements. From the defendant's viewpoint, the remedy requested by the plaintiff poses a potential cost in the millions of dollars. If the purpose of the jurisdictional amount is to allow into federal courts only those cases that are sufficiently important in dollar terms, this case satisfies that policy.

8. In each of the following instances, two claims have been asserted in a complaint filed in federal court, and the only basis for federal jurisdiction is diversity of citizenship. [Read the first two subsections of the Supplemental Jurisdiction statute, 28 U.S.C. §1367(a) and §1367(b).] Assume both of the joined claims are part of the same case or controversy and that both plaintiffs are joined pursuant to Rule 20. **Can the federal court adjudicate Claim 2 in each set of circumstances?**

(a)

P-1 (Iowa)—Claim 1 (Tort: $120K)— D (Nebr.)
P-2 (Texas)—Claim 2 (Contract: $50K) —

Explanation

Yes, supplemental jurisdiction supports Claim 2 under these circumstances.

(a) Rule

In Exxon Mobile Corp. v. Allapattah Services, Inc., 545 U.S. 546 (2005), the Supreme Court held that so long as one plaintiff satisfied the jurisdictional amount requirement in a diversity case supplemental jurisdiction extended to insufficient but related claims by plaintiffs joined under Rule 20 or Rule 23. Section 1367(b)'s requirement of "original jurisdiction" over a "civil action" demands complete diversity. If complete diversity exists, however, § 1367(b)'s language does not withdraw supplemental jurisdiction from joined plaintiffs merely because of the insufficient amount of their claims.

Application

Yes, claim 2 under these circumstances fits within the supplemental jurisdiction of the court. Since P-1's claim is for an amount that exceeds $75,000, the court can also adjudicate the related claim of P-2 as supplemental to claim 1.

(b)

P (Nebr.)—Claim 1 (Tort: $120K)— D (Nebr.)
—Claim 2 (Contract: $50K)—D (Iowa)

Explanation

(b) Sorry! This is a trick question. Complete diversity does not exist, and therefore supplemental jurisdiction cannot support adjudication of either claim.

(c)

P (Iowa) —Claim 1 (Tort: $45K)— D (Nebr.)
—Claim 2 (Tort: $50K)—

Explanation

Multiple claims by one party against another can be aggregated to satisfy the amount requirement.

(c) Rule:

Although no clear justification exists for this conclusion, federal courts generally allow the aggregation of multiple claims asserted between one claimant and against one defending party. Aggregation of multiple claims is allowed even if those claims are not related sufficiently to satisfy supplemental jurisdiction.

Application

Addition of these two claims gives an aggregate of $95,000. Since that aggregate exceeds $75,000, the amount requirement has been satisfied.

(d)

P-1 (Iowa)—Claim 1 (property: $45K)—D (Nebr.)

P-2 (Texas)—Claim 2 (property: $45K)—

Explanation

Although claims by multiple parties generally cannot be aggregated to satisfy the amount requirement, these claims may arise from a common and undivided right or title.

(d) Rules

(1) Claims asserted by multiple parties generally cannot be aggregated. (2) An exception to this general rule applies when the two claims arise from a common and undivided right, title, or interest. That exception operates more sensibly in a property context when multiple parties have undivided interests in the property on which their claims are based.

Application

Under the general nonaggregation rule, these two claims would fail to satisfy the amount requirement individually and cannot be added together in order to do so. If, however, the two plaintiffs were suing to establish their ownership of a single tract of land worth $90,000, their two claims would satisfy the common undivided interest exception and would justify aggregation. Under those circumstances, the two claims are identical, and they only differ with respect to the division of any judgment.

9. Assume the plaintiff, a citizen of Texas, has sued the defendant, a citizen of Texas, in Texas state court for the state-created tort of defamation. In her original pleading in state court, the plaintiff alleges that the defendant's libelous statement is not protected by the First Amendment to the U.S. Constitution. She specifically alleges that she is a private person suing another private person for defamation and is, therefore, not bound to plead and prove actual malice. Actual malice is an extra element added by the First Amendment to any defamation cause of action brought by public officials or public figures. Assume further that the plaintiff cannot succeed if the First Amendment requires her to prove that the defendant acted with actual malice. **Can the defendant remove this case to federal court?**

Explanation

Since diversity removal is not possible, this case could only be removed based on federal question jurisdiction, and the plaintiff's complaint mentions federal law only in anticipation of that defense.

Rules

(1) Under the authorization of § 1441(a), the defendant can remove this case from state to federal court only if the federal court would have had original jurisdiction had it been filed there. (2) The well-pleaded complaint rule therefore applies both to original and to removal jurisdiction based on federal question jurisdiction. That rule requires a court to consider only those allegations in the plaintiff's pleading that state a prima facie cause of action and not any allegations that seek to anticipate or avoid a possible defense. (3) If the cause of action thus identified was created by federal law, federal question jurisdiction exists. (4) As a general rule, state law creates common law causes of action, such as ones in tort. (5) A state cause of action that relies on an important issue of federal law can be deemed sufficient to give rise to federal question jurisdiction. However, the Supreme Court created this exception in the *Smith* case and reaffirmed it in the *Grable* case, and both cases involved state causes of action that depended on a federal issue that could have had significant effects on the operations of the federal government.

Application

In these facts, the well-pleaded allegations of the plaintiff's pleading describe a state cause of action in tort. Any allegations of the plaintiff about the actual malice requirement of the First Amendment are in anticipation of the defendant's contention that this element must be satisfied by the plaintiff. Such federal allegations are, therefore, not found in the well-pleaded allegations of the plaintiff's pleading. Although the plaintiff's state cause of action would be affected by the determination of a constitutional issue, she does not base any element of her cause of action on the application of that federal law, and a decision on that issue does not pose a danger to the operations of the federal government. Since the plaintiff could not have successfully invoked the original federal question jurisdiction of a federal district court, the defendant cannot remove it to that court.

10. The plaintiff brought suit in Utah state court against the defendant, a national bank chartered by the federal government and located in Utah. The plaintiff contends that the bank induced her to obtain a loan using her prospective income tax refund as collateral, and that its loan agreement violated the laws of Utah restricting the amount of interest a lender can charge for a loan. She has asserted a state cause of action seeking damages for this violation of state law. The defendant removed the case to federal court in Utah, and there contends that the plaintiff's real cause of

action is under the National Bank Act. That federal statute sets the interest rates that a federal bank can charge, and it expressly creates a federal cause of action for violation of that restriction. Furthermore, the federal statute declares that no cause of action other than this federal one may be asserted against a national bank for excessive interest. **Can the defendant remove?**

Explanation

The defendant can remove because it can successfully allege that the federal claim for relief preempts any state cause of action the plaintiff could bring.

Rules

(1) A plaintiff who has both a state and a federal cause of action can choose to assert only the state cause in state court and thereby avoid removal, assuming the absence of diversity. (2) When a valid federal statute sets a standard, any inconsistent state law is preempted. This results from the operation of the Supremacy Clause of the Constitution. However, this "substantive" preemption of state law would be asserted as a defense to a state cause of action, and, under the well-pleaded complaint rule, a federal defense cannot create federal question jurisdiction. (3) When a federal statute creates a federal cause of action and, in addition, preempts all state causes of action on the same subject, a court must assume that the plaintiff's allegation of a preempted state cause of action is, in fact, a statement of the preempting federal cause of action. (4) This "remedial preemption" shows that Congress intended to provide a federal forum for the legal issues involved and that federal question removal should exist. See Beneficial National Bank v. Anderson, 539 U.S. 1 (2003).

Application

The defendant can remove this case to federal court based on the concept of remedial preemption. The National Bank Act expressly created a federal cause of action for those claiming that a national bank charged excessive rates of interest, and the statute also preempted all other causes of action that would bear on that question. Therefore, the plaintiff's state cause of action was really a federal cause of action because that's the only thing it could be. More to the point, congressional creation of such remedial preemption shows that Congress intended to make a federal court available through removal by removing a plaintiff's ability to assert only a state cause of action.

11. The plaintiff, a citizen of Oklahoma, filed suit in federal court alleging that on August 12, 2006, two police officers arrested him in Norman, Oklahoma, and beat him solely because he was cruising the streets of the downtown area of the city. These two officers are citizens of Oklahoma as well. The plaintiff alleges that their actions violated his federal constitutional rights and, in addition, that the beating also violated the tort law of Oklahoma. He seeks damages against the two officers pursuant to the federal civil rights cause of action authorized in 42 U.S.C. § 1983, and he also seeks damages from the officers by asserting the tort cause of action for assault and battery under Oklahoma law. **Can a federal court adjudicate the state tort claim?**

Explanation

Yes, the federal court has supplemental jurisdiction over the state claim because it arises from a common nucleus of operative fact with the federal claim.

Rules:

(1) The federal cause of action clearly establishes federal question jurisdiction over the federal claim. (2) Section 1367(a) authorizes federal courts that have original jurisdiction to adjudicate claims that would not be within their original jurisdiction when those state claims are so related to the federal claims that they form part of the same case or controversy. (3) The Supreme Court's decision in *Gibbs* established that when a federal and a state claim arise from a common nucleus of operative fact they form part of the same controversy.

Application

In this case, the beating of the plaintiff is the common event that gives rise to the federal and to the state cause of action. Therefore, these claims form part of the same case or controversy. Since the federal court has original jurisdiction over the federal claim, it will have jurisdiction to adjudicate the state claim as well.

12. The plaintiff, a citizen of Florida, filed suit and asserted tort claims against defendant-1, a citizen of New Jersey, and defendant-2, a citizen of New York in New York state court on March 1, 2005, seeking $100,000 in damages against each defendant.
    (a) Can the defendants remove on March 15, 2005?
    Assume the plaintiff settled his claim against defendant-2 in April of 2006, and gave notice to defendant-1 of defendant-2's dismissal on May 1, 2006.
    (b) Can defendant-1 remove on May 15, 2006?
    What if the plaintiff had originally asserted a federal civil rights claim, instead of a tort claim, against defendant-1 that arose from the same facts

that gave rise to her personal injury claim against defendant-2. The plaintiff's claim against defendant-2 was, therefore, a state tort claim.
(c) **Can the defendants remove both claims to federal court if they do so in a timely manner?**

Explanation

(a) Rule

Defendants cannot remove on diversity grounds if one of them is a citizen of the state in which the suit has been filed. See § 1441(b).

Application

Since defendant-2 is a citizen of New York and the suit was filed in New York, these defendants cannot remove on diversity grounds.

(b) Rule

Even though the defendant sought to remove this case within 30 days after it became removable for the first time, defendants cannot remove on diversity grounds more than a year after suit was filed in state court. See § 1446(b).

Application

Defendant-1 could remove only on diversity grounds, and his removal would come more than one year after the plaintiff initiated this suit in New York state court on March 1, 2005. As a result, defendant-1 cannot remove.

(c) Rule:

If the plaintiff could have filed his suit in federal court originally, a federal court would have jurisdiction over the case upon removal.

Application

If the plaintiff had alleged a federal claim against one defendant and a closely related state claim against the other, both could remove to federal court. The federal claim against defendant-1 would be supported by federal question jurisdiction, and the state claim against defendant-2 would be supported by supplemental jurisdiction under § 1367(a).

CHAPTER 5

PERSONAL JURISDICTION

A. Terminology

Amenability—From the court's standpoint, this term refers to its ability to force a defendant to defend himself in that court. From the defendant's standpoint, the term refers to his vulnerability to a court's jurisdiction. If a nonresident has had minimum contacts with the forum state, he is amenable to the jurisdiction of a court of that state and can be forced to litigate there.

In Personam **jurisdiction**—This phrase refers to the jurisdiction a court has over the person of the defendant.

In Rem **jurisdiction**—Although no longer sufficient under due process, a court could at one time obtain jurisdiction over a nonresident defendant's local property. The court was said to have acquired *in rem* jurisdiction—that is, jurisdiction only over the "res" or the property.

General appearance—A defendant who appeared to defend himself on the merits of a claim was said to have made a general appearance, which means that he waived his objection to personal jurisdiction.

General jurisdiction—A court can obtain jurisdiction over a nonresident defendant in regard to any cause of action if that defendant has substantial, continuous, and systematic contacts with the forum state.

Special appearance—A defendant can avoid making a general appearance if he, instead, made a special appearance in the court solely for the purpose of challenging that court's jurisdiction. This is not a requirement in federal court.

Specific jurisdiction—A court can obtain jurisdiction over a nonresident defendant in regard to a specific cause of action if the defendant's contacts with the forum state are related or give rise to that cause of action.

Transient jurisdiction—A court can acquire jurisdiction over a nonresident individual if personal service of process is made on the defendant while he is voluntarily within the forum state.

B. The Constitutional Problems

1. Amenability and Notice

Personal jurisdiction consists primarily of two constitutional problems. The first concerns what is often referred to as the defendant's "amenability" to service of process. amenability depends on whether the Due Process Clause of the Fourteenth Amendment prevents the forum state court from asserting its judicial power over a nonresident defendant who has been served outside the borders of that state. This problem concerns the constitutional limit on a court's territorial reach or, more to the point, its power to force a person residing outside the forum state to litigate in it. The identifying characteristics of this problem therefore consist of the following: a court in the forum state asserts its power (jurisdiction) through service of process (summons and a copy of the complaint) on a defendant residing and located outside the forum state, and the defendant objects properly.

The second constitutional problem arises also from the Due Process Clause but concerns the efficiency of the means used to deliver the initial information about a lawsuit to the defendant. This due-process notice problem focuses on the likelihood that the delivery method will provide actual notice to the defendant. Again, the primary constitutional concern is with the fairness of the procedure being used to initiate a lawsuit. In an adversary system, one can hardly contend that a judgment was fairly entered if the defendant was not notified that a lawsuit had been brought against him.

2. Complications

a. Corporate Residence

Corporate defendants cause many of the modern jurisdictional problems. Unlike a natural person, a corporation does not have a single physical being which can be found within a state's borders. A corporation is an abstraction that can only be represented by its officers, employees, or shareholders. These individuals represent the corporation, but do not wholly embody it. Therefore, service on one or more of them (even in the forum state) generally satisfies the notice requirement, but does not alone satisfy the amenability requirement of due process. It is for this reason that a court cannot obtain the benefits of transient jurisdiction merely because the plaintiff made personal service on the officers or shareholders of a nonresident corporation in the forum state.

The law has traditionally assigned corporations residence or citizenship because those concepts do not apply easily to what are often sprawling but coherent organizations. For purposes of personal jurisdiction, federal law assigns to a corporation legal residence in the state in which it was incorporated. If, therefore, a plaintiff sues a corporation incorporated in the forum state, that court has general jurisdiction over the corporation.

An inordinate number of large corporations have been incorporated in Delaware because of the tax and other benefits offered by that state, but primarily operate in other states. Therefore, a plaintiff suing such a corporation in a state other than Delaware is seeking to assert personal jurisdiction over a nonresident.

b. Long-Arm Statutes

A court that could constitutionally exercise extraterritorial jurisdiction may be unable to do so because it lacks *statutory* authority. In general, federal and state courts do not have power to exercise extraterritorial jurisdiction in the absence of legislatively conferred authority. State laws and Rule 4 of the Federal Rules of Civil Procedure uniformly authorize the issuance of process, and therefore the assertion of jurisdiction, throughout the forum state. However, to assert jurisdiction over defendants found outside the forum state, either a state or federal statute must provide that authority. A statute may do so by either declaring the amenability of nonresident defendants under certain circumstances or by allowing service on nonresidents under those circumstances. Because due process has always allowed jurisdiction to reach those found or served within the forum state, laws allowing a court to extend its reach outside the forum state became known as "long-arm statutes."

Each state has such a law for civil cases, and federal courts can use the long-arm statute of the state in which they are located. Modern state enactments of this sort have tended to allow local courts to exercise jurisdiction over defendants to the extent allowed by due process. However, state long-arm statutes need not authorize extraterritorial jurisdiction to that extent. For example, a state might allow its courts to exercise jurisdiction over nonresident corporations but only if they are doing business in the state. This "doing business" language may not allow jurisdiction if the corporation has limited but purposeful contacts that satisfy due process. The Constitution does not require states to extend jurisdiction to the due process limit; it merely prevents state courts from going beyond that limit.

c. Federal Courts and Personal Jurisdiction

The Fourteenth Amendment, by its terms, limits only the power of state courts. However, a federal court has authority under Rule 4 of the Federal Rules of Civil Procedure to use state long-arm statutes as authority in extending its jurisdictional reach beyond the borders of the state in which it is located. Federal long-arm statutes exist only for special cases—statutory interpleader, for example. If a federal court uses a federal long-arm statute, the Fifth Amendment's Due Process Clause, which includes essentially the same language as the Fourteenth Amendment's Due Process Clause, provides the jurisdictional limit. The Fifth Amendment generally allows jurisdiction throughout the United States—the sovereign reach of the federal government.

In most of the private litigation in federal court, a federal long-arm statute will not exist, and the plaintiff must rely on state statutes. State long-arm statutes can be used in diversity cases or even when the claim arises under federal law. Whenever a plaintiff in federal court uses a state long-arm statute, the due process limit on states applies to determine the federal court's jurisdiction over the defendant. That particular due process limit requires a nonresident to have minimum contacts with the forum state.

d. Subject Matter Jurisdiction Distinguished

The objection to personal jurisdiction is a personal right based on the Due Process Clause. It, therefore, can be lost through waiver, through contract (consenting ahead of time to jurisdiction in designated courts), or through estoppel.

Objections to the assertion of federal subject matter jurisdiction, on the other hand, arise because of the limited judicial power allowed federal courts in Article III of the Constitution. The specificity of these grants implies a limited subject matter jurisdiction, and this limit prevents judicial usurpation of powers belonging to other branches of the federal government and preserves the role of state courts. Article III therefore does not confer constitutional rights on individuals. Instead, it allocates governmental powers in our federal system, and federal courts cannot exercise powers not assigned to the judicial branch by Article III. This characteristic shows why individual litigants cannot cause a federal court to ignore defects in subject matter jurisdiction, regardless of whether the reason is called waiver, consent, or estoppel.

3. Full Faith and Credit

Prior to the ratification of the Fourteenth Amendment in 1868, the Full Faith and Credit Clause provided the only constitutional limit on a court's assertion of jurisdiction. That provision, Article IV § 1, reads as follows:

> Full Faith and Credit shall be given in each State to the public Acts, Records, and judicial Proceedings of every other State. And the Con-

gress may by general Laws prescribe the Manner in which such Acts, Records and Proceedings shall be proved, and the Effect thereof.

The implementing statute, 28 U.S.C. § 1738, mandates that the judicial proceedings of any state "shall have the same full faith and credit in every court within the United States ... as they have by law or usage in the courts of [the state] from which they are taken." As a result, § 1738 requires each state to enforce the judgments of sister states, and requires the responding state to enforce that judgment to the extent the state issuing the judgment would have done so. The statute has its most significant, practical effect when a court enters a judgment against someone whose assets are located outside the forum state. Under these circumstances, the judgment must be enforced (or executed) where the judgment-debtor's property is located. Since the original court has no power in the second state, its judgment has to be first accepted for enforcement by the courts of the second state.

Section 1738 has long been interpreted to require the second or enforcing state to enforce only the *valid* judgments of another state. In order to be a valid judgment and therefore enforceable under full faith and credit, a judgment must have been entered with personal jurisdiction. Prior to the Civil War, the courts had generally adopted a territorial approach to jurisdiction as a means of accommodating the conflicts of state sovereignty that could develop when one state exercised jurisdiction over persons or property located in another state. This approach consisted of two geographical principles for determining jurisdiction. The first principle was that a state court could assert jurisdiction over persons and property located within that state. The second principle held that a court could not exercise jurisdiction over persons or property located outside the forum state. These two principles governed the validity of judgments enforced in a second state, but did not apply to enforcement of the judgment in the issuing State. *See, e.g.,* Lafayette Insurance Company v. French, *et al.,* 59 U.S. 404, 406 (1855).

4. Due Process and State Sovereignty

Civil procedure casebooks ordinarily begin coverage of personal jurisdiction with the Supreme Court's decision in Pennoyer v. Neff, 95 U.S. 714 (1878). In this landmark case, the Court for the first time applied the Due Process Clause of the Fourteenth Amendment as a constitutional limit on state courts' power over parties. That clause declares that no state shall "deprive any person of life, liberty, or property, without due process of law." To give meaning to due process in this context, the Court adopted the *in personam* and *in rem* territorial principles that had given structure to jurisdictional analysis in full-faith-and-credit situations. It held that due process permitted the assertion of jurisdiction over those persons or that property found within the borders of the forum state, but it prohibited any direct assertion of jurisdiction over persons or property located outside the state.

By placing these restrictions in the Due Process Clause, the Supreme Court made all judgments vulnerable to a constitutionally based jurisdictional challenge. Under § 1738, the territorial principles were used only to prevent enforcement in a state other than the forum state. Once they were absorbed into due process, even the forum state could not enforce one of its own judgments that was entered without jurisdiction.

Pennoyer held that due process required a proper assertion of judicial authority over either a person found within the area subject to a state's sovereign power—*in personam* jurisdiction—or over property located within the state and belonging to the defendant—*in rem* jurisdiction. The court, or the plaintiff on its behalf, was required by due process to satisfy one or the other, but not both, of these categories. Furthermore, evidence of a proper assertion of sovereignty had to be proved in *in personam* cases by personal service of process on the person of the defendant while he was present in the forum state. Few would argue that a state should not have power to regulate even nonresidents who were present in its territory, and personal service proved the defendant's presence.

In the absence of an *in personam* basis for jurisdiction, a state court could satisfy due process only by initiating an *in rem* action. This alternative required the formal proof of sovereignty by seizure of local property (the *res*). When the state court needed power over property located in the state, it was required to prove the validity of its sovereignty by asserting control over that local property at the outset of litigation. A court's satisfaction of either requirement allowed it to validly assert jurisdiction, but *in rem* jurisdiction was constitutionally limited in that the state court could only impose a judgment to the extent of the local property's value.

By restricting jurisdiction to defendants who were present within the state, the Supreme Court in *Pennoyer* avoided conflicting jurisdictional claims (or just conflict) among the states. This was not an abstract danger because, as noted above, judgments against outsiders frequently had to be enforced in the outsider's home state. The courts of that second state might understandably resent a foreign judgment entered unfairly against a local resident. The territorial principles had the traditional pedigree gained through use in full-faith-and-credit cases, and they made sense in a constitutional system created, in part, to moderate interstate hostility. The Civil War had ended only thirteen years before the *Pennoyer* decision, and those circumstances emphasized the need to reduce friction and encourage cooperation among the states.

Although providing fair notice to the defendant was not the primary motive of the Court's decision, personal delivery of the papers outlining the nature of the lawsuit gave such notice to the defendant and provided him an opportunity to appear and defend himself. The Court's territorial principles also protected out-of-state defendants who were served in their own states from being forced to travel over ill-formed and hazardous roads to what, in that day, would almost always have been a distant forum. Because travel was difficult, a substantial percentage of defendants would suffer hardship if forced to litigate outside their home states. The difficulties and danger of travel might have prevented some defendants from even appearing to defend themselves or from defending themselves fully.

5. Due Process and Fairness

a. International Shoe v. Washington

As society became more mobile and corporate business more interstate, *Pennoyer*'s strict territorial limits on jurisdiction became more troublesome. They prevented a plaintiff from suing in his home state even though a nonresident defendant's business activity in that state had caused plaintiff's harm. This problem was exacerbated by the rule that a corporation had no real existence, and therefore no residence, outside the state of its incorporation. A corporation thus could do business in a state in which it was not incorporated but not be present in that state for purposes of jurisdiction.

The Supreme Court sought to adapt *Pennoyer*'s principles by using the legal fiction that held that a nonresident corporation was present (as a person could be) in the forum state if it did a sufficient amount of business there. If the corporation was present in the forum state, jurisdiction could attach through service on its local officials. On occasion, the Court modified it legal fiction by concluding that a nonresident corporation had "impliedly" consented to jurisdiction in the forum state by doing a sufficient amount of business there. A corporation caught by this fiction had no intention of consenting to the forum state's jurisdiction, and often had fashioned its interstate activities to avoid jurisdiction. Both the presence and consent fictions were based on the reasonable conclusion that a corporation should not be allowed to engage in extensive business activities in the forum state and then escape that state's jurisdiction because of incorporation in another state.

More troublesome, however, was the test used by the courts to determine when a nonresident corporation had done enough business to justify application of either fiction. That doing-business test turned solely on whether the defendant corporation had engaged in a sufficient quantity of business activity. In some cases, such as when a corporation established its principal place of business in the forum state, the test was not difficult to apply. However, when the corporation engaged in buying and selling in the state without having a local office or local employees, it was difficult to decide whether that corporation should be within the state's power.

Application of the test solely by reference to the quantity of business activity in a state could not yield predictable outcomes in the absence of some arbitrary line drawn, for example, on the amount of revenue obtain in the state. The test was also difficult to apply because it had no underlying principle or rationale other than the analogy to individual presence. As a result of these difficulties, interstate businesses were encouraged to carefully design their organizational structure and activities to ward off assertions of jurisdiction in those states where they engaged in business activity.

The Supreme Court changed the basic focus of due process from corporate "presence" to "minimum contacts" when it decided International Shoe Co. v. State of Washington, 326 U.S. 310 (1945). More particularly, the Court altered its interpretation of due process at least as that interpretation was applied to extraterritorial *in personam* jurisdiction. The State of Washington filed suit in one of its own courts to force the International Shoe Company to make payments to the state's unemployment compensation fund. The state assessed these payments as a percentage of the wages an employer paid to employees in the state. International Shoe was incorporated in Delaware, and had its principal place of business in St. Louis, Missouri. Over a period of years, it had hired commissioned salespersons in Washington to sell its shoes to residents of that state. These salespersons were given one shoe of each set as a model, and they could only take orders for the shoes. Those orders had to be approved by and filled through shipments from the St. Louis office. International Shoe had no office or officers located in Washington, and it did not produce any of its shoes there. In short, International Shoe had designed its business so that it could profit from Washington buyers without engaging in that amount of business activity necessary to make it vulnerable to jurisdiction there.

In the *International Shoe* case, the Supreme Court jettisoned the fictions of corporate presence or consent, and introduced the new concept of minimum contacts. After *International Shoe,* therefore, a court's assertion of jurisdiction over a nonresident defendant, whether a corporation or an individual, depends on whether that defendant had sufficient minimum contacts with the forum state. The Court did not ask whether the International Shoe Company was doing enough business in Washington to be deemed present there or whether its local business activities proved that it had consented to that jurisdiction. Instead, the Court concluded that jurisdiction was constitutionally permitted because due process depends on the "quality and nature of the activity in relation to the fair and orderly administration of the laws."

When a corporation enjoys the privilege of profit-making activity in a state, that state provides the legal order and protection that enables that open market. By taking advantage of the benefits provided at the expense of that state, the Court reasoned, the nonresident corporation must be held responsible for the obligations it incurs or the wrongs its commits in that state. Since the obligations sued upon by the State of Washington were incurred because of International Shoe's activities in that state, the Court held that the assertion of jurisdiction satisfied the notions of fair play and substantial justice embodied in the Due Process Clause.

Under the Court's reasoning in *International Shoe*, a state court can constitutionally assert power over nonresidents whose activities in the forum state gave rise to the plaintiff's claim. By knowingly engaging in these local activities, such a defendant would have had sufficient minimum contacts and, therefore, would not be *unfairly* disadvantaged by local litigation. In addition, even when the plaintiff's claim was unrelated to the defendant's local activity, a nonresident's continuous and systematic local activities could justify jurisdiction.

It should be noted at the outset that *International Shoe* does not establish an undifferentiated fairness test that can be satisfied whenever a defendant would suffer no great inconvenience by suit in a particular state. Instead, the minimum contacts approach forces a court to determine whether jurisdiction would be fair and reasonable given the *relationship between the defendant and the forum state*. It is not determinative, therefore, that a nonresident defendant resides only a short distance from the border of the forum state. That nonresident must still have had minimum contacts with the forum state before due process allows jurisdiction.

b. No Constitutional Exception for In Rem Jurisdiction

In Shaffer v. Heitner, 433 U.S. 186 (1977), the Court abolished the constitutional fiction that had distinguished *in rem* and *in personam* jurisdiction for due process purposes. It recognized in *Shaffer* that *in rem* jurisdiction represented an assertion of judicial power over individuals and their property interests rather than over the things themselves. Today, therefore, *in rem* proceedings, as they may still be labeled for other purposes, are recognized for due process purposes as suits against the owner of the property seized. Because of this, due process requires that the owner, if an outsider, must have had minimum contacts with the forum state. Minimum-contacts analysis thus proceeds as if the (*in rem*) claim were asserted directly against the owner of local property even if the only issue is ownership of that property.

The decision in *Shaffer*, which involved an assertion of quasi in rem jurisdiction, does not undermine a state's power in what would be a true *in rem* action to determine title to local property. When competing claims are asserted to ownership of local property, a nonresident's claim to that property amounts to a purposeful contact that is related to the claim on which the suit is based. This sort of related and purposeful contact should always be sufficient for specific jurisdiction over that nonresident defendant.

c. The Continuing Influence of Pennoyer

Pennoyer continues to influence due process analysis even after *International Shoe*. It does so first by forcing us to begin analysis with a focus on the forum state's territory and on the defendant's relationship with that territory. Even when a state allows its courts to extend their jurisdiction over nonresidents, the statutes that allow such extraterritorial jurisdiction are known as "long-arm statutes." Thus, the original constitutional limits established in *Pennoyer* influence the terminology and the analytic framework of personal jurisdiction.

The Supreme Court's interpretation of due process in *Pennoyer* has been expanded rather than rolled back in *in personam* cases. As a consequence, *in personam* jurisdiction acceptable under *Pennoyer* remains as acceptable grounds of jurisdiction today. The effect, therefore, of the Court's decision in *International Shoe* has been to expand the due process limits to allow greater extraterritorial jurisdiction over defendants not found in the forum state. The Supreme Court's decision in *Shaffer v. Heitner* in 1977 makes clear, however, that *Pennoyer* does not provide an *in rem* exception to the rules concerning jurisdiction over defendants. After *Shaffer*, every assertion of jurisdiction is about the liabilities of a defendant, and therefore one must always satisfy the rules for personal jurisdiction over a defendant.

The decision in *International Shoe* apparently did not reject *Pennoyer's* rule that allows *in personam* jurisdiction over a nonresident individual defendant who happens to be served with process while within the borders of the forum state. As noted below, this "transient jurisdiction" remains valid, at least in part because such jurisdiction was traditionally accepted, beginning with *Pennoyer*. The Supreme Court's modern acceptance of general jurisdiction over corporations incorporated in the forum state and over foreign corporations doing business in a continuous and systematic way also carries forward grounds of jurisdiction that were accepted as constitutionally sufficient under *Pennoyer*.

C. The Current Law of Personal Jurisdiction

1. Minimum Contacts

When an objection to jurisdiction has been properly asserted and maintained, a court's assertion of jurisdiction satisfies due process only when the defendant has sufficient "contacts" with the forum state. The analysis of contacts comes in two forms: general jurisdiction and specific jurisdiction. Hence, there exist two routes through which due process can be satisfied when a court asserts its power over a nonresident defendant.

a. General Jurisdiction

General jurisdiction contains several subcategories that reflect a modern acceptance of those instances in which personal jurisdictional was justified under *Pennoyer*.

(a) (RESIDENCE) A defendant who is deemed in law to be a resident in the forum state typically has no due process objection to any assertion of jurisdiction in that state.

- An individual who is domiciled in the forum state can be sued there on causes of action that arise outside that state and even when he is served outside the forum state.
- A corporation that is incorporated in the forum state can be sued there even on causes of action that arise outside that state.

(b) (TRANSIENT JURISDICTION) A court can constitutionally assert its jurisdiction over a nonresident individual defendant, though not over a corporate defendant, by serving that defendant while present within the borders of the forum state.

(c) (CONTINUOUS AND SYSTEMATIC CONTACTS) A court can constitutionally assert its jurisdiction even as to causes of action arising outside the forum state over a nonresident individual or nonresident corporation who does a substantial amount of business in the forum state.

- The defendant must have continuous, systematic, and (probably) substantial contacts with the forum state.
- And the assertion of jurisdiction must not violate our traditional conception of fair play and substantial justice.

b. Specific Jurisdiction

Specific Jurisdiction requires a showing:

- that the plaintiff's cause of action arose from a contact
- that the defendant purposefully caused in the forum state; and
- that the assertion of jurisdiction does not violate our traditional conception of fair play and substantial justice.

c. Consent, Waiver, and Estoppel

The Due Process Clause provides the defendant with a personal defense rather than an absolute limitation on judicial power. Therefore, the defendant can refuse to assert the defense, or waive his right in a contract. That defense can also be lost by the defendant's failure to assert it in a proper manner. A court can prevent a defendant from asserting his due process defense when he fails to comply with the discovery orders of the court relating to minimum contacts, and he can also be barred from asserting the defense through application of the doctrine of issue preclusion.

2. General Jurisdiction

If a nonresident defendant has not voluntarily waived his personal defense to jurisdiction and has not involuntarily waived that defense by procedural error or by disobedience of a related court order, a court of the forum state can constitutionally assert jurisdiction over him only by satisfying one of the two categories of jurisdiction—specific or general jurisdiction.

a. Residence

General jurisdiction begins with the conclusion that persons or corporations, which "reside" in a state, should be subject to the jurisdiction of its courts generally—that is, for the adjudication of any claim or cause of action. An individual resides in the forum state when he has his domicile in that state. A corporation bears the same relation to the forum state when it was incorporated in that state. In both cases, the resident defendant can be forced to litigate in that state without regard to the place where the cause of action arose.

b. Transient Jurisdiction

Under *Pennoyer v. Neff,* a court of the forum state could assert jurisdiction over an individual defendant who was served with process while physically located within the borders of that state. Premised on the notion of a state's authority over those within its territory, this form of judicial power turned solely on the defendant's physical presence and not on his connection with the forum state. In other words, the tradition established by the Supreme Court's interpretation of the Due Process Clause in *Pennoyer* allowed jurisdiction over defendants who were merely passing through the state. Their presence within that state's territory was as transients rather than as residents.

A state certainly needs to exercise its law enforcement power over transients who might violate that state's laws while present in its territory. However, transient jurisdiction gave a state's courts power to force transients to return and defend themselves against causes of action that might have only limited relation to the forum state. In these cases, therefore, one might well have contended that, after the Supreme Court's decision in *International Shoe*, transient jurisdiction would depend on whether those transients had minimum contacts with the forum state.

In Burnham v. Superior Court, 495 U.S. 604 (1990), the Supreme Court upheld jurisdiction based on local service made on a defendant who was visiting the forum state. In upholding this transient jurisdiction, the Court, without a majority opinion, unanimously upheld jurisdiction over a husband (and father) who was served with process in a divorce suit while in the forum state for business purposes and to visit his children. Justice Scalia, for a plurality, reasoned that such jurisdiction was valid because it had been traditionally accepted and was well recognized in 1868 when the Fourteenth Amendment was ratified. Justice Brennan, joined by three justices, reasoned that tradition was important but not determinative. However, he concluded that the assertion of jurisdiction under the facts in *Burnham* was fair. He reasoned that the defendant should have known of the risk, had benefited from his presence in the forum state, and would not be greatly inconvenienced by returning to litigate.

Burnham had not sent his wife and family to the forum state, and neither his business activities there nor the visit to his children gave rise to the divorce action. A court of that state could not, therefore, have exercised specific jurisdiction over him. Furthermore, his contacts with the forum state were certainly not sufficiently continuous and systematic to support general jurisdiction over him. Even though one might conclude, as did Justice Brennan, that litigation in that state would not cause Burnham any great inconvenience, the facts do not satisfy *International Shoe*. *Burnham* thus adds support for the conclusion that those *Pennoyer*'s principles that *allowed* jurisdiction in *in personam* cases remain valid today.

c. Continuous and Systematic Contacts

Many businesses have chosen, for tax purposes or other reasons, to incorporate in the State of Delaware. For similar reasons, other corporations may incorporate in foreign countries. However, if these companies have established their principal place of business in the forum state, they cannot legitimately dispute the fairness of having to defend themselves in suits filed there. Little unfairness results in such jurisdiction even when the claim asserted by the plaintiff arose wholly from the corporation's activities in another state or country. It should be noted that a forum state's choice of law rules may require that these claims be decided according to the substantive law of the state or country where the claim arose. The existence of jurisdiction over the corporation therefore does not mean that the forum state's substantive law will control its liabilities.

The Supreme Court has only twice addressed the concept of general jurisdiction with respect to a nonresident corporation's continuous and systematic contacts with the forum state. In Perkins v. Benquet Consolidated Mining Co., 342 U.S. 437 (1952), the Court upheld Ohio's jurisdiction over a Philippine corporation which had its principal office in that state, even though the claim arose elsewhere. During World War II, the mining company used Ohio as its corporate headquarters because the Japanese had occupied the Philippines. The corporation's president maintained his office, stored the corporate files, held directors' meetings, and generally ran what existed of the corporation's business in Ohio. The Court upheld jurisdiction because of the significance and quantity of these contacts even though unrelated to the plaintiff's claim.

In Helicopteros Nacionales de Colombia, S.A. v. Hall, 466 U.S. 408 (1984), a Colombian helicopter company agreed in Texas to ferry a joint venture's employees among several work sites in Peru where the joint venture was constructing a pipeline. On one of those trips in Peru a helicopter crashed killing four workers. The survivors of the four employees brought suit for wrongful death in Texas. Helicopteros, the Columbian company, had no office or agent located in Texas, had never performed services in Texas, and owned no property in the state. It had, however, purchased most of its helicopters and their parts in Texas, had sent pilots for training in the state, and had received payments under its agreement with the joint venture from a Texas bank. The Court concluded that these contacts were insufficient for general jurisdiction, noting that sporadic purchases in the forum state cannot alone sustain general jurisdiction.

With only these extremes as guides in applying the general jurisdiction brand of minimum contacts, lower courts have been somewhat erratic in deciding what a sufficient quantity of unrelated contacts is. The lower courts generally demand that the contacts extend over a reasonable period of time prior to suit and that they not be trivial. *Helicopteros* seems to undermine the weight to be given periodic or even frequent purchases in the forum state, and *Perkins* suggests that the local presence of offices and employees carrying on corporate business would strongly support jurisdiction. The contacts should be sufficient if they seem to show that the corporation has knowingly established corporate residence in the forum state and that the state has sufficient reason to adjudicate even non-local claims against the corporation.

However, a finding of continuous and systematic contacts for general jurisdiction is most difficult when a nonresident corporation has no established office in the forum state. The courts look first "for some kind of deliberate 'presence' in the forum state, including physical facilities, bank accounts, agents, registration, or incorporation." See Gator.Com Corp. v. L.L.Bean, Inc., 341 F.3d 1072, 1077 (9th Cir. 2003). In addition, courts determine whether the company "has engaged in active solicitation toward and participation in the state's markets, i.e., the economic reality of the defendant's activities in the state." *Id.* As a general rule, therefore, continuous and systematic activities are more likely shown by physical presence of business assets or at least by a substantial volume of sales in the state.

d. Reasonableness Factors

A number of lower federal courts have also applied the reasonableness inquiry to determine the existence of general jurisdiction, at least when the contacts are not clearly sufficient or insufficient. See, *e.g.*, Lakin v. Prudential Securities, Inc., 348 F.3d 704, 713 (8th Cir. 2003); Gator.Com Corp., 341 F.3d at 1080–1081. In applying the reasonableness factors, the courts tend to use them only to deny jurisdiction when the defendant's contacts seem only barely to satisfy the requirement of continuous and systematic contacts. See *Lakin,* 348 F.3d at 713. The Supreme Court has not required this inquiry for general jurisdiction, and the reasonableness factors seem unsuited for application when jurisdiction is to be justified without regard to the claim asserted. The reasonableness (or *gestalt*) factors require the weighing of five interests: (1) of the plaintiff to have a forum, (2) of the state to provide her that forum, (3) of the defendant to avoid serious inconvenience in litigation, (4) of the interstate system in the efficient resolution of disputes, and (5) the interest in furthering fundamental substantive social policies. (See the discussion in the following section on specific jurisdiction.)

3. Specific Jurisdiction

This form of jurisdiction is "specific" because it is derived from the conclusion that nonresidents should not be constitutionally protected when they seek to avoid litigation in the forum state concerning a cause of action that arose from the specific harm they caused in the forum state. The three steps required for specific jurisdiction (purposeful contact, relation to the cause of action, and reasonableness) appear to operate in the following manner.

a. Relatedness

The Supreme Court has focused most of its attention on the purposefulness requirement and less on the relationship between the defendant's contacts and the claim asserted by the plaintiff. Little difficulty exists when the defendant's purposeful actions lead directly to the plaintiff's injury in the forum state. In other words, the defendant's actions give rise to a claim when those actions lead, in a logical sequence, to the forum-state injury on which the plaintiff's claim is founded. When the plaintiff's injury occurs outside the forum state, the connection becomes more difficult to establish. In *Helicopteros*, the plaintiffs' decedents had been hired in Texas for pipeline construction in Peru where they were killed by the alleged negligence of a Colombian helicopter company. Justice Brennan, in dissent, attempted to show the connection between the workers' hiring in the forum state (Texas) and their deaths in Peru. He argued that, instead of giving rise to the claim, the defendant's efforts in Texas to obtain the contract to ferry the workers in Peru were sufficiently related to the subsequent claim. Justice Brennan's difficulty arose largely because the plaintiffs and their decedents were not residents of Texas and the accident did not occur in Texas.

b. Purposeful Contacts

The specific jurisdiction category of minimum contacts represents the most significant extension of a courts' constitutional authority under the *International Shoe* decision. Jurisdiction of this sort exists when a nonresident has purposefully sought a benefit from activity in or affecting the forum state that gave rise to the plaintiff's claim. These circumstances necessarily make the assertion of jurisdiction over that nonresident both fair and reasonable in the *International Shoe* sense and, therefore, sufficient under due process.

Specific jurisdiction requires only the most minimal of contacts if those contacts are purposeful and give rise to the plaintiff's claim. The starkest example of specific jurisdiction's reach appears in McGee v. International Life Ins. Co., 355 U.S. 220 (1957). In this decision, the Supreme Court upheld the jurisdiction underlying a California state court judgment based on what could be described as one contact with that state by a Texas insurance company. The defendant, International Life, had assumed the obligations of another company that had insured the life of a California resident. International Life mailed a reinsurance certificate to this insured, thereby establishing a contractual relationship with that California resident. The company refused to pay after the insured's death, and the beneficiary sued in California. The record did not show any other business activity by International Life in California, and it had no office or agent located in the state. The Court emphasized the substantial connection that the insurance contract had with California and the state's manifest interest in providing its resident a forum. The California forum was especially important to the plaintiff because she probably could not have afforded to litigate in Texas. And, because the defendant had reached into the state seeking the contract on which the suit was based, jurisdiction over it was not unfair or unreasonable.

In distinguishing *McGee*, the Court noted in Hanson v. Denckla, 357 U.S. 235 (1958) that some act of the defendant must show that it had purposefully availed itself of the privilege of conducting activities within the forum state. Purposeful availment requires affirmative conduct by the defendant "which allows or promotes the transaction of business within the forum State," or the purposeful direction of a foreign act that has an effect in the forum state. Sinatra v. National Enquirer, Inc., 854 F.2d 1191, 1195 (9th Cir. 1988).

i. Foreseeability

In World-Wide Volkswagen v. Woodson, 444 U.S. 286 (1980), the Supreme Court ruled that to be purposeful a contact must be such that the defendant could foresee being haled into the forum court. With such foreknowledge, the defendant can avoid contact with the forum state or protect itself from the risk by purchasing more insurance. The requirement of foreseeability thus demands that the defendant know of its contact with the forum state beforehand and be able to exercise such control that it could avoid the contact and thereby avoid the risk of litigation in that forum.

In *World-Wide Volkswagen*, a retail vendor sold a car at its New York lot to New York residents. The purchasers then decided to move to Arizona in their car but on the way had an accident in Oklahoma. The plaintiffs sued the retailer and its New York distributor in Oklahoma, and the Oklahoma courts held that jurisdiction over the New York defendants existed under these circumstances. The Supreme Court reversed, holding that these defendants did not have a purposeful contact with Oklahoma even though they might foresee one of their cars being driven to and having an accident in that state. Because the defendants could not control the travels of the plaintiffs and did not purposefully act so as to cause an effect in Oklahoma, sufficient minimum contacts did not exist.

ii. Contacts of the Plaintiff

The Court held that the actions of the *plaintiffs* do not count toward satisfaction of the requirement that the defendant have had a purposeful contact with the forum state. Also, a defendant's contacts with the forum state cannot be purposeful if they were caused by actions of parties or persons over whom the defendant has no control. In *World-Wide Volkswagen*, the plaintiffs caused the connection with Oklahoma, while the defendants had never attempted to do business in that state.

iii. Stream of Commerce

A corporation can have a purposeful contact with a forum state through activity that occurs outside that state if its activities are designed to have an effect in that state. For example, a corporation might sell its products in one state to a second company with full knowledge that those products will be regularly sold by the second company in the forum state. If such knowledge exists, the company presumably also has control over the contact because it can refuse to put its products into a "stream of commerce" that it knows will flow into the forum state. By continuing to supply the second company with products, the defendant purposefully avails itself of the benefits of doing business in the forum state.

In Asahi Metal Industry Co. v. Superior Court, 480 U.S. 102 (1987), five justices agreed that a company need only have knowledge that its products may end up in the forum state, so long as its sales to the intermediary are substantial. Four other justices insisted that purposefulness requires something beyond knowledge of the possibility that the goods will reach the forum state. This group would require additional conduct indicating the defendant's intent to serve the forum state. In *Asahi*, the Japanese third-party defendant, who was challenging jurisdiction, had sold valves in Taiwan for tire tubes constructed by a Taiwanese corporation. The Japanese corporation knew that the tire tubes to which it contributed value assemblies were sold in the United States, and could predict that some percentage of those would be sold in California. The five-justice majority concluded that this knowledge allowed the Japanese corporation control over its risk of litigation in California. These facts, in their opinion, proved that the Japanese corporation had sufficient, though weak, purposeful contacts.

iv. Contacts Through the Internet

The use by business organizations of the Internet has caused federal courts some difficulty, both in using contacts through the Internet to justify specific jurisdiction and in using the nature and quality of those contacts to establish general jurisdiction. The majority of federal courts use the sliding scale approach often identified as arising from the decision in Zippo Mfg. Co. v. Zippo Dot Com, Inc., 952 F.Supp. 1119 (W.D.Pa. 1997). In seeking to determine whether a defendant fell within the general jurisdiction of a court in Texas, the Fifth Circuit explained its adoption of the sliding scale approach in the following statement.

> The *Zippo* decision categorized Internet use into a spectrum of three areas. At the one end of the spectrum, there are situations where a defendant clearly does business over the Internet by entering into contracts with residents of other states which "involve the knowing and repeated transmission of computer files over the Internet...." In this situation, personal jurisdiction is proper. At the other end of the spectrum, there are situations where a defendant merely establishes a passive website that does nothing more than advertise on the Internet. With passive websites, personal jurisdiction is not appropriate. In the middle of the spectrum, there are situations where a defendant has a website that allows a user to exchange information with a host computer. In this middle ground, "the exercise of jurisdiction is determined by the level of interactivity and commercial nature of the exchange of information that occurs on the Website." We find that the reasoning of *Zippo* is persuasive and adopt it in this Circuit.

Mink v. AAAA Development LLC, 190 F.3d 333, 336 (5th Cir. 1999) (Citations omitted).

The sliding scale analysis leaves something to be desired as a tool for determining the existence of general jurisdiction because it does not provide a standard with which to decide whether the defendant's contacts were sufficiently continuous and systematic. See *Lakin*, 348 F.3d at 712. On the other hand, Internet contacts that give rise to the plaintiff's cause of action can normally be characterized as purposeful in light of established standards and thus yield a clearer finding in regard to specific jurisdiction.

c. Reasonableness Factors

Even though a majority of justices in the *Asahi* decision held that Asahi's contacts with California were sufficiently purposeful, the Court denied that state jurisdiction after considering the reasonableness factors. Eight justices held jurisdiction unconstitutional because its assertion under these facts would violate our traditional notions of substantial justice and fair play.

In making this determination, the Court considered (a) the interests of the plaintiff in having the local forum, (b) the inconvenience thereby caused defendant, and (c) the interests of the forum state in providing its resident a local forum and in regulating the conduct on which the suit is based. In addition, the Court spoke of interests in (d) efficient resolution of disputes and in (e) furthering fundamental substantive social policies. In *Asahi,* the plaintiff, a California resident, had already settled his claims against the defendants, including the Taiwanese corporation. The Taiwanese corporation wanted to continue litigation of its third-party claim for contribution against Asahi, the Japanese corporation, in California. The third-party plaintiff undoubtedly feared the prospect of seeking indemnity for a substantial United States judgment in a Japanese court. However, California had no interest in providing a forum for two foreign corporations, and Asahi was more than a little inconvenienced by suit in this distant forum. Neither efficiency nor any substantive policy was furthered by allowing this litigation in a California court.

Insistence on purposeful contacts by the defendant, which are also related to the plaintiff's claim, dominates the inquiry into fairness as that concept was intended by *International Shoe.* The reasonableness factors therefore arrive on the scene as generalized considerations designed for the rare case which cannot be cleanly decided on the basis of the first two steps. They become important only when the conclusions about purposefulness and relatedness do not cut forcefully in one direction or the other. The reasonableness factors cannot sustain jurisdiction in the absence of a purposeful contact, *see World-Wide Volkswagen,* but can invalidate jurisdiction when only a weak showing of purposefulness has been made, *see Asahi.* As one lower court explained:

> [T]he reasonableness prong of the due process inquiry evokes a sliding scale: the weaker the plaintiff's showing of the first two prongs (relatedness and purposeful availment), the less a defendant need show in terms of unreasonableness to defeat jurisdiction. The reverse is equally true: an especially strong showing of reasonableness may

serve to fortify a borderline showing of relatedness and purposefulness. (citations omitted)

Ticketmaster-New York, Inc. v. Alioto, 26 F.3d 201, 210 (1st Cir. 1994).

4. Consent, Waiver, and Estoppel

a. Consent

Waiver is a term used to describe a defendant's knowing consent to an assertion of jurisdiction that could have been challenged. For example, a nonresident defendant may contractually waive his personal due process right to object to a court's assertion of jurisdiction. These contractual provisions provide an opportunity for a party, usually the party with the greater bargaining power, to set the location of a suit that might arise from a disagreement about the terms or conditions of a contract. The parties can agree that any suit can be brought, for example, in the courts of Texas, and both parties would agree to waive any objection based on personal jurisdiction that arose solely because of the location of the forum court. The parties can also agree that only the courts of Texas will have jurisdiction over a suit arising from their contract, and a defending party could object based on this contractual provision when the plaintiff brought suit in another state. In the absence of a contractual waiver, the defendant can waive his objection merely by not raising that defense or by affirmatively consenting to the court's jurisdiction.

b. Waiver

Unfortunately, waiver has also been used to describe legal conclusions rather than intentional actions. In two instances, the law prevents a defendant from objecting to a court's personal jurisdiction as a matter of law and may label these conclusions as examples of waiver. Waiver in this sense is better described by the term "estoppel." The law bars or estops the assertion of jurisdiction when the defendant has failed to follow the proper procedure in raising the issue (thus "waiving" his constitutional objection) or when he has already had his day in court on that issue. The latter concept is better known as collateral estoppel or issue preclusion.

In federal court, Rule 12 of the Federal Rules of Civil Procedure regulates the method by which a defendant must raise his objection to personal jurisdiction. In general, Rule 12 requires the defendant to raise that objection in his first paper response to the plaintiff's complaint. A defendant can file a pre-answer motion to dismiss the complaint, but is not required to do so. If he files such a motion, he must include his objection to personal jurisdiction. A failure to include the objection in a preanswer motion causes its "waiver." If the defendant does not file a preanswer motion, his first responsive paper would be the answer. A failure to include his objection to personal jurisdiction in the answer (or in a quick amendment) again causes waiver. In these instances, the defendant may well have intended to assert the defense but have lost his right to do so by a procedural misstep.

In some states, defendants are required to assert an objection to personal jurisdiction in their first paper without including any other defensive material. These states refer to this as a "special appearance" procedure. If the defendant does not file a proper special appearance, he has made a "general appearance," which means that he has "consented" to jurisdiction. These special procedures do share one basic principle; they both insist that a defendant make this objection early in the litigation.

c. Estoppel

If a nonresident defendant challenges jurisdiction in the forum state but loses, he might thereafter also lose on the merits. If he has no assets in the forum state, the plaintiff must bring that judgment for enforcement to the defendant's home state. In that state, the plaintiff must file an enforcement suit in a local court and notify the defendant of that action. If the defendant again seeks to challenge the forum states' judgment for lack of personal jurisdiction, he will be collaterally estopped from doing so. Today, most jurisdictions refer to this bar as issue preclusion.

D. Hypotheticals and Explanations

1. A small corporation known as Digital Heaters, Inc., (DHI) obtained a patent and began production of a digital hot-water heater. DHI is incorporated in New York and has its *only* place of business in that state. DHI purchased a list that includes the names, physical addresses, and e-mail addresses of individuals who have exhibited an interest in high-tech items similar to the digital water heater. DHI then sent an ad for its water heater over the Internet to the e-mail addresses of the persons on its list. A Texas resident responded to the ad and ordered a water heater from DHI. After its installation in her home in San Antonio, the water heater exploded, causing the purchaser personal injuries and property damages.

She brings a tort claim against DHI in a Texas state court seeking $3 million in damages.
Personal jurisdiction in Texas? Explain.

Explanation

Yes, the Texas court has specific jurisdiction over DHI.

Rule

[Assume the absence of consent, waiver, or estoppel.]

(1) The Texas court can constitutionally assert jurisdiction over a nonresident if that defendant falls within the court's specific or general jurisdiction. Since DHI is incorporated in New York and has no office or place of business in Texas, general jurisdiction does not support this assertion of jurisdiction. (2) Specific jurisdiction can be found if (a) DHI's contacts with Texas gave rise to the plaintiff's cause of action (relatedness); (b) those related contacts were purposeful (purposeful contact); and (c) jurisdiction would not violate our traditional notions of substantial justice and fair play (the reasonableness factors—consider interests of the plaintiff and the forum state, convenience of the defendant, the efficiency of the interstate system, and the need to support fundamental substantive policies).

Application

(**Relatedness**) DHI's solicitation of the Texas resident led to the sale of the water heater to that resident and the placement in her home in Texas. DHI's placement of the allegedly defective water heater in the plaintiff's home in Texas was the direct cause of explosion that caused the injuries for which the plaintiff now sues in tort.

(**Purposefulness**) DHI had knowledge of the physical location of the persons to which it sent its solicitations. It, therefore, knowingly reached into the forum state in order to make a sale to a Texas resident. This contact was purposeful in the sense that it was deliberate and in the sense that DHI had control over the location of the contact. Unlike the *World-Wide Volkswagen* case, this defendant was not drawn involuntarily into a contact with the forum state because of the unilateral act of the plaintiff. This assertion of jurisdiction more closely compares with the California court's assertion of jurisdiction over the Texas insurance company in the *McGee* decision. In that case, the Texas insurance company sent a reinsurance letter to a California resident, who accepted that offer, paid his premiums from California, and then died in that state. His mother, as the named beneficiary, was also a resident of California. She sued in that state to enforce the contract, and the Supreme Court held that the one purposeful contact of the defendant in creating this contractual relationship with a California resident was sufficient to satisfy what we now call specific jurisdiction.

(Reasonableness Factors) Unlike the *Asahi* decision, the Texas court has a strong case for purposefulness and, in addition, a strong interest favoring the plaintiff's ability to sue in her home state where she was solicited. Moreover, the forum state has an interest in providing that forum to provide a remedy to one of its residents. If the plaintiff does not obtain a readily accessible forum for her tort claim, her support may well fall upon the taxpayers of Texas. These interests were not present in the *Asahi* decision because there the plaintiff had settled and had been removed from the case, and the opposing parties were both foreign corporations. The inconvenience to the defendant, a Japanese corporation, was not counterbalanced by any interest in favor of keeping the case in California.

2. A small corporation known as Digital Heaters, Inc., (DHI) obtained a patent and began production of a digital hot-water heater. DHI is incorporated in New York and has its *only* place of business in that state.
DHI sold one of its water heaters to a New York couple. The couple moved to New Jersey six months later and took their water heater with them. Shortly thereafter, the water heater exploded, injuring the couple and damaging their New Jersey home. The couple sued DHI in New Jersey and personally served its chief executive officer while she was visiting a New Jersey nightclub.
(a) Can the New Jersey court constitutionally assert personal jurisdiction DHI? Explain.
(b) Suppose DHI owned a vacant lot in New Jersey which it intended to use as a future office. Would formal seizure of that local land give the New Jersey court jurisdiction? Explain.
(c) If DHI annually sold 120 of its water heaters (out of a yearly production of 200) in New Jersey, would that fact help the couple establish jurisdiction in New Jersey? Explain.

Explanation

(a) As the facts are presented, the New Jersey court's assertion of jurisdiction must satisfy the requirements of specific jurisdiction.

Rule

(1) In the *Burnham* decision, the Supreme Court held, for different reasons, that the tradition of transient jurisdiction supported the constitutionality of jurisdiction over a nonresident individual defendant who had no min-

imum contacts with the forum state. (2) The nonresident defendant must have itself purposefully caused a contact with the forum state that gives rise to the plaintiff's cause of action.

Application

That tradition of allowing transient jurisdiction does not support the assertion of jurisdiction over DHI, the corporate defendant, merely because its president was served with process in the New Jersey. The individual defendant was "present" within the forum state in *Burnham*, but no one officer of DHI embodies that corporation. However, if the corporation appoints an agent for service of process in a state, that fact generally has been taken as a limited consent to the jurisdiction of a court of that state for claims arising from the corporation's local activity.

DHI's only possible New Jersey contact that could also be said to give rise to the plaintiff's cause of action occurred when it sold a water heater to the plaintiffs when they were domiciled in New York. That couple, not DHI, took the water heater to New Jersey and created the connection on which they now base the New Jersey court's assertion of jurisdiction. This "contact" with New Jersey fails to satisfy the purposefulness requirement for specific jurisdiction because these facts resemble the facts of the *World-Wide Volkswagen* decision.

In that case, the Supreme Court held that a defendant cannot be charged with a purposeful contact with a second state when it sold a car in one state to domiciliaries of that state, who then drove the car to the second state where the accident occurred. The Court held that the defendant did not have a purposeful contact with a state into which its product was taken by the plaintiff. Under these circumstances, the defendant did not deliberately reach into the forum state and had no control over the location of the product. In like manner, this hot water heater was sold in New York to New Yorkers, but was taken by those consumers to New Jersey. This case provides even a stronger case against purposefulness because this product is not mobile, as was the car sold to the plaintiffs in the *World-Wide Volkswagen* case.

(b) This appears to be an attempt by the plaintiffs to use the location of real property in the forum state as a justification for personal jurisdiction over its nonresident owner.

Rule

(1) After the Supreme Court's 1977 decision in *Shaffer v. Heitner*, the ownership of local land (or other property) by a nonresident defendant cannot

alone be sufficient to satisfy the due process limitations on jurisdiction. (2) In the absence of consent, waiver, or estoppel, all assertions of jurisdiction must satisfy either the requirements of specific or general jurisdiction.

Application

If DHI's only contact with New Jersey is its ownership of this land in the state, that ownership can stand as a contact with the state. However, that contact has no relation to the cause of action asserted by the plaintiff in this case. Therefore, although purposeful, the contact does not satisfy the relatedness requirement for specific jurisdiction. The plaintiff might argue that the ownership of land, assuming the land has a substantial value and has been owned for a sufficient number of years, counts as a continuous and systematic contact giving rise to general jurisdiction in the New Jersey court. However, the *Shaffer* decision shows that ownership alone cannot be sufficient. At best, the ownership of this one parcel of land would be considered an isolated or sporadic contact insufficient to satisfy the continuous-and-systematic-contacts requirement for general jurisdiction.

(c) Rule

The New Jersey court can exercise general jurisdiction over a nonresident corporation that engages in continuous, systematic, and substantial business sales within the state. A corporation that so substantially and so regularly reaps the benefit of doing business in the state would not be unfairly treated by an assertion of jurisdiction even though the cause of action does not arise from DHI's contacts with New Jersey.

Application

Once the facts show that, in addition to the ownership of land, DHI sells 120 of the 200 water heaters it produces each year to residents in New Jersey, the argument for general jurisdiction becomes much stronger. By selling a majority of its annual production in New Jersey, DHI has directed its attention and its products to the residents of that state. One would want to know what revenue was created in New Jersey from the sale of the 120 water heaters and how long DHI had been doing such a quantity of business with New Jersey. Even though DHI's New Jersey sales may not create a huge amount of revenue, it can be said that this pattern shows that DHI has a major presence, considering its size, in the State of New Jersey.

3. A small corporation known as Digital Heaters, Inc., (DHI) obtained a patent and began production of a digital hot-water heater. DHI is incorporated in New York and has its *only* place of business in that state.

   DHI entered a contract to sell every water heater it produces to Interstate Distribution Corporation (IDC), which is incorporated and has its only office in Massachusetts. IDC takes delivery and title to DHI's water heaters in New York and thereafter ships them to retail stores in New York, Massachusetts, and Connecticut. After being injured by an exploding water heater, a purchaser in Connecticut brought suit in that state against DHI and IDC.

   (a) **Can the Connecticut court constitutionally assert personal jurisdiction over both defendants? Explain.**

   Assume, instead, that IDC ships the water heaters to all 50 states and to Europe. Neither DHI nor IDC modifies the water heaters for the climate in any location.

   (b) **Could the Connecticut court assert jurisdiction over DHI? Explain.**

Explanation

Yes, the Connecticut court can assert specific jurisdiction over both defendants.

(a) Rule

A manufacturer who places its product in the "stream of commerce" with knowledge that it will be sold in the forum state cannot escape having that sale counted as both a related and a purposeful contact with the forum state. After the conflict between the justices on this issue in *Asahi*, the lower federal courts have been inconsistent in finding that more than mere awareness of the distribution was sufficient to make a manufacturer amenable in the state of sale. Some courts hold that the manufacturer must have done something further to benefit from sales in the forum state.

Application

(DHI as defendant) The stream-of-commerce metaphor prevents a manufacturer from avoiding the usual application of minimum contacts by using intermediary corporations that purchase and then distribute its products. DHI has more control over that distribution system than did the Asahi company in that case. Asahi was a component manufacturer, selling tire tube valve assemblies to a Taiwanese corporation that produced the tire tubes and distributed them in the United States. DHI produces the final product and, therefore, has greater control over the distributor of its products and the location of the ultimate sales. In this instance, IDC distributes DHI's water heaters to only three states, DHI should be held to have knowingly and deliberately sent its products into those states for the purpose of profiting from their residents. Since the sale to the Connecticut consumer, can be traced to the purposeful act of DHI, it should be within the specific jurisdiction of the Connecticut court.

(IDC as defendant) The assertion of jurisdiction over IDC in Connecticut rather easily satisfies the three requirements of specific jurisdiction because that corporation distributed the water heaters in the forum state to retail stores. Since IDC distributed the allegedly defective water heater to the retail store that sold it to the plaintiff, IDC's contact gave rise to the cause of action and was purposeful. The reasonableness factors would not show such unfairness that the assertion of jurisdiction would violate our traditional notions of justice and fair play. Although unnecessary in this case, the plaintiff could argue general jurisdiction because of the continuous and systematic business activity of IDC in Connecticut.

(b) Application

The distribution of the water heaters in 50 states and Europe brings these facts closer to those of *Asahi* in regard to the purposefulness of DHI's contacts with Connecticut. Again, however, we can distinguish DHI's position in the distribution system from that of Asahi, a component manufacturer. First, DHI not only had knowledge that it was sending its products into 50 states, including Connecticut, it had greater control over the distribution system. Unlike Asahi, DHI could direct its distributor to avoid any state when it chose not to do business there. Moreover, this hypothetical does not involve the assertion of jurisdiction of an American court over a foreign corporation, such as Asahi, that had only done business in the direct sense in another foreign country with another foreign corporation.

[Note: In considering the relatedness and purposefulness requirements for specific jurisdiction, nothing was said of the proximity of Connecticut to New York or Massachusetts. The fact that the defendants were not required to travel to a distant forum does not play a role until their interests are considered as part of the reasonableness-factors inquiry. In *Asahi*, the California forum's distance from Japan, as well as the unfamiliarity of the American legal system, weighed against jurisdiction over the Japanese corporation.]

4. A small corporation known as Digital Heaters, Inc., (DHI) obtained a patent and began production of a digital hot-water heater. DHI is incorporated in New York and has its *only* place of business in that state.

The contract (partially described above) between DHI and IDC resulted from a solicitation by IDC's marketing director. He went to New York to discuss a business relationship with DHI as it was beginning production of digital water heaters. As a result of this discussion, executives from the two corporations met in New York and there negotiated and signed the contract making IDC the exclusive distributor of DHI's water heaters. IDC was to take title and delivery of all of DHI's water heaters at its plant in New York. A provision in the contract required application of Massachusetts law to any dispute arising from the agreement. After several years of this relationship, DHI refused to deliver water heaters to IDC. IDC then sued DHI in a Massachusetts state court for breach of contract.

Can the Massachusetts court constitutionally assert personal jurisdiction over DHI? Explain.

Explanation

Rule

A defendant who purposefully enters an extensive contractual relationship with a party located in another state thereby brings himself within the specific jurisdiction of a court of that state when it adjudicates a cause of action arising from that relationship. In the *Burger King* case, the Supreme Court held that a Michigan individual who knowingly entered a franchise relationship with a Florida franchisor was within the jurisdiction of a Florida court for purposes of a suit for breach of the franchise agreement. See Burger King Corp. v. Rudzewicz, 471 U.S. 462 (1985).

Application

As in the *Burger King* case, DHI knew it was entering a long term distribution contract with a Massachusetts corporation. The contract's requirement that Massachusetts law apply to any conflict arising from the contract proves that awareness. One might distinguish *Burger King* by arguing that there the defendants had taken the initiative in seeking a franchise agreement from a Florida corporation. In this case, IDC took the initiative and was the instigator of contractual negotiations, and IDC held those negotiations in New York. The contract was signed in New York and was thereafter performed wholly in New York. Since DHI was a "passive customer" in respect to the arrangements and IDC was the party that took the initiative, one might well argue that DHI's entering into that distribution contract was not a purposeful contact with Massachusetts.

[Note: The choice of law provision in this contract does not require that any lawsuit arising from the contract be brought in the courts of Massachusetts. The parties could have included such a clause—called a forum-selection clause—in the contract, and it would have stated that any suit must be brought in Massachusetts. Such a forum-selection clause would operate as DHI's consent to any future suit in Massachusetts, and would prevent it from challenging jurisdiction in that state.]

CHAPTER 6

STATE LAW IN FEDERAL COURT: THE *ERIE* DOCTRINE

A. Terminology

Common law—In this chapter, the common law is used primarily as a characterization of law made by judges. It should be distinguished from constitutional law, statutory law, or Federal Rules made under statutory authority.

Preemption—The Supremacy Clause of the Constitution makes the Constitution and all federal laws made pursuant to the Constitution the supreme law of the land. If a federal law is authorized under the Constitution it will preempt—that is, displace—any inconsistent state law.

Procedural law (civil)—This phrase refers to the rules that govern the manner or means by which a civil action must be adjudicated. The primary procedural guides for litigation in federal district courts are the Federal Rules of Civil Procedure and the Federal Rules of Evidence.

Statute—Legislatures consist of elected representatives of the people, and these bodies enact laws that usually must be presented to the chief executive for approval. Once approved, these laws will be included in the body of statutes that bind those within the authority of that legislature.

Substantive law—This phrase refers to the law that regulates our behavior or conduct. Law has a substantive effect in its primary stage when it prohibits certain conduct, such as reckless activity, and a further substantive effect when it creates a mechanism, such as a suit for damages in tort, by which the prohibition can be enforced.

Rules Enabling Act—This federal statute, 28 U.S.C. § 2072, delegates to the Supreme Court part of Congress's power to promulgate rules of procedure for federal courts. The Federal Rules of Civil Procedure were promulgated according to the process established in this statute and first came into effect in 1938. The statute cautions that the rules established should not "abridge, enlarge or modify any substantive right."

Rules of Decision Act—This federal statute, 28 U.S.C. § 1652, requires, in the absence of preempting federal law, application of state law as rules of decision in civil actions tried in federal court "in cases where they apply." Rules of decision are usually thought of as substantive rules, and state substantive law applies in any civil case in which a federal court adjudicates a state cause of action.

B. The Nature of *Erie* Problems

1. Summary of the Problems

A true *Erie* problem exists when in deciding an issue necessary to a state cause of action a federal court must resolve a conflict between a federal judge-made rule or practice and a state law. Courts often say that *Erie* requires a federal court in diversity cases to apply state substantive law and federal procedural law. This is roughly accurate, but *Erie* and its rules apply in federal question cases when the federal court has to determine a supplemental state claim. In other words, *Erie* applies whenever a federal court must adjudicate a state-law cause of action. One might also say that this form of *Erie* problem focuses primarily on the nature of the state law in asking whether it is substantive, as that term is used for purposes of *Erie* analysis.

The other type of problem that a federal court encounters when adjudicating a state-law cause of action can be called a preemption problem, or a Rule preemption problem. This sort of difficulty arises in an *Erie*-type setting—that is, when a federal court is deciding an issue necessary to a state cause of action. However, preemption analysis begins with a requirement that the court resolve a conflict between a Federal Rule of Civil Procedure and state law. One begins by asking whether that Rule is valid—that is, does it fall within the power of Congress as a procedural rule and within the power delegated to the Supreme Court by Congress in the Rules Enabling Act. The Act prohibits a rule that might "abridge, enlarge, or modify any substantive right." However, the Supreme Court has presumed that Federal Rules of Civil Procedure are valid.

The second part of the preemption analysis is the most controversial and confusing. If a Rule is valid, the court must find that it directly and indisputably conflicts with the state law that would have been applied if the case was in state court. In its more recent decisions, the Supreme Court has generally read the pertinent Rule narrowly in order to avoid preempting state laws that appear substantive in the *Erie* sense. This modern trend suggests that one should begin his analysis of an *Erie*-type problem by determining the substantive effect of the otherwise applicable state law.

2. Overview of an *Erie* Problem

The two problems summarized above can be seen as two different forms of the problem caused in part by the Supreme Court's decision in 1938 in the landmark case entitled *Erie Railroad v. Tompkins*. In that decision, the Court held that a federal court, when adjudicating a state cause of action must apply the rules of decision (or substantive law) adopted in the state in which the federal courts sits, whether those rules were created by the highest court of the state or by the state's legislature. The most significant holding of *Erie*, therefore, was that when a federal court adjudicates a cause of action created by state law it must apply the substantive law of that state.

Most frequently, federal courts adjudicate a state cause of action when they take jurisdiction under the general diversity statute, § 1332(a). The general diversity statute allows federal jurisdiction even when no federal law is involved, and therefore all claims will exist solely because of the authority of state law. However, in federal question cases, a federal court can take supplemental jurisdiction over a state claim that shares a common nucleus of operative fact with the federal claim. In adjudicating this supplemental state claim, the rules of *Erie* apply as they would in a diversity case. See Felder v. Casey, 487 U.S. 131, 151 (1988) (the Supreme Court spoke in this case of "pendent jurisdiction" because the decision was issued before the judge-made concepts of pendent and ancillary jurisdiction were displaced by the statutory form of supplemental jurisdiction created in 28 U.S.C. § 1367).

In 1938, the same year in which the Supreme Court announced its decision in *Erie*, the Court also promulgated the Federal Rules of Civil Procedure under authority delegated to it by Congress in the Rules Enabling Act of 1934, 28 U.S.C. § 2072. Therefore, in 1938, the Court both demanded that federal district courts apply a distinct set of procedural rules in civil cases but also that they apply state substantive law when adjudicating state claims. Because of these two events, federal district courts are said to be obligated in a diversity case (or whenever adjudicating a state claim) to apply state substantive law while applying federal procedural law.

3. Federal Common Law

In Texas Industries Inc. v. Radcliff Materials, Inc., 451 U.S. 630 (1981), the Supreme Court listed those areas in which federal courts have specialized power to create substantive legal rules. If a federal court creates a common law rule authorized by the Constitution or by a federal statute, that law preempts inconsistent state rules. However, Congress, as the legislative branch of the federal government, can preempt federal common law by statute unless that common law implements the Constitution.

Although the Supreme Court in the *Erie* decision stated that federal courts had no power to create federal general common law, federal courts clearly have power to create federal common law in special areas. That special federal common law exists where state law would be inappropriate. In suits between states before the Supreme Court, the law of one state should not control its disputes with another state. No special body of state admiralty law existed in 1787 when the Constitution was drafted, and state law would not be appropriate in regulating conflicts that arise outside state borders. For many of the same reasons, federal law controls disputes implicating the nation's relations with foreign nations. Federal common law may be used to protect the federal government from discriminatory state law, or in those instances in which the lack of a uniform rule would seriously endanger federal programs.

The common law power of federal courts can be exercised, under limited circumstances, within areas of Congress's constitutional authority. Instead of legislatively creating statutory law in an area of its authority, Congress can authorize, either expressly or by necessary implication, federal courts to create federal common law in that area. Federal judges have also created private causes of action to enforce federal statutory prohibitions when they conclude that this remedy was intended by Congress. In addition to the more obvious creations of common law, federal courts create rules when they interpret federal positive law (the Constitution, a federal statute, or one of the Federal Rules) or when they engage in the interstitial law-making necessary to realize Congress's programmatic intent.

In each instance, federal courts either ignore state law or override it when engaged in their law making. The current Supreme Court, though conservative in the social sense, has added to the areas in which federal courts can create common law. In Boyle v. United Technologies Corp., 487 U.S. 500 (1988), the Court immunized contractors that provide products to the United States from suits under state law for design defects. The government-contractor defense applies to immunize a contractor from state tort liability for design defects when it can prove:

- that the U.S. approved reasonably precise specifications,
- that the equipment supplied conformed to these specifications, and
- that the contractor warned the U.S. about any dangers that were known to it but not to the U.S.

At least one lower federal court has expanded that immunity to prevent state tort claims against contractors who have service contracts with the Government. The same three requirements must be satisfied, but the Government must have established reasonably precise requirements for maintenance. See Hudgens v. Bell Helicopters, 328 F.3d 1329 (11th Cir. 2003).

In addition, the Supreme Court held in the Semtek International Inc. v. Lockheed Martin Corp., 531 U.S. 497 (2001) that federal common law rules of res judicata controlled the enforcement of judgments issued by federal courts. The Court held in that case that no reason existed to apply a uniform federal res judicata rule for diversity cases. Therefore, even though federal common law rules will control other federal court judgments, state law has been adopted to determine the scope of federal judgments entered in diversity cases.

4. Substantive or Procedural Law

The clearest example of "substantive law" would be found in a court decision or legislative act that created (or rejected the creation of) a cause of action. One state might, for example, allow a cause of action against someone who negligently inflicted emotional distress on the complaining party. Once the existence of that cause of action became public, individuals and businesses would tend to avoid those actions that would make them liable under that cause of action. Retail businesses might decide that they would not halt someone suspected of shoplifting because of the higher risk of liability resulting from this new cause of action. In this sense, the law's creation of a separate right to sue alters the primary (out-of-court) behavior of citizens. Substantive law thus tells citizens how they should act by establishing a risk of civil liability. Although civil suits provide the tool for enforcement, a state creates substantive law to order the behavior of its citizens by punishing someone for bad behavior. The state also can protect citizens from liability and thus allow particular behavior.

"Procedural law," on the other hand, regulates the process of enforcing these causes of action in courts; it tells a person, or her lawyer, about the manner or means of commencing and maintaining a civil suit adjudicating a substantive cause of action in court. While substantive law acts upon a particular type of conduct, and the conditions that must exist before that behavior makes the actor liable in court, procedural law applies generally to all causes of action, whether in tort, contract, or unjust enrichment. Difficulties arise in the application of *Erie*'s dictates because these general definitions resolve easy cases but do not help when a federal court must decide whether to apply a state law that falls in that uncertain area between procedure and substance.

Moreover, a law can appear procedural, in that it tells a party how to proceed in court, but be designed to achieve a substantive goal. For example, a rule giving state judges discretion in tort cases to reverse jury verdicts that seem excessive establishes the procedural standard for a motion for new trial. However, by limiting jury awards in tort cases, the rule also resembles a cap on tort damages, which would represent a policy decision to protect defendants in tort cases. In other words, the rule causes a substantive tort reform limitation on the value of tort cases even though it appears in a procedural form. Since federal district judges follow a judge-made rule that gives them far less control over jury verdicts in tort cases, refusal to apply the state law in federal court would entice plaintiffs to invoke federal jurisdiction, if available, in order to avoid the judicial oversight of jury verdicts. See Gasperini v. Center for Humanities, Inc., 518 U.S. 415, 429–30 (1996). That would allow nonresident plaintiffs to change the law that significantly affected their tort claims by choosing federal court.

5. Rule Preemption

Courts most frequently speak of preemption when a federal statute supersedes an inconsistent state law in federal or state court. The federal statute annuls the application of the state law by virtue of the Supremacy Clause of the Constitution (Article VI, cl. 2), which makes the Constitution, and constitutionally authorized federal law, supreme in a conflict with state law.

Rule preemption refers to the use of one of the Federal Rules of Civil Procedure to supersede a conflicting state law even in a diversity case in federal court. Unlike a federal statute or the Constitution, the Federal Rules of Civil Procedure operate only in federal court and, therefore, can conflict with state law only in that forum. Although federal courts have authority to apply federal judge-made procedural rules unless they conflict with a state substantive law, different considerations apply when that federal procedure is compelled by the Federal Rules of Civil Procedure.

The Federal Rules of Civil Procedure are promulgated by the Supreme Court through the Judicial Conference, but Congress has the authority to prevent them from becoming effective. Nevertheless, the Federal Rules of Civil Procedure are not federal statutes, and are primarily the product of the judicial branch. However, Congress has authorized this method of rulemaking in the exercise of its constitutional power over the creation and uniform operation of lower federal courts. The existence of this constitutional source of authority for the Federal Rules of Civil Procedure thus distinguishes Rule-preemption questions from true *Erie* problems involving the application of federal judge-made rules.

6. A Hypothetical to Explain *Erie* (Sue Jones v. Doctor Smith)

Assume that a plaintiff, Sue Jones, is a citizen of Texas and has filed suit seeking damages of $250,000 in federal court in New York against Dr. John

Smith, a citizen of New York. Ms. Jones has alleged a state cause of action for medical malpractice against Dr. Smith and has invoked jurisdiction based solely on the existence of diversity of citizenship. Assume further that the highest New York court created this claim in order to authorize suit against health care providers, whether individuals or entities, whenever their negligence caused the plaintiff physical injury. Under the state's common (judge-made) law applicable in negligence cases, a plaintiff can recover punitive damages against health care providers. Punitive damages are those available, in addition to compensatory damages, when the defendant's actions were reckless or grossly negligent.

After many years of experience with punitive damages in medical malpractice suits, the New York legislature enacted a law that provided doctors a defense that effectively prevents the recovery of punitive damages in malpractice suits against them. Although punitive damages are generally available in tort actions in New York, the state legislature created this absolute defense to punitive damages awards solely as a protection for physicians in civil suits. The legislature deemed this to be such a fundamental protection that it provided in the statute that this defense could not be waived even if the defendant failed to plead it. The legislature had identified jury awards in New York for punitive damages in medical malpractice suits as one cause for the substantial rise in medical malpractice insurance rates, which has contributed to the rapidly increasing cost of medical care in the state. In order to avoid this consequence, the legislature enacted the statute, hoping that the defense it has provided would convince insurers to lower medical malpractice insurance rates, thereby reducing the upward pressure on medical care costs.

In bringing her diversity action in federal court, Sue Jones alleged in her complaint that Dr. Smith acted recklessly when he punctured her intestinal tract while performing a liposuction procedure on her in his Manhattan clinic. For that reason, she claimed he should be liable for punitive damages. Dr. Jones's lawyer failed to assert his state statutory defense in his answer. One year after filing his answer, Dr. Jones has asked permission of the federal court to amend his answer to include this defense.

Ms. Smith has discovered older federal cases that, she claims, establish a federal judicial practice of refusing, for general policy reasons, to interfere with a jury's power to award punitive damages when defendants acted recklessly. On the basis of these cases, she has objected to Dr. Jones' motion to amend his answer to add the defense as authorized by the state statute. She also supports her opposition to his amendment by asserting that Rule 8(c) of the Federal Rules of Civil Procedure makes his objection to punitive damages an affirmative defense, which under the Rule is waived if not included in defendant's answer.

a. True Erie Question

The defendant's motion to amend and the plaintiff's response raise both a true *Erie* question and a preemption problem. First, let's consider the true *Erie* question. Should the federal court use state law (creating the defense); or should it, instead, apply the conflicting federal judicial practice of not interfering with a jury's decision to award punitive damages? Under *Erie*, the federal court must apply the state's defense to punitive damage awards if the state law is substantive in the *Erie* sense—that is, if it is the type of state law that *Erie* required federal courts to apply when adjudicating state claims. As we will see later in this chapter, the modern test for determining whether a state law is substantive focuses on *Erie*'s twin aims. The test asks whether ignoring state law will change the outcome of the case from what it would have been in state court and, if so, whether that difference will cause forum shopping or serious harm to the rights of parties involuntarily drawn into federal court.

New York laws establish the medical malpractice cause of action that allows the plaintiff to recover a judicial remedy. In this instance, however, the state legislature also created a defense to that cause of action to prevent the recovery of punitive damages. If we recognize that the state law which creates the cause of action for medical malpractice is substantive, we must recognize that the state law which reduces the possible liability under that cause of action is also substantive. In policy terms, we can see that the state has purposely designed its law to serve both the purpose of compensating ill-treated patients *and* of protecting physicians (or their insurance companies) from large punitive damages awards. Therefore, the state created a defense—a procedural device—solely as a tool for enforcing its policy of reducing the upward pressures on medical care costs.

In the *Erie* decision, the Supreme Court held that a state law having such an effect could not be displaced by a contrary policy decision made at the whim of the federal judge who is adjudicating the state's cause of action. The Supreme Court held in *Erie* that a federal judge has no general law-making power that would allow him to alter the main elements of a cause of action that exists solely because of decisions by state law-making authorities. The state legislature has the power to abolish the common law claim for malpractice, but it chose instead to leave that claim in place for compensatory damages but to prohibit the recovery of punitive damages. If a federal court altered this outcome, it would significantly frustrate the state's efforts to use law to achieve its policy goal, which in this instance was to reduce one source of upward pressure on health care costs.

Individual citizens and businesses are presumed to have knowledge of what the law prohibits or allows, and they depend on such knowledge in regulating their conduct. Businesses hire lawyers to advise them of the law that affects their actions and that define the economic risks they must take. If liability is likely, a business will reduce its risks by purchasing insurance or by choosing to avoid that activity. A wise individual might well do the same. Unfairness results when citizens rely on state law to plan their conduct and to assess their risks, but then find this law changed significantly solely because they were drawn into federal court. In this context, the exercise of discretion by a federal judge that changes a state law claim appears both unfair to the hapless defendant and an intrusion on the rightful role of the state.

In the hypothetical medical malpractice suit based on state law, no interest of the United States Government demands federal court interference with state law. If no Federal Rule of Civil Procedure, no federal statute, or no provision of the Constitution of the United States applies, a federal judge would have no justification if he decided in accordance with federal judicial practice, or in accordance with his own sense of justice, that the affirmative defense provided by state law to this suit could not be applied. One might argue that the federal judicial policy was part of the judge-jury relationship in federal court, and that relationship was influenced if not controlled by the Seventh Amendment to the Constitution. However, federal judges do not need to control federal juries to the extent of creating rights for them to adjudicate. Therefore, we can assume that no federal interest justifies such a decision, unless one believes federal judges are inherently wiser and more just than state judges.

b. Rule Preemption Question

However, a rule preemption question has been raised by the plaintiff's assertion that Federal Rule of Civil Procedure 8(c) demands a finding that Dr. Jones has waived his defense to punitive damages. Federal Rule 8(c) expressly requires that a defendant "[i]n pleading to a preceding pleading ... shall set forth affirmatively" any objection that constitutes "an avoidance or affirmative defense." The defense to punitive damages appears at least in part to be an avoidance defense in that the defendant can prevent an award of punitive damages even if the plaintiff proves that he was reckless in puncturing her intestinal tract.

If that's the case, Rule 8(c), by demanding that a defendant include that defense in his answer, seems to conflict with the state statute, which allows the defense even if not properly asserted. If we assume further that the state's determination—that pleading error cannot block the defense—is an integral part of the substantive defense to punitive damage awards, we seemingly have a conflict between a substantive state law and a procedural federal law.

Furthermore, unlike the federal common law rule allowing a jury to determine punitive damage awards, this federal law was created pursuant to a federal delegation of power to the Supreme Court in the Rules Enabling Act of 1934. The Constitution of the United States delegates to Congress the power to create, and to provide for the operation of, the lower federal courts. Under these circumstances, the federal law that conflicts with state law does have its source, though indirectly, in the Constitution. The existence of a constitutional source distinguishes the Rule preemption problem from the true *Erie* problem.

In our hypothetical problem, therefore, the federal court faces an apparent conflict between a substantive state law and a valid federal procedural law promulgated pursuant to a constitutionally authorized congressional delegation of power. If Federal Rule 8(c) is valid, and it will be presumed so, it preempts any conflicting state law even when that state law is substantive in the *Erie* sense. *Erie* concerned the use of unauthorized federal common (judge-made) law to displace state substantive law. The Supremacy Clause of the Constitution declares that federal law enacted pursuant to the Constitution will preempt any conflicting state law.

A second question must be answered however. That is whether Federal Rule 8(c) directly and necessarily conflicts with the state law that imposes the defense against punitive damages regardless of proper pleading by the defendant. One way of avoiding the conclusion that these two directly conflict is to ask whether they can both be applied and given full effect in the same case. If so, they are not in conflict. If we recognize that calling something an "affirmative defense" is a legal way of demanding that it be affirmatively pled, the state statute actually declares that his defense to punitive damages does not have to be affirmative plead and is therefore not an affirmative defense. Rule 8(c) deals only with the procedure a defendant must follow in federal court in regard to affirmative defenses. If state law declares that the bar to punitive damages in medical malpractice suits is not an affirmative defense, Federal Rule 8(c) says nothing about the method of pleading this bar. The two laws therefore are not in conflict, and the state law is not preempted by Rule 8(c).

As noted earlier, the Supreme Court has tended to read an apparently conflicting Federal Rule narrowly so as to avoid preempting a substantive state law. Although the Court has not provided a clear guide for those who must predict the outcome of such conflicts, it clearly has sought to protect the ability of states to control the nature of substantive state rights and goals. Unfortunately, that protection comes at the cost of uncertainly about the meaning of the Federal Rules of Civil Procedure in diversity cases.

C. Background and Development

1. The Common Law

The term "common law" can be used in at least three different ways. In the first year of law school, most students are required to enroll in the common law courses of torts, contracts, and property. These courses cover many of the fundamental legal principles that were developed by the common law courts of England. When one speaks of the common law, therefore, these are the bodies of law that first come to mind. One might also speak of the common law in contrast to the law of equity. The chancery or equity courts in England developed the law of equity to provide relief not available in the common law courts. The equity courts are, therefore, most frequently remembered for their creation of the injunction and other equitable remedies—that is, nonmonetary judicial relief.

The third way in which the term common law is used emphasizes the creation of that law by judges rather than by legislatures. The equity courts also made substantive law through the development of private causes of action (claims for relief) in regard to such matters as trusts or for recovery for unjust enrichment. In this manner, both the courts of common law and of equity created judge-made law to establish and adjudicate causes of action. It is this judge-made nature of law—also known as common law—which has significance in this chapter.

The Rules of Decision Act (RDA), originally enacted as part of the First Judiciary Act of 1789, currently exists in § 1652 of Title 28 and reads as follows:

> The laws of the several states, except where the Constitution or treaties of the United States or Acts of Congress otherwise require or provide, shall be regarded as rules of decision in civil actions in the courts of the United States, in cases where they apply.

The Supreme Court in Swift v. Tyson, 41 U.S. 1 (1842), held that the "laws of the several states" language of the RDA did not include state common law. In this way, the Court allowed federal courts to apply their own version of the common law even in adjudicating diversity cases. In 1938, the Supreme Court in *Erie* concluded that the Constitution did not confer such a general power to make common law on federal courts and reinterpreted "laws of the several states" to include the substantive law of a state, whether statutory or common law.

2. *Swift v. Tyson*

In Swift v. Tyson, 41 U.S. 1 (1842), Tyson had given Norton a bill of exchange in payment for the purchase of certain land Norton and another man purportedly owned. Norton also owed Swift money, and to obtain cancellation of that debt he transferred Tyson's bill of exchange to Swift. When Tyson learned that Norton did not own the land, he refused to pay. Swift sued Tyson on the bill in a claim based on state law, but he sued in federal court in New York based on diversity of citizenship jurisdiction. Tyson sought to defend himself by proving that the bill was issued because of Norton's misrepresentation.

Swift claimed he was a bona fide purchaser and, as such, was not bound by deficiencies in the agreement between Tyson and Norton. Swift could prove he was a bona fide purchaser only by showing that he had given valuable consideration for the bill. He had paid for its endorsement by canceling Norton's debt to him, but cancellation of a pre-existing debt was not valuable consideration under New York case law. However, the Supreme Court instead applied a federal judge-made, commercial law rule which accepted such consideration as sufficient.

The Court concluded that even though the Rules of Decision Act required federal courts to apply the "laws of the several states," a state judge-made rule on the general commercial law was not one of these laws. The Court believed a federal court could use general reasoning to find the proper rule in the body of commercial law principles just as would a state court. Congress, the Court reasoned, did not intend the "laws of the several states" language of the RDA to include the judge-made law of a state. The Court therefore held that the RDA required application only of the statutory law of a state and of those state court opinions which established local law with regard, for example, to rights in local land.

By avoiding application of state judge-made law in diversity cases, federal courts were able to create their own rules in adjudicating state claims. The Court's holding in *Swift* allowed federal courts to ignore state substantive law and apply a federal rule even when that rule altered the result of the case. Such an intrusion on the power of states would have been less troublesome if the Court had restricted the effect of *Swift* to the field of commercial law. However, subsequent decisions extended the *Swift* rule to matters involving the civil law in general.

3. *Erie R.R. v. Tompkins*

By 1938, however, judges had come to recognize that state common law was *created* because of policy reasons and was enforced because of the governmental authority of a state. In addition to allowing federal court interference with this policy making, *Swift* had introduced an unnecessary source of unfairness. The variation between the common law applied in federal and state courts located in the same state could alter the course of that litigation solely because federal diversity jurisdiction existed. Rights and liabilities recognized under a state's common law could thus be changed simply by moving a state claim into federal court. This lack of uniformity discriminated against local residents who had to abide by local law but whose rights could be altered at the option of a nonresident litigant.

The decision in Erie R.R. v. Tompkins, 304 U.S. 64 (1938) began with Harry James Tompkins' accident one Friday night in 1934. The accident occurred in Tompkins' hometown in Pennsylvania as he was walking on a path that ran parallel to the railroad tracks of the Erie Railroad. As one of Erie's trains passed, he was struck and seriously injured by something (probably a door) protruding from the train. Tompkins sued the railroad in a New York federal court even though the accident had occurred in Pennsylvania. His lawyers resided in New York, and they might have feared that both state and federal courts in Pennsylvania would apply the law of that state which imposed a higher burden on proving his state tort claim. Tompkins could obtain personal jurisdiction because the railroad was incorporated in New York, and incorporation made the railroad subject to service of process in that state.

Under Pennsylvania common law, Tompkins had been a trespasser while on the path running alongside the tracks and, therefore, the railroad owed him only the duty not to act recklessly. If Pennsylvania law controlled, therefore, Tompkins would have to prove fault beyond mere negligence. However, the federal trial court in New York ruled that, because of the rule established in *Swift*, federal common law controlled. Under federal common law, as the federal judge saw it, Tompkins was required to prove only negligence. And at trial, Tompkins proved negligence to the jury's satisfaction and was awarded a verdict.

The Supreme Court reversed, and remanded the case for application of the Pennsylvania law. To reach this decision, the Court could have simply held that state common laws were the "laws of the several states" which the Rules of Decision Act (RDA) required federal courts to apply. However, the Court went beyond this reinterpretation of the RDA and held that the "course pursued" under *Swift* was unconstitutional. It held that Congress has no general constitutional power to impose substantive rules of common law on a state. Furthermore, the Court reasoned, the Constitution provided federal courts no power to make federal general common law.

a. Congress's Constitutional Power

The Court's reasoning clearly had a firm basis in fundamental constitutional principles. Even though Congress has specific enumerated powers to make substantive law, it certainly does not possess a *general* power to enact any substantive law it desires. Congress could have exercised its specific power over interstate commerce to enact a statute regulating the liabilities of such interstate creatures as railroads. However, it had not done so and, furthermore, had not delegated such power to the federal courts. Therefore, the federal courts cannot look to Congress's specific legislative powers as authority for their making of common law.

Hence, the course pursued under *Swift* was unconstitutional because federal courts were exercising an authority to make substantive law in diversity cases which had neither a constitutional nor a statutory basis. First, by displacing state common law under the *Swift* rule, federal courts had assumed a power not assigned to them in the Constitution, thereby usurping powers expressly reserved by the Tenth Amendment for the states and state courts. Second, even if federal courts had limited their common law to the specific areas of Congress's constitutional authority, that judicial lawmaking would represent a usurpation of the preeminent law-making power of the legislative branch. Therefore, the courts could not constitutionally assume undelegated legislative functions without violating the principles which maintain the Constitution's mandate for separation of powers.

Courts could only point to the judicial power allowed under Article III over diversity cases. However, the Court's statement in *Erie* that no clause of the Constitution purports to confer power to formulate federal general common law means that this language in Article III does not alone support such authority. Even if Article III as a whole authorizes some common law powers, Congress must confer those powers by statute before lower federal courts can exercise them. In *Erie,* the Supreme Court held that neither the RDA nor the general diversity statute conferred common law power in diversity cases.

The oft-stated general rule of *Erie* is that federal courts apply state substantive law and federal procedural law in adjudicating state claims. This substantive-procedural distinction can cause confusion for at least two reasons. First, states may seek to have a substantive effect through laws which regulate judicial procedure. Therefore, identifying a state law as procedural does not end analysis. Second, federal courts can apply the substantive law announced in the Constitution and in federal statutes even when that federal law displaces state law in a diversity case.

What is not so obvious is that federal courts do have a limited common law power. They can create and generally apply judge-made rules to regulate their operations. As a matter of fact, *Erie* problems exist because the federal judiciary does have this power to create judge-made *procedural* rules. If they lacked this power, the *Erie* conflict would be illusory because in every instance a federal judge-made rule would be invalid. For example, federal district judges apply their own standard for determining whether the jury has been swayed unduly by emotion in granting a verdict. Instead of invalidating this rule, the

Supreme Court in *Gasperini* (discussed below) merely refused to apply the rule because it would have displaced state substantive law.

Discussing true *Erie* and Rule preemption problems is a simplified way of considering the opposing interests that dominate this analysis. One starts by identifying the context in which these problems arise. A federal court, respecting the limits imposed by the constitutional system, seeks to adjudicate a claim for relief which depends for its existence solely on the governmental authority of a state. In this context, one has the impression that, of course, the court should use any state law that would regulate the claim were it adjudicated in state court. No federal interest justifies altering the outcome of a state claim merely because the federal judge prefers a rule that the state has rejected. However, must the federal judge apply the state's rules of procedure in adjudicating the state law claim? Should federal judges be required to comply with a state procedure that bars a judge from commenting on the evidence when federal judges have long followed the practice of exercising such a power in their management of jury trials?

If the Constitution authorizes a Federal Rule of Civil Procedure or a federal judicial practice, that federal authority should displace state law because our constitutional system recognizes the need for supremacy of federal law. The Supremacy Clause of the Constitution declares that the laws of the United States derived from or enacted pursuant to the Constitution must displace inconsistent state law. Therefore, even when a state law is bound up with substantive policies, constitutional authority for a conflicting federal rule causes the displacement of state law to the extent it is inconsistent with the federal rule. *Erie* and preemption problems can thus arise only when that constitutional authority for a federal rule either does not exist or does not require the displacement of state substantive law.

At the extremes, one need only recognize either the absence of a clear line of constitutional authority, leaving no reason for displacing state law, or the presence of that authority, calling for preemption by federal law. As one moves between these extremes, however, the need for federal supremacy weakens. In addition, the need to enforce state law in federal court may be strong in one case but weak in another. For example, no federal court would casually disregard a state's decision that a plaintiff seeking the benefit of its tort claim must prove the absence of his contributory negligence in order to prevail. However, a state law which mandates the filing of a complaint on 14-inch paper does not implicate our concern for the role of the states or for litigational fairness sufficiently to require displacing a federal judge-made rule calling for pleadings on 11-inch paper. *Erie*'s command was fired by the need to respect that law which represents a state's efforts to regulate behavior within its borders; it does not require blind deference to every state decision.

Although not usually identified as preemption, the Constitution of the United States can defeat the application of state law in either state or federal court. Assume that a city's officials have sued in state court, asserting a state law civil nuisance claim, to close a bookstore for its sale of pornographic materials. In response, the defendant interposes a defense based on the Freedom of Speech Clause of the Constitution. The state law which authorizes a civil claim prohibiting the sale of pornographic material represents a policy decision aimed at protecting the general public from dissemination of such materials. That state claim is thus a substantive law—that is, one primarily motivated by the desire to protect the citizenry at large. However, if the Freedom of Speech Clause prevents closure of the bookstore, that state law cannot be validly applied; it would be defeated, or preempted, by the supreme law of the Constitution.

Preemption by a federal statute differs from preemption by the Constitution because a litigant can challenge the validity of a federal statute but not the validity of the Constitution. A constitutional rule, once announced, cannot be defeated by its inconsistency with a higher law because no such law exists. On the other hand, a federal statute can be inconsistent with the Constitution and for that reason invalid. The Constitution can be used to invalidate a federal statute in two ways. The first way is by questioning Congress's *constitutional power*. Congress can exercise only those powers assigned to it in the Constitution. If a federal statute represents the exercise of a power beyond Congress's constitutional authority, the statute is invalid for that reason. The second way of invalidating a federal statute is by showing that it invades *constitutional rights*. Congress may enact a statute based in one of its enumerated powers—say, its power over interstate commerce—which collides with a constitutional protection for individual rights, such as the Freedom of Speech Clause. If that is the case, the federal statute, in this application, would be invalid. Because conflicts between federal statutes and state law do not typically involve constitutional rights, a litigant would normally use only the constitutional-power challenge to avoid preemption.

Preemption by a federal statute occurs after two steps have been followed. First, preemption does not become an issue unless the federal statute and state law appear to be in conflict. Therefore, a court must determine that this conflict is inescapable rather than merely apparent. Second, if the conflict is real, the litigant seeking application of state law prevails only by successfully challenging the constitutionality of the statute. If the litigant fails in this challenge, preemption occurs and the federal statute displaces state law.

Rule preemption also operates in a similar fashion; it operates only after satisfaction of these two requirements—inescapable conflict and validity. First, a court must determine that the Rule directly and indisputably conflicts with a state law. Can both the Rule and the state law apply in the same case without either being seriously disturbed? If so, no direct conflict exists and Rule preemption will not operate. Second, if a Rule indisputably conflicts with state law, the Rule must be valid—that is, it must fall within both the constitutional power of Congress and the statutory power regulating the Rule's promulgation.

The Federal Rules of Civil Procedure were created pursuant to Congress's constitutional power to enact procedural rules to regulate the federal courts. Both Article I and Article III authorize Congress to create the lower federal courts. That authority, combined with the constitutional power to do what is necessary and proper to achieve this end, is easily broad enough to support promulgation of rules that regulate the operation of the courts Congress creates. Congress, however, did not itself promulgate the Federal Rules of Civil Procedure. Instead, it delegated authority to propose such rules to the Supreme Court in the Rules Enabling Act of 1934 (REA), found in § 2072 of Title 28. The REA reads, in part, as follows:

> (a) The Supreme Court shall have the power to prescribe general rules of practice and procedure and rules of evidence for cases in the United States district courts (including proceedings before magistrates thereof) and courts of appeals.
>
> (b) Such rules shall not abridge, enlarge or modify any **substantive right.**

Newly proposed Rules go through an elaborate process before becoming effective. Section 2074 requires the Supreme Court to transmit any proposed Rule to Congress no later than May 1 of the year in which the Rule is to become effective. The proposed Rule cannot become effective earlier than December 1 of that year. In the interim, Congress may pass legislation to block the Rule from taking effect or to rewrite the Rule as it sees fit.

In theory, a federal court determines validity by asking whether Congress could have itself enacted the Rule within its constitutional powers over court procedure. In asking this question, a court recognizes that Congress's power extends to those Rules which might have both procedural and substance aspects. If the Rule comes within Congress's constitutional power, the court asks whether the Rule actually proposed by the Supreme Court comes within the language of the REA. In reality, courts *presume* the validity of any Rule which is arguably procedural. A presumption of statutory validity is justified because of the careful review presumably given by Congress to insure that proposed Rules come within the limit imposed in the REA. Furthermore, without such presumptive validity, litigants could not rely on a uniform application of the Federal Rules of Civil Procedure in diversity cases.

b. The Consequences of Erie

After *Erie*, a few points are clear. In diversity cases, federal courts have to apply state substantive law whether it is found in state statutes or state court decisions. Because *Erie* emphasized the necessity of applying state *substantive* law—law which represents state decisions about rights and liabilities—federal courts can still apply federal *procedural* rules. The courts can, it would seem, even apply federal judge-made procedural rules (procedural common law) unless such rules interfere with the application of state substantive law. As became clear in later cases, however, no clear divide between substantive and procedural law exists to make the distinction an easy one to draw.

4. *Guaranty Trust Co. v. York*

Guaranty Trust Co. v. York, 326 U.S. 99 (1945) began when Ms. York sued the Guaranty Trust Company in federal court for breach of its fiduciary duty and sought the equitable remedy of an accounting. Guaranty had been the trustee for individuals who held particular corporate notes. This diversity suit came well after the state statute of limitations had expired, and Guaranty pleaded that defense. York claimed that her suit was in equity and that, therefore, the equitable doctrine of laches rather than a statute of limitations should apply. It was clear that were the statute of limitations applied, York would lose. However, if a federal judge could use his own discretion to decide whether her delay was unreasonable—apply laches, in other words—she might well have the opportunity to litigate her suit on the merits.

York had two arguments to counter the application of *Erie*. First, at the time of this decision, the Rules of Decision Act required application of state law in "suits at common law." (The RDA was amended in 1948 to apply to civil actions.) York's suit was for an equitable remedy and, therefore, seemed to fall outside the language of the RDA. The Supreme Court held against her on this point by concluding that the RDA and *Erie* applied to equity suits. The Court reasoned that in diversity cases seeking equitable relief federal courts were called upon to adjudicate state-created causes of action (as in *Erie),* and the plaintiff's request for an equitable (instead of a damages) remedy did not change that fact. Therefore, the Court held that in any diversity case when a federal judge-made rule—here, the rule of laches—conflicted with state substantive law, the principles of *Erie* controlled.

York also contended that if *Erie* applied it required application only of the substantive law of the state. The federal court could apply its own procedural law. York argued that in New York choice-of-law cases its courts labeled statutes of limitations as procedural. She thus concluded that the New York statute of limitations was procedural in this case and need not be applied. The Supreme Court held that *Erie*'s mandate did not turn on labeling or on any abstract definition. The Court reasoned that laws can be procedural or substantive depending on the purposes for which this distinction was being made. For example, in choice-of-law matters courts defined as procedural that law which was integral to their basic mode of operation. They would then consider borrowing from other states only other types of law, which they labeled substantive.

In diversity cases ruled by *Erie*, on the other hand, a federal court must apply state law to maintain a uniformity of outcome in cases which could be brought either in a federal or a state court of the same state. The lack of such uniformity had been one of the principal evils of the *Swift* regime which the Court in *Erie* sought to end. Therefore, federal courts should not apply a federal judge-made rule which significantly altered the outcome of a case from what would have been reached in a state court of that state. If that change in the outcome would occur, the conflicting state law should be deemed substantive in the *Erie* sense and, to maintain uniformity of result, applied in place of the federal judge-made rule.

The Court in *York* thus created an outcome-determinative test that implemented *Erie*'s mandate for uniformity of result far better than would an attempt to distinguish substantive from procedural rules. However, the test also swept too many laws into the substantive law hopper. Even variations between indisputably procedural rules could become outcome determinative whenever state law imposed a terminal penalty for a failure to comply. For example, a state law requiring use of paper of a certain size for pleadings might require dismissal of a case for noncompliance. Would a federal court's insistence on its own paper length not alter the outcome of a case by preventing the dismissal which would occur in state court? What if the state law was to be applied in a diversity case after the applicable statute of limitations had expired?

The consequences of a blanket outcome-determinative test thus threatened litigants' confidence in the Federal Rules of Civil Procedure, which had become effective in 1938, the year in which *Erie* had been decided. Weighing against the policies of *Erie* therefore was the federal interest in providing uniform federal procedural rules on which federal court litigants in every state and in every civil action could rely.

5. *Byrd v. Blue Ridge Rural Electric Cooperative*

Although the decision in Byrd v. Blue Ridge Rural Electric Cooperative, 356 U.S. 525 (1958) did not involve a Federal Rule of Civil Procedure, it provided some support for the federal interest in having reliable and uniform federal procedural rules. It also provided support for the notion that federal judges could make their own procedural common law rules.

In remanding this diversity case to the district court for another trial, the Supreme Court was asked to decide whether the federal trial judge should determine whether the tort plaintiff was an employee of the defendant at the time he was injured (the state rule) or whether this issue should be submitted to the jury (the federal judge-made rule). If the plaintiff was an employee of the defendant, the plaintiff would be prevented from bringing the tort action by South Carolina's workers' compensation statute.

The South Carolina Supreme Court had held that such questions were to be answered by the judge and not by the jury. *Guaranty Trust*'s outcome-determinative test required the Supreme Court to ask whether failure to apply the state rule would substantially alter the outcome from what it would have been in state court. That test did not, however, yield a definite answer in this case. The outcome might just as easily be the same with either rule. One might guess that a judge would more strictly follow the law while a jury might tend to be more sympathetic to an injured worker. However, federal judges possess the power to control a jury and, if necessary, to grant a new trial should the verdict be against the great weight of the evidence.

In the absence of any certainty, the Court recognized the strong policy supporting the ability of federal courts to operate as an independent system for the administration of justice. The Court also concluded that the state supreme court's rule was not integral to the substantive provisions of South Carolina's statute and, therefore, appeared to be procedural rather than substantive. Furthermore, the relationship between a federal judge and jury was an essential characteristic of the federal system. The federal rule—submitting such factual issues to the jury—was strongly influenced, although not required, by the Seventh Amendment. (The Seventh Amendment requires federal, but not state, courts to preserve the right to jury trial in actions at common law.) The Court concluded that under these circumstances its role was to determine whether the federal interest should yield to the policies favoring application of state law. Since the outcome-determinative test did not make a strong case for application of state law, the Court ruled that the federal rule should control.

Byrd's contribution to *Erie* analysis arises because of the apparent freedom it gives federal courts to weigh the federal interest supporting the application of a federal rule against the state interest represented by the state law. This approach is commonly referred to as a balancing of the interests—those favoring application of the state rule against those favoring application of the federal rule. However, the Court's balancing occurred only after it found that the outcome-determinative test was inconclusive. If the policies of *Erie* strongly mandated application of the state rule, one must assume that federal interests represented by a federal judge-made rule would not have prevailed unless that rule was directly required by the Constitution.

6. *Hanna v. Plumer*

In initiating a state tort claim in federal court, the plaintiff in Hanna v. Plumer, 380 U.S. 460 (1965), relied on Rule 4 of the Federal Rules of Civil Procedure to serve process by leaving the papers at the defendant's home with his wife. However, the defendant was the executor of the estate of the alleged tortfeasor (in an auto accident), and Massachusetts' law limited the methods of service on executors. That state law required service either through in-person delivery of process or through the filing of a notice in the registry of the probate court within one year of the executor's being empowered to act. The defendant/executor in *Hanna* refused to accept service as performed in this case and, after the one-year limitations period had expired, moved for summary judgment. The district court granted the motion, and the court of appeals affirmed. These courts reasoned, in part, that the Massachusetts rule was integral to the one-year statute of limitations which, in accordance with *Guaranty Trust*, was a substantive law.

a. Part 1: The Twin Aims Test

The Supreme Court reversed. In ordering application of Rule 4, the Court conceded that the use of federal law *at this point* would substantially alter the outcome of the suit from what it would have been if controlled by the state service rule. In responding to this outcome-determinative argument, the Court explained that *Guaranty Trust*'s approach was never intended to provide an automatic and conclusive criterion. Instead, that decision had attempted to serve the policies enunciated in *Erie*, and those policies did not require application of this state rule. In modifying the *Guaranty Trust* analysis, the Supreme Court in *Hanna* noted that *Erie* had two major policies or aims. One aim was to prevent discrimination against residents whose rights had been made to vary under *Swift* simply because they were subject to suit in federal court by nonresidents. *Erie* had been designed to avoid this inequitable administration of the laws. The other aim of *Erie* was to discourage the forum shopping which had occurred under *Swift* largely because federal courts had insisted on applying their own versions of law to decide state law claims.

Application of the Federal Rule in the *Hanna* case did not undermine either of the twin aims of *Erie* because, the Court reasoned, doing so would not encourage forum shopping or cause the inequitable administration of the laws.

The Court held that application of Rule 4 instead of the stricter state service rule would not cause future litigants to choose federal court. Both rules were designed to accomplish the same thing—actual notice. Because the defendant received actual and timely notice of the suit, Rule 4's allowance of delivery to his wife at their home also did not deprive the defendant of any substantial right.

b. Part 2: Rule Preemption

In part 2 of its opinion, the Court stated the ultimate reason for its holding. It concluded that when a Federal Rule of Civil Procedure was valid and pertinent to the issue, the Federal Rule applied in place of a conflicting state law. The Court held that *Erie* did not provide the appropriate test when a Federal Rule of Civil Procedure conflicted with state law. Instead, *Erie* applied only when a federal judge-made rule, having no constitutional basis, was used to displace an indisputably substantive state law. The absence of a general constitutional power to make substantive common law created the problem in *Erie*. However, constitutional power directly supports creation and application of the Federal Rules of Civil Procedure. Congress has express power to create the lower federal courts and must have the necessary power to establish the housekeeping rules by which these courts are to be operated. In exercising this broad power, Congress also can regulate matters that fall within the hazy area of mixed substantive and procedural effects if it adopts rules which are rationally capable of classification as procedural.

For these reasons, the Court concluded that a federal court must follow an applicable Federal Rule of Civil Procedure unless it finds that the Rule is invalid because it falls outside the constitutional power of Congress or the power delegated in the Rules Enabling Act (REA). Justice Harlan, in his concurring opinion, criticized the majority for oversimplifying the essence of *Erie*. He believed that *Erie* was concerned with those "primary decisions respecting human conduct which our constitutional system leaves to state regulation." 380 U.S. at 475. In addition, he was troubled by the Court's test for determining the validity of a Federal Rule, which he characterized as an "arguably procedural, ergo constitutional" test. *Id.* at 476.

In this regard, Justice Harlan accurately described the strong presumption of validity which the Court attached to the Federal Rules of Civil Procedure. That presumption of validity was the primary accomplishment of the *Hanna* decision. In addition, the Court's dicta in part 1 of its opinion established a new approach to be used in determining unadorned *Erie* problems. In doing so, it modified *York*'s outcome-determinative test by requiring a focus on the twin aims of *Erie*. That new test, at least in its forum-shopping stage, requires one to look at a federal rule's influence on future litigants rather than solely at the problems it causes in a particular case because of the past actions of the parties.

7. *Gasperini v. Center For Humanities, Inc.*

The issues in Gasperini v. Center For Humanities, Inc., 518 U.S. 415 (1996), arose because New York required its trial and appellate courts to grant a new trial (or to order a remittitur) whenever a jury award deviates materially from what would be reasonable compensation. Federal district judges normally apply their own standard in ruling on new trial motions; they grant such motions only if the alleged excessiveness of a jury's damage award shocks the conscience of the court. The New York standard allowed a judge to impose a remittitur when a jury verdict "materially deviated" from similar damage verdicts. (A remittitur, or reduction in a damages award, can be ordered by a judge through his power to grant a new trial. In effect, the judge tells the plaintiff that a new trial will be ordered unless the plaintiff accepts the reduction.)

In the Court's opinion, a state statute placing a cap on damages would clearly be a substantive law. New York's materially-deviates standard accomplished the same objective even though it did so through a procedural rule that did not automatically limit damage awards. By this analogy, the Court identified New York's standard as one having a substantive effect even though that effect was achieved through a procedural means.

In *Gasperini*, the Supreme Court held that the substantive thrust of New York's materially-deviates standard for judicial review of excessive verdicts required that standard's application by federal trial judges sitting in New York in diversity cases. The Court held, however, that federal appellate courts could not exercise such freedom in reviewing jury awards. Federal appellate courts must, instead, review a district court's denial of such a motion under an abuse of discretion standard because this standard is required by the Reexamination Clause of the Seventh Amendment. The limits imposed by that clause, as well as practical reasons, outweighed the state interests in having the materially deviates standard used by appellate courts of the federal system.

The Court began its analysis by noting that in diversity cases federal procedural rules and state substantive law were to be used in adjudicating state claims. After admitting the difficulty often encountered in distinguishing substantive from procedural law, the Court briefly discussed the methods by which federal courts made that determination. First, the Court noted that *Guaranty Trust* identified state law as substantive (in the *Erie* sense) whenever its displacement by federal law would significantly alter the outcome of a case from what that outcome would have been in state court. In order to prevent this outcome-determinative approach from being triggered by every variation, the Court in *Hanna* had concluded that analysis must be guided by the twin aims of *Erie*—that is, the prevention of forum shopping and of the inequitable administration of the laws.

a. Preemption

The Seventh Amendment's Reexamination Clause states that "no fact tried by a jury, shall be otherwise re-examined in any Court of the United States, than according to the rules of the common law." This clause has been interpreted to restrict the power of federal courts in reviewing the decision of a jury. However, federal *trial* courts have long been permitted to examine the excessiveness of a jury's verdict upon a motion for new trial. But, the Court held in *Gasperini* that the shock-the-conscience standard used by federal trial courts for determining excessiveness was not mandated by the Seventh Amendment. Therefore, these courts could examine an award in accordance with state law without violating the Reexamination Clause. However, the Court concluded that the influence of the Reexamination Clause argued against allowing a federal *appellate* court to use the New York standard.

Even though New York law was deemed substantive in the *Erie* sense, Federal Rule of Civil Procedure 59(a) appears to establish a conflicting federal standard. Rule 59(a) reads, in part, as follows: "A new trial may be granted ... for any of the reasons for which new trials have heretofore been granted in actions at law in the courts of the United States." In his dissent in *Gasperini*, Justice Scalia argued that this language required establishment of a federal standard for deciding new trial motions. The Court countered Justice Scalia's point by concluding that this language merely authorized federal trial judges to grant new trials. The Court refused, however, to read Rule 59(a) as establishing or mandating the creation of a federal standard by which that excessiveness was to be determined. In this way, it refused to interpret the Rule broadly and avoided disturbing the substantive effect of the state law.

Until *Gasperini* has been further explained by the Court, one should be (and I am) hesitant to declare that it announces any radical departure from existing *Erie* and Rule preemption analysis. What we do know is that the Court began its analysis by attempting to discover the substantive *effect* of an apparently procedural state standard. It found that substantive effect by equating the New York rule to an indisputably substantive law—a statutory cap on damages. Once the substantive effect of the state rule had been established, the Court narrowly interpreted a potentially applicable Federal Rule of Civil Procedure to avoid wholly displacing the state rule. The twin-aims approach of *Hanna* was briefly brought into play to show that the policies represented by this approach supported application of the state rule. It is reasonable to assume that the Court will follow these steps in the same sequence in future cases.

D. Rules and Analysis

In following the multi-step process outlined below, take the perspective of an advocate. If you seek clear answers to every *Erie* or Rule preemption problem, you may become frustrated. As an advocate, you are obliged to accurately identify the issue and to make the best legal argument available to your client under the facts and law. In preparing this argument, you will notice the weakness of your own contentions and the strength of the arguments that could be made against you. By being aware of these strengths and weaknesses, you are better able to make an estimate of your client's chances of prevailing in court, and are less likely to freak out looking for the "right" answer.

1. *Erie* Problems

This problem arises when in adjudicating a state cause of action, a federal court confronts a conflict between a federal judge-made rule (or practice) and a state law. Although federal courts have power to promulgate and enforce federal judge-made rules that are procedural in nature, they cannot displace substantive state law with those rules. As generally stated, a federal court must apply state substantive law when adjudicating a state cause of action but can apply federal procedural law.

(a) SUBSTANTIVE LAW: One might begin by asking whether the conflicting state law is substantive in the legal sense in that it creates, defines, or limits a cause of action. Furthermore, one might also ask whether the state law is substantive in the political sense in that it appears to effectuate a state policy that relates to the ordering or protection of state residents. If a federal court can answer either question in the affirmative, it is likely to apply that state law.

(b) OUTCOME DETERMINATIVE: If the state law is not clearly substantive in either the legal or political sense, ask (i) whether application of the federal common law, instead of state law, would have such an effect on the outcome of the litigation that this effect would cause parties to forum shop between state and federal courts in the future (because of the different rules applied in each). (ii) Would application of the federal common law, instead of state law, have such an effect on the outcome of the litigation that this effect would deprive the party drawn involuntarily into federal court of a significant protection that would have been available in state court? If you answer either of these "twin-aims" questions in the affirmative, the court should strongly incline toward applying the state law.

(c) BALANCING: Does a strong federal interest directly and necessarily require the application of the federal judge-made rule? For example, does the federal law directly regulate the judge-jury relationship that emanates from the constitutional right to jury trial in federal court, conferred by the Seventh Amendment to the Constitution? If a federal interest appears to demand application of the federal common law, consider the substantive nature of state law and the answers given to the twin-aims questions. If those considerations weigh heavily in favor of applying state law, the state law probably should be applied.

2. Rule Preemption Problems

This problem arises when in adjudicating a state cause of action a federal court confronts an apparent conflict between a Federal Rule of Civil Procedure and state law. The courts generally declare that two requirements must be satisfied before the Federal Rule preempts the state law. First, the Federal Rule must be deemed valid. The Rule must be within the rule-making power of Congress under the Constitution. And it must not violate the limits set in the Rules Enabling Act, which primarily bars a Rule from abridging substantive rights. Second, a valid Rule must indisputably conflict with a state law before it will displace that law.

(d) VALIDITY: Is the Federal Rule valid in that it would have a primarily procedural effect if it applied to this diversity case? The Federal Rules generally will be presumed valid. However, in its decision in Semtek International Inc. v. Lockheed Martin Corp., 531 U.S. 497 (2001), the Supreme Court interpreted Federal Rule 41(b) so that it could not itself create the judgment on the merits needed for claim preclusion. The Court cited the Rules Enabling Act as one reason for reading the Rule so that it could not transform a dismissal with prejudice into a judgment on the merits. If that had been the effect of Rule 41(b), the Court reasoned, it would have violated the prohibition against abridging substantive rights contained in the Rules Enabling Act.

(e) PERTINENCE: Finally, does the Federal Rule inescapably conflict with the state law? If the court has determined that the state law is substantive or outcome-determinative, it will search for a reasonable alternative reading of the Federal Rule that leaves the state law intact. That seems to have been one of the Supreme Court's motives in wholly ignoring the broader meaning of Rule 59(a) available in *Gasperini*. Therefore, the presumptive validity of the Rules will cause courts to interpret them narrowly when to do otherwise would interfere with the substantive effect of state law. At some point, presumably, a Federal Rule of Civil Procedure will preempt even a state law with a substantive effect. The Supreme Court may not yet have discovered that Federal Rule.

E. Hypotheticals and Explanations

Erie causes little difficulty at the extremes. A state law that, for instance, prevents a tort remedy for medical malpractice except upon proof of gross negligence changes the primary element of that cause of action. Ignoring that law would mean that a federal court was creating a cause of action that the state would not allow. On the other extreme, a state law that establishes a special procedure for challenging the personal jurisdiction of a court of that state regulates all cases without regard to their elements. If Federal Rule 12 provides a significantly different procedure for raising that issue, a litigant in federal court should be allowed to depend on the Rule as a guide. However, matters are not always so clear. In these instances, one must narrow the problem to a manageable issue and apply the pertinent rules in light of the general policies discussed above.

1. The plaintiff brought a state tort claim in federal court based on diversity. He filed the complaint within two years after the tort claim arose, but served the defendant more than three months after the state statute of limitations expired. The forum state's statute of limitations requires "commencement" of such a tort claim within two years after the date on which the claim arose. However, a service requirement is part of the state's limitations statute, and it requires a plaintiff both to file the complaint *and* *serve* the defendant within the two-year period in order to toll (satisfy) the statute. In contrast, Rule 3 of the Federal Rules of Civil Procedure reads as follows: "A civil action is commenced by filing a complaint with the court." In response to the defendant's motion for summary judgment, the plaintiff contends that in federal court Rule 3 preempts the state's service requirement and requires only the filing of a complaint. In addition, the plaintiff has numerous federal cases to prove that federal judges have long believed that both federal and state statutes of limitations were tolled by filing alone. **Does the state service requirement control?**

Explanation

Rule

(1) If Rule 3, which we will assume is valid, directly and inescapably conflicts with the state service requirement, the Rule will displace state law and apply in federal court. (2) If Rule 3 does not apply, state law will apply if application of the federal common law rule would cause forum shopping or the inequitable administration of the laws.

Application

The service requirement was designed to make certain that defendants received actual notice of such suits within the limitations period. In this way, the service requirement reinforces the policies of the statute of limitations. The *Guaranty Trust v. York* decision provides authority for the conclusion that the statute of limitations itself has a substantive effect. Even though *York*'s outcome-determinative test cannot completely resolve the question any longer, it compels one to recognize the substantive nature of a limitations requirement. More particularly, the service requirement shows that the state seeks to further one of the primary values of a statute of limitations, which is to protect the defendant's right of repose. Under the service requirement, a potential defendant can know with precision when the threat of a lawsuit has ended. However, if filing the complaint alone were sufficient, service could occur several months after the end of the limitations period. Application of the federal common law rule would thereby deprive defendants of the important interest of repose that they enjoy under state law. The state service requirement appears rather clearly to be a substantive law and to be applicable under the twin-aims modification of the outcome-determinative test.

Because the state service requirement appears to be substantive, Rule 3 cannot have a primarily procedural effect when it displaces that rule. Rule 3 enjoys a strong presumption of constitutional and statutory validity, and will under *Hanna* displace the state service requirement if the two directly conflict. On the other hand, the Supreme Court in *Gasperini* seemed to suggest, by the manner of its analysis, that lower courts should narrowly interpret a Federal Rule when to do otherwise would cause that Rule to displace a state's substantive law. Because the state service requirement has a clear substantive effect, Rule 3 should be interpreted, if possible, in a way which would avoid a direct conflict with the state law.

Rule 3 can be read solely as a guide advising a plaintiff of the first action one is to take in order to begin a civil action in federal court. Setting the point of commencement at the date of filing without regard to service has usefulness because it represents the plaintiff's invocation of judicial power and is the date to which jurisdictional rules refer. For example, complete diversity of citizenship must exist at the time of commencement. If one of the parties has moved his or her home, the court will determine the citizenship of that party on the date of commencement—that is, when the plaintiff filed the complaint. Commencement was also intended to serve as the beginning point for some time limits set in the Federal Rules of Civil Procedure. For example, Rule 56(a) allows the filing of a motion for summary judgment as early as 20 days after commencement. In addition, the Advisory Committee's Notes express uncertainty about Rule 3's application to statutes of limitations. In short, the Rule was created to have effects other than the tolling of a statute of limitations. It can therefore be reasonably interpreted to apply in this federal case without having to displace the state tolling rule. If so, Rule 3 and the state service requirement are not in direct conflict, and both can be applied in this case.

Application of the state service requirement does not interfere with the judge-jury relationship in federal court or contradict any part of the Seventh Amendment. One might conjure a federal interest in allowing federal courts to determine, according to a uniform rule, the method by which any statute of limitations was tolled. However, such an interest lacks the weight provided the federal rule in *Byrd* by the Seventh Amendment.

Also, once one determines that failure to apply the state rule would frustrate the state's substantive policies and would violate *Erie*'s purposes, only an extraordinarily important federal interest should be sufficient to allow application of the federal rule. In *Byrd*, the substantive nature of the state law was questionable at best. In fact, that state law appeared merely to allocate decisionmaking authority between the judge and jury. Since *Byrd* preceded *Hanna*, the twin-aims questions were not asked. Presumably, neither forum shopping nor the inequitable administration of the laws would have been the obvious result of applying the federal rule considered in *Byrd*. The federal interests supporting the federal rule thus were compelling, and the state interest in having its procedural rule applied in federal court was very weak. Therefore, when *Erie* does command application of state law, the balance may tip in favor of the federal rule only when the Seventh Amendment compels that conclusion.

In Walker v. Armco Steel Corp., 446 U.S. 740 (1980), the Supreme Court began with a Rule preemption analysis to determine the conflict between Rule 3 and a state service requirement. It concluded, however, that the service requirement was an integral part of the state's statute of limitations by finding that the two state laws had a common effect. Because the statute of limitations was undeniably substantive in the *Erie* sense, any integral part of it would be substantive too. Thereafter, the Court interpreted Rule 3 to avoid a conflict with the state law, although it stated that it was not interpreting the Rule narrowly. However, having found that Rule 3 did not preempt the state law, the Court applied *Hanna*'s twin-aims approach and held that this test required application of the state law.

2. Although the state generally allows punitive damages in tort cases, the Illinois legislature recently enacted a statute that amends state law in regard to pleading. Under the amended Illinois Rules of Civil Procedure, a plaintiff cannot plead a demand for punitive damages unless, after a non-jury hearing at which the defendant is invited to attend, the judge concludes that the plaintiff has sufficient evidence to make a prima facie case for such damages. If the judge finds that the plaintiff has stated such a prima facie case, the plaintiff may amend her pleading to include a demand for such damages. A plaintiff cannot recover punitive damages unless they have been included in her pleading.

   In a tort complaint filed in federal court in Illinois based on diversity jurisdiction, the plaintiff included allegations for punitive damages. In contending that Illinois law does not control, she cited Federal Rule of Civil Procedure 8(a), which states that any pleading in federal court which sets forth a claim for relief must, in part, contain: "a demand for judgment for the relief the pleader seeks." She contends also that Federal Rule 9 requires her pleading of punitive damages because it requires that "[w]hen items of special damages are claimed, they shall be specifically stated." [Punitive damages are special damages.] The plaintiff also contends that federal judges routinely hold that the right of a party to obtain punitive damages is a question for the jury not the judge in federal court.

   Does Illinois law apply?

Explanation

The Federal Rules do not conflict with the state law, and the latter is clearly substantive under the twin-aims analysis.

Rules

(1) If either Federal Rule 8(a) or 9 directly conflict with the Illinois law, those Rules will preempt the state law and allow the plaintiff to plead her right to punitive damages. The Supreme Court's modern tendency is to narrowly interpret any Federal Rule that appears to conflict with a substantive

state law. (2) If the Rules do not apply, the federal judge-made practice of leaving punitive-damage questions to the jury should not displace the Illinois rule if to do so would cause forum shopping or the inequitable administration of the laws.

Application

This Illinois law appears procedural because it is part of the Illinois Rules of Civil Procedure and deals with pleading requirements. However, the purpose of the Illinois rule is to reduce the ability of plaintiffs to gain the advantages of arguing punitive damage issues and introducing evidence to show the reprehensible nature of the defendant's action. Under the twin-aims analysis, the court asks whether application of the federal practice of sending such issues to the jury rather than deciding them in a non-jury hearing would violate either of the twin aims of *Erie*. Application of that federal common law would encourage plaintiffs to forum-shop because they could then avoid the troublesome Illinois law in federal court. And, if the federal common law applied, defendants drawn involuntarily into federal court would lose an important protection that they would enjoy in state court when sued in tort. In short, the twin-aims test shows that the Illinois law should be applied in place of the federal common law rule.

Federal Rule 8(a) requires anyone stating a claim to make a demand for the relief she seeks, but that Rule does not require a pleader to describe a type of damages that she cannot recover. The Illinois law directly prevents recovery of punitive damages unless the judge finds the plaintiff has a prima facie case for such damages. This plaintiff therefore has no right to those damages when filing her original complaint and thus is not in violation of Rule 8. Rule 9 requires the pleading of unusual or special damages to give the defendant notice of what might otherwise be a surprise. In this case, no surprise is likely. Furthermore, the plaintiff cannot recover these special damages under Illinois law until the court holds its prima-facie-case hearing and approves such a pleading. Neither of these Federal Rules therefore requires the pleading of a remedy that the plaintiff cannot recover under the substantive law. And Illinois provides that substantive law in creating and defining the cause of action that the plaintiff asserts.

One might argue that the federal common law rule that sent questions about punitive damages to a jury should be balanced against the interest supporting application of the state rule. The balancing of interests in the *Byrd* decision began with a determination that no strong interest supported application of state law. Here, just the opposite is the case. This state rule is substantive under the twin-aims approach and should be applied unless it indisputably conflicts with federal positive law. Since no such conflict exists, we must determine whether a strong federal interest requires application of the federal common law rule. In *Byrd*, the Supreme Court held that the federal rule that sent mixed issues of fact and law to the jury was an essential characteristic of the federal judicial system. That conclusion was based, in part, on the application in federal, but not in state, courts of the Seventh Amendment to the Constitution which preserves the right to jury trials in civil cases. The Seventh Amendment "influences" (and therefore authorizes) the rules controlling the judge-jury relationship in federal court. In this case, the state law defines the nature of the remedies that a plaintiff can recover under Illinois tort causes of action. If the substantive law does not allow a plaintiff to recover punitive damages, she has no issue for the jury to decide. The state law thus does not conflict with a federal rule authorized by the Seventh Amendment.

3. A tort suit has been removed to a federal court in Texas on the basis of diversity. The defendant contends that the plaintiff's negligence contributed to the accident that forms the basis of her suit and that she cannot recover for that reason. The federal courts have long applied the traditional common law rule of contributory negligence under which the plaintiff loses any right to recover if she was negligent to any degree. However, Texas law allows proportionate recovery under its comparative negligence system so that a plaintiff can recover when the defendant is more negligent than she. The defendant, however, cites Federal Rule 8(c) which states that "[i]n pleading to a preceding pleading, a party shall set forth affirmatively … contributory negligence … and any other matter constituting an avoidance or affirmative defense. **Does Texas law apply?**

Explanation

Federal Rule 8(c) merely requires the pleading of affirmative defenses, leaving to the substantive law the creation or definition of those defenses.

Rules

(1) If Federal Rule 8(c) directly conflicts with the Texas law, the Rule will preempt the state law and, presumably, would call for the application of the common law rule of contributory negligence. (2) If the Rule does not apply, the federal judge-made practice of applying contributory negligence should not displace the Texas rule if to do so would cause forum shopping or the inequitable administration of the laws.

Application

Application of the federal common law rule instead of the Texas rule would cause nonresident defendants to forum shop through removal and would deprive plaintiffs of an important protection provided by state law. Defendants would definitely want a court that would apply the draconian contributory negligence rule in order to bar any recovery by an even slightly negligent plaintiff. In addition, a plaintiff forced into federal court by the fortuity of diversity jurisdiction would lose the protection provided plaintiffs by the comparative negligence rule.

Federal Rule 8(c) was not intended to create any particular affirmative defense; a court would read it to require the affirmative pleading of such defenses as contributory negligence or its replacement. Furthermore, a reading of Rule 8(c) that gave it the effect of creating a more severe defense to state causes of action would diminish substantive rights in violation of the Rules Enabling Act, which authorizes the promulgation of rules so long as they do not enlarge or abridge substantive rights.

PART III

PREPARING THE CASE

CHAPTER 7

PLEADINGS AND THE
CLAIM FOR RELIEF

A. Terminology

Affirmative defense—These are defenses that the defendant must allege in his answer in order to give the plaintiff sufficient notice. Failure to plead an affirmative defense causes waiver of that defense. This category includes defenses based on a statute of limitations, res judicata, a statute or frauds, or contributory negligence. See Rule 8(c).

Amendment—In many circumstances, a party can file a new pleading to take the place of one that is deficient in some way. These can also be used to add or change causes of action or even to change or add a defendant. See Rule 15(c).

Answer—This is the pleading that the defendant prepares in response to the allegations of the complaint. It can contain denials, defenses, and claims for relief.

Cause of action—This is the manifestation of the law's recognition that one suffering harm because of a particular form of wrongful conduct by another should have a judicial remedy. A plaintiff cannot prevail in court unless she pleads and proves each element of her cause of action. It is her ticket to ride.

Claim for relief—This is the same thing as a cause of action. The Federal Rules of Civil Procedure uses "claim for relief" to avoid carrying forward the pleading and procedural restrictions that were attached to a cause of action under the old common law.

Complaint—This is the plaintiff's initial pleading in which she describes the reason for the court's subject matter jurisdiction, the elements of her claim for relief, and the remedy she seeks.

Material fact—Facts are material to the extent they sustain the elements of a cause of action or an affirmative defense to it. The plaintiff must satisfy each element of her cause of action by proving those facts that by law establish the element. One does not prove negligence; one proves the defendant, for example, was driving his car at an excessive rate of speed when he collided with the car driven by the plaintiff.

Motions—Since pleadings are limited, most papers filed are motions or the responses to them. A request for relief from the court will typically be sought through the filing of a motion for that relief.

Pleadings—These are the formal documents that the parties must file with the court and serve on each other setting out the claim for relief and the response to it. In federal practice, only two pleadings are frequently used—the complaint and the answer.

Relation back—An amended pleading that adds a new cause of action or a new defendant after the running of a statute of limitations can avoid that defense if it relates back to the time, before the end of the limitations period, when the original pleading was filed. See Rule 15(c).

Reply—When the defendant includes in his answer a counterclaim and calls it that, the plaintiff must file a responsive pleading to the counterclaim. That responsive pleading is called a reply.

Supplemental pleading—This pleading is used to bring into an existing suit information about relevant transactions that have occurred after the original complaint was filed.

B. Substantive Law

1. Elements of the Claim for Relief or Cause of Action

In order to sue someone successfully, the plaintiff must be able to plead and prove at least one cause of action. The Federal Rules of Civil Procedure speak instead of a claim for relief, but whether called a cause of action or a claim for relief, the legal right to bring a private lawsuit comes in these packages of substantive law. Each depends on the satisfaction of specific requirements. One can better understand the requirements for pleading in federal court by gaining a sense of the concept of a claim for relief

The claim for relief and the defenses form the foundational unit of a lawsuit, and understanding the pleadings requires one to understand a few basic propositions about claims and defenses. In federal court, Rule 8(a) of the Federal Rules of Civil Procedure describes the pleading requirements for a "claim for relief." The claim-for-relief terminology replaces references to the concept of a cause of action that was primarily used in state procedural systems. Those systems had imposed various onerous procedural burdens on the pleader of a cause of action. For example, one pleading a cause of action in some state systems was required to make proper factual allegations to support each element (or requirement) of a cause of action and of the remedy sought. The framers of the Federal Rules of Civil Procedure dropped the cause-of-action terminology in order to avoid confusing federal pleadings with those requirements.

If one ignores the different pleading requirements attached to a federal claim for relief as opposed to a state cause of action, the substance of the two concepts are the same. Both stand as legal expressions of approval for judicial remedies when the plaintiff satisfies a preordained set of requirements or "elements." For example, the common law cause of action for breach of contract requires the plaintiff to prove the following elements in order to obtain a judicial remedy:

- A valid contract existed between the plaintiff and defendant;
- The parties are in privity;
- The plaintiff performed her contractual obligations;
- The defendant breached the contract; and
- That breach caused the plaintiff's injury.

The plaintiff must, in addition, prove the extent of her injury in accordance with the law that rules contract damages, but that judicial remedy can be awarded only if she can prove each and every element of the cause of action. Should she fail to prove any one of the listed elements, she loses on the breach of contract cause of action, and no relief can be granted by the court.

Claims for relief (or causes of action) always depend on proof that the defendant's action has violated the law. As a result, a plaintiff recovers only for wrongful action that causes her damage. In a breach of contract claim, the courts of a state have, through judge-made (or common law), declared that failure to live up to one's formal agreements is unlawful. A breach of contract is thus prohibited as a legal wrong, and the common law of every state enforces this prohibition by giving those harmed by the wrong a private right to sue. Common law causes of action thus contain a legal prohibition, and they provide a cause of action, which is the enforcement mechanism by which this prohibition is enforced. A federal or state statute may prohibit certain action (as unlawful) and, in addition, provide authority for private parties to enforce that prohibition through civil suits. For example, the common law generally provided no judicial remedy for the heirs of someone killed through the negligence of a tortfeasor. State legislatures have uniformly changed that common law rule by enacting what are called "wrongful death statutes" that describe the wrong and provide a cause of action to the beneficiaries of the deceased who are named in the statute.

In some instances, a plaintiff will use two federal laws to support both the legal prohibition that underlies his claim and the authority for the claim for relief she asserts. For example, the Constitution prohibits state action that deprives someone of her fundamental right to freedom of expression, but it contains no express authority for the affirmative enforcement of that prohibition through a private suit for damages. Section 1983 of Title 42 of the United States Code authorizes a private right of action to recover damages and injunctive relief for injuries caused by unconstitutional acts committed under color of state law. Although no statute authorizes a private suit for damages against federal officials, the Supreme Court has created a limited damages action against federal officials. See Bivens v. Six Unknown Named Agents of Federal Bureau of Narcotics, 403 U.S. 388 (1971).

Be careful, however, to remember that a law may prohibit certain action—dumping effluent in a river, for instance—but not authorize enforcement of that prohibition through private civil suits. This means that someone owning land that abuts the river cannot sue for harm caused his land. She may have some political recourse by contacting her representative or by complaining to the appropriate federal agency, but she will not be able to sue. This is another way of saying that no one has a constitutional right to sue anyone who causes her harm. Congress may have refused to allow private suits in order to have enforcement only by an administrative body such as the Environmental Protection Agency. In choosing administrative enforcement rather than private suits, Congress may have sought to provide a more efficient decision-making process and a more uniform set of environmental rules. On the other hand, a cynic might contend that the nonexistence of private suits suggests that the polluter has more political influence in Congress than those injured by the polluter.

2. Material Facts

One might loosely say that a plaintiff must prove the elements of her claim, and the defendant must prove the elements of any affirmative defense. For instance, a plaintiff setting out to prove a breach of contract begins by showing that her agreement with the defendant satisfies the legal requirements of a contract. One may state the first requirement, as I have, by requiring the plaintiff to prove the existence of a contract—that is, a legally binding agreement. However, in order to prove the existence of a contract, the plaintiff must instead allege and prove specific facts that support the conclusion that the parties entered a contract. One may allege that, through correspondence, the plaintiff offered to supply 1,000 units of a particular product, as described in the attached specifications, at a price of $23,000 per unit. In a letter, the defendant accepted this offer and agreed to pay according a schedule outlined in that letter. The parties may have put all of the details of their agreement in a separate document, entitled the "Contract." By describing these documents and by attaching them to the complaint, a plaintiff provides the basis of her claim, and she can then use the details contained in those documents to prove that she performed (or offered to perform) in accordance with the conditions of the agreement, but the defendant failed to pay for the products delivered at the specified price.

In this manner, the plaintiff has made the allegations of fact which, if proved, will satisfy the elements of her breach of contract cause of action. These specific factual allegations are "material" to the cause of action in that when they are proved they sustain each and every element of the cause of action. In simple terms, the plaintiff must plead and prove the specific facts that establish each legal element of her cause of action. That factual matter is material to the cause of action because precedents will support a finding that, once proved, a factual proposition sustains the finding that a contract existed. One searches judicial opinions for those breach-of-contract cases that most closely resemble the facts of the client's problem. Those cases will suggest the character of facts needed to sustain each element of the cause, and then one can sue if the client's factual claims fit those precedents.

C. Pleadings

1. Overview

Rule 7. The only pleadings are (1) the complaint, (2) the answer, (3) a reply to an answer that contains a counterclaim denominated as such, (4) an answer to a cross claim, (5) a third-party complaint, and a (6) third-party answer. The court can (but rarely will) order a reply to an answer or to a third-party answer.

Rule 8(a). A pleading containing a claim for relief must contain (1) a jurisdictional statement, (2) "a short and plain statement of the claim," and (3) a demand for the relief sought.

Rule 8(b). A defending party shall either admit or deny the averments upon which the adverse party relies. Denials shall be specific, but the pleader can effectively deny an averment by stating that he is "without knowledge or information sufficient to form a belief as to the truth of an averment." Although the Rule suggests that a defendant can make a blanket denial of the plaintiff's averments, Rule 11 requires an attorney to certify that he has sufficient reason for making such a statement. A defendant ordinarily should either specifically admit designated averments and deny the remainder ("qualified general denial"), or specifically deny designated averments and admit the rest ("specific denial").

Rule 8(c). Affirmative defenses must be asserted or they are waived. These defenses typically are ones that defeat the plaintiff's claim even if that claim is otherwise proved. The running of a statute of limitations is the affirmative defense we have discussed most frequently in this book.

Rule 8(d). If a responsive pleading is required to a previously filed pleading, the averments of that filed pleading must be denied or they are admitted. Rule 7 indicates which pleadings require a response. If no responsive pleading is required to a filed pleading—say to an answer that doesn't contain a counter-claim—then the averments of that pleading are deemed to have been denied.

2. Burden of Pleading

In the United States, courts generally operate as passive decision-makers in civil cases; they do not investigate the claim or gather evidence themselves for the resolution of the issues. Instead, the burden of doing so falls on the litigants. The plaintiff therefore has the burden both of pleading and proving the elements of her claim. The Supreme Court refers to this as the default rule; "plaintiffs bear the risk of failing to prove their claims." Schaffer v. Weast, 126 S.Ct. 528, 534 (2005). The defendant normally has the burden of pleading and proving those affirmative defenses which can defeat a claim, but controversy can develop when one seeks to discover whether a particular proposition is part of the plaintiff's claim or an affirmative defense to it.

The law places the greatest burden on the plaintiff because it is she who seeks to use the court's governmental power to enforce rights against the defendant. In the broadest sense, the plaintiff must prove her legal right by establishing a claim for relief. More particularly, the law creates claims through the elaboration of multiple requirements (or elements), and the plaintiff has the burden of satisfying all of these requirements in order to succeed in court. If the plaintiff fails to satisfy any requirement of her claim, she loses.

The law divides the plaintiff's burden into three parts, each being governed by different rules. The plaintiff's obligation begins with the burden of pleading. In order to prove the material facts needed to establish each element of her claim, the plaintiff has the burden of production; this is the burden of coming forward with some evidence to prove those material facts. The plaintiff then must bear the burden of persuasion, and that burden requires her to persuade the fact-finder, which we will assume is a jury, that her evidence "outweighs" the contrary evidence of the defendant. Each of these burdens places the plaintiff at a certain risk.

The plaintiff invokes the jurisdiction of the court on the basis of her claim and bears the burden of pleading each of its elements. As a claimant, one need not enter allegations to cover every possible barrier—that is, a claimant is not required to negate all possible counters. At some point, issues critical to the ultimate judgment become the responsibility of the defendant. The substantive law, therefore, decides which matters are classified as elements of a claim and which are to be defenses. In making this determination, tradition often controls. Much of that tradition is evidenced by Rule 8(c)'s listing of affirmative defenses, and the burdens to be allocated in modern litigation may be guided by finding similarities with common law claims and defenses. As a practical matter, one looks to the precedents to answer these questions.

When still in doubt, one might assume a defendant should bear the burden of pleading those matters which are peculiarly within his knowledge. In some cases, however, even this consideration will not allow reliable prediction because burden allocation will be made for policy reasons. A legislature or court (in making common law) may allocate the burden on some issue in order to encourage or discourage particular claims for relief. For example, the Supreme Court has placed the actual malice (knowing-falsity) burden in public figure libel actions on the plaintiff to protect free speech interests even though knowledge as to that issue lies peculiarly within the control of the defendant.

3. The Complaint

We tend today to assume that every wrong can be remedied in a private lawsuit. The materials discussing the need for a claim or cause of action prove that this assumption is inaccurate. One cannot hope to succeed by merely complaining about a defendant's responsibility in causing the plaintiff a loss of some sort. It is not enough to prove that the defendant is a bad guy; he must have harmed the plaintiff through actions the law deems wrongful. In addition, the law must permit the plaintiff, rather than some governmental agency, to punish him for his unlawful acts through a private right of action.

Rule 8(a) of the Federal Rules of Civil Procedure requires every pleading which sets forth a claim for relief to include:

(1) a short and plain statement of the grounds upon which the court's jurisdiction depends…,
(2) a short and plain statement of the claim showing that the pleader is entitled to relief, and
(3) a demand for judgment for the relief the pleader seeks.

The reference in Rule 8(a) to a statement of the courts grounds of jurisdiction reflects the principle of limited subject matter jurisdiction that characterizes federal but not state courts. Because of that concern, one seeking to invoke a federal court's jurisdiction must always plead and, if challenged, prove that the court has subject matter jurisdiction. One need not plead the existence of personal jurisdiction or of venue.

A defendant can challenge the plaintiff's statement of his claim by moving to dismiss that claim under Rule 12(b)(6). Dismissal should be granted when the plaintiff has failed "to state a claim upon which relief can be granted." In considering a Rule 12(b)(6) motion, a court should construe the complaint in a light most favorable to the plaintiff and accept all of the factual allegations as true. See Jackson v. City of Columbus, 194, F.3d 737, 745 (6th Cir. 1999). A plaintiff's allegations even when favorably viewed can fail to state a claim in various ways:

(1) by making allegations that are wholly ambiguous [see also Rule 12(e)];
(2) by complaining of a harm for which no cause of action exists [not showing up for her wedding];
(3) by failing to make allegations to support each element of a cause of action; or
(4) by making unhelpful conclusory allegations ["he discriminated against me"].

Rule 1 of the Federal Rules of Civil Procedure commands that the Rules be "construed and administered to secure the just, speedy, and inexpensive determination of every action." Faced with that command and their ever-increasing dockets, lower federal courts have encouraged plaintiffs to provide sufficient factual allegations in their complaints. The Sixth Circuit in the *Jackson* case held that to survive the defendant's motion to dismiss his racial discrimination claim the plaintiff must include in his complaint "factual allegations that provide direct evidence of a discriminatory motive." *Id.* at 751. In the absence of specific allegations that would, if proved, support each element of the plaintiff's claim for relief, the defendant is left with the obligation to research the elements of possible claims in order to discover evidence that bears on the material facts. Because the burden of pleading falls on the plaintiff, one might well argue that she should include more than conclusory statements of her right to recover.

The Supreme Court has, however, held otherwise at least in employment discrimination cases. In Swierkiewicz v. Sorema, 534 U.S. 506 (2002), the Court unanimously held that a plaintiff's pleading obligation under Rule 8(a) does not extend beyond giving the defendant fair notice of the claim and of its grounds. See *id.* at 512. This simplified requirement of notice pleading rests on the existence of liberal discovery rules and summary judgment motions to clarify the factual issues or to dispose of unmeritorious claims. *Id.* Unless the specific exceptions of Rule 9 apply, the simplified pleading standard applies to all civil actions. *Id.*

Although notice pleading appears to remove much of the burden of pleading from the plaintiff, one should realize that lawyers who repeatedly provide district judges with obscure and inept pleadings may well face judicial hostility and Rule 11 sanctions. Rule 11 of the Federal Rules of Civil Procedure requires a pleader to make a reasonable inquiry such that she can certify that the claim is warranted by existing law and that the factual allegations are likely to have evidentiary support. Having done the legal research and having queried the client and other potential witnesses about the facts, the plaintiff's lawyer should have sufficient information to plead the claim. Although Rule 11 does not have the bite it once possessed, the court can, in response to ill-supported claims, punish attorneys, law firms, or the parties by appropriate sanctions, such as payment of fines to the court or payment of compensation to the opposing party. Even if a lawyer avoids sanctions for sloppy pleading, the legal community quickly tags that person with a reputation that will not serve him well in front of judges or in his dealings with other lawyers.

Rule 10(a) of the Federal Rules of Civil Procedure imposes further requirements to the form of a complaint. The original complaint must include in its caption (at the top of the first page) the names of all of the parties. This listing of plaintiffs and defendants appears on the left side and can become rather extensive. In subsequent pleadings, the caption need only contain the name of the first or primary plaintiff and defendant, followed typically by "*et al.*" ("and others"). In the very top and center of the caption, the plaintiff must name the court in which the case is to be filed. On the right side of the caption, she must include the file number. Centered over the body of the complaint the plaintiff must state the designation or type of the document—that is, "Plaintiff's Original Complaint with Demand for Jury Trial." Rule 10(b) requires the plaintiff to make averments (specific allegations) of her complaint in numbered paragraphs, and advises the pleader to restrict any one paragraph to a statement of a single set of circumstances. The numbering allows the defendant to respond to allegations in the complaint by reference to those numbers. If each of plaintiff's paragraphs briefly states a single set of circumstances, a denial or admission by the defendant can also be more concise and clear.

4. The Answer

a. Challenges to the Complaint

Once the defendant receives the complaint either by service or through waiver of service, he can choose to file either an answer or a preanswer motion. If the defendant chooses to begin with an answer, he will include (1) any available objections to jurisdiction, service, venue, and nonjoinder; (2) any challenge pursuant to Rule 12(b)(6) contending that the plaintiff has failed to state a claim upon which relief can be granted; (3) denials and admissions directed at the allegations of the complaint; (4) any affirmative defenses, such as those listed in Rule 8(c); and, (5) any Rule 13 counterclaims or Rule 14 third-party claims he may have. [*Note: Discussion of claims by the defendant has been left for the chapter on joinder.*]

The defendant may challenge the plaintiff's claim by contending pursuant to Rule 12(b)(6) that even if all of plaintiff's allegations were proved she could not be given a judgment under law. If the plaintiff has attempted to state a recognized claim, the defendant can argue that she failed to allege a material fact needed to satisfy one of its elements. The latter ground of legal insufficiency—failure to allege an element—can also provide the basis for a no-evidence motion for summary judgment. By filing this motion after the discovery period has ended, the defendant can contend that the plaintiff has failed to acquire *any* evidence to support one element of her claim. Remember, the plaintiff has both the burden of pleading and the burden of proof in regard to *all* elements of her claim. Failure to have any evidence to support a material fact needed to sustain even one element of her claim for relief means, at this time, that she must lose as a matter of law.

b. Denials

Since the plaintiff will lose on the merits of her claim if she fails to sustain each and every element of the claim, a defendant begins by using denials to challenge the factual allegations of the complaint. If the defendant can defeat the proof of a material fact—that is, one the plaintiff must prove in order to establish one of her elements—the defendant prevails on the merits and thereby wins judgment.

In order to dispute the existence of any such material fact, the defendant must begin by denying the plaintiff's allegations in regard to that fact. Normally he must specifically deny designated paragraphs in the complaint or the averments within a paragraph. Although Rule 8(b) technically allows a defendant to use a general denial—that is, to respond by denying each and every allegation of the complaint—Rule 11 requires a good faith inquiry into the facts that would usually make such a response inappropriate. It is difficult to imagine a plaintiff whose complaint was inaccurate in every particular. Therefore, a defendant would almost never be justified in denying every allegation of the complaint.

In most cases, therefore, the defendant's answer should consist of admissions and denials. If the defendant knows which material facts the plaintiff must plead and prove to establish the claim for relief, he thereby can identify those allegations that must be denied, if possible. The defendant can present his denials in three ways. If the defendant can legitimately deny many of the complaint's allegations, he may admit the few he cannot deny but generally deny the rest. The defendant can use the opposite tact by specifically denying a few allegations and generally admitting the rest. Finally, the defendant can make either a denial or an admission to every averment. A defendant who cannot gather sufficient information at the pleading stage to deny or admit particular factual allegations may state that he is "without knowledge or information sufficient to form a belief as to the truth of an averment," and Rule 8(b) gives this statement the effect of a denial.

c. Affirmative Defenses

Another type of defense that challenges the plaintiff's claim on the merits is known as an "affirmative defense"—that is, one that must be affirmatively pled by the defendant. These defenses were known as confession and avoidance defenses under the common law. The defendant confesses (or assumes) the validity of the plaintiff's claim for relief, but asserts a defense that defeats the claim anyway. For example, a defendant might concede that a claim was otherwise valid but prevail on the merits by showing that it was brought after the applicable statute of limitations has expired. Under the Federal Rules of Civil Procedure, a defendant can assert an affirmative defense without giving up his right to dispute the material facts underlying the plaintiff's claim. In other words, asserting an affirmative defense does not waive any right to challenge the plaintiff's claim, but the defendant's failure to affirmatively plead such a defense in his answer can bar its later assertion in the case.

Affirmative defenses operate by trumping the plaintiff's claim for relief even when all of its elements have been proved. For instance, under the common law, a plaintiff who proved the defendant's negligence had caused her injuries would still lose her suit if the defendant proved that the plaintiff's negligence also contributed to those injuries. This contributory negligence defense completely defeated negligence claims.

Rule 8(c) of the Federal Rules of Civil Procedure contains an illustrative list of affirmative defenses. Other affirmative defenses arise from statutes. Perhaps the best known, and most troublesome generally for plaintiffs, are statutes of limitations. These statutes require particular claims to be brought in a court of competent jurisdiction within a set period after the claim arises. A plaintiff's failure to comply with such a prescription is punished by the entry of judgment for the defendant no matter how valid the plaintiff's claim.

Although federal courts generally cannot exercise common law power to displace state law causes of action, they have exercised greater law-making authority in creating affirmative defenses to federal claims. The Supreme Court created the qualified immunity defense even though Congress, in establishing the statutory § 1983 claim did not include such a defense in its statute. Under this defense, a state official who has violated the plaintiff's current constitutional rights may nevertheless defeat a claim for damages if his actions, *when taken*, were not in violation of clearly established constitutional law. Adopting such a protection for government officials sued in their personal capacity makes sense in that those officials should not be financially punished for making a decision that was not wrongful when made. On the other hand, the government that gives those officials government power to cause harm ordinarily pays those judgments.

D. THE PROBLEM OF PLEADING

As a default rule, the law places burdens on the plaintiff both to plead and to prove the cause of action, and the failure to carry those burdens can lead to a legal decision on the merits against her. The plaintiff has the obligation to plead that claim for relief sufficiently and to gather and bring forward evidence to sustain each requirement of the claim.

1. Hypothetical

In the beginning, a client arrives at the lawyer's office with her story of a wrong done her by someone else. Clients tend to provide a lawyer a broad range of information, some of which may be relevant to a legally recognized claim for relief and some of which may be legally insignificant. Relevance, at this point, means little more than that the information could tend to prove or disprove facts that are material to a recognized claim for relief. After hearing the client's story, the lawyer will search the case law to discover a claim that fits the information the client provides.

Suppose Jane Schmidt, the client, complains that she had been employed as an executive assistant by a state official, Harlan James. She had been the Deputy Administrator for the state's agricultural agency, and Mr. James during all relevant times was its chief administrator. Although she invested many years of competent service, Mr. James fired her by a letter delivered to her on February 4, 2005.

Ms. Schmidt contends that Mr. James fired her because she provided a newspaper reporter a copy of the 2004 Annual Report that she submitted to Mr. James on January 7, 2005. She was required by her job description to prepare and submit to the chief administrator an annual report concerning the agency's major activities and expenditures of the previous calendar year. However, her report concerning 2004 contained information that was critical of Mr. James's handling of the agency's annual budget. She delivered a copy of her 2004 report to a newspaper reporter on January 17, 2005, and he wrote a front page article criticizing Mr. James for his profligate ways. This article, published on January 31, 2005, stirred a great deal of controversy, and a legislative committee had been appointed to investigate the allegations contained in that article and in Ms. Schmidt's annual report.

Mr. James fired Ms. Schmidt by having his secretary deliver to her a letter on Friday, February 4 at 5 p.m., which contained only the following:

> Ms. Schmidt, your employment with this agency is hereby terminated, and you are required to remove all private possessions from your office and to leave your keys to this office before permanently vacating these premises on this, the 4th day of February, 2005.

Mr. James has not at any time provided further explanation for his decision to fire Ms. Schmidt. As noted above, she was fired within a week after the local newspaper published its story based on information gathered from Ms. Schmidt's 2005 annual report. The newspaper had published information from Ms. Schmidt's report that described how Mr. James had spent millions of taxpayer dollars on his travel to other countries. Ms. Schmidt was quoted as complaining that the budget for her own research programs had been cut in half in order to preserve sufficient funds for Mr. James's travel. The author of the newspaper article had discovered on his own that Mr. James had spent over $1 million on his travels in 2004 and that he had spent over three weeks during the year visiting the cities of Paris, London, and Prague. The author questioned the amount of the expenditure and asked what one could learn about agriculture by staying in five-star hotels in these exotic European cities.

It is clear that Ms. Schmidt has no long-term contract of employment with the state or with its agricultural agency. Under state law, she was an employee at will—that is, one who could be fired without good cause. Because state law ranked her position at a managerial level, state statutory and administrative law did not provide her civil service protections. She also cannot assert a tort cause of action under the state's common law because the courts of her state have stubbornly prohibited wrongful termination claims in tort by state employees. State law therefore does not give Ms. Schmidt any remedy against either the state or her supervisor for his termination of her employment. Assume that this conclusion holds even though the supervisor fired her without good cause or because of outright meanness.

2. Claim for Relief

However, since the harm was caused her by a state official, a federal statute appears to provide her a cause of action for the violation of her right to freedom of expression. Section 1983 of Title 42, United States Code, provides statutory authority for a claim seeking damages or injunctive relief against a state official who has violated the client's constitutional rights. That statute provides:

> <u>Every person</u> who, under <u>color of any statute, ordinance, regulation, custom, or usage, of any State</u> or Territory or the District of Columbia, subjects, or causes to be subjected, any citizen of the United States or other person within the jurisdiction thereof to the <u>deprivation of any rights, privileges, or immunities secured by the Constitution and laws</u>, shall be liable to the party injured in an <u>action at law, suit in equity, or other proper proceeding for redress</u>....
> (*Emphasis added.*)

For our purposes, § 1983 authorizes a private right of action to any person who claims that a state official (who acts under "color" of state law) violates the constitutional rights of the plaintiff. The plaintiff can seek relief as in an action at law—that is, damages—and can also seek equitable remedies, such as injunctive relief ordering Mr. James to reinstate her in her old job.

After further legal research, Ms. Schmidt's lawyer concludes that her free speech rights, as incorporated in the Due Process Clause of the Fourteenth Amendment, have been violated. Preliminary research into cases in which government employees were allegedly fired because of the exercise of their freedom of speech indicates that two broad elements are required for a successful § 1983 claim of this sort. First, one must prove that the harm was caused through state action. A state official who acts within the scope of his employment with the state represents the government. In that regard, Ms. Schmidt need only show that she complains of action by Mr. James as a state official.

That state action must violate the Constitution, and Ms. Schmidt contends that the termination of her government employment was a punishment imposed in violation of her rights of free speech. The federal court cases that have dealt with the constitutional "whistleblower protection" for the free speech of government employees have provided a rather elaborate set of requirements that Ms. Schmidt must satisfy. The elements of her § 1983 claim that Mr. James fired her because of her disclosures to the public are the following:

(1) First, the plaintiff must show that the defendant is a government official in order to satisfy the color-of-law requirement. In this case,

no dispute will exist about whether Mr. James is the head of the
state's agricultural agency or about whether he acted as such when
he took the action that Ms. Schmidt claims violated her freedom of
expression.

(2) Next, the plaintiff must show that when she publicly disclosed the information contained in her 2004 Annual Report that she spoke as a
citizen on a matter of public concern. See Garcetti v. Ceballos, 126
S.Ct. 1951, 1958 (2006).

(3) If she can satisfy the preceding requirement, she possesses a possible
free-speech claim, but she must show that her free-speech interests
outweigh the state's interest in promoting the efficiency of the agricultural agency. See Mack v. Augusta-Richmond County, Georgia,
365 F.Supp.2d 1362, 1374 (S.D. Ga. 2005). The Supreme Court has
noted that a government agency has broader discretion as an employer than it would as a regulator, but the "restrictions it imposes
must be directed at speech that has some potential to affect the entity's operations." *Garcetti*, 126 S.Ct. at 1958.

(4) As a final requirement, the plaintiff must provide a prima facie case
to show that the defendant terminated her employment because of her
protected speech. To do so, she has the obligation to prove by a preponderance of the evidence that her speech played a substantial part
in Mr. James's decision to fire her. See *Mack*, 365 F.Supp.2d at 1374.

If the plaintiff satisfies the fourth element of her claim, the burden shifts
to Mr. James to prove by a preponderance of the evidence that he would have
made the same decision even in the absence of the protected speech. In other
words, Mr. James can rebut Ms. Schmidt's contention that he fired her because of the information she fed the newspaper reporter by making a convincing showing that he fired her because of some reason other than her protected speech. If Mr. James succeeds in this effort, he will have disproved the
material facts needed to sustain her fourth element—the requirement that she
show that his violation of the First Amendment caused her harm.

Although not listed as an element of Ms. Schmidt's free-speech claim for
relief, she should include some allegations to counter Mr. James's qualified
immunity defense. That defense shields executive government officials from
damage suits arising from discretionary acts unless they took those actions in
violation of what was then clearly established law. In short, to overcome the
qualified immunity defense, a plaintiff seeking damages from a government
official in his personal capacity must show that the defendant's action was
clearly unconstitutional when it occurred and is unconstitutional when the

court decides the issue. Some federal appellate courts impose the burden of pleading the affirmative defense of qualified immunity on the defendant, but the burden of proving that the defendant violated clearly established constitutional rights falls on the plaintiff. *See, e.g.*, Atteberry v. Nocona General Hospital, 430 F.3d 245, 253 (5th Cir. 2005).

If you were representing either party in this suit, you would have to pay special attention to the recent Supreme Court decision in *Garcetti v. Ceballos*. In that decision, the Court held that when public employees make statements pursuant to their official duties, they are not speaking as citizens for First Amendment purposes, and the Constitution does not protect them. See *Garcetti*, 126 S.Ct. at 1960. In that decision, the public employee argued that he had been disciplined because of a memo that he delivered to his superiors. Since he was paid to write such memos, the Court held that he was acting as a government employee rather than as a citizen. As the Court explained, the "First Amendment does not prohibit managerial discipline based on an employee's expressions made pursuant to official responsibilities." *Id.* at 1961. This major precedent will force the plaintiff to argue that she was fired because of her communications with the reporter not because of her report to Mr. James. Mr. James, on the other hand, can defeat her claim by proving that his motive was the report not the newspaper article.

Now, let's do the complaint. Remember, Ms. Schmidt has the burden of pleading the elements of her claim but need not provide specific factual allegations to sustain each element. As a general rule, however, a lawyer would appear more competent if he or she provided sufficient factual information to indicate the basic contentions in regard to each element. And that is the rule I follow below. Some pleaders may, however, prefer to be more or less wordy depending on their style and their choice of tactics.

[Please be aware that his hypothetical is fabricated to serve as an example. I made up the agency, the parties, the controversy, and the law firms and their addresses.]

3. Complaint

UNITED STATES DISTRICT COURT
FOR THE NORTHERN DISTRICT OF GEORGIA
ATLANTA DIVISION

Jane SCHMIDT,	}	
Plaintiff.	}	
v.	}	Civil Action File No. _____
	}	

Harlan JAMES, in his   }
personal capacity,   }
     Defendant.   }

COMPLAINT AND DEMAND FOR JURY TRIAL

JURISDICTION

1. Jurisdiction is founded on the existence of a federal question. This action arises under the Freedom of Speech Clause of the First Amendment of the Constitution, as made applicable to the states by incorporation in the Due Process Clause of the Fourteenth Amendment. The action is brought pursuant to Title 42 United States Code § 1983, and jurisdiction is specifically conferred in Title 28 United States Code §§ 1331 and 1343(3). [Look at Form 2 of the Table of Forms appended to the Federal Rules of Civil Procedure.]

PARTIES

2. Plaintiff Jane Schmidt is an individual who is a citizen of the State of Georgia, residing in Atlanta.
3. Defendant Harlan James is an individual who is a citizen of the State of Georgia and who is sued here in his personal capacity. The Defendant may be served with process at his place of residence, which is located at 3405 Baskerville Road in Atlanta, Georgia.

CLAIM

4. On February 4, 2005, Defendant Harlan James, who was then and is now the Chief Administrator of the Georgia Agriculture Commission (GAC), an agency of the State of Georgia, wrongfully discharged Plaintiff Jane Schmidt, who at the time of her discharge was the Deputy Chief Administrator of the GAC. Defendant Harlan James was at that time acting within the course and scope of his office. [*Element # 1*]
5. The Plaintiff was hired by the State of Georgia on January 10, 1994, and from 1999 until her termination was employed as the Deputy Chief Administrator of the GAC. Since 1999, Defendant Harlan James, the Chief Administrator of GAC, has been her supervisor and immediate superior.
6. In performing his annual personnel evaluations of the Plaintiff as his deputy, Defendant Harlan James has since 1999 rated her overall job performance no lower than "superior," which is the next highest rating in the five-level ranking of employees. Harlan James, as her supervisor, rated her competence in her job as "superior" on December 18, 2004, less than two months before he fired her. [*Element # 3*]

7. As one of the Plaintiff's duties as Deputy Chief Administrator, she compiled an annual report describing the major activities of the GAC and its major expenditures. On January 7, 2005, she submitted a copy of her Annual Report for 2004 to Mr. James and forwarded the original to the Agriculture Committee of the Georgia legislature. In her annual report, the Plaintiff provided extensive details about the Defendant's use of the GAC budget to pay for the travels in Europe of himself and his family. On January 10, the Plaintiff Harlan James sent to the Plaintiff Jane Schmidt an interoffice memo that confirmed his receipt of her Annual Report for 2004. This memo did not contain any criticism or comment on the substance of the annual report. [*Element # 2, not fired because of report*] The Defendant has not to date communicated to the Plaintiff any criticism of that report. [*Element # 2, not fired because of report*]

8. On January 17, 2005, while not present at her place of employment or on duty as an employee, the Plaintiff was contacted by Zachary Lane, a reporter for the Atlanta Express-News, a daily newspaper with a wide readership in the state. Before contacting the Plaintiff, Mr. Lane had acquired information from a source independent of the Plaintiff suggesting that the Defendant had spent millions of dollars in GAC funds in order to pay for the first-class travel of his family to the tourist centers of Europe. Mr. Lane initiated his interview with the Plaintiff in order to question her concerning the travel budget of Defendant Harlan James.

9. In answering Mr. Lane's questions, the Plaintiff conveyed accurate information about the Defendant's budgetary decisions in 2004, which at that time were matters of general interest and of value and concern to taxpayers of the State of Georgia. [*Element #2*] In order to bring the issue to the public with only the most accurate information, the Plaintiff gave Mr. Lane a copy of the 2004 Annual Report she had compiled and had submitted earlier to the Plaintiff.

10. That annual report provided documentary evidence to show that during 2004 Mr. James had spent approximately $1 million from the taxpayer funds available to the GAC to pay for his travels in Europe. These funds covered the expenses of Mr. James, his wife, and his three children. The great expense of these travels can be explained in part by noting that the Defendant and four members of his family traveled on commercial airlines and exclusively in first-class seats when they flew to and returned from Europe, and they flew first class between cities in Europe. Furthermore, in each European city they visited, the family stayed in expensive five-star hotels.

11. In addition, the Defendant used $72,000 in GAC funds to pay for the purchase of various items of clothing and furniture in Paris, France. He also used approximately $12,000 in GAC funds to pay for purchases in London, and $16,000 in GAC funds to pay for purchases in Prague in the Czech Republic.

12. During these travels through Europe in 2004, Mr. James and his family spent slightly over three weeks (23 days) visiting Paris, London, and Prague. These travels do not have any discernible value to either the GAC or to the taxpayers of Georgia.

13. On January 31, 2005, Mr. Lane published the initial installment of two-part investigative article in the Atlanta Express-News. This first installment began on the front page of that edition, and his second and final installment was published on the front page of the February 1 edition of the newspaper. Both installments concerned Defendant Harlan James and his use of taxpayer money to pay for the expenses for his personal travel in 2004. The two-part series of articles caused a vigorous public debate that was featured for over a week in the Georgia mass media. [Element #2] As a consequence of this media coverage, the Georgia legislature appointed a legislative subcommittee to investigate the charge made in those articles.

14. Three days after the final installment of Mr. Lane's series of articles appeared in the Atlanta Express News, the Defendant reacted to the Plaintiff's contributions to that series of articles by causing his secretary to hand-carry a single-sentence termination letter to the Plaintiff. [Element # 4] This termination letter was delivered to the Plaintiff at 4:45 p.m. on February 4, 2005, and notified her that her employment with the State of Georgia and with the GAC had been terminated as of that day. A copy of the termination letter is attached hereto and incorporated for all intents and purposes.

15. The Defendant's action as a state official was taken solely because she had exercised her right to engage in political speech by responding truthfully in the unsolicited interview with a reporter as described above. [Element # 4] The Defendant took no action against the Plaintiff upon the submission of her annual report three weeks earlier, but he moved with great dispatch to terminate her employment three days after the publication of that information in a newspaper.

16. At no time, before or after her termination, has the defendant notified the plaintiff of any complaint about her work; about any difficulties with her relationships with other employees in the office; about the competence with which she performed her official duties, including the 2004 Annual Report; or concerning any negative aspect of her efforts as an employee. Nor has the Defendant provided the Plaintiff with any explanation of the cause for her termination. [Element # 3]

17. As noted above, the Defendant's official action terminated the Plaintiff's employment with the GAC because of her exercise of free speech as a responsible citizen in communicating information of public importance. The termination of the Plaintiff's employment had no relation to the efficiency, ef-

fectiveness, or other legitimate purpose of the GAC at the time it occurred, and the Defendant terminated the employment of the Plaintiff in violation of her rights as clearly established in the Supreme Court precedent in Pickering v. Board of Education, 391 U.S. 563 (1968). The Defendant's action in terminating the employment of the Plaintiff was clearly unconstitutional when it occurred, and that action remains unconstitutional today.

18. As a direct and proximate result of the Defendant's wrongful termination of her employment, the Plaintiff has suffered:

- Lost earnings because she has been unable to secure employment;
- Damage to her earning capacity;
- Damage to her reputation and good name, which will continue to cause her injury in the future;
- Mental anguish; and
- Damage to her retirement or other job related benefits.

It was also necessary for the Plaintiff to hire the undersigned attorney to file and prosecute this lawsuit. Upon judgment, Plaintiff is entitled to an award of attorney fees and costs pursuant to Title 42 U.S.C. § 1988(b).

DEMAND FOR JUDGMENT

Wherefore, premises considered, the Plaintiff respectfully requests that the Defendant be adjudged liable in his personal capacity [*This is a special pleading required because of the Eleventh Amendment*], to pay all damages to which the plaintiff is entitled, with prejudgment interest, and including attorney's fees. The Plaintiff requests that the Defendant be required to pay all costs of court, and she asks for such other and further relief to which she may be entitled under the law.

DEMAND FOR JURY TRIAL

The Plaintiff in this action demands a jury trial on all issues for which she has a right to jury trial.

June 8, 2006   /s/_____

                                           Short, Baxter, & Hook
                                           A Professional Corporation
                                           By: Levander Short
                                           Georgia State Bar No. _____
                                           4235 Holland Avenue, Suite 430
                                           Atlanta, Georgia 30309
                                           [telephone]
                                           [fax number]

Attorneys for Plaintiff
Jane Schmidt

[Rule 19(c) requires the listing of interested persons who were not joined. Local rules regulate the line spacing and other details of the pleading, and will require the plaintiff to attach a civil cover sheet giving general information about the suit. You should consult Forms 3 through 18 in the Table of Forms appended to the Federal Rules of Civil Procedure for other examples of complaints.]

4. Answer

In our hypothetical, Ms. Schmidt's firing (on February 4, 2005) occurred more than a year before the defendant could have received service of process in this suit. (The complaint was signed on June 8, 2006.) The defendant's lawyer might be alerted by this delay about the possibility of a limitations bar. In researching the law as it pertains to § 1983 actions, he would discover that this federal law does not include a statute of limitations. Instead, federal courts apply the appropriate state statute of limitations. In this instance, let's say the defendant finds that Georgia generally requires state tort causes of action to be commenced in a court of competent jurisdiction within two years of the date on which the cause arose. However, the Georgia legislature has also imposed a special one-year limitations period on persons bringing state tort causes of action against state officials. The defendant would look for case precedents to argue that this one-year limitations period applies as well to a federal § 1983 cause of action against a Georgia state official.

IN THE UNITED STATES DISTRICT COURT
FOR THE NORTHERN DISTRICT OF GEORGIA
ATLANTA DIVISION

Jane Schmidt,	}	
Plaintiff.	}	
v.	}	Civil Action File No. _____
	}	[Use number assigned by clerk.]
Harlan James, in his personal	}	
capacity,	}	
Defendant.	}	

ANSWER

Defendant Harlan James, in his personal capacity, files this his original answer to Plaintiff Jane Schmidt's original complaint.

FIRST DEFENSE

1. Defendant admits the allegation of jurisdiction in paragraph 1 of the Plaintiff's complaint.

2. Defendant admits the allegation in paragraph 2 of the Plaintiff's complaint.

3. Defendant admits the allegation in paragraph 3 of the Plaintiff's complaint.

4. Defendant admits the allegations in paragraph 4 of the Plaintiff's complaint, but the Defendant denies that he wrongfully terminated Plaintiff's employment.

5. Defendant admits the allegations in paragraph 5 of the Plaintiff's complaint.

6. Defendant admits the allegations in paragraph 6 of the Plaintiff's complaint, but denies that the evaluation as "superior" in GAC practice means anything other than unremarkable performance.

7. Defendant admits the allegation in paragraph 7 of the Plaintiff's complaint, but denies the implication that the Defendant did not communicate criticism of the Plaintiff's Annual Report of 2004 to other officials of the GAC and discuss with them the need to replace her.

8. Defendant is without knowledge or information sufficient to form a belief as to the truth of the allegations in paragraph 8 of the Plaintiff's complaint.

9. Defendant denies the allegation in paragraph 9 of the Plaintiff's complaint that she gave reporter Lane "accurate information" about the Defendant's budgetary decisions for 2004 and the allegation that the communication of her inaccurate information served the "general interest and of value and concern to taxpayers." The Defendant is without knowledge or information sufficient to form a belief as to the truth of her statements about what documents she provided reporter Lane.

10. Defendant denies the allegation in paragraph 10 of the Plaintiff's complaint that the Defendant "spent approximately $1 million from … taxpayer funds" on his personal travels because much of the money used by the Defendant for his travels came from campaign contributions that he had received when he was contemplating a campaign for Governor of the State. The Defendant admits the other allegations of paragraph 10 of the Plaintiff's complaint.

11. Defendant denies the implication in paragraph 11 of the Plaintiff's complaint that the expenses listed were paid by taxpayer funds. Most of the listed payments by GAC were ultimately reimbursed from the Defendant's private funds, and the rest were paid from campaign funds available for the personal expenses of the Defendant under State law. The Defendant admits the other allegations of paragraph 11 of the Plaintiff's complaint.

12. Defendant denies the allegations in paragraph 12 of the Plaintiff's complaint.

13. Defendant admits the allegations in paragraph 13 of the Plaintiff's complaint, but denies that the articles communicated information that was of general public interest.

14. Defendant denies the allegation in paragraph 14 of the Plaintiff's complaint that he terminated her employment because of the newspaper articles or because of the public's reaction to them. Defendant admits the remaining allegations in paragraph 14 of the Plaintiff's complaint.

15. Defendant denies the allegation in paragraph 15 of the Plaintiff's complaint that he terminated her employment because her exercise of free speech in communicating with reporter Lane. Defendant admits the factual allegation in paragraph 15 of the Plaintiff's complaint that he fired her three weeks after her submission of the Annual Report of 2004, but denies the irrational suggestion that this time period proves that the Defendant had disregarded the insulting and insubordinate statements contained in that report.

16. Defendant admits the allegations in paragraph 16 of the Plaintiff's complaint, but denies the implication that he had any obligation to give the Plaintiff, an at-will employee under his authority, any explanation of his decision to terminate her employment. Defendant also denies that his failure to communicate his reasons to her is evidence that he had not discussed his intent to terminate her employment because of the statements she made in the Annual Report of 2004.

17. Defendant admits the allegation in paragraph 17 of the Plaintiff's complaint that his official action terminated her employment with the GAC, but denies that he took that action because of any reason other than her incompetent performance of her official duties—that is, the compilation of the Annual Report of 2004. Defendant denies that he acted because of her exercise of free speech, that she was acting as a "citizen in communicating information of public importance," or that his action "had no relation to the efficiency, effectiveness, or other legitimate purpose of the GAC at the time it occurred. Defendant denies the allegations in paragraph 17 of the Plaintiff's complaint that his termination of her employment was clearly unconstitutional on February 4, 2005, or that her termination is unconstitutional under current law.

18. Defendant denies the allegations in paragraph 18 of the Plaintiff's complaint because he is not liable to the Plaintiff in any respect. [See Rule 8(d). The Defendant's failure to deny the amount of damage does not amount to an admission.]

SECOND DEFENSE

19. The Plaintiff's claim is barred by the applicable state statute of limitations because the Plaintiff did not file her complaint within one year of the termination of her employment.

THIRD DEFENSE

20. The Defendant's termination of the Plaintiff's employment did not violate any clearly established constitutional or federal statutory right, and, for that reason, the defense of qualified immunity makes him immune from this damage suit.

PRAYER

21. For these reasons, the Defendant asks the court to enter judgment that the Plaintiff take nothing, that the court dismiss the Plaintiff's suit with prejudice, that the court assess costs against the Plaintiff, and that the court award the Defendant all other relief to which he is entitled.

July 20, 2006

/s/_____

Hadley, Baxendale & Middleburg
A Professional Corporation
By: Jonas Middleburg
Georgia State Bar No. _____
6201 Lee Boulevard, Suite 520
Atlanta, Georgia 30308
[telephone]
[fax number]
Attorneys for Defendant
Harlan James

Certificate of Service

I have served the Defendant's Answer on Levander Short, attorney for Plaintiff, by mail addressed to him at 4235 Holland Avenue, Suite 430, Atlanta, Georgia 30309 on July 20, 2006.

_____

Jonas Middleburg

[I've omitted Rule 12(b) objections or claims permitted by either Rule 13 or 14. See Form 20 of the Table of Forms appended to the Federal Rules of Civil Procedure for examples of an answer presenting defenses under Federal Rule 12(b) and subsequent claims for relief.]

5. Reply

Although the defendant can file a third-party complaint or an answer to a cross-claim, the only other distinct form of pleading is the reply. The plaintiff files a reply only when the defendant's answer contains a counterclaim labeled as such. Because Rule 7(a) requires a response to such an answer, Rule 8(d) applies and would require a court to deem the allegations of the counterclaim admitted unless denied. For this reason, the plaintiff must either admit or deny the allegations of the counterclaim or risk entry of judgment on the pleadings. The plaintiff's reply therefore resembles an answer but need only include responses to the counterclaim. In addition to denials, the plaintiff can contest the legal sufficiency of the counterclaim and assert any available affirmative defenses.

6. Preanswer Motions

Rule 12 gives a defendant the option of responding to the complaint by serving the plaintiff's lawyer with an answer or by serving a preanswer motion to dismiss the complaint. Both normally must be served on the plaintiff's lawyer within 20 days after service of process on the defendant. This period can be longer if, for example, the defendant chooses to waive service of process. *See* Rule 12(a)(1)(B).

If a defendant chooses to serve a preanswer motion to dismiss, he need not prepare an answer unless the motion is denied. In this fashion, the preanswer motion saves the defendant, at least for a time, from the burden of drafting an answer. A preanswer motion can include objections to subject matter or personal jurisdiction, to service of process or to the process itself, to the venue of the action, to the legal sufficiency of the claim, or to the failure of the plaintiff to join a party who must be joined under Rule 19. *See* Rule 12(b)(1)–(7). If the motion is granted, the case will be dismissed, unless the absent person can be joined under Rule 19(a). If the court denies the motion, the defendant will have at least 10 days in which to serve his answer to the plaintiff's claim.

Objections to personal jurisdiction, to venue, to service, and to process can be lost if, being available at the time, the defendant does not assert them at the first opportunity. Rule 12(g) makes clear that, unlike state special-appearance procedures, waiver does not occur because a waivable defense is joined with any other objection. Instead, waiver under the Federal Rules is a penalty for the tardiness of a defendant in raising threshold personal objections.

Rule 12(h)(1) describes waiver in the following terms:

> [A waivable defense] is waived (**A**) if omitted from a [preanswer] motion, or (**B**) if it is neither made by [preanswer] motion ... nor included in a responsive pleading or an amendment thereof permitted by Rule 15(a) to be made as a matter of course.

Under this language, waiver occurs if either of the alternatives, (A) or (B), has occurred. That is, omission of the defense from a preanswer motion causes waiver of that defense because of subsection A. Subsection B, when read alone, might lead one to believe that the defendant can save a defense omitted from a preanswer motion by including it in the answer. However, a defense omitted from a preanswer motion has already been waived because of subsection (A). As a general rule, therefore, a waivable defense (personal jurisdiction, venue, service, or process) is lost whenever the defendant omits it from the first responsive paper he files under Rule 12.

7. Amendment of Pleadings

Rule 15 provides a pleader with the ability to correct or supplement a pleading. An amendment completely replaces the pleading amended. One must therefore be careful not to omit something important that was included in the original. A supplemental pleading is used to bring before the court events occurring subsequent to the commencement of the suit, while an amendment may be used to include prior events of which the party was ignorant at the time of commencement.

Only amendments of or supplements to *pleadings* are expressly allowed by Rule 15. Neither Rule 12 nor Rule 15 provides for the amendment of a motion, but the courts have exercised discretion to allow amendments to include omitted, waivable defenses at least when the new motion is filed well before the hearing or decision on the original.

a. Amendments as a Matter of Course

Rule 15(a) provides for the amendment of pleadings as a matter of course, by leave of court, or by written consent of the adverse party. A party may amend a pleading once as a matter of right (without seeking anyone's permission) if the amendment is served on the opposing party before a required responsive pleading is served. Put another way, the plaintiff can amend as a matter of course if she serves the amended complaint before the defendant serves an answer to the original complaint. A preanswer motion is not a pleading, so the plaintiff can still serve an amended complaint after a preanswer motion is served. The last sentence of Rule 15(a) requires the opposing party to respond to the amended pleading either within the time remaining for response to the original or within 10 days, whichever is the longer period.

If no responsive pleading is required, a party may amend once as a matter of course if the amendment is served within 20 days of the service of the original or before the action is placed on the trial calendar, whichever comes first.

For example, a plaintiff is not allowed to file a responsive pleading under Rule 7(a) to an answer which does not contain a counterclaim, denominated as such. Therefore, the defendant can amend that answer once as a matter of course before the 20-day period has expired, unless the action has been placed on the trial calendar.

b. Amendment by Consent or by Leave of Court

If the period within which an amendment may be served as a matter of course has expired, a litigant may amend with the written consent of the adverse party or by leave of court. A party seeking leave to amend should attach the proposed amendment to his motion for leave to amend. Leave to amend is within the discretion of the district court, but leave should be freely given in the absence of undue delay, bad faith or dilatory motive, repeated failure to cure deficiencies, undue prejudice to the opposing party, or futility of amendment.

c. Amendments at Trial

Rule 15(b) governs amendments to the pleadings once trial has begun. If issues raised at trial by a party are not supported by the pleadings but are tried by the express or implied consent of the parties, these issues are to be treated as if they had been raised by the pleadings. The pleadings may be amended to conform to the evidence, but failure to amend does not affect the trial on these issues. This result applies also when the issues raised are not supported by the pretrial order on which the case was brought to trial.

If the opposing party objects to evidence because it is beyond the scope of the pleadings, the court can allow an amendment of the pleadings to conform to the evidence, unless to do so would cause the objecting party prejudice in maintaining a defense. Under this rule, an objecting party must show how admitting the evidence will cause him prejudice. Because Rule 15(b) requires that amendments should be freely granted, the objecting party has the burden of proving prejudice. The primary concern is that the objecting party may be surprised by the new evidence and unable to respond adequately. If surprise is caused, the court has power under the last sentence of Rule 15(b) to admit the evidence but grant the objecting party a continuance of the trial.

d. Relation Back — Avoiding Limitations

A problem may arise where the plaintiff satisfies the applicable statute of limitations by the commencement of an action but finds it necessary to amend the complaint after the statutory period has expired. Under Rule 15(c), a late amendment can "relate back" to the date of the original pleading. Rule

15(c)(2) allows new claims in an amendment to relate back if those claims and the claims asserted in the original complaint arose from the same transaction or related series of transactions. If the amended pleading does relate back, and if the date of the original pleading was within the limitations period, the amendment cannot be barred by limitations.

If an amendment states a different claim for relief, the amendment will relate back if the law which provides the statute of limitations would allow relation back. In most instances, this means that the plaintiff can obtain relation back for an added state claim if state law provides a more liberal rule than does Rule 15(c). If state law does not, the court will allow the amendment to relate back only when the new claim arises from the same transaction which gives rise to the claim stated in the original. If both claims arose from the same transaction, the defendant had sufficient notice. He should be aware that a dispute encompasses all claims that fairly arise from that transaction. Because knowledge of these claims is attributed to the defendant, he cannot complain when, after the limitations period, a new theory of liability is introduced.

e. Relation Back of an Amendment Adding a New Party

Rule 15(c)(3) allows relation back of an amendment which changes the party against whom a claim is asserted if:

(1) the claim asserted in the amendment arose out of the transaction set forth in the original; and

(2) within the 120-day period after filing the complaint, which is allowed by Rule 4(m) for service of process, the party to be brought in by amendment:

(a) "received such notice of the institution of the action that the party will not be prejudiced in maintaining his defense on the merits," and

(b) "knew or should have known that, but for a mistake concerning the identity of the proper party, the action would have been brought against the party."

Although the Rule also applies to parties whom the plaintiff fails to name as a defendant, it was primarily designed to protect plaintiffs who served but mistakenly misnamed the defendant. The 120-day period was chosen because Rule 4(m) allows the plaintiff 120 days after filing in which to serve defendants, and should have the same time beyond commencement in which to communicate the required information to mistakenly named or omitted defendants.

In addition, the notice required by the Rule does not have to be given through the formal means of service of process. Timely knowledge of the institution of the suit may be inferred from other circumstances, but the evidence must show that during the 120-day period the added defendant not only knew of the suit but also knew or should have known that but for a mistake he would have been the person sued. If the added defendant had knowledge of this sort, he would not be prejudiced in maintaining a defense by the delay in joining him as a defendant.

f. Supplements to Pleadings

Rule 15(d) allows the filing of a supplemental pleading, but, unlike Rule 15(a), requires a party through motion to seek leave of court before filing such a pleading. The purpose of a supplemental pleading is to state transactions, occurrences, or events which have happened subsequent to the commencement of the action. In this manner, a continuing transaction or pattern of events can be brought before the court so that all elements of the dispute and all harm caused by these events can be considered in a single proceeding.

A difference in the claim asserted in a supplemental pleading may cause difficulty on rare occasions because of the running of the applicable statute of limitations. Ordinarily, one would not expect the limitations period to have expired as to events occurring subsequent to the commencement of suit, but delay in processing cases through the judicial system makes such problems possible. Under these circumstances, the provisions of Rule 15(c) have been applied even though this provision does not refer expressly to supplemental pleadings. Relation back to the date of the original pleading may, therefore, be allowed where the original pleading gave fair notice to the defendant that the wrongful conduct was of a continuing nature and the supplemental pleading is addressed to the same conduct.

E. Hypotheticals and Explanations

1. The plaintiff brought a Title VII claim against her employer, contending that she was fired because she was African-American. After describing her 20-year employment with the defendant, her qualifications for the job, and the summary termination, she included the following: "The defendant, who is white, fired me solely because I'm black." After being served with this complaint, the defendant filed a Rule 12(b)(6) motion, contending that the plaintiff has not stated a claim upon which relief can be granted. **How should the judge rule on that motion?**

Explanation

The judge should deny the motion and allow the parties to find evidence of discrimination through discovery.

Rules

(1) In considering a Rule 12(b)(6) motion, a court should construe the complaint in a light most favorable to the plaintiff and accept all of the factual allegations as true. (2) A plaintiff's pleading obligation under Rule 8(a) does not extend beyond giving the defendant fair notice of the claim and of its grounds.

Application

The plaintiff has not omitted an element of her discrimination cause of action. At most, she has failed to make allegations with sufficient particularity to satisfy the defendant. At the beginning stage of litigation, the plaintiff has no power to force the defendant to disgorge information about his motives. She, therefore, can only make conclusory allegations about his motives or use the factual information available to her to show the likelihood of an illegitimate reason for her termination. As in Swierkiewicz v. Sorema, 534 U.S. 506 (2002), the court can conclude that the plaintiff has asserted a discrimination in employment cause of action under Title VII. Her only failing was that she did not allege any direct evidence showing with particularity the defendant's discriminatory motive. That failing comes from her inability to use formal discovery and thereby to force the defendant to answer her questions about his motive.

2. The plaintiff filed a tort claim in federal court in Ohio on September 1, 2006, alleging that the defendant was negligent in constructing the farm machinery that it sold to the plaintiff and that its negligence caused the plaintiff's damages. The plaintiff served the defendant with process on September 15, and the Ohio statute of limitations expired on September 20. On October 17, the plaintiff moved for leave to file an amended complaint that substitutes a products-liability claim for the negligence claim asserted in the original. **Can the defendant successfully block this amendment based on the statute of limitations?**

Explanation

No, the court should grant leave to file the amended complaint because the new products-liability theory for recovery relates back to the original filing within the limitations period.

Rule

Rule 15(c)(2) allows new claims in an amendment to relate back if those claims and the claims asserted in the original complaint arose from the same transaction or related series of transactions.

Application

To benefit from relation back, the plaintiff must have filed the original complaint in a timely manner. State law may also require service on the defendant within the limitations period. A federal court must apply that state requirement as well. See *Walker v. Armco*. If the plaintiff made a timely filing and service within the statute of limitations with her original filing, "relation back" means that court assumes the similar timeliness of the amended complaint. Changing the legal claim from negligence to a products-liability claim will be supported by relation back so long as the two claims arose from the same transaction. If that is the case, the defendant will not have been surprised by the new claim. In essence, Rule 15(c) requires the defendant to recognize that the plaintiff may assert any legal claim supported by the factual basis for the dispute and be ready to defend each of those claims.

3. The plaintiff filed her complaint in federal court against the Los Angeles Police Department and the City of Los Angeles contending that her constitutional rights were violated by two unknown (to her) Los Angeles police officers. Her original complaint was filed 15 days before the applicable limitations period lapsed. After filing the original complaint, she learned the identities of the two police officers and named them as defendants in an amended complaint that she served on them six months after the original was filed. She alleges however that the two officers must have known of the suit within 120 days after the original complaint was filed. They contend that the statute of limitations bars the amended complaint. **Should the federal court accept the amendment?**

Explanation

No, the amendment adding these parties does not satisfy the relation back requirements of Rule 15(c)(3).

Rule

Rule 15(c)(3) allows relation back of an amendment which changes the party against whom a claim is asserted if: the claim asserted in the amendment arose out of the transaction set forth in the original; and within the 120-day period after filing the complaint, which is allowed by Rule 4(m) for service of process, the party to be brought in by amendment: "received such notice of the institution of the action that the party will not be prejudiced in maintaining his defense on the merits," and "knew or should have known that, but for a mistake concerning the identity of the proper party, the action would have been brought against the party."

Application

In this case, assume the two police officers concede that they knew about the plaintiff's suit at least within 120 days of its filing, largely because their superiors would have required them to assist in the defense of the suit. The plaintiff would have to prove that they knew the failure to name them as a defendant was a "mistake." However, she failed to name them because she lacked knowledge of their identities rather than because of a mistake as to their identities. Strictly interpreted, Rule 15(c)(3) establishes only mistake as a ground for allowing relation back to a complaint that adds new parties. One reason for doing so might be that the plaintiff should have been more diligent in seeking the identity of the two officers. If she was actually mistaken about their identity, she might have failed to take action. See Worthington v. Wilson, 790 F.Supp. 829 (C.D. Ill. 1992).

CHAPTER 8

Parties and Claims

A. Terminology

Class action—This joinder device allows a few named parties to bring suit as representatives of a large number of unnamed persons who have suffered similarly from the defendant's pattern of harmful action. The unnamed members of this class are described by reference to the common harm they have suffered. A claim can be brought against a class of defendants as well, and a defendant class will be described by reference to the allegedly unlawful common action by which the unnamed members harmed the plaintiff.

Compulsory counterclaim—This is a counterclaim that Rule 13(a) requires a party to assert in this lawsuit. The Rule requires assertion because the counterclaim arises from the same transaction or occurrence that gave rise to the opposing party's claim against the counterclaimant. The Federal Rules of Civil Procedure require the assertion of related counterclaims, and the defendant waives or loses his compulsory counterclaim by failing to assert it.

Counterclaim—This is a claim made back against one who has asserted a claim against you. You and that other party are opposing parties because she has asserted a claim against you. Typically, the defendant files this responsive claim for relief against the plaintiff.

Cross-claim—This is a claim for relief asserted against a co-party. If, for example, a plaintiff joins two defendants in her lawsuit, the defendants are in opposition to the plaintiff. At the time the complaint is filed, those defendants are co-parties in respect to each other. Co-parties become opposing parties after one asserts a cross-claim against the other.

Derivative action—If minority shareholders of a corporation become disturbed by the wasteful activities of corporate executives or directors, they can bring an action on behalf of all shareholders. This action is derivative because any damages recovered are paid by the defendants to the corporation for the benefit of all shareholders.

Impleader—This is a claim asserted by the defendant in a third-party complaint filed against someone who was not named in the suit by the plaintiff, and the defendant's impleader claim must allege that the impleaded party is liable to him for some part of his liability to the plaintiff.

Interpleader—This joinder procedure allows the holder of a fund to escape the risk of multiple liability that might befall her if she gives the fund to one of many claimants to it. She escapes this risk by submitting the fund into the registry of a court and by forcing all of those claimants to litigate their adverse claims in that court.

Joinder of claims—One speaks of joinder of claims when one plaintiff asserts multiple claims against a single defendant. Some other Federal Rule must first authorize the claiming party to assert her first claim against a defending party. If so, Rule 18 allows, but does require, the claiming party to add any other claim she has against the defending party.

Joinder of parties—One speaks of joinder of parties when the plaintiff joins with other plaintiffs or chooses to assert claims against multiple defendants. The requirements of Rule 20 determine whether all of the parties on one side or the other can be joined in one lawsuit.

Third-party plaintiff/third-party defendant—When the defendant asserts an impleader claim against a new party, the defendant is known as the third-party plaintiff in respect to this third-party action. The party against whom the claim is made is known as the third-party defendant.

B. Proper Parties

1. Real Party in Interest

Rule 17(a) requires every action to be prosecuted in the name of the real party in interest. Under the Rule, anyone asserting a claim must be the person whom the law protects with the substantive right sought to be enforced. The real party requirement provides the defendant with a procedural objection to protect him against the possibility of being subjected to a second suit by the true "owner" of the claim.

The real party requirement applies most comfortably to common law claims for relief. Newer claims made for injunctive or declaratory relief and based on constitutional or statutory rights cannot as easily be said to have a clearly defined owner. In these cases, the real party is determined by asking whether the plaintiff has standing to sue. As indicated earlier, the plaintiff must have suffered a personalized injury in fact caused by the allegedly wrongful action, and that injury must be redressable by a favorable judgment.

Although Rule 17(a) controls the manner of pleading in federal court in a diversity action, state law determines the owner of the substantive right being asserted. Where federal substantive law creates the claim, that law will govern. Rule 17(a) allows executors, administrators, guardians, trustees of an express trust, and others who possess such a legal right to bring suit on behalf of another. These representatives would, of course, normally be proper parties, and at one time were generally able to invoke diversity jurisdiction based on their own citizenship without considering the citizenship of those they represent.

However, § 1332(c)(2) deems the legal representative of an incompetent, an infant, or of the estate of a decedent to be a citizen only of the state in which the deceased was domiciled at his death, or in which the incompetent person or minor is domiciled.

Rule 17(a) does not describe the manner in which an objection based on the absence of a real party in interest is to be made, but it would not seem of any great significance whether the objection were raised in the answer or in a preanswer motion to dismiss. The objection should, however, be raised promptly after the defect becomes known by the defendant or it may be deemed to have been waived. For example, assume that a beneficiary under an express trust sues the defendant for harm caused the trust assets. Even though the trustee of an express trust is the real party in interest, the defendant may waive that objection by not making it in a timely fashion. Although an objection that the plaintiff lacks standing to sue is constitutional and cannot be waived, this beneficiary can satisfy the injury in fact test even though the law doesn't recognize her right to sue.

2. Capacity to Sue or be Sued

Only a party asserting a claim for relief need be a real party in interest. However, every party must have capacity. Capacity refers to the personal qualification of one to participate as a party in federal court. An individual may, for example, be a real party in interest because he possesses a right of action against a tortfeasor but not have capacity to sue on his own behalf because he is a minor. A state may consider administrators to be real parties in regard to a suit on behalf of an estate but still deny administrators appointed by another state capacity in its courts.

Capacity to sue or be sued is generally determined by state law, but federal law applies, as provided in Rule 17(b), in three instances. First, a partnership or unincorporated association is given capacity to sue or be sued as an entity regardless of state law when the suit is to enforce a right given by the Constitution or the laws of the United States. Second, the capacity of a receiver appointed by a federal court is governed by Title 28 United States Code §§ 754 and 959(a). Third, Rule 17(c) itself authorizes suit by a next friend or guardian ad litem on behalf of an infant or incompetent person who does not have a duly appointed representative.

In other than these three instances, state law determines the capacity of a party to sue or be sued in federal court. The further question, however, is which state's law is to apply. Rule 17(b) requires, as to natural persons not acting as representatives of others, the federal court to determine capacity by looking to the law of the state in which that individual is domiciled. The capacity of a corporation created under state law is determined according to the law of the state of its incorporation. The capacity of a corporation created by federal law is determined by that federal law. The capacity of all other parties is determined by the law of the state in which the federal court is located.

Rule 9(a) states that a party is not required to plead affirmatively the existence of capacity to sue or be sued except where such allegation may be necessary to show the existence of subject matter jurisdiction. One wishing to challenge the capacity of another party must, under Rule 9(a), do so through a specific negative averment including "such supporting particulars as are peculiarly within the pleader's knowledge." Failure to comply with this requirement can result in the waiver of this objection.

C. Joinder of Parties and Claims

1. Overview

Rule 8(a) of the Federal Rule of Civil Procedure requires every pleading that states a claim for relief to include a statement of the subject matter jurisdictional ground for that claim unless the court already has jurisdiction. As a aid to analysis, one can treat a claim for relief as the essential subject matter jurisdictional unit. If the court has jurisdiction over a claim for relief, it also has power to adjudicate all issues raised in determining that claim or the defenses asserted against it. Because the presence of a party requires the existence of a claim for relief, either asserted by or against that party, a focus on the claim is helpful as well in highlighting any jurisdictional problem which might arise when parties are being named or joined.

The question of whether certain parties or claims may be included in a pleading cannot be adequately answered without considering two requirements. Every claim for relief must be supported by some ground of subject matter jurisdiction *and* be permitted by the Federal Rules of Civil Procedure. First, a federal court must have either an independent ground of subject matter jurisdiction or supplemental jurisdiction under § 1367 in order to adjudicate any claim. Second, the pertinent Federal Rule must allow the naming or joinder of a particular party or the assertion of a particular claim.

The original claim in the complaint must have an independent ground of subject matter jurisdiction and, therefore, cannot be supported by supplemental jurisdiction. If the plaintiff invokes federal question jurisdiction, the original claim is the federal claim used to support that jurisdiction. A joined state law claim may then enjoy supplemental jurisdiction. If the plaintiff invokes only diversity jurisdiction, all claims asserted in the complaint will be supported by that jurisdiction.

If the defendant responds by asserting a counterclaim in the answer, that counterclaim must be supported by an independent ground, such as federal question or diversity jurisdiction, or it must be supported by supplemental jurisdiction. A "permissive" counterclaim must have an independent ground for jurisdiction because it, by definition, would not be sufficiently related to the original claim to enjoy supplemental jurisdiction. Cross-claims and Rule 14 claims must arise from the same transaction as the original claim and will, for that reason, be within the court's supplemental jurisdiction. In pleading claims which fall within the court's supplemental jurisdiction, the defendant need not state their jurisdictional grounds because Rule 8(a) requires such only if an independent ground is needed.

A plaintiff must also consider the procedural requirements for including parties and claims in the complaint. Although there are limits, the Federal Rules of Civil Procedure generally provide for liberal joinder of parties and claims. The named plaintiff must, however, be a real party in interest who has capacity to sue, and the named defendant must have capacity to be sued. There must be a sufficient relationship between co-parties before they can be joined on either side of the litigation, and some persons not included may be so necessary to the full and fair adjudication of the controversy that they cannot be left out. Also, a person left out of the litigation may move for intervention on either side.

Modern federal litigation can involve multiple plaintiffs, defendants, and third-party defendants, and multiple claims, cross-claims, counterclaims, third-party or other Rule 14 claims. Because of these complications, it is wise to begin one's analysis by diagramming the litigation, much as teachers once required of students seeking to learn the parts of a sentence. This practice allows one to highlight the relevant characteristics of claims and the proper position of parties.

-Key to Diagrams

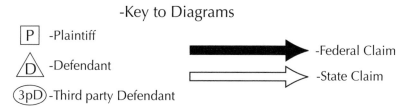

For example, consider the following diagram of a possible diversity case:

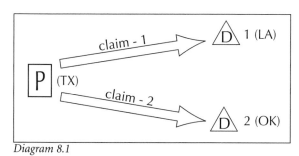

Diagram 8.1

The plaintiff in this hypothetical action has asserted two claims which we will assume are substantially identical except that they are against two defendants. Assume all claims asserted or which might be asserted arise from the same transaction or occurrence that is the subject matter of the two claims asserted by the plaintiff. If the $75,000+ amount requirement of § 1332 is satisfied as to each of these claims, diversity jurisdiction exists over the case as stated in the complaint because complete diversity of citizenship exists between the plaintiff and defendants. The complaint would, of course, have named only the plaintiff and the two defendants.

Once subject matter jurisdiction is established over the case stated in the complaint (assuming no indispensable party is omitted), jurisdiction over the claims asserted therein continues without regard to subsequently joined claims or parties. Later claims may be dismissed and additional parties may be dropped, but the jurisdiction of the parties and claims stated in the complaint persists.

Assume further that defendant-2 asserts a cross-claim against defendant-1 in its answer and an impleader claim in a third-party complaint against a third-party defendant. The procedural questions are whether the cross-claim satisfies Rule 13(g) and whether the third-party claim satisfies Rule 14. Another question defendant-1 might ask is whether he must now assert any related claim he has against defendant-2—that is, would that claim be a compulsory counterclaim. The answer is yes. See Diagram 8.2 below.

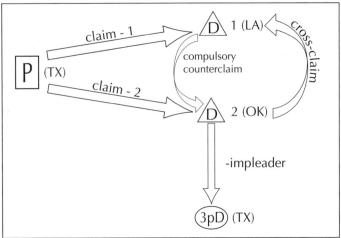

Diagram 8.2

Defendant-2's cross-claim and impleader claim would, if proper under Rule 13(g) and Rule 14, be supported by supplemental jurisdiction because those Rules require an original cross-claim and an original third-party claim to arise from the same transaction which gives rise to the plaintiff's claim. Furthermore, complete diversity exists between defendant-2 and the parties against whom the claims were asserted. Therefore, assuming the claims satisfied the jurisdictional amount, these claims also would have an independent ground of jurisdiction.

Assume next that the third-party defendant, after being served, decides to include in his answer to the third-party complaint a state law claim against the plaintiff. He may do so under Rule 14 if that claim arises from the transaction which gives rise to the plaintiffs claim against Defendant-2. If it does, that claim would be supported by supplemental jurisdiction and would not fail even though both parties are citizens of Texas.

2. Joinder of Parties

Joinder of parties may cause procedural as well as jurisdictional problems. Rule 20(a) permits joinder of parties regardless of whether relief sought by or against them is sought jointly, severally, or in the alternative. The Rule provides that parties "need not be interested in obtaining or defending against all the relief demanded." Rule 20(a) does, however, have two specific requirements that must be satisfied: (1) the claims by or against multiple parties must arise from the same transaction or occurrence, and (2) some question of law or fact common to the joined parties must arise in the action.

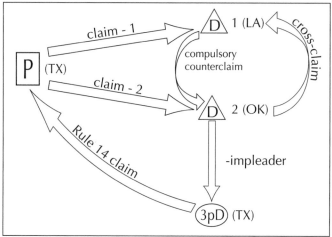

Diagram 8.3

In order to arise from the same transaction or occurrence, claims need only arise from events which are reasonably related; these events need not be absolutely identical. This requirement has, for instance, been satisfied by plaintiffs injured by the same general policy of racial discrimination allegedly practiced by the defendant. This broad view of the underlying transaction furthers the purposes of Rule 20, which are to promote trial convenience and to expedite the final determination of disputes without multiple lawsuits.

For example, a large number of plaintiffs may be joined in one suit when their claims arise from a single defect in the product sold them by a manufacturer because joinder will save judicial time and litigation expense. However, were there no common defect, a single proceeding might become overly complicated because of the different facts that would have to be proved or disproved. In such a case, the multiple parties would face a more expensive preparation and could not share the fruits of their efforts as well because of their different interests.

To satisfy Rule 20's second requirement, all questions of law or fact need not be common to the claims by or against the multiple parties. For example, a common question of law can exist even though multiple claimants have suffered different injuries. The common-question requirement also should be applied with the purposes of Rule 20(a) in mind. To the extent common questions dominate, allowing joinder of the parties prevents multiple litigation of similar issues. If the common issues are minor and the differences so serious that confusion, inconvenience, and unnecessary expense are caused, joinder should be denied.

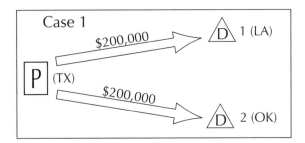

Assume, for instance, the plaintiffs were riding in a car that was struck by a car driven by the defendant. In seeking damages for their injury in this accident, they can join their individual tort claims against that defendant in the same complaint. Rule 20 is satisfied because both claims arise from the accident—the common occurrence—and both claims will require adjudication of the same factual and legal issue of the defendant's negligence in causing that accident. If these plaintiffs were struck by a business vehicle, they might well choose to join the defendant's employer with the defendant. Their claims against the employer and employee would arise from the same transaction and give rise to a common issue of negligence, with only the addition of the evidence necessary to establish the employer's liability through the doctrine of *respondeat superior*.

In an even simpler situation—Case 1 outlined below in Diagram 8.4—the plaintiff joins two defendants and seeks joint or several relief based on the same claim. In a three-car accident, the driver struck from the rear sues the other two drivers. Thus, an almost identical negligence claim has been effectively asserted twice—once against the first defendant, and again against the second defendant. The plaintiff thus alleges that one of the two defendants negligently caused her injuries and should be liable. In another hypothetical, (Case 2), two plaintiffs have joined to assert the same claim against a single defendant. Assume that in the three-car accident two of the drivers have determined that the accident was caused by the third driver. In Case 1 and Case 2, a defending party might challenge the complaint for failure to satisfy Rule 20's two requirements. That challenge would be unsuccessful in these hypotheticals because the claims by or against the multiple parties necessarily arose from the same occurrence and contained numerous common issues.

a. Consolidation, Severance, and Separate Trials

Civil actions involving common questions of law or fact but pending in different district courts may be transferred to one district for coordinated or consolidated pretrial proceedings pursuant to the procedures set forth in

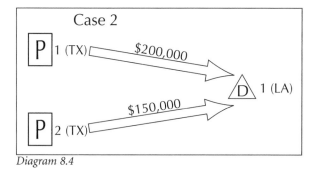

Diagram 8.4

Title 28 U.S.C. § 1407. This transfer must be made by the judicial panel on multidistrict litigation authorized under this section. This pretrial consideration allows the expeditious handling of a large number of cases, such as in the asbestos litigation, without depriving the plaintiffs of their chosen forum for trial. Consolidation of cases for all purposes may occur pursuant to Rule 42(a) whenever actions pending before the same court involve a common question of law or fact. Consolidation can be ordered in these instances even though joinder of parties would not have been proper under Rule 20(a).

A consolidation under Rule 42(a) can be ordered by a court on its own motion, but the court will not merge the cases so as to deprive a party of a substantial right he would otherwise have had. Rule 42(a) thus provides a tool with which a district court can control its docket, expedite the trial of related cases, and eliminate unnecessary duplication of effort. Although consolidation cannot be granted if there exists no common question of law or fact, a court has great discretion otherwise in deciding whether the risks of prejudice and confusion of the jury arising from a common trial are outweighed by the risk of inconsistent adjudication of common issues and the extra burden or expense placed on the parties and witnesses by separate suits. In balancing these risks, the court can also consider using cautionary instructions to the jury and other controls to reduce the risk of prejudice or jury confusion.

In contrast to the consolidation allowed by Rule 42(a), the last sentence of Rule 21 authorizes the severance of *claims*. Severance creates two suits where there was one, and these suits can then be taken to judgment independently. Claims severed for pretrial purposes can, however, be consolidated for trial. Without creating two independent suits, a court, pursuant to Rule 42(b), can order separate trials for any claim or issue to further "convenience or avoid prejudice, or when separate trials will be conducive to expedition and economy."

Because Rule 42(b) authorizes a separate trial on any separate issue, the court may bifurcate the trial—that is, send only part of the case to trial. The court might, say, choose to hold trial initially on the issue of liability alone. Only if the plaintiff prevails on the liability issue would a second trial on the issue of damages be required. The value to the defendant (and disadvantage to the plaintiff) arises in personal injury cases because evidence concerning the seriousness of plaintiff's injuries can be excluded as irrelevant to the issue of liability. A defendant might move for bifurcation because she believes that her liability cannot be proved and, therefore, does not wish unnecessarily to prepare for a trial on damages. The defendant may also contend that the liability issue will be prejudiced by the introduction of gruesome evidence of the plaintiff's injuries. A federal court can order a bifurcated trial in a diversity case even though the law of the forum state prohibits separate trials of this sort. The *Erie* doctrine does not require the application of state law because a valid Federal Rule of Civil Procedure addresses the issue in dispute.

3. Joinder of Claims

In addition to joining parties, a plaintiff, or any other party for that matter, can freely join multiple claims against the same opposing party. Rule 18 imposes no limits on the joinder of claims. However, it only allows the addition of a claim to another claim that has been properly asserted under another Rule. Furthermore, Rule 18 applies only when that added claim is directed against the same party as the first claim. If a claimant asserts the second claim against an additional party, Rule 20 applies instead of Rule 18.

Rule 18 of the Federal Rules of Civil Procedure makes clear that there is no procedural limitation to a party's ability at the pleading stage to join multiple claims against a single opposing party. It states that any claimant may join as many claims as he has against an opposing party, whether legal, equitable, or maritime, with his original claim, counterclaim, cross-claim, or third-party claim, and he may assert these joined claims as independent or alternative claims. Under Rule 18(b), a claimant may even join a claim which would not be enforceable until after the original had been prosecuted to a conclusion. As an example, Rule 18(b) states that a "plaintiff may state a claim for money and a claim to have set aside a conveyance fraudulent as to him without first having obtained a judgment establishing the claim for money."

More difficult problems arise when multiple claims are asserted against or by multiple parties. For example, suppose the plaintiff asserts a claim for the breach of a commission contract against the defendant for whom the plaintiff acquired a customer, but also asserts a claim against that customer, named as a second defendant, to attach any payments to be made to the first defendant. Suppose also that the plaintiff joins an additional breach of contract claim against the first defendant for failure to pay commissions on other sales. This case thus involves both joinder of claims and joinder of parties. Rule 18 allows the joinder of the two claims against the first defendant, but Rule 20 must be consulted to decide whether the two defendants can be joined as parties. The distinction between joinder of parties and of claims can be diagrammed in the following manner:

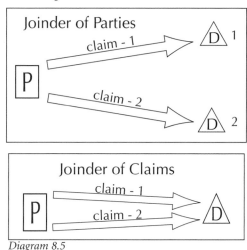

Diagram 8.5

Although Rule 18 itself places no procedural limitation on the claims joined against an opposing party, that party may move under Rule 42(b) for a separate trial of the multiple claims in order to avoid undue delay or prejudice. Rule 18 does not require joinder of claims, but the doctrine of res judicata may operate to prevent subsequent litigation of a claim which arises from the transaction which gave rise to the claim that has been adjudicated.

As one observes from these graphic representations, the joinder of parties always effectively creates a new claim that either is asserted by an additional party or asserted against an additional party. No party appears in a lawsuit unless she either asserts a claim or is defending against a claim. In turn, each claim must be sustained by the substantive law, permitted by the pertinent Federal Rule of Civil Procedure, and supported by some ground of subject matter jurisdiction.

Unless an independent basis supports original jurisdiction, added claims have nothing to supplement under § 1367. In diversity cases, the plaintiff's complaint may include numerous claims if he satisfies the requirements of complete diversity and seeks a sufficient amount in controversy. In the graphic below, these requirements have been satisfied. Rule 20 governs joinder in Case 1 and Case 2 (Diagram 8.4 above), but in Case 3 below, Rule 18, governing joinder of claims, controls. Rule 18 permits, without restriction, the procedural joinder of claims.

Case 3

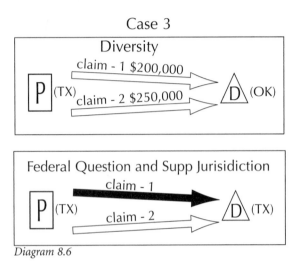

Diagram 8.6

However, Rule 18 can only grant procedural permission for the joinder of claims. For example, it allows the joinder of a federal claim with an additional state claim in a federal question case between nondiverse parties. However, the state claim must be supported by supplemental jurisdiction, and the absence of supplemental jurisdiction would prevent adjudication of the state claim in federal court even though Rule 18 allowed its joinder.

Rules 13 and 14 authorize the assertion of claims in pleadings subsequent to the original complaint, either in the answer or in a third-party complaint. If a defending party alleges a procedurally proper claim under one of these Rules, Rule 18 authorizes that party to join any other claim he may have against the same opposing parties. In other words, other of the Federal Rules of Civil Procedure authorize the assertion of particular subsequent claims for relief. Once one of these subsequent claims has been properly asserted, the claiming party can, as a procedural matter, join any additional claim against the same party regardless of whether that additional claim is related to the first claim.

D. Subsequent Claims

1. Counterclaims and Cross-Claims

A counterclaim is typically a claim for relief asserted by the defendant against the plaintiff and is included in the defendant's answer. However, parties other than the original defendant can assert counterclaims, and counterclaims can be asserted against parties other than the plaintiff. Because compulsory counterclaims can be lost if not asserted, one must know their identifying characteristics. A counterclaim is a claim which a party has against any "opposing party" at the time of serving a pleading. An opposing party is one who has already asserted a claim for relief against the party. A party against whom a claim has been asserted therefore "counters" that claim with a claim back against the one who has asserted a claim against him.

For example, the plaintiff becomes an opposing party in respect to the defendant by asserting the original claim against him. The defendant's claim against the same plaintiff is therefore always a counterclaim. Rule 13 effectively permits a defendant to assert *any* claim for relief against the plaintiff; it thus does not limit the *assertion* of counterclaims. However, Rule 13(a) *requires* the assertion of counterclaims that arise from the transaction which gives rise to the original claim. These "compulsory" counterclaims must be asserted in the suit, or they will be lost through the operation of Rule 13(a) and the doctrine of res judicata. Rule 13(b) permits the assertion of any counterclaim regardless of its relationship with the opposing party's claim. This "permissive" counterclaim can be asserted or not at the defendant's discretion. No penalty is imposed to prevent a defendant from saving a permissive counterclaim for subsequent litigation, but supplemental jurisdiction does not support unrelated counterclaims.

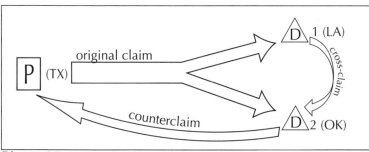

Diagram 8.7

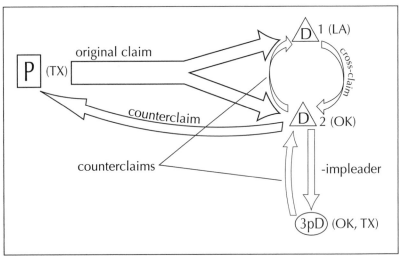

Diagram 8.8

A cross-claim is a claim for relief asserted against a co-party. Rule 13(g) limits cross-claims to those arising from the transaction which gives rise to the claim against the co-parties, and a cross-claim may be a claim over for contribution or indemnity. The Rule does not require assertion of a cross-claim. Co-parties are those who have been joined on either side of the litigation and who have not asserted a claim against one another. See Diagram 8.7 below.

A claim asserted between co-defendants makes them opposing parties. However, the initial claim between them is a cross-claim, not a counterclaim, because when it is asserted the defendants are not in opposition. Once a cross-claim is asserted, a responsive claim by the defendant who was the object of that cross-claim will be a counterclaim and, therefore, can be compulsory. A third-party defendant becomes an opposing party to the third-party plaintiff because of the claim asserted in the third-party complaint. His claim against the third-party plaintiff would, therefore, be a counterclaim, and a compulsory one *if* it arises from the transaction giving rise to the third-party plaintiff's claim. See Diagram 8.8 above.

If the third-party defendant initiates a claim against the plaintiff, a related responsive claim by the plaintiff is between opposing parties, and is therefore a compulsory counterclaim. Section 1367(b) expressly prevents the use of supplemental jurisdiction by plaintiffs to circumvent the requirement of complete diversity. If the plaintiff becomes a defending party, because of the third-party defendant's claim, he should be allowed to use supplemental jurisdiction if such is needed. Even though the availability of jurisdiction might be questioned, a plaintiff's assertion of the claim should protect him against a res judicata (or Rule 13) bar to subsequent litigation.

Rules 13 and 14 speak of subsequent claims which arise from the same transaction as that which gives rise to the original claim of the plaintiff. In a practical sense, this requirement seems largely the same as § 1367(a)'s requirement that supplemental claims arise from the same case or controversy which the plaintiff brings before the court. This language in § 1367 has been interpreted to require that claims arise from a "common nucleus of operative fact." Both the transaction and the common-nucleus inquiry point to the shared facts underlying the claims. See Chapter 4 for a discussion of supplemental jurisdiction.

Related claims are allowed primarily because their adjudication in one suit makes efficient use of judicial resources by having one court determine common issues of fact and law. The parties also tend to reduce their litigation expenses when all facets of their dispute can be resolved in one court. Therefore, courts might ask whether the issues of fact and law raised by the claims are largely the same, whether res judicata would bar a subsequent suit on the added claim, or whether substantially the same evidence supports or refutes the two claims.

2. Impleader and Rule 14 Claims

A defendant has a limited right under Rule 14 of the Federal Rules of Civil Procedure to bring in persons not joined by the plaintiff. He can implead only a person who is or may be liable to him for all or part of the plaintiff's claim against him. The defendant can thereby join, as a third-party defendant, someone who by contract has agreed to indemnify the defendant for any liability to the plaintiff. He also can implead a joint tortfeasor from whom he has a right to receive contribution. As a procedural rule, however, Rule 14 does not supply the claim for relief. That claim must be found in the applicable substantive law. Rule 14 thus permits the assertion of such "claims over" against the third-party defendant *if* they exist under state or federal law. A defendant cannot implead a third party merely because he believes that party, and not he, is liable to the plaintiff. For example, a defendant might believe that another driver in a three-car accident was the cause of the accident involving the defendant and the plaintiff. He cannot, for this reason alone, implead this other driver. In other words, a defendant cannot use impleader to tell the plaintiff whom to sue.

By restricting impleader, Rule 14 limits the ability of the defendant to complicate the plaintiff's suit. One can imagine how defendants might otherwise burden litigation by the addition of new parties and new claims, causing the plaintiff to lose control of its progress. Having made this point, however, one must recognize that Rule 18 opens the door for the joinder of other claims. If a proper impleader claim has been asserted, Rule 18 permits the defendant to join *any* claim he may have against the third-party defendant without respect to the limitations of Rule 14. By allowing such liberal joinder of claims, Rule 18 would seem to frustrate the purpose of Rule 14's limitation. Rule 14 limits the ability of defending parties to complicate the plaintiff's civil action, but Rule 18 opens the door to unrelated claims once Rule 14 has been satisfied. However, if the joinder of unrelated claims unduly complicates the litigation and its management, the court can use its discretion to sever those claims. In addition, Rule 18's free-joinder policy is subject to the further requirement that all claims have some ground of subject matter jurisdiction.

Other Rule 14 claims are allowed, but they all must arise from the transaction which gives rise to the plaintiff's original claim. Other Rule 14 claims include the following: (1) A third-party defendant can assert a claim against the plaintiff if it arises from the transaction which gives rise to the plaintiff's claim. This is not a counterclaim or a cross-claim because, prior to its assertion, these parties are not opposing or co-parties. (2) The plaintiff can assert a claim against the third-party defendant. This is not a counterclaim unless the third-party defendant has already asserted a claim against the plaintiff.

b. Impleader Procedure

For purposes of the third-party action, the defendant is known as the third-party plaintiff, and those joined thereby are known as the third-party defendants. The defendant/third-party plaintiff can file a third-party complaint without leave of court if he does so within 10 days after serving his answer. After this period, the third-party complaint may be served only with leave of court. A court may deny leave if it finds the third-party action will unduly complicate and lengthen the trial.

Aside from the limitations imposed by Rule 14(a), the pleading rules generally apply to third-party actions in the same manner as they do to original actions. The defendant, for instance, must comply with Rule 11 before signing any paper filed with the federal court. The defendant serves the third-party complaint and summons in accordance with Rule 4 because he is asserting the court's jurisdiction over someone not previously brought within that jurisdiction. Once served, the impleaded party responds to the third-party complaint in accordance with Rule 12. The third-party defendant must admit or deny the allegations of the third-party complaint in accordance with Rule 8(b) and allege any affirmative defenses in accordance with Rule 8(c). She also must assert any counterclaim deemed compulsory under Rule 13(a), and may assert permissive counterclaims or cross-claims. Only a claim asserted by a third-party defendant against the third-party plaintiff is a counterclaim.

In addition, Rule 14(a) allows a third-party defendant to assert any defenses which the third-party plaintiff may have but has not asserted against the original plaintiff. Even though the liability of the third-party defendant is derived from the liability of the third-party plaintiff, the third-party defendant cannot be made to suffer for the original defendant's lack of diligence in defending against the original claim. Rule 14 permits the third-party defendant to assert a claim, arising from the transaction giving rise to the original claim, directly against the plaintiff. This is not a counterclaim because prior to its assertion those were not opposing parties, but is merely another Rule 14 claim. Furthermore, if the plaintiff has a claim against the third-party defendant which arises from the same transaction that gives rise to the original claim, she can assert it directly against the third-party defendant. Unless the third-party defendant had previously asserted a claim against the plaintiff, the plaintiff's claim would not be a counterclaim. It would be another Rule 14 claim.

c. Supplemental Jurisdiction

It bears repeating that the procedural provisions of Rule 14 cannot expand the subject matter jurisdiction of a federal court. As a result, claims properly asserted under Rule 14 also must be supported by their own ground of subject matter jurisdiction. If not, they must be dismissed. Rule 14 allows the assertion only of claims arising from the same transaction as does the plaintiff's original claim. Under most circumstances, therefore, supplemental jurisdiction provided by § 1367 supports Rule 14 claims by defending parties. As noted, Rule 14 allows the plaintiff to assert related claims for relief directly against a third-party defendant. In a diversity case, however, the plaintiff's assertion of a related state claim against a nondiverse third-party defendant would not be supported by an independent ground of jurisdiction. Section 1367(b) prevents plaintiffs from using supplemental jurisdiction in a case founded solely on § 1332 to initiate a claim against the nondiverse third-party defendant.

E. Omission of Interested Persons

1. Compulsory Joinder or Dismissal

A plaintiff, by design or omission, does not always sue all of the parties necessary to a lawsuit. If she does not join a person who has an interest in the litigation or one whose absence may cause prejudice to those who are parties, any party may object pursuant to Rule 19. The defendant can include the objection in the answer or in a preanswer motion, or the court may raise the issue on its own motion. To alert the court to this problem, Rule 19(c) requires the listing in any pleading which includes a claim for relief of persons interested in the action but not joined.

Although the issues raised by a Rule 19 motion should be brought to the court's attention at an early stage in litigation, Rule 12(h)(2) states that "a defense of failure to join a party indispensable under Rule 19" may be made in any pleading by motion for judgment on the pleadings, or at the trial. It may even be raised for the first time at the appeal stage because the judgment might otherwise work an injustice on those interested persons who are not parties. The interested person might, for example, have a claim against the assets of an estate which the judgment would confer on the plaintiff, and asserting a claim or recovering relief against that plaintiff might pose serious practical difficulties.

If the Court accepts the objection, there are two possible outcomes under Rule 19: either the plaintiff is ordered to join the absent party or the plaintiff's complaint is dismissed. First, a court considers the factors listed in Rule 19(a) to determine whether an absent person should be joined *if feasible.* Joinder would not be feasible if that person cannot be brought within the court's personal jurisdiction or if joinder would deprive the court of subject matter jurisdiction. Joinder also may not be feasible because the presence of that party would make the venue of the action improper; however, joinder should be ordered initially. If after being joined, that person makes a timely and valid objection to venue, then his joinder would not be feasible and he must be dismissed as a party. Second, if the court concludes that joinder is not feasible, it must decide whether "in equity and good conscience" the action should be dismissed.

a. Joinder When Feasible

To determine whether an absent person is someone who should be joined if feasible under Rule 19(a), the court must decide that:

(1) in his absence complete relief cannot be accorded among those already parties, or

(2) he claims an interest relating to the subject of the action and is so situated that the disposition of the action in his absence may,

    (i) as a practical matter impair or impede his ability to protect that interest or

(ii) leave any of the persons already parties subject to a substantial risk of incurring double, multiple, or otherwise inconsistent obligations by reason of his claimed interest.

If the court answers yes to either (1) or (2), the interested person must be joined.

b. Dismissal When Joinder Not Feasible

The analysis of Rule 19(b) problems presupposes that supplemental jurisdiction cannot be used to support the joinder of the outsider. Section 1367(b) expressly states that, in a diversity case, supplemental jurisdiction cannot support claims by plaintiffs against persons made parties under Rule 19 or claims by persons proposed to be joined as plaintiffs under Rule 19. If supplemental jurisdiction were available, a plaintiff could create diversity jurisdiction by omitting essential but nondiverse parties, assuming the court would order their joinder.

If joinder of a party who should be joined under Rule 19(a) is not feasible, the court must consider the factors listed in Rule 19(b) to determine whether the case must be dismissed. The four interests to be examined under Rule 19(b), as restated by the Supreme Court in Provident Tradesmens Bank v. Patterson, 390 U.S. 102 (1968) case, are:

(1) the plaintiff's interest in having a forum;
(2) the defendant's interest in avoiding multiple litigation, or inconsistent relief, or sole responsibility for a liability he shares with another;
(3) the interest of the outsider whom it would have been desirable to join; and
(4) the interest of the courts and of the public in complete, consistent, and efficient settlement of controversies.

Rule 19(b) also directs a district court to consider the possibility of shaping relief to avoid harm to the defendant or to the outsider.

The interest of the plaintiff in having a forum speaks initially to her need for an available alternative. If the plaintiff has access to a state court which would be convenient to her and to the witnesses, less reason exists to continue the case in federal court. This is especially so when the federal court has no special interest or expertise in solving what are state law issues of greater concern to the state courts. The theoretical existence of another forum does not, however, automatically outweigh the plaintiff's choice of a forum. A plaintiff may face a statute of limitations bar when the case is refiled in state court. In addition, when the Rule 19 issue has not been raised until after trial, as was the case in *Provident Tradesmens*, the plaintiff has an added interest in retaining the judgment.

The defendant may understandably wish to avoid any multiple or inconsistent liability which might arise as the result of the failure of plaintiff to join someone. This could occur when the absent person has a claim against the defendant for the same property or because of the same harm that is before the federal court. A defendant cannot, however, make a strong claim of prejudice if he did not promptly raise the issue. Also, a defendant's claim of prejudice need not be given determinative weight when he could have impleaded or otherwise have joined the absent person.

The interest of the outsider need only be affected in a practical way. For instance, the possibility that the absent person may be hindered by the precedent established in his absence weighs in favor of joinder or dismissal. The absent person has no obligation to intervene in the suit to protect his interests, and he may well be unable to do so because his presence would not be supported by supplemental jurisdiction. An outsider also can be affected by the difficulty he will experience after judgment in protecting his interest in the property claimed by the plaintiff. It is even more obvious that prejudice could be caused an absent person who would be financially harmed by a judgment in favor of the plaintiff. For example, by winning the judgment a plaintiff might thereby gain possession of particular assets which she could then dispose of, leaving nothing for the absent person to acquire in a subsequent suit.

The fourth interest is that of the public and of the courts in providing complete and adequate relief to settle the whole of a dispute. Any judgment entered should provide adequate relief to the plaintiff and avoid, if possible, the chance of subsequent litigation. In some instances, a suit between the existing parties could end without yielding an enforceable judgment. For example, a suit against an excess insurer—contractually liable, say, for any amount over $100,000—which omitted the primary insurer—liable for any amount up to $100,000—could yield a judgment below $100,000, leaving the court with no power to enter judgment against anyone.

Before dismissing a case under Rule 19(b), however, a court should determine whether it can re-shape the relief requested to reduce any prejudice. For example, funds to which an absent person may have a claim can be withheld pending the termination of any subsequent litigation. The district court also might reduce any recovery in the final judgment by the amount which might be claimed or attributable to an absent party. Where, however, the parties and the absent person have claims which exceed the value of the fund or property sought, there may be no form of remedy which both provides adequate relief to the parties and protects the interests of the absent person. In this case, the court may be forced to dismiss the case, forcing the plaintiff to refile elsewhere.

2. Intervention

A person who is omitted from an action in federal court may intervene and thereby become a party on either side of the litigation. Rule 24(c) of the Federal Rules of Civil Procedure requires an intervenor to file a motion detailing the grounds for intervention along with a pleading setting out the claim or defense for which intervention is sought. The intervenor then serves the motion and pleading according to Rule 5(b) on the attorneys for all parties. Formal service of process under Rule 4 is not necessary because the intervenor need only serve the existing parties, who are already within the jurisdiction of the court. By voluntarily entering a federal action, the intervenor waives any objection she might otherwise have had to the court's personal jurisdiction, or to the venue of that action.

Rule 24 does not make intervention compulsory, and the doctrine of res judicata does not require a person to intervene in an action which affects her interests. A person might nevertheless choose to intervene because a judgment could have adverse consequences for her, because she has an interest which can best be protected by participation, or simply because intervention may be more convenient and less expensive than initiating a new action.

In addition to the different procedural requirements set forth in Rule 24, a court must consider the requirements of subject matter jurisdiction. These problems arise primarily in diversity cases when the citizenship of an intervenor is the same as that of a party she intends to oppose in the action. Section 1367(b) declares that, in diversity cases, supplemental jurisdiction cannot support claims by plaintiffs against nondiverse persons joined under Rule 24 or claims by nondiverse persons seeking to intervene under Rule 24. Because § 1367(b) operates to withdraw the supplemental jurisdiction that would otherwise exist under § 1367(a)—that is, over claims by or against intervenors which arise from the same case or controversy—the denial of supplemental jurisdiction could only be in regard to intervenors as a matter of right. As a result, intervenors can only exercise a right to intervene when their presence would be supported by an independent ground of subject matter jurisdiction.

a. Intervention by Right

Rule 24(a) provides a right to intervene in two instances. The first, which is discussed in Rule 24(a)(1), occurs when one having an unconditional right to intervene pursuant to a federal statute makes timely application to do so.

On example of such a statute is 28 U.S.C. §2403, which allows the United States government to intervene when the constitutionality of an Act of Congress is drawn into question. This statute also allows a state to intervene when one of its statutes is being challenged as unconstitutional.

Second, Rule 24(a)(2) sets out four requirements which must be satisfied before any other intervenor will have such a right.

(1) The application for intervention must be timely.
(2) The applicant must have an interest relating to the property or transaction which is the subject of the action.
(3) The applicant must be so situated that the disposition of the action in her absence may as a practical matter impair or impede her ability to protect that interest.
(4) However, an applicant has no right to intervene if her interest is adequately represented by those who are already parties.

Although the timeliness requirement applies both to intervention of right under Rule 24(a) and intervention by permission under Rule 24(b), courts more frequently forgive delay by one who has an interest which may be impaired by her absence. Because timeliness decisions do not turn solely on how quickly after commencement the motion is served, a court will also consider the justifications for that delay and the prejudice caused the opposing party.

One can sometimes better evaluate the claimed interest of an intervenor in an indirect manner by considering how refusal to allow intervention would impair her ability to protect the interest. The character of an interest can thus be more appropriately described by reference to the harm caused by denial of intervention. The impairment requirement must also be considered in light of the Rule's mandate to consider the practical consequences for the potential intervenor by adjudication in her absence. Although the operation of res judicata is not the test, this doctrine may suggest practical as well as a legal impairments of one's ability to protect an interest. Moreover, even though a judgment cannot have claim or issue preclusive effect on an absent person, it can cause a practical disadvantage sufficient to satisfy Rule 24(a). This may occur simply through the prospect of stare decisis if the judgment deals, for example, with particular land. Where the entry of a judgment will not significantly impair the right of the intervenor and that right could be protected by subsequent litigation, there would be insufficient impairment to justify intervention of right.

In considering whether to deny the motion to intervene, the court must determine the adequacy of representation. A party to the action must, at a minimum, represent the interests of the intervenor and not have claims which undermine those interests. The original burden on the intervenor in regard to representation is the minimal one of showing that representation of her interest may be inadequate, not that it necessarily will be. A governmental entity may be presumed to represent the interests of the public and, therefore, to block intervention of right. But this presumption can be overcome by showing that the intervenor seeks protection for a narrower interest than the government. Intervention should therefore be allowed where the interests of the parties are significantly different from, even though not adverse to, those of the intervenor. If the interests of the intervenor and of one who is already party to the suit are identical, intervention will usually be denied unless there is either evidence of collusion or of a lack of diligence on the part of the purported representative. For example, an otherwise representative government official may decide not to appeal, and an intervenor might seek to intervene to appeal a judgment by contending that the official no longer provides adequate representation.

b. Permissive Intervention

A federal court may give permission to intervene whenever a federal statute establishes a conditional right to intervene or when an applicant's claim or defense and the main action have a question of law or fact in common. Rule 24(b)(2) does not require an intervenor to have any particular interest in the subject matter of the main action, but the court cannot permit intervention unless an independent ground of subject matter jurisdiction supports the presence of the intervenor.

The common question of law or fact requirement provides minimal restraint on a court's discretion. This is the same language used to allow consolidation of cases under Rule 42(a) and should be construed with the same liberality. Even though joinder of a party under Rule 20 requires both a common question and a common underlying transaction, the latter requirement does not restrict permissive intervention. As a practical matter, potential intervenors often contend either that they have a right to intervene or that they should be permitted to intervene. If no right exists, the court weighs the benefits to its docket of allowing intervention (assuming the frustrated intervenor may file her suit in a separate action) against the burdens intervention will cause the other parties and the jury confusion which might result. The court may also condition its permission to intervene on, for example, the intervenor's agreement to engage in limited discovery or not to seek relief which would unduly delay or complicate the case.

F. Unusual Joinder Procedures

1. Class Actions

A class action is a joinder device which allows large numbers of individuals having the same or a similar interest to unite as parties in one action. It can also provide a procedure by which an action may be pursued even though the individual members of the class do not have the resources to sue or a sufficient claim to justify individual suits. A class action under Rule 23 overcomes these practical barriers by allowing similar claims or defenses to be united in one action under the control of named representative members of the class.

In 1966, Rule 23 was substantially revised to require a functional analysis of the propriety of a class action according to the circumstances of each case. To accomplish this end, Rule 23(a) sets out four requirements which every class action must meet. In addition to satisfying these four requirements, one who seeks certification of a class must satisfy the requirements of either subsection (1), (2), or (3) of Rule 23(b). Satisfaction of these requirements must be properly pled, and the class must be defined in the pleading with specificity.

The first requirement of Rule 23(a) is that the class be so numerous that joinder of all members is impracticable. There is no reason for the use of a class action if the members could be adequately joined individually. Second, there must be questions of law or fact common to the class, but all questions need not be common to all members of the class. This requirement is closely related to the need for similarity of interest reflected in the Rule's subsequent requirements. Third, the claims or defenses of the representative parties must be typical of the claims or defenses of the class. The fourth, and closely related, requirement is that the representative parties must fairly and adequately protect the interests of the class. This representation is essential for a judgment's binding effect on the unnamed members of the class. To determine the adequacy of representation, courts look at the experience and ability of the representatives' counsel and are alert for any inconsistency between the interests of the representatives and those of the unnamed members of the class.

In addition to satisfying these four requirements, the class must fit into one of the three categories outlined in Rule 23(b). A Rule 23(b)(1) class is one in which prosecution of individual actions by or against the members of the class would create the risk of inconsistent adjudications that establish incompatible standards of conduct for the party opposing the class. A 23(b)(1) class also is appropriate where individual adjudications would, as a practical matter, be dispositive of other members' interests or would substantially impair or impede their ability to protect their interests.

A Rule 23(b)(2) class is appropriate where declaratory or injunctive relief is sought against a party who has acted on grounds generally applicable to the class. A (b)(2) class would exist where a public official had acted in an unconstitutional manner to the detriment of numerous individuals. A desegregation or other civil rights class action would be an example.

Rule 23(b)(3) provides for certification of a class when common questions of law or fact predominate over questions affecting only individual members. In addition, it must be shown that a class action would be a better way of adjudicating the controversy. The Advisory Committee states, in its Notes to the 1966 Amendments, that (b)(3) "encompasses those cases in which a class action would achieve economies of time, effort, and expense, and promote uniformity of decision as to persons similarly situated without sacrificing procedural fairness." A court must consider the interests of the class members in handling their own suits, the extent of existing litigation involving the controversy, the desirability of concentrating the litigation in a single forum, and the difficulties inherent in handling the litigation as a class action. The Advisory Committee suggests that private damage claims arising out of an antitrust violation might fall within (b)(3), but the claims arising out of a large scale accident would not. In the latter example, the different questions of liability, of damages, and of available defenses would make mass tort cases inappropriate for class handling.

As soon as is practicable, the court must determine whether it will certify a class action. A class may be certified with respect to particular issues or divided into subclasses, and the judge may exercise discretion to order further notice during the litigation or to impose conditions on the representatives. Because the members of a (b)(3) class will have less in common, Rule 23(c)(2) requires prompt individual notice to all members who can with reasonable effort be identified. They are to be advised of their ability to opt out of the class by request or to appear through their own counsel.

In determining the existence of diversity jurisdiction in a class action case, the court will consider only the citizenship of the named representatives of the class and not that of the unnamed members of the class. Some class actions will encounter difficulty in satisfying the $75,000+ amount requirement of the diversity statute because aggregation of insufficient claims made by multiple parties cannot be used to satisfy the amount requirement. However, the Supreme Court has held that supplemental jurisdiction does support an insufficient claim by one plaintiff when joined with another plaintiff who does satisfy the amount requirement if those plaintiffs were joined either under Rule 20 or Rule 23. See Exxon Mobil v. Allapattah, 545 U.S. 546 (2005).

2. Derivative Actions

Derivative actions are suits typically brought by minority shareholders as class actions to complain of some wrong done the corporation for which those in control of the corporation will not seek a remedy. The shareholders assert a derivative right because they must assert a claim which belongs to the corporation. The derivative nature of the action is also evidenced by the requirement that the relief sought must be for the benefit of the corporation.

Rule 23.1 requires the complaint to be verified and to include an allegation that the plaintiffs were shareholders or members at the time of the transaction of which they complain or that their shares or membership devolved by operation of law. In addition, a derivative action may not be maintained unless the plaintiffs will fairly and adequately represent similarly situated shareholders, and it may not be dismissed or compromised without the approval of the court after notice to the other shareholders. The plaintiffs must allege that the action is not for the purpose of collusively creating federal jurisdiction and must allege with sufficient particularity the demands made by them to obtain the relief they desire from the officers or directors of the corporation. This demand requirement allows the directors an opportunity to determine whether they wish to oppose the corporation's alleged claim. Although the plaintiffs need not continue efforts to urge the directors to take action where these efforts have proven futile, the plaintiffs must make specific allegations to show that they have exhausted all corporate remedies before bringing suit.

In diversity cases, state substantive law will be applied to determine whether a derivative action may be brought even though the requirements of Rule 23.1 control the manner of pleading. States generally impose the demand requirement, but different conditions may be imposed by state law to distinguish a derivative from a direct action. A corporation is a necessary party to a derivative action because its right of action is being asserted. In diversity cases this would cause a problem if the corporation were aligned in the position of plaintiff against the directors who would often have the same citizenship as the corporation. The Supreme Court has, however, adopted an "antagonism" rule in derivative actions which results in the alignment of a corporation on the defendant's side of the litigation.

3. Interpleader

Interpleader is a procedure which can be used by one who holds property or a fund of money that is claimed by two or more adverse parties. Typically, the holder of the fund, the "stakeholder," has no claim to the fund but does not wish to release it to one of the claimants for fear another claimant will then sue it for the same fund. To escape the danger of multiple liability, the stakeholder may interplead all adverse claimants and require them to settle their dispute in one action. Interpleader claims are not limited to original actions but may be asserted in a counterclaim or cross-claim.

To bring an interpleader action, therefore, there must exist the danger to the stakeholder of at least multiple vexation through litigation of nonfrivolous claims in regard to a single fund. In addition, the claimants to the fund must be adverse to one another such that all cannot be satisfied from the fund. A typical example occurs when each of several claimants demands the total proceeds of an insurance policy. The claims need not be mutually exclusive if it is clear that together they would more than exhaust the fund.

Two types of interpleader actions exist in federal court: one under federal statutes and the other under Rule 22 of the Federal Rules of Civil Procedure. A federal court can assume subject matter jurisdiction of a statutory interpleader action brought pursuant to 28 U.S.C. § 1335 if (1) the fund or stake is of the sum or value of $500 or more, (2) at least two or more adverse claimants of diverse citizenship exist, and (3) the stake (or a bond acceptable to the court) is deposited in the registry of the court. Congress has power to confer such "minimal diversity" jurisdiction (between only two or more adverse claimants) because Article III's allowance of diversity jurisdiction does not require complete diversity between the plaintiff (stakeholder) and the defendants (claimants). The complete diversity requirement applies only as a statutory restriction of § 1332, and § 1335 is an independent jurisdictional grant. If statutory interpleader is brought, 28 U.S.C. § 1397 provides that venue is proper in any judicial district in which one or more of the claimants reside. Section 2361 authorizes the service of process in a statutory interpleader action wherever in the United States a claimant resides, and also expressly authorizes the federal court to enjoin any state or other federal judicial proceeding affecting the fund.

Rule interpleader is brought under Rule 22 of the Federal Rules of Civil Procedure. Rule 22 does not affect jurisdiction or venue and only provides the procedural device of interpleader. A stakeholder must, therefore, satisfy the usual requirements for subject matter jurisdiction, personal jurisdiction, and venue. Thus, a Rule interpleader action must be supported by jurisdiction under either § 1331 or § 1332. If diversity jurisdiction is invoked to support Rule 22 interpleader, the stakeholder, as the plaintiff, must be of a citizenship which is diverse from each one of the claimants who are viewed as defendants. The $75,000+ amount requirement for general diversity also must be satisfied.

In addition, process must be served in accordance with Rule 4 of the Federal Rules of Civil Procedure, and the general venue statue, §1391, would control in determining whether the venue of the action was proper.

Assuming the procedural requirements for an interpleader claim are satisfied, the citizenship of the parties will allow the following choices. If the stakeholder, as plaintiff, and the claimants, as defendants, all have the same state of citizenship, an interpleader action must be brought in state court unless Rule interpleader could be brought on the ground of federal question jurisdiction. No matter what may be the citizenship of the stakeholder or of the other claimants, if the citizenship of at least two of the claimants is diverse, statutory interpleader may be brought in federal court. If the claimants all have the same state of citizenship but the stakeholder has diverse citizenship, Rule 22 interpleader can be brought in federal court on the basis of the general diversity statute. If the stakeholder's citizenship is different from that of the claimants and two claimants have diverse citizenship, the stakeholder can choose to use either Rule or statutory interpleader.

Rule 22 interpleader does not provide any express authority for a federal court to enjoin state proceedings even when those proceedings also involve some of the same adverse claims. The federal Anti-Injunction Act, 28 U.S.C. §2283, prevents a federal court from enjoining state proceedings unless that injunction is expressly authorized by federal law. Section §2361 provides that express authorization in a statutory interpleader action and allows federal enjoining of state proceedings. Despite the procedural advantages of statutory interpleader, one might choose Rule interpleader, if available, because Rule 22 does not expressly require the deposit of the fund with the court. If the court does not order the deposit of the fund, the stakeholder can retain its use throughout the pendency of the litigation.

4. Substitution

Rule 25 provides for the substitution of any party who becomes unable to proceed because of death, incompetence, transfer of interest, or replacement in office. Substitution simply replaces a party with someone who represents the same interest. If either the plaintiff or the defendant dies during the pendency of an action and that action survives under the applicable substantive law, a motion for the substitution of the legal representative of the deceased may be made by any party or by the deceased's legal representative or successor. If subject matter jurisdiction validly existed between the original parties, substitution of the legal representative does not destroy that jurisdiction: the representative simply steps into the shoes of the original party. This would be the effect if the representative had brought the suit originally under § 1332(b)(2).

A motion for substitution must be made within 90 days of the time a "suggestion of death" is placed on the record. Although a party's death may have occurred many months before, the suggestion of death places that fact in the record of the court proceeding and starts the 90-day period. This period can be expanded or extended by motion in accordance with Rule 6(b) of the Federal Rules of Civil Procedure. Both the suggestion of death and the motion for substitution must be served according to Rule 5 on all existing parties and according to Rule 4 on those who are to be made parties to the action by the substitution. These papers can be served on those to be substituted in any federal judicial district.

Rule 25(d) provides for the automatic substitution without motion of a public official who is replaced for any reason during the pendency of an action. This rule prevents the action from abating solely because an official leaves office. A public official may, under Rule 25(d)(2), sue or be sued by his official title rather than by name. If suit is in the official's name, proceedings subsequent to her replacement shall be in the name of her successor, and a misnomer not affecting the substantive rights of the parties will be disregarded.

G. HYPOTHETICALS AND EXPLANATIONS

1. Andrew (NY) was riding in a car with Bertha (NY) in Oklahoma when her car collided with a car driven by Carter (OK). Some evidence exists to suggest that Bertha swerved because she was distracted by Andrew's clowning in the car. After the accident, Carter notified his employer, Denim Creations, Inc. (incorporated in Delaware with its principal place of business in Oklahoma), of the accident. Denim responded by denying that Carter was acting within the scope of his employment. Andrew and Bertha have now brought suit, an original claim (oc), in federal court in Oklahoma against Carter and Denim, based solely on diversity jurisdiction. [Assume all claims satisfy the jurisdictional amount.]
Carter was the first defendant to file an answer. His answer included a (a) claim against Bertha, contending that she had negligently caused the accident in which he had suffered personal injury. (b) Carter's answer also included a claim against Denim, contending that under his employment contract Denim is obligated to provide him legal defense and to indemnify him for any liability in this suit. In an answer filed later, Denim as-

serted a (c) claim against Andrew, (d) a claim against Bertha, and (e) a claim against Carter. Each of these claims by Denim sought compensation for the damage to the company car Carter was driving. **Are these claims by Carter and Denim permitted under the Federal Rules, and can they be maintained in federal court?**

Explanation

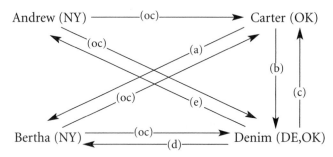

The claims by Carter and Denim are permitted by Rule 13 and will be supported by supplemental jurisdiction.

Rules

(1) Under Rule 13(a) a defendant must assert as a counterclaim any claim he has against an opposing party if that counterclaim arises out of the transaction or occurrence that is the subject matter of the opposing party's claim. (2) Under Rule 13(g), a party may assert a cross-claim against a co-party if either that cross-claim arises out of the transaction or occurrence that gave rise to the original claim or includes an assertion that the party against whom it is asserted is liable for all or part of the claimant's liability to the plaintiff. (3) Under § 1367 (a), supplemental jurisdiction supports the adjudication of all claims (by defendants) that arise from a common nucleus of operative fact with the original claim.

Application

Carter's claim back against Bertha is a counterclaim against an opposing party. Because it arises from the same accident that gave rise to Bertha's claim against him, this counterclaim is compulsory. It, therefore, must be asserted in the suit. Because this counterclaim arises from the same event that gave rise to the original claim, it will also share a common nucleus of operative fact with the original claim and would, therefore, be supported by supplemental jurisdiction. However, supplemental jurisdiction is not needed because Carter's counterclaim is supported by diversity jurisdiction because the parties are diverse. Carter's claim against Denim is a cross-claim because when asserted it was directed against a co-defendant. Cross-claims must also be factually related to the original claim under Rule 13(g) but can include a claim for indemnity, which is what Carter is seeking against Denim. The cross-claim against Denim does not have support in diversity jurisdiction because both defendants have Oklahoma citizenship, but any cross-claim that satisfies Rule 13(g) will arise from the same common nucleus of operative fact as the original claim and thereby gain supplemental jurisdiction under § 1367(a).

Please note that § 1367(b) withdraws supplemental jurisdiction in diversity cases in order to prevent a plaintiff from circumventing the complete diversity requirement. That subsection does not withdraw supplemental jurisdiction from claims asserted by defendants.

Denim asserted claims for its property damage against Andrew and Bertha. These are counterclaims because Andrew and Bertha are opposing parties. These claims are also compulsory counterclaims because they both arise from the same accident that gave rise to the original claims by Andrew and Bertha. Because complete diversity exists between Denim on one side and Andrew and Bertha on the other, diversity jurisdiction would support the counterclaims, but § 1367(a) would have provided supplemental jurisdiction if diversity had not existed. Denim's claim against Carter appears to be a cross-claim because Carter and Denim began as co-defendants. However, when Carter asserted his cross-claim against Denim, they became opposing parties, and Denim's later claim becomes a counterclaim. Because Denim's claim against Carter arises out of the same accident that gave rise to the original claims, it is a compulsory counterclaim and must be asserted in this suit. Because Denim and Carter share citizenship in Oklahoma, diversity jurisdiction does not support Denim's claim against Carter. However, that claim arises from the same accident and would be supported by supplemental jurisdiction.

2. [Assume that all claims mentioned in this problem seek damages in excess of $75,000.] In 2006, Microdata, Inc. (MD) (incorporated in Delaware and having its principal place of business in Oregon) entered a contract with Bloom Cement Company, Inc., (incorporated in Delaware and having its principal place of business in California) and with Pots Engineering Company, Inc., (incorporated and having its principal place of business in California). Bloom and Pots were obligated under the contract to build a 25-story parking garage on the MD campus in Oregon.

As a condition for entering the agreement, MD demanded that Bloom and Pots provide it with a performance bond that guaranteed they would complete the construction. Hokum Insurance Company, Inc. (incorporated in New York and having its principal place of business in California) provided the performance bond insuring MD against the possibility that either or both of the two contractors would fail to perform. As a condition for it to take on this risk, Hokum required Bloom and Pots to indemnify it for any money it might have to pay MD because of their failure to complete the construction project.

Before the building was completed, Bloom and Pots began to squabble and thereafter refused to work together on the project. The building had to be completed by a third construction company hired and paid by Hokum. However, MD refused to accept the finished building, complaining of shoddy construction, and sued—filed an original claim (oc) against—Hokum in federal court in Oregon.

Hokum filed a preanswer motion to dismiss, contending that no subject matter jurisdiction existed over MD's suit because Bloom was both an indispensable and a nondiverse party that must be joined. (a) **Should the case be dismissed for this reason?**

The district court denied the preanswer motion, and Hokum then filed its answer. Along with its answer to MD's complaint, Hokum filed a third-party complaint (1) against Bloom and Pots, claiming that they are liable to it under their indemnity agreement for any amount it is or may be liable to MD. The third-party complaint and summons were properly served on Bloom and Pots. (b) **Can Hokum maintain these claims against Bloom and Pots in this federal court?**

Bloom filed its answer to this third-party complaint first and in it denied liability to Hokum and asserted a claim for damages (2) against Pots for the financial loss Pots allegedly caused Bloom when it (Pots) provided deficient engineering plans for the project. You represent Pots, and your client insists that it also suffered financial injury caused by Bloom's breach of the construction contract. However, Pots does not wish to assert that claim against Bloom in this federal suit. It wishes, instead, to save the claim for a later suit in a California state court. (c) **Can Pots wait until this federal suit ends and then assert its claim against Bloom in a separate suit?**

After Hokum impleaded Bloom and Pots, MD amended its complaint to add breach-of-contract claims (3) directly against Bloom and Pots for the losses it (MD) suffered because of their failure to complete the construction project. (d) **Can the federal court adjudicate MD's claims against Bloom and Pots?**

Explanations

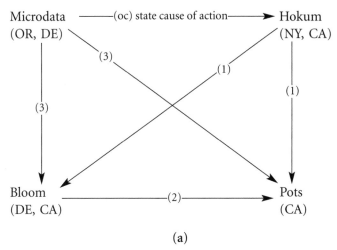

(a)

No, although Bloom cannot be joined as a nondiverse defendant, Bloom's absence from the complaint does not harm either the interests of the defendant or of Bloom.

Rule

If joinder of a party who should be joined under Rule 19(a) is not feasible, the court must consider the factors listed in Rule 19(b) to determine whether the case must be dismissed. The four interests to be examined under Rule 19(b), as restated by the Supreme Court in *Provident Tradesmens Bank v. Patterson*, 390 U.S. 102 (1968) case, are:

- the plaintiff's interest in having a forum;
- the defendant's interest in avoiding multiple litigation, or inconsistent relief, or sole responsibility for a liability he shares with another;
- the interest of the outsider whom it would have been desirable to join;
- the interest of the courts and of the public in complete, consistent, and efficient settlement of controversies; and
- the ability to shape relief so as to lessen any prejudice.

Application

Remember, this issue arises before Hokum asserts its own claims against Bloom or Pots, and is in response to the complaint that names it alone as the defending party. Under Rule 19(a), the joinder of Bloom was not feasible because if added as a defendant, Bloom's presence would have defeated diversity jurisdiction. Analysis therefore moves to consideration of the factors listed in Rule 19(b). The primary focus under Rule 19(b) is whether continuation of the suit in the absence of Bloom would have been unfair to either Bloom or Hokum. Considering these parties' interests, a court would conclude that although Bloom has a legitimate concern for the outcome of this litigation, it would not be bound under res judicata by any issue or judgment entered in its absence. Hokum complains of Bloom's absence, but Hokum does not lose anything because of the plaintiff's failure to join Bloom. Hokum would save money by having all of these issues determined in one suit, and that can occur only by having Bloom and Pots in the suit. Those corporations might become judgment proof in the interim, and their absence from this suit would frustrate the ability of Hokum to enforce its indemnity clause. However, those problems can be easily avoided by Hokum's filing of a third-party complaint to implead both Bloom and Pots. No strong interest compels dismissal of the complaint, and the case should therefore go forward.

(b)

Hokum can assert these claims under Rule 14, and they will be supported by supplemental jurisdiction.

Rules

(1) Under Rule 14, a defending party can implead any person who is liable to it for all or part of its liability to the plaintiff, and that claim must arise from the same transaction or occurrence that gave rise to the plaintiff's claim. (2) Impleader claims necessarily arise from a common nucleus of operative fact with the plaintiff's claim and will thus be within a federal court's supplemental jurisdiction authorized by § 1367(a).

Application

The claims made by Hokum against Bloom and Pots are Rule 14 impleader claims. An impleader claim can be asserted by a defendant against a person who was not joined in the original complaint. The defendant thus becomes a third-party plaintiff as to the impleader, and the new party becomes a third-party defendant. The defendant must assert a claim that makes the third-party defendant secondarily or derivatively liable—that is, the claim must assert that this party is liable to the defendant only to the extent the court finds the defendant liable to the plaintiff. A defendant cannot implead a person by contending that the plaintiff should have joined that person; the defendant cannot allege a "he's liable, but I'm not" claim under Rule 14. As derivatively liable, the third-party defendant can only be liable for the amount a court finds the defendant owes the plaintiff. If the plaintiff doesn't prevail, the third-party defendant cannot be liable solely because of an impleader claim.

Rule 14 thus requires that an impleader claim arise from the transaction or a logically related series of transactions that gave rise to the plaintiff's claim. MD sued Hokum for the defective completion of the construction contract, and Hokum's claims against Bloom and Pots arise from its contractual requirement that these parties indemnify it for claims such as this one by MD. Since the third-party plaintiff has citizenship in California, as do both of the third-party defendants, the claim lacks the complete diversity required by § 1332.

Hokum can support the impleader claims by using § 1367 to establish supplemental jurisdiction over both. As already indicated, these claims arise from the contractual relationships that arose from the agreement to construct MD's parking garage. All claims seem therefore to arise from a common nucleus of operative fact in a manner sufficient to justify supplemental jurisdiction under § 1367(a). Section 1367(b) does not deprive the court of jurisdiction because it applies only to prevent the use of supplemental jurisdiction over claims made by plaintiffs.

(c)

No, Pots must assert the claim it has against Bloom because that claim is now a compulsory counterclaim.

Rule

A claim by a party against one who has asserted a claim against that party is a counterclaim, and if this counterclaim arises from the same transaction as the initial claim its assertion is compulsory. Failure to assert a claim that is a compulsory counterclaim prevents later assertion of the claim.

Application

Bloom's claim against Pots was a cross-claim. A cross-claim is a claim asserted by one party against a co-party. Co-parties are those who are on the same side of litigation, but who have not asserted claims against one another. When Hokum impleaded both Bloom and Pots, they became third-party defendants and were co-parties in opposition to Hokum. Once Bloom asserted a claim for damages against Pots, they ceased being co-parties and became opposing parties, at least in respect to their mutual contest over which caused the other damages in the completion of the MD contract.

Since the cross-claim made Bloom and Pots opposing parties, the responsive claim that Pots wishes to assert against Bloom for the financial injury that was allegedly caused to Pots by Bloom's breach of contract must be a counterclaim. This counterclaim rather clearly arises from the same contractual obligations the two owed MD, and the performance (or nonperformance) of these obligations gave rise to Bloom's claim against Pots. As such, Pots' claim is deemed to be compulsory under Federal Rule 13(a). Under the Rule, Pots' failure to assert its claim in this litigation means that it cannot thereafter assert the claim. It would thus be unable to save the claim for later suit in California state court. This effect of the compulsory counterclaim rule operates because of Rule 13(a) and is not limited by res judicata rules. In a sense, it is a legislatively declared rule of claim preclusion. The policy served is, however, the same. If Pots could freely litigate its claim against Bloom in another suit, the adjudication of Bloom's claim against Pots would be a waste of judicial resources.

(d)

No, MD cannot maintain its claim against Bloom, but can maintain its claim against Pots in federal court.

Rule

(1) Rule 14 allows a plaintiff to assert claims against third-party defendants if those claims arise from the same transaction that gave rise to the plaintiff's original claim. (2) When MD amends its complaint to assert claims against the third-party defendants, diversity jurisdiction will allow only those claims against diverse parties. (3) Supplemental jurisdiction will not support the adjudication of claims by a plaintiff in a diversity case against parties joined pursuant to Rule 14.

Application

Rule 14 allows the original plaintiff to assert claims against the third-party defendants so long as these arise from the same transaction as the original claim. Here, MD seeks to recover its damages caused by the allegedly deficient completion of the parking garage. Although the contract giving rise to Hokum's liability is different from the contract signed between MD and Bloom and Pots, a "transaction" includes logically related events or actions, such as these two contracts. Therefore, MD can assert its claims against Bloom and Pots under Rule 14.

Even though Rule 14 authorizes the assertion of these claims by MD, the court must have a subject matter jurisdictional basis for each claim. In adding a claim directly against Pots, MD can use diversity as its ground for jurisdiction. The law deems MD a citizen of Delaware (its state of incorporation) and of Oregon (its principal place of business) and Pots a citizen of California (its state both of incorporation and of its principal place of business). Therefore, diversity supports the claim against Pots.

MD cannot however sustain the claim against Bloom. The law deems Bloom a citizen of Delaware (its state of incorporation) and of California (the state of its principal place of business). Since diversity cannot support that state-law breach of contract claim (and federal question cannot as well), MD can only seek to establish jurisdiction through the supplemental jurisdiction statute, § 1367. The "common nucleus" requirement of § 1367(a) would be satisfied by the same analysis that showed this claim arose from the same transaction as the original claim. However, § 1367(b) prevents the use of supplemental jurisdiction in a wholly diversity case when the use of that jurisdiction would allow the plaintiff to circumvent the complete diversity requirement of § 1332. In respect to the claim against Bloom, this case presents the same relevant facts as the *Kroger* decision, which was the basis for the enactment of § 1367(b). The Supreme Court in *Kroger* prevented the use of "pendent jurisdiction," the common law predecessor of supplemental jurisdiction, when used by the plaintiff to join a nondiverse party. See Owen Equipment & Erection Co. v. Kroger, 437 U.S. 365 (1978).

CHAPTER 9

NOTICE REQUIRED BY DUE PROCESS

A. TERMINOLOGY

Constructive notice—Under limited circumstances, the state can allow a plaintiff to satisfy the requirement of service by using publication or posting even though those methods of delivering information are unlikely to provide actual notice.

Personal service—This phrase refers to personal (in-hand) delivery of process to the defendant.

Process—In federal practice, the plaintiff must deliver a copy of the complaint and a summons, which has been signed and sealed by the clerk of a federal district court.

Service—Service of process refers to the delivery of those papers to the defendant.

Substituted service—This refers to methods for delivery of process other than personal service.

B. Providing Notice and
an Opportunity to Appear

1. Overview

If a court finds that the means used to give defendant service of process is constitutionally deficient, it will dismiss the case for lack of jurisdiction. Thus, a constitutional failure in giving sufficient notice robs a court of power over the defendant. In some instances, jurisdiction can be reasserted by the subsequent use of a constitutionally sufficient means of notice. In this regard, these dismissals for lack of jurisdiction differ from dismissals based on the conclusion that a defendant had insufficient minimum contacts with the forum state. The latter form of dismissal effectively ends the jurisdiction of any court of the same state.

A federal court also may dismiss suits for failure of the plaintiff to comply with the requirements of Rule 4 of the Federal Rules of Civil Procedure. That Rule describes the manner in which process can be legitimately served on a defendant. Failure to comply with the guidelines of the Rule justifies the quashing of service, but the court ordinarily would allow the plaintiff to again attempt service in accordance with the Rule.

Letting someone know about a suit against them seems rather basic, especially in a system dependent on the adversarial presentation of issues for decisionmaking. However, over the years, some of the methods used to give notice have been remarkably ineffective in notifying anyone. In *Pennoyer v. Neff*, the Supreme Court in 1878 had little difficulty in approving publication notice in an *in rem* action. At that time, most states allowed a plaintiff in *in rem* actions to serve all persons interested in the property at issue by publishing information about the case in a local newspaper. That act of giving notice was always unlikely to inform anyone, except very lonely people who regularly read those boring recitations hidden in the back pages of the newspaper. Even less likely was the possibility that interested persons who resided outside the forum state would, through happenstance, fall upon this information.

Courts referred to publication as constructive notice, which was to say they merely assumed, as a matter of law, that the publication of information satisfied the defendant's right to notice. The Supreme Court rationalized this method of serving process in *in rem* actions by assuming that nonresident owners of land would have a local caretaker. That local caretaker would notify the owner of any action against the land. Of course, the local caretaker, if he existed, might not read the back pages of the newspaper, but he would be alerted, reasoned the Court, by a second requirement of *in rem* actions. The Court insisted that jurisdiction in an *in rem* action must begin with a court's attachment or seizure of the local property. Unfortunately for the local caretaker, this might mean only that the plaintiff placed some sort of stop order on the deed records. These *lis pendens* (litigation pending) notices prevent sale or the encumbering of the land, but they do not do much, for example, to notify a local apartment manager hired by the absent landlord. The Court has recognized the emptiness of this fiction, and in the *Mullane* case (discussed below) concluded that publication notice can satisfy due process only when the identity and whereabouts of interested parties cannot be discovered with due diligence.

The Court's analysis of *in personam* actions in *Pennoyer* culminated with its requirement that such actions be initiated with personal service of process within the forum state. Personal delivery of process to the defendant is the means most likely to provide actual notice of the lawsuit. In addition, the Court in *Pennoyer* saw personal service as a useful ritual to memorialize a court's assertion of jurisdiction over someone within its territorial authority. Personal service has continued to stand as a model method for giving the defendant actual notice of a suit even though today it need not be accomplished while the defendant is located in the forum state. In some states, courts refer to substituted service as any means other than personal service. In Federal Rule 4, for example, process may be left with someone of suitable age and discretion residing in the dwelling place of the defendant.

The different terms used in regard to the problem of service of process can probably best be understood when one looks at the mechanics of the procedure. In a simple sense, the plaintiff has the obligation to serve—that is, to deliver to the defendant those papers which adequately inform a defendant of the suit and of what is required for an adequate response. This procedure has significance beyond the notification of the defendant because it serves as the official act by which a court asserts its jurisdiction. A defendant who has not been served and who has not waived service is not within the jurisdiction of the court and nothing the court does binds that person. Because of this significance, all jurisdictions provide specific rules for service of process. A plaintiff cannot informally notify the defendant, but must comply with the service-of-process rule of that court system in order to obtain jurisdiction unless the defendant surrenders the right to service. Furthermore, process must be served on the defendant or on someone who stands in the legal position of the defendant for purposes of service of process. A foreign corporation doing business in a state can be required to appoint a local agent for service of process. Service is effective only if made on this duly appointed agent, but not on, say, a defendant's lawyer (unless the lawyer has been officially appointed as an agent for receipt of process).

It is helpful to note that a defendant does not have a constitutional right to actual notice. A constitutional right that demanded actual notice in every case would encourage willful avoidance of service and unnecessary litigation over this threshold issue. To describe the right another way, the plaintiff does not have the constitutional obligation to prove that the defendant was actually notified. Instead, the defendant has a constitutional right to insist only that the legal means used in serving him with process was reasonably likely to give him actual notice. Proof showing that the defendant failed to receive notice because of no fault of his own will, however, provide the defendant a powerful nonconstitutional argument for setting aside a default judgment.

2. Nature of Due Process Rights

The Constitution of the United States contains two Due Process Clauses— one in the Fifth Amendment, limiting the federal government, and the other in the Fourteenth Amendment, limiting state and local governments. The Fifth Amendment's Due Process Clause states that "[n]o person shall ... be deprived of life, liberty, or property, without due process of law." The Fourteenth Amendment's Due Process Clause states that "[n]o State shall ... deprive any person of life, liberty, or property, without due process of law." Both clauses have been interpreted to impose the same essential limitations on courts. Unless stated otherwise, assume that the "due process of law" required in the two clauses has the same meaning.

As a prerequisite for the entry of a valid judgment, courts are bound to follow the dictates of due process in civil actions. In a sense, due process controls the actions of courts because courts use governmental power to apply law to individuals. Other government actions are not so pervasively bound by due process. For example, due process does not directly limit the legislative process because legislatures act upon groups rather than on individuals. After a law's enactment, however, executive officials will enforce that law against individuals; and that enforcement against the individual, whether before a court or an administrative agency, must proceed according to a fair procedure— that is, one which satisfies due process.

The Due Process Clauses thus require government to follow fair procedures whenever it seeks to deprive an individual of life, liberty, or property. A plaintiff invokes the jurisdiction of a court in a civil case to obtain a judgment against the defendant. If the plaintiff seeks injunctive relief, he thereby seeks to prevent the defendant from exercising his liberty to engage in some behavior. If the plaintiff seeks a monetary remedy, the judgment, once final, can be executed against the movable or immovable property of the defendant. In either case, the court is asked to use its governmental power to deprive the defendant of either liberty or property. Because all civil suits (and all criminal prosecutions) threaten one or more of the protected interests (life, liberty, or property), courts must always follow constitutionally mandated procedures.

3. Waiver and Estoppel

A party's objection to the unconstitutionality of a service procedure is a personal right. Being a personal right, it is one that the defendant can lose by failing to assert it in a timely or proper manner. If a defendant in federal court has been served through a constitutionally deficient method of service, he may challenge service in a motion to dismiss or a motion to quash service. A motion to quash, instead of one to dismiss, should be directed at the plaintiff's first effort at service because she can correct that deficiency with proper service. A defendant may choose to file a preanswer motion pursuant to Federal Rule 12(b), and that Rule lists insufficiency of process (failure to include both the complaint and summons) and insufficiency of service (failure to serve according to Rule 4 or due process) as two objections that can be included in the motion. Rule 12 (h) provides for the waiver of these two objections if they are not included in a preanswer motion that the defendant filed for other reasons. However, a defendant need not file a preanswer motion, and can, instead, respond initially with an answer. If he then omits either of these two grounds (insufficiency of process or of service) from the answer or an amendment, he waives them.

If the defendant challenges the sufficiency of service after a federal default judgment has become final, he will do so through a motion to set aside the judgment as void under Federal Rule 60(b)(4). This challenge to a constitutionally deficient method of service will, if successful, invalidate any judgment entered in violation of due process. The Rule 60(b)(4) challenge is available to the defendant because, under those circumstances, he has never had his day in court on the issue of due process. If, on the other hand, he participates in the litigation, he must comply with the required procedure for raising that objection, or he loses his constitutional objection under due process.

Waiver—in the sense of consenting to suit without service of process—can result from an agreement in a contract. The Supreme Court has held that parties to a contract may agree in advance to surrender their right to service of process. In these situations, however, the waiving party typically has little or no bargaining power, and may not understand the significance of such a provision even if he reads it. Although such contractual provisions are not per se unconstitutional, they may be vulnerable to a due process attack if the contract is one of adhesion, if there is a great disparity in bargaining power, and if the defendant has received nothing for the waiver.

C. Determining the Unconstitutionality of Service

1. Predeprivation Service

The timing of the notice becomes critical when the plaintiff seeks to move against the defendant or his property before notifying him of the action. The general rule in civil actions is that predeprivation notice is required. Before adjudicating claims against a defendant, a court must provide him with notice and an opportunity to appear and defend himself. Since our adversary system draws its justification largely from the assumption that both sides have an equal chance to present their arguments, notice which precedes any final decision seems obviously necessary.

Due process, therefore, generally requires predeprivation notice. In simple terms, that means the notice must precede any action by the court which would affect the rights or obligations of the defendant. However, in rare instances, notice has been deemed sufficient when given after a property interest of the defendant has been affected. These cases often involve a creditor's action against a delinquent debtor in which the plaintiff/creditor obtains a judicial order preventing the defendant from removing his property. If the defendant receives notice of a suit seeking repossession of his property before that property is seized, he has a motive to remove or hide the property. When seizure is the first notice to the defendant, the plaintiff can be assured that the property will be protected until judgment.

These seizure orders frequently appear as writs of attachment or sequestration. Attachment typically allows seizure of assets in the defendant's possession, and sequestration permits the plaintiff to seize the defendant's assets in the hands of a third party such as a bank. A court can also issue a temporary restraining order (TRO) without giving the defendant prior notice. These "ex parte" orders (issued without participation of the other party) are available only when the plaintiff will suffer irreparable harm if forced to give prior notice to the defendant.

2. Ineffective Means of Service

The primary Supreme Court precedent on this issue is Mullane v. Central Hanover Bank & Trust Co., 339 U.S. 306 (1950). In *Mullane*, the trustee of a common trust, established pursuant to New York law, brought a judicial proceeding to settle its accounts in regard to the operation of the trust. This settlement of accounts threatened to deprive beneficiaries of property because it would effectively terminate any claims they might have against the trustee because of its actions up to that point. In addition, the settlement constituted judicial approval of the trustee's fees for operating the trust, and that approval would preclude the beneficiaries from challenging those fees as excessive.

New York law allowed the trustee to satisfy its service obligation to the beneficiaries by publication of information about the proceeding in a local newspaper. Publication notice had been deemed sufficient in *in rem* actions by assuming that an absent owner always had a local custodian to receive notice of any challenge to his title. In this instance, the custodian of the beneficiaries' property was the trustee, and the trustee was seeking to terminate any claims they might have for its actions. Therefore, the trustee could not use the local custodian fiction to ignore the ineffectiveness of publication notice because it was adverse to the absent beneficiaries in this controversy.

The Supreme Court held that the transmission of process (or of the information constituting process) by publication in a local newspaper was constitutionally insufficient when, with due diligence, the plaintiff could discover the name and location of an interested person. If such information was available, the trustee could use the mail to give actual notice to the known beneficiaries. The trustee had, in fact, communicated with the beneficiaries in this manner when the common trust was created, and could do so again without incurring unreasonable costs.

In some instances, the interest of known beneficiaries may have been changed by assignment or testamentary transfer. The trustee would be hard put to discover all of the new beneficiaries and their addresses without expending substantial amounts of money. The states had developed the common-trust device to allow large numbers of small trusts to combine in one trust in order to obtain efficiencies of scale and to take advantage of better investments. If the due process requirements imposed such substantial expenses on its operation, the benefits of a common trust would be lost. However, the

Court concluded that due process demanded only that the method used for service of process was reasonably calculated under the circumstances to give actual notice. Under these circumstances, the Court held that the publication procedure was sufficient for the unknown beneficiaries but not for the known beneficiaries. The unknown beneficiaries were, after all, persons whose identity and whereabouts the trustee could not discover using reasonable diligence, and, therefore, publication was sufficient because no other more effective means were readily available.

Although the Court in *Mullane* did not expressly abolish the *in rem* fiction which allowed the publication form of process serving, it did emphasize the need to use means for service which were reasonably calculated to give actual notice. As the Court explained, the state need not require the best method for delivering process. It should, however, require a method which either is likely to convey actual notice or which is not substantially less likely to do so than other feasible and customary methods. Since, as to the known beneficiaries, publication was not likely to provide actual notice, the existence of a more effective and feasible alternative—using the mail—made the publication procedure unconstitutional.

The posting of notices—another form of constructive notice—also proved vulnerable to due process challenge. In Schroeder v. City of New York, 371 U.S. 208 (1962), the city, in addition to publication, posted notices of a pending condemnation on trees and poles in the vicinity of the landowner's property. This additional effort did not help much because the notices were not posted on the owner's land and they did not mention his name. In Greene v. Lindsey, 456 U.S. 444 (1983), a Kentucky statute provided for service of process in forcible entry and detainer actions by posting the summons on the door of the tenant's apartment. The evidence in *Greene* indicated that not infrequently the plaintiff's notices were removed by children or other tenants in the housing project where the defendant lived.

In both cases, the plaintiff had a more effective means by which to deliver process. The City of New York had information about the name and address of the property owner in its own records, and the landlord could send process through the mail to the tenants he intended to evict. Therefore, the use of posting in each case was constitutionally insufficient because of two conclusions. First, the means at issue were ineffective in giving actual notice. And, second, the plaintiffs had an inexpensive and more effective means available.

Once the problem moves beyond posting and publication, a challenge to a means allowed by the state becomes more difficult. The mails may not always run on time or deliver every letter, but a law allowing their use could not be condemned for using a wholly ineffective means. Because personal service appears to be the most effective means for giving actual notice, a less effective means might always seem vulnerable to a due process challenge. However, the Court's analysis in *Mullane* indicates that expense must also be considered. A plaintiff, such as the trustee of a common trust, may confront the need to give notice to a large number of interested persons. Under those circumstances, personal service may be more effective but not feasible. As the Court has stated, a state need not use only that procedure which is most likely to give actual notice, but "where an inexpensive and efficient mechanism ... is available to enhance the reliability of an otherwise unreliable notice procedure, the State's continued exclusive reliance on an ineffective means" is not satisfactory under due process. *Greene v. Lindsey*, 456 U.S. at 455.

3. Pre-Judgment Knowledge of Ineffective Service

If a plaintiff uses an otherwise effective method of service while knowing that the defendant is not likely to be informed of the suit, reliance on that method of service does not satisfy due process. In Covey v. Town of Somers, 351 U.S. 141 (1956), the Supreme Court held that a notice of foreclosure that was mailed, as well as posted and published, was constitutionally deficient because town officials knew that the property owner was incompetent and unprotected by a guardian. *Id.* at 146–47. In a similar situation, the Court held mailed notice to a vehicle owner's home address was insufficient when the state was charged with knowledge that he was in prison at the time of service. Robinson v. Hanrahan, 409 U.S. 38, 40 (1972) (*per curiam*).

More recently, the Supreme Court has affirmed this approach to the requirements of due process. In Jones v. Flowers, 126 S.Ct. 1708 (2006), the state sought to notify a property owner of its intent to sell his real property for a tax delinquency and of his right to redeem the property by paying the delinquency. The state provided this notice by sending a letter by certified mail to the defendant, Jones, at the address of the real property. No one was present to sign for that letter, and no one retrieved it from the post office in the 15-day period it was held there. The letter was, therefore, returned "unclaimed" to the state. Shortly before the public sale of the property, the state published a notice of the sale in a local newspaper. Because no bids were received, the state was allowed to negotiate a private sale of the property, and Mrs. Flowers submitted an offer. Before the sale, the state again sent notice to Mr. Jones by certified mail, but that second letter was also returned "unclaimed" to the state.

After Mrs. Flowers purchased the property, she delivered an eviction notice to the property which was served on the daughter of Mr. Jones, who was living in the house. The daughter notified Mr. Jones of the tax sale, and he brought suit in state court challenging the notice as being insufficient under due process. The Arkansas Supreme Court held that the certified mail notice was sufficient under due process and upheld the sale. The Supreme Court of the United States granted certiorari and reversed. The Supreme Court reaffirmed the proposition that due process does not require a defendant to receive actual notice. It also recognized that its precedents supported the conclusion that service by certified mail was constitutionally sufficient because such service was reasonably calculated to reach the intended recipient when sent. See *id.* at 1714. However, the Court distinguished these precedents by noting that in the cases cited the government had attempted notice by mail and had heard nothing indicating that service had gone awry. *Id.*

The Court held that with knowledge of the failure of service in a particular case before judgment, the state should have taken additional reasonable steps to notify Mr. Jones if it was practicable to do so. The Court discussed the likelihood that service through certified mail would be less likely to give actual notice to the property owner than notice by regular mail. A letter sent by regular mail would be left with other mail, and could have been opened by a tenant. In addition, the Court noted that in this instance the state was likely to be more effective by posting a notice of sale on the property's front door or by sending the notice to "occupant." See *id.* at 1719. The Court also held that the state could not avoid the due process requirement to use a reasonably effective method of service by imposing an obligation on the property owner to furnish a current address. On the other hand, the state does not have the constitutional obligation to search for a property owner's current address when he has failed to inform the state of that address.

One might wonder whether the Court's decision in *Flowers* undermines the oft-stated proposition that due process does not require actual notice. Justice Thomas, in his dissent in *Flowers*, noted that in *Covey* and *Robinson* the government had knowledge before sending notice that the defendant's mental state or location made mailed notice unlikely to provide actual notice. In *Flowers*, however, the state had no knowledge that sending its notice letter by certified mail would fail to reach the defendant until after that letter was returned unclaimed. Justice Thomas complained that the Court's rule has no natural end point. When, for example, does newly acquired information of failed notice require the state to use additional measures? See *id.* at 1724.

In the Supreme Court's decision in Dusenbery v. U.S., 534 U.S. 161 (2002), the Court held that certified mail service on a prisoner was sufficient under due process. The challenge arose from a prisoner complaining about the seizure of cash by the United States Government. The Federal Bureau of Investigation (FBI) sent prior notice of an administrative forfeiture proceedings by certified mail addressed to the prisoner at the federal prison where he was being confined. Prison staff signed for the certified mail and then typically delivered the letter to the prisoner during mail call. The prisoner contended that this procedure was deficient because the Bureau of Prisons should have required the prisoner to sign for his certified mail. That procedure would be more likely to assure actual receipt of notice. The Court held that the process used was constitutionally sufficient even though other methods would be more certain to prove that a prisoner had actually received notice.

Dusenbery appears to be a case in which the Court held that, in the absence of early notice that service failed, use of a reasonably effective means of delivery cannot be deemed unconstitutional merely because a more effective means exists. As so interpreted, that decision is consistent with the *Flowers* case. It would seem, therefore, that these cases support the conclusion that a defendant cannot challenge the constitutional sufficiency of a service procedure after judgment has been entered by proving that he did not receive actual notice of the suit. That may partially answer the question asked by Justice Thomas in *Flowers*.

4. Post-Deprivation Service

Requiring notice and an opportunity to be heard reduces the high risk of erroneous or unjustified seizures that would fall on defendants if only plaintiffs were pleading their case in *ex parte* proceedings. The danger of error or unfairness exists in any *ex parte* procedure (one in which only one side appears). That danger is reduced if a judge, rather than a court clerk, must approve a seizure order and must do so on the basis of specific allegations showing a preexisting interest. In these instances, constitutional analysis balances the risk of error that might harm a defendant against the practical gain in protecting the plaintiff's property from removal or waste by the defendant. If the defendant is judgment proof, the only recovery a plaintiff can obtain is return of the property secured by a lien. If the defendant is notified that the plaintiff seeks return of the secured property before the property is seized, the defendant has little reason to maintain it in good condition and no reason to make it available to subsequent seizure by the plaintiff.

Another example of *ex parte* action that may occur before notice is the temporary restraining order (TRO). Once served on the defendant, this order effectively restrains him in order to protect the plaintiff from a feared irreparable harm. A TRO may be issued under Rule 65(b) of the Federal Rules of Civil Procedure for a period of 10 days. Only a judge can issue a TRO and can do so only when "it clearly appears from specific facts shown by affidavit or by the verified complaint that immediate and irreparable injury, loss, or damage will result" before the adverse party could be brought before the court. In addition, the attorney applying for a TRO must certify in writing the efforts she has made to notify the other party, and she must explain whether notice has been given or, if not, the reasons for not having done so. Because conditions must indicate that the plaintiff's need for immediate action is great, issuing a TRO for a 10-day period without prior notice does not violate due process.

In Mitchell v. W. T. Grant, 416 U.S. 600 (1974), the plaintiff/creditor obtained sequestration (a preliminary seizure of property) under a Louisiana statute which allowed relief only to lienholders. The Louisiana procedure required a verified affidavit containing specific rather than conclusory allegations proving the existence of the lien, of the debt, and of the delinquency. In addition, a judge, rather than a clerk or other court employee, had to authorize the seizure. Once the assets were sequestered, the defendant could seek dissolution of the writ, and in the hearing on this issue the burden of proof fell on the plaintiff. The Supreme Court upheld the sequestration by distinguishing the Louisiana law from those which allowed property to be seized at the unchecked discretion of the plaintiff. A defendant's assets could not be frozen when the writ was issued by a clerk based on general claims of debt.

A plaintiff may need to freeze a defendant's checking or savings account before the defendant can move these funds. In some instances, a defendant can hide his assets during litigation and thereby make any ultimate judgment unenforceable. However, a plaintiff who can prevent a defendant from using his checking and savings accounts during litigation has gained an advantage which could enable her to force a settlement without regard to the merits. The Louisiana law prevented the worst abuses by plaintiffs because it allowed seizure only in cases in which a lien existed and because it required specific allegations showing a right to recover. In addition, these allegations had to be presented to a judge who would be more likely than a clerk to resist issuing a writ on inconclusive grounds.

D. Service of Process in Federal Civil Actions

Rule 4 is the primary guide for service of process in federal court. As a general rule, plaintiffs, rather than the United States Marshal's Office, must accomplish service or obtain the defendant's waiver of his right to service. Rule 4 provides various methods for delivering information about the commencement of an action to a defendant and, in this manner, also establishes service as the symbolic act representing a court's assertion of jurisdiction. A federal court is not authorized to create its own rules for asserting its jurisdiction but instead must find its authority either in the Federal Rules of Civil Procedure or in federal statutes.

Rule 4 applies whenever the plaintiff or any other party seeks to assert a federal court's power over someone who has not already been brought within that court's jurisdiction. For example, in bringing a third-party action under Rule 14, a defendant must serve third-party defendants in accordance with Rule 4. Rule 5 of the Federal Rules of Civil Procedure controls the service provided a party over whom the court has already acquired jurisdiction. It requires only informal delivery of papers to each party's attorney by mail, by personal delivery, or by leaving a copy of the paper at the attorney's office. The informality reflects an emphasis on providing timely information without the concern for symbolism. Furthermore, the presence of a party in litigation, especially while represented by an attorney, provides him protection against adjudications without notice.

Service or waiver of service must occur within 120 days from the date of filing. See Rule 4(m). Original process includes a copy of the complaint and the summons (*see* Form 1, appended to the Federal Rules). Among other information provided the defendant, the summons describes the time within which a defendant must answer the complaint (20 days after service), and it describes the consequences of a default. Typically, the plaintiff's attorney completes a summons form before filing suit in federal court. After the complaint is filed, the clerk of the court attaches the court's seal and his or her signature.

Before delivering process, the plaintiff can send to the defendant by first-class mail a document that gives him notice of the suit and requests that he waive service of process. See Rule 4(d), and see Form 1A and 1B. This notice and request for waiver can be sent to a defendant who is an individual, a corporation, or an association. By waiving service, a defendant does not lose the ability to object to the venue of the suit or to the court's personal jurisdiction.

If an attorney has the obligation of serving a defendant in federal court or in overseeing the process server, her first step would be to identify the type of defendant to be served. The obvious distinction arises between individual and organizational defendants. You would next determine the location of the defendant. Provisions, other than the ones mentioned here, apply if the defendant is located outside the United States.

Service on an individual who is found in the United States can be delivered according to the law of the state in which the federal court is located or according to the law of the state in which service is to be completed. The plaintiff can have process delivered personally to an individual defendant, delivered to the defendant's agent by appointment or by law, or left with at the defendant's dwelling house or usual place of abode with someone of suitable age and discretion then residing therein. See Rule 4(e).

Process addressed to a corporation or association found in the United States can be delivered personally to an officer, or to a managing or general agent of the defendant. The plaintiff can also deliver process to the defendant's agent by appointment or by law. When delivered to an agent assigned to the defendant by a statute, a copy of process must be mailed to the defendant if the statute so requires. See Rule 4(h). In addition, Rule 4 allows the plaintiff to serve both individuals and organizations by any means authorized under the law of the forum state or by the law of the state in which process is to be delivered. If either state allows first-class mail delivery of process to a defendant, for example, the plaintiff can deliver process in that manner even though Rule 4 does not itself allow mailed service of process.

1. Legal Power to Serve

Except in regard to transient jurisdiction (service within the forum state on an individual who isn't a citizen), service or waiver of service activates jurisdiction but does not create it. In other words, service represents the formal assertion of a court's power and thus a prerequisite to adjudication, but service generally does not confer jurisdiction. The court can quash service, but still adjudicate the plaintiff's claims after he has properly served the defendant. The quashing of service differs from a dismissal for lack of personal jurisdiction, therefore, because the dismissal means that neither the forum court nor any other court of the forum state has power over the defendant.

Furthermore, federal courts do not have common law power to authorize service on particular defendants. Therefore, federal courts must find authority to serve a particular defendant in Rule 4 of the Federal Rules of Civil Procedure. Rule 4(k) provides the basic authority for service on defendants according to their location. It acts primarily as a reference to those legal authorities that allow service by federal courts. Rule 4(k)(1)(A) allows service on any defendant who could be subjected to jurisdiction by the courts of general jurisdiction in the state in which the district sits. Since state trial courts can universally issue process for service on any defendant found in the forum state, a federal court has the same authority. The only question of federal authority arises in regard to defendants not found in the forum state. Rule 4(k)(1)(A) authorizes a federal court to issue process for service on a defendant who could be reached by a state court through the forum state's long-arm statute. The vast majority of state long-arm statutes allow service to the extent permitted by the Fourteenth Amendment's Due Process Clause. Approximately six states have more restrictive statutes. When that is the case, a federal court in that state generally has no greater power to issue process beyond the reach of a state court.

Federal courts can extend the reach of their service if a federal law allows them to do so. Rule 4(k)(1)(D) allows a federal court to serve a defendant outside the forum state, regardless of the availability of a state long-arm statute, when a federal statute provides the authority. This Rule refers however to the relatively few instances in which a federal statute authorizes nationwide service by a federal court that is adjudicating a substantive federal claim. One example is found in the Securities Exchange Act, 15 U.S.C. §78aa (2000). When a plaintiff brings a claim created by that statute, she can serve the defendant in any federal judicial district in which he is an inhabitant or wherever he may be found. Rule 4(k)(1)(C) refers to §1335 of Title 28 U.S.C., which provides a similar power of nationwide service when the plaintiff has brought a statutory interpleader action in federal court.

Federal Rule 4(k)(2) itself adds another limited long-arm provision. It authorizes a federal court to serve process on a defendant who would not be covered by any other legal authority. This so-called "fall-back" provision operates only when (1) the plaintiff asserts a federal claim, (2) no state court would have jurisdiction over the defendant, and (3) that jurisdiction would not violate the Constitution. This provision therefore applies in a rare case in which the defendant resides outside the United States, has not caused sufficient minimum contacts with any one state, but has contacts with the United States that are sufficient to satisfy the Fifth Amendment Due Process Clause. The Due Process Clause of the Fifth Amendment, rather than of the Fourteenth Amendment, applies to a federal court's assertion of jurisdiction under a federal long-arm statute to adjudicate a federal claim. Under those circumstances, due process requires only that the defendant have sufficient minimum contacts with the United States because that is the jurisdiction asserting power over her. If a federal court uses a state long-arm statute, it can only use that authority to the extent a state court could do so. A state court's use of such a statute would be limited by the due process demand that it show the defendant had minimum contacts with the forum state.

2. Service and Statutes of Limitations

Rule 3 of the Federal Rules of Civil Procedure states that a "civil action is commenced by filing a complaint with the court." Commencement is the point at which the citizenship of the parties is to be determined for diversity purposes, the time at which residence is determined for venue purposes, and the point from which various time periods set in other of the Federal Rules might be measured. The Supreme Court held, in Walker v. Armco Steel Co., 446 U.S. 740 (1980), that Rule 3 does not displace a requirement of service adopted by a state as part of its statute of limitations. In that case, the state required service of process to toll its statute of limitations. That statute of limitations was applicable in the *Walker* case because it was based on diversity of citizenship jurisdiction and therefore was to be adjudicated according to state substantive law. The plaintiff filed the complaint within the limitations period but served process outside that period. The Supreme Court held that Rule 3 did not preempt the state tolling provision, and therefore the case had to be dismissed as barred under the state statute of limitations.

Federal statutes of limitations refer to particular federal statutory causes of action. Some of these statutes of limitations expressly require only the filing of the complaint to commence an action so as to satisfy the limitations command. If this is the case, the federal statute controls and filing would satisfy the limitations requirement without reference to Rule 3. Other federal statutes may only refer generally to "commencement," and that term would be defined by reference to Rule 3 in the absence of other intent by Congress.

E. Hypotheticals and Explanations

"[N]or shall any State deprive any person of life, liberty, or property, without due process of law."

1. The plaintiff brought suit in federal court in Oregon seeking to establish title to local land, and named a nonresident defendant as an adverse claimant to that land. In compliance with state law, the plaintiff published a copy of her complaint in a local newspaper once a week for four consecutive weeks. In addition, state law required the posting of the same information on trees or structures on the land, and the plaintiff complied with this requirement as well. The defendant, whose name and address is listed in the Oregon deed records of this land, failed to learn of the suit before the Oregon court terminated his interests in the land in favor of the plaintiff. The defendant later discovered that the Oregon judgment had terminated his title to the Oregon land. The defendant moved to set aside the judgment pursuant to Rule 60(b)(4) of the Federal Rules of Civil Procedure by contending that the judgment is void for lack of notice sufficient under due process. **Will he prevail?**

Explanation

The methods allowed under law for attempting to notify the defendant (publication and posting) were unlikely to give him actual notice. Because the plaintiff could have learned the address of the defendant with only minimal effort, she could have sent a copy of the process to the defendant by regular mail. That method of delivering information is inexpensive and much more efficient in providing interested parties actual notice.

Rules

(1) Because the court in Oregon deprived him of his property, that court must provide the defendant with due process. (2) In order to make a successful due process challenge to the judgment, the defendant must prove that the means allowed for delivery of process was seriously ineffective and that a feasible and more effective means existed.

Application

The use of publication or posting for delivering notice to interested parties is very unlikely, even when used together, to give those parties actual notice. Due process does not automatically invalidate the use of publication and posting however. If the interested parties could not be identified or located with due diligence, the Supreme Court in *Mullane* concluded that publication would be sufficient simply because no better means existed. The defendant must, therefore, first show that a more effective method of providing actual notice existed. The Court in *Mullane* held that the postal service could provide an effective means for delivering process. The mail also ordinarily would be an inexpensive means for serving persons whose name and address were known.

In this case, therefore, the only remaining question would be whether the plaintiff, with due diligence, could have identified the defendant as an interested party and have discovered his address. If that information appears in the local deed or tax records, the plaintiff could have obtained the information with only a little diligence. The fact that she did not suggests that she did not want to give notice. Whatever her motives, the law cannot allow the plaintiff to depend solely on publication and posting notice under these circumstances.

2. The State of Utah allows service on any defendant by leaving process with someone of suitable age and discretion in the defendant's "usual place of abode." A defendant seeks to set aside a default judgment entered against him because he contends that this service provision vio-

lates due process. He proved that, shortly before process was left at his home with his wife, she had learned of his affair with the couple's teenaged babysitter. She immediately banned him from the family home and had failed to inform him of the service. **Was this service constitutionally defective?**

Explanation

Assuming that neither the plaintiff nor the court knew of this failure of notice, the service would be constitutionally sufficient.

Rule

As the Supreme Court stated in *Jones v. Flowers*, the defendant does not have a constitutional right to actual notice under due process. Instead, due process merely requires the state court to use a method of delivering process that is likely to give the defendant actual notice.

Application

Delivery to a person of suitable age and discretion residing in the defendant's home is a reasonably efficient method by which to give him actual notice. This defendant failed to receive actual notice because of an unusual set of circumstances. Therefore, his experience does not indicate an inherent deficiency in the method of service. The defendant does not have a constitutional right to be served by the most efficient method of providing actual notice, which would be personal service. Serving this defendant by mail, an efficient and inexpensive alternative, was just as likely to deny him actual notice under these circumstances.

3. The tax assessor's office in Georgia sends tax delinquency notices to property owners by first-class mail. In 2004, that office mailed a tax delinquency notice to Jack Roe, the record owner of a rural tract of land. That notice was returned to the assessor's office with a notation from the postal service stating that it could not deliver the mail to Jack Roe because he did not maintain a mail box at that rural address. The assessor sent a further notice to Roe stating that his property would be sold at auction if he did not pay his delinquent taxes. That notice also was returned with the same notation showing that it was not delivered. The assessor's office sold Jack Roe's land at the tax sale auction. Roe has now brought suit to set aside the tax sale. **Was the mailed notice to Roe constitutionally insufficient?**

Explanation

Although serving a defendant with process through the mail is ordinarily a reasonably efficient method of giving actual notice, the state cannot proceed to deprive him of his property after it knows that he has not received of notice.

Rule

Because the state had knowledge that no actual notice had been given to Roe before it proceeded to terminate his property interest, its action was comparable to reliance on an inherently inefficient method of service. When the state has feasible and reliable alternative methods by which to deliver process, the existence of those alternatives prevents the state from relying on a method that has proved itself insufficient.

Application

This case differs from the previous one because in that instance the court had no reason to know the delivery method had failed to provide the defendant actual notice. It learned of this failure only after the tax sale had been completed. However, in *Jones v. Flowers*, the state sent process by certified mail, return receipt requested, and its letter was returned unclaimed each time. The state proceeded with the tax sale knowing that its delivery method had failed, and the Supreme Court held the sale invalid. The Court concluded that the state had not provided "notice reasonably calculated, under all the circumstances, to apprise interested parties of the pendency of the action." The tax sale was invalidated because, in addition to the state's knowledge that its letters had been returned, it could have taken reasonable additional steps that were likely to notify the defendant.

In this case, using first-class mail has failed to give the defendant notice, and the state knew of this failure before selling Roe's land. The state could have used one of the alternative methods of service that the Court mentioned approvingly in *Flowers*. It could have caused the notice of foreclosure to be posted on the fence, gate, or trees of the defendant's land. This posting would be likely to give him actual notice and allow him the opportunity to protect his interests in the property.

CHAPTER 10

DISCOVERY

A. Terminology

Deposition—An oral deposition allows the questioning of a witness or party under oath in front of a stenographer who produces a verbatim transcript of the proceeding. A deposition upon written questions requires the stenographer or other official to present written questions to the deponent and record his answers.

Interrogatories—These are written questions drafted by an attorney that can only be sent to another party. That party must serve written answers under oath or his objections to particular interrogatories within 30 days.

Opinion work product—The legal theories, notes, or plans of an attorney concerning the litigation cannot be obtained even with a showing of need. This privilege has also been called the absolute privilege or the attorney work product privilege.

Privilege—In discovery matters, a privilege provides either absolute or limited protection from demands for relevant information. The attorney-client privilege, for example, protects confidential communications by a client with his attorney. The divulgence of privileged matters to third parties waives the privilege.

Qualified work product—Documents or tangible things prepared in anticipation of litigation or trial by the attorney for one party need not be surrendered to another party unless that party has some special need and inability to obtain the same information.

Request for admission—A party may send another party requests that he admit the accuracy of statements made in the requests or the genuineness of documents attached to the requests.

Request for production—A party may demand that another party produce documents described and listed in the demand or that the party allow entry on or inspection of his land. A party can use a *subpoena duces tecum* to require a nonparty witness to bring documents to his deposition for inspection and copying.

B. OVERVIEW

1. Informal Discovery

Lawyers begin investigating their cases long before they use the power of a court to aid them in doing so. This informal discovery period occurs before the lawsuit is filed and the discovery rules are engaged. Before filing a complaint, the plaintiff's lawyer conducts a preliminary investigation to determine whether the facts justify alleging the proposed claim for relief. This preliminary investigation typically includes the gathering of evidence from friendly witnesses who are willing to divulge information. The defendant's lawyer usually knows of the plaintiff's proposed claim well before the complaint is filed. If not, service of the complaint informs the defendant of the nature of the claim. At this point, the defendant must engage in a preliminary investigation in order to file an answer.

Rule 11 of the Federal Rules of Civil Procedure requires that lawyers engage in a reasonable inquiry before filing pleadings in federal court. The inquiry must be sufficient to allow one signing a pleading to certify that its claims or defenses are warranted by law (or at least by a reasonable legal argument) and that the factual allegations have, or are likely to have, evidentiary support. Therefore, the preliminary investigation must be sufficient to permit a lawyer, through factual knowledge and legal research, to make at least an educated guess about the validity of a client's case.

2. Depositions before Suit or Pending Appeal

Rule 27 permits the taking of a deposition before commencing an action to perpetuate testimony. It allows such a deposition only upon order of the court and only by a person who expects to bring an action but is unable to do so. That person must file a verified petition including specific allegations showing that he expects to be a party to an action cognizable in a federal court. He must include a description of the subject matter of the expected action, the facts to be established by the proposed testimony and the reasons for desiring it, the names or a description of the persons he expects will be adverse parties and their addresses, and the names and addresses of the persons to be examined and the substance of the testimony to be elicited. These restrictions make sense when one considers the potential for harassment and the unfairness inherent in allowing unrestricted preaction discovery during the negotiation stages of a conflict.

Rule 27 also allows a deposition to acquire testimony pending appeal. This deposition may take place only after an appeal has been taken or before the time for taking an appeal has expired. The motion must show that the movant needs the deposition because the evidence may not exist later. Rule 27(b) does not control when one wishes to obtain a deposition to aid in collecting a judgment; instead, Rule 69(a) provides authority for the use of federal or state discovery rules to enable one to enforce a judgment.

C. Formal Discovery

1. Purposes

One pursues at least two legitimate objectives through formal discovery. First, a lawyer obtains evidence to use at trial or in response to the evidence of his opponent. That is the primary purpose of the discovery enterprise. Second, one needs to know what the opposing party and witnesses will say at trial to prepare for cross-examination and to prepare rebuttal evidence. In addition, by questioning witnesses one learns about their demeanor and its likely effect on the jury. Depositions also allow one to test the certainty of these witnesses through a detailed examination outside the jury's view.

The discovery rules facilitate enlightened decisions on the merits of the case and remove much of the sporting nature of litigation by preventing parties from hiding information until it can be used to surprise the other party at trial. Unfortunately, the liberality of the discovery rules also permits abuse, and some critics argue that discovery often operates largely as a tool for the harassment of opposing parties and witnesses. One also may encounter opposing lawyers who frustrate even legitimate inquiries, and their roadblocks require time-consuming and expensive efforts to carry out discovery procedures.

After the pleadings are closed, the parties begin the formal discovery phase. Formal discovery can begin when the court enters a scheduling order that describes the period during which discovery is to be completed. This order also sets the time within which the parties must disclose witnesses having discoverable information, relevant documents, computations of the requested damages, and any insurance agreements bearing on the alleged liability. Rule 26(f) requires parties to meet before the scheduling order is entered to decide when they will make these initial disclosures. After this first wave of disclosures, the parties must provide a detailed report of the testimony expected from expert witnesses. Shortly before trial, the parties provide each other, and the court, a list of all witnesses who will testify and of all documents or exhibits that will be presented at trial.

Disclosures reduce the amount and cost of discovery. Sometimes, the matter in controversy will not warrant extensive or expensive discovery, and the disclosure provisions may supply sufficient information for the parties to enter settlement negotiations or, if necessary, to try the case. A lawyer approaches the discovery phase of litigation knowing that he can force disclosure of information that is relevant to any potential issue in a case. However, even information relevant to the subject matter of the litigation can be protected from discovery by the assertion of privileges or by protective orders. The opposing party might, for example, refuse to disclose information because of the work product privilege of Rule 26(b)(3). Or, the opposing party might seek an order pursuant to Rule 26(c) to protect a trade secret or to limit discovery for other reasons.

2. Disclosures

Rule 26(a): Required Disclosures

(1) Initial Disclosures. Except [as] specified in Rule 26(a)(1)(E) or [as stipulated or ordered], a party must, without waiting for a discovery request, provide to other parties:

(A) [WITNESSES] the name and address of those having discoverable information that the disclosing party may use to support its claims or defenses, unless solely for impeachment, identifying the subjects of the information;

(B) [DOCUMENTS] a copy or description of all documents, data compilations, and tangible things that are in the control of the party and that the disclosing party may use to support its claims or defenses, unless solely for impeachment;

> [The initial disclosure obligation of subdivisions (a)(1)(A) and (B) has been narrowed to identification of witnesses and documents that the disclosing party may use to support its claims or defenses. "Use" includes any use at a pretrial conference, to support a motion, or at trial. The disclosure obligation is also triggered by intended use in discovery, apart from use to respond to a discovery request; use of a document to question a witness during a deposition is a common example. The disclosure obligation attaches both to witnesses and documents a party intends to use and also to witnesses and to documents the party intends to use if—in the language of Rule 26(a)(3)—"the need arises."
>
> A party is no longer obligated to disclose witnesses or documents, whether favorable or unfavorable, that it does not intend to use.]
>
> Fed.R.Civ.P. 26(a)(1), Advisory Committee note to 2000 amendment.

(C) [DAMAGES] a computation of damages claimed by the disclosing party, making available unprivileged evidentiary material on which a computation is based; and

(D) [INSURANCE] a copy of any insurance agreement by which an insurer may be liable to pay the judgment.

(E) [EXCEPTIONS] The following categories of proceedings are exempt from initial disclosure under Rule 26(a)(1): judicial review of an administrative record, habeas corpus or other challenges to criminal convictions, an action brought pro se, an action to quash an administrative summons or subpoena, an action by the US to recover benefit payments or to collect on a student loan, an ancillary proceeding, or an action to enforce an arbitration award.

(2) Disclosure of Expert Testimony.

(A) [TRIAL EXPERTS] A party shall identify all experts who may be used at trial.

(B) [EXPECTED TESTIMONY] If an expert is specially employed or regularly employed to provide expert testimony, a party shall provide a report signed by that expert describing his or her expected testimony and qualifications.

(C) [TIMING] Unless otherwise directed by the court, these disclosures are to be made at least 90 days before the trial date and, for rebuttal experts, within 30 days after the disclosure by the other party.

(3) Pretrial Disclosures. Except as to evidence that may be presented solely for impeachment purposes, a party must, at least 30 days before trial, provide the other parties the following information:

(A) [TRIAL WITNESSES] the name, address, and telephone number of each witness the party intends or may call;

(B) [DEPOSITION EVIDENCE] the designation of that testimony which will be presented by deposition and a copy of the pertinent parts of the deposition; and

(C) [EXHIBITS] the appropriate identification of each document or exhibit that the party expects to offer or may offer if the need arises.

(4) Form of Disclosures; Filing. All of the disclosures mentioned above shall ... served, and promptly filed.

3. Discovery Devices

If the disclosures are not sufficient, the parties can, during the designated discovery period, use the devices authorized in the discovery rules. These Rules and their provisions allow the following:

Depositions (Rules 30 and 31)

- may be taken of any party or nonparty witness (may request a nonparty witness to produce documents with a *subpoena duces tecum*),
- but no more than 10 depositions may be taken without leave of court, and
- a deposition is deemed to last one day of seven hours (running over means you're taking two depositions).

Interrogatories (Rule 33)

- may be sent only to another party,
- and consist of no more than 25 questions,
- to be answered under oath within 30 days.

Requests for Production or Inspection (Rule 34)

- may be made only to another party
- for inspection of land or for copying documents.

Mental or Physical Examination (Rule 35)

- may be taken only of another party or of someone within the custody and control of another party,
- and by leave of court, given when good cause exists for inquiring into that party's condition and when that condition is in controversy.

Requests for Admission (Rule 36)

- may be sent only to another party,
- and admissions can be used for the pending action only.

4. Discoverable Information in General

In general, the scope of party-controlled discovery includes any matter, not privileged, that is relevant to the claim or defense of any party, including the existence, description, nature, custody, condition, and location of any books, documents, or other tangible things and the identity and location of persons having knowledge of any discoverable matter. The scope of discovery can be expanded, if the court finds good cause to order discovery of any matter relevant to the subject matter involved in the action.

Relevant information need not be admissible at the trial if the discovery appears reasonably calculated to lead to the discovery of admissible evidence. For example, a plaintiff claiming personal racial discrimination might seek information about discrimination complaints in the same plant as evidence of a company policy. In order to be "relevant to" some fact, materials must tend to prove or disprove the existence of that fact. "Subject matter involved in the action" refers to claims or defenses other than those stated in the pleadings.

Rule 26(b)(1) allows each party to seek, as a matter of course, discovery of matters that are relevant to the disputed issues raised by the pleadings. Moreover, Rule 26(b)(1) provides that a party cannot validly object to discovery on the ground that the information will be inadmissible at trial if it "appears reasonably calculated to lead to the discovery of admissible evidence." This language distinguishes the relevance standard used for discovery from the relevance rules used to decide admissibility of evidence at trial. Although Rule 26(b)(1) permits discovery of any nonprivileged matter that is relevant to the claim or defense, information gathered through discovery does not automatically become admissible in evidence at trial. Rules 26–37 of the Federal Rules of Civil Procedure open the door for the gathering of information, but the restrictions imposed by the Federal Rules of Evidence limit the evidence and testimony that can be presented to the jury.

A district court has power under Rule 26(b)(1) to protect a deponent (one being deposed) from burdensome or harmful discovery requests. This Rule allows the court in which the case is pending, upon good cause shown, to issue a protective order where justice requires the protection of a party or person from "annoyance, embarrassment, oppression, or undue burden or expense." A party may make a motion for a protective order, or a non-party deponent may move to prevent the taking of a deposition. The court may act on its own initiative, after giving the parties reasonable notice, to prevent such abuses.

D. DISCOVERY PRIVILEGES

Analysis of the scope of discovery requires an understanding of the rules that restrict discovery. Privileges prevent a party from obtaining discovery of relevant information. The attorney-client privilege, the Fifth Amendment's privilege against self-incrimination, and state law privileges thus may prevent the gathering of helpful information. Also, Rule 26(b)(3) limits the discovery of the work product of a party and its attorney. Rule 26(b)(4) limits discovery from other parties' nontestifying experts, and Rule 35 requires court approval when one seeks a mental or physical examination.

1. The Attorney-Client Privilege

Federal courts protect the attorney-client privilege as a matter of federal common law when adjudicating federal claims.

> The privilege applies only if (1) the asserted holder of the privilege is or sought to become a client; (2) the person to whom the communication was made (a) is a member of the bar of a court, or his subordinate and (b) in connection with this communication is acting as a lawyer; (3) the communication relates to a fact of which the attorney was informed (a) by his client (b) without the presence of strangers (c) for the purpose of securing primarily either (i) an opinion on law or (ii) legal services or (iii) assistance in some legal proceeding, and not (d) for the purpose of committing a crime or tort; and (4) the privilege has been (a) claimed and (b) not waived by the client. The burden is on the proponent of the attorney-client privilege to demonstrate its applicability.

Hawkins v. Stables, 148 F.3d 379, 383 (4th Cir. 1998) (Citations omitted).

In Upjohn Co. v. U.S., 449 U.S. 383 (1981), the Supreme Court held in regard to a federal claim that when a corporation was the client for purposes of the attorney-client privilege, the privilege applied to the confidential communications of corporate employees beyond the executives or the "control group" that governed the corporation. As outlined by one federal court, the attorney-client privilege applies to current employees when their conversations:

> (1) were made to the corporate counsel, acting as such; (2) were made at the direction of corporate supervisors for the purpose of securing legal advise from counsel; (3) concerned matters within the scope of the employees' corporate duties; and (4) the employees were sufficiently aware that they were being questioned in order that the corporation could obtain legal advice.

U.S. ex rel. Hunt v. Merck-Medco Managed Care, LLC, 340 F.Supp.2d 554, 556–557 (E.D.Pa. 2004).

Although the attorney-client privilege extends beyond the control group of a corporation under the federal common law, the Supreme Court's common law rule applies only in federal court when the federal court is not adjudicating a state cause of action. Many state courts continue to limit the scope of the privilege to those executives who have the authority to control the operations of a corporation.

2. Work Product Immunity

The work product immunity from discovery protects the privacy of lawyers and other representatives of a litigant in preparing the case. This privilege protects the form of that preparation rather than information relevant to the issues. The papers developed through a lawyer's informal investigation thus may be protected, but the facts relevant to the issues that may be included in those papers are not. However, the surrendered "facts" cannot include the legal opinions and impressions of an attorney concerning the litigation because these are absolutely protected.

The privacy of an attorney's preparation helps to protect a client's interest in competent legal representation. A client does not, however, have a legitimate interest in obtaining legal advice in the furtherance of an ongoing criminal or fraudulent scheme. This "crime-fraud" exception to the attorney-client privilege applies as an exception to the work product immunity even when opinion work product is involved.

The work product immunity was first established by the Supreme Court in its decision in Hickman v. Taylor, 329 U.S. 495 (1947). In *Hickman*, the plaintiff demanded disclosure by the defendant's attorney of any written statements he had taken from witnesses to a tugboat accident. These witnesses were survivors of the accident in which the plaintiff's decedent had drowned, but they were available for depositions and had given testimony at a formal investigation shortly after the accident. In addition, the plaintiff demanded that the defendant's attorney write down his recollection of conversations with witnesses and supply any other memoranda he had prepared about the sinking of the tug.

The Court held that the defendant need not surrender the written statements taken by its attorney or supply the plaintiff with his recollections or with notes of his mental impressions of the case. The Court concluded that public policy required protection for an attorney's work done in preparation for litigation or for trial. If one could readily obtain such materials through the discovery rules, lawyers would avoid putting their mental impressions, plans, thoughts, or other work in writing to avoid having a less diligent opponent take the benefit of his preparation. Discovery would thus interfere with his obligation to provide diligent and competent legal representation to the public.

The privilege established in *Hickman* has been codified with some changes in Rule 26(b)(3) of the Federal Rules of Civil Procedure. The Rule provides differing degrees of protection for two types of work product. First is work product created through efforts to gather evidence in a case. The documents and tangible things prepared in this process are given only qualified protection. The second type of work product, opinion work product, includes the mental impressions, conclusions, opinions, or legal theories of an attorney or other representative of a party concerning the litigation. Courts give this latter type almost absolute protection.

3. Qualified Work Product Privilege

If discovery is requested for material relevant to the claims or defenses of the parties, a party may assert a qualified privilege against surrendering:

- documents and tangible things
- that were prepared in anticipation of litigation or for trial
- by or for a party or by or for a party's agent.

Such matters may be obtained only under the following circumstances:

- the discovering party has (1) a substantial need for the materials and (2) cannot by other means obtain a substantial equivalent without undue hardship, or
- the person who gave the statement is requesting a copy of it.

As stated above, there are three requirements for application of the qualified work product privilege. First, the privilege is restricted to documents and tangible things, and this restriction derives from the nature of the privilege itself. It protects what a lawyer has *produced*, rather than the facts he has discovered. A lawyer who prepares a case before suit by taking statements from witnesses and photographs of the accident scene should not be forced to surrender these products of his diligence once suit is filed.

On the other hand, the opposing lawyer must have access to relevant facts. The narrow scope of the privilege derives from the need to allow discovery of such factual information even though it may be contained in the work product of a lawyer. The protection for documents and tangible things therefore does not include the information a lawyer obtained even through great effort and expense. For example, a lawyer who uses his own efforts and money to discover an important eyewitness cannot use the work product privilege to prevent disclosure of that witness's identity.

The second requirement is that the qualified immunity applies only to documents and tangible things which were prepared for trial or for particular anticipated litigation. To prove that one prepared a document in anticipation of litigation, the party can show that he had information of a specific claim which would likely lead to litigation. Under these circumstances, a court looks for the primary motivation for the creation of the document. Was it created to prepare for impending litigation, or was it instead created in order, for example, to satisfy legal reporting requirements or for record keeping during the regular course of business? In other words, a document prepared in the normal operation of a business, though with an eye toward that business's liability, would not be prepared in anticipation of particular litigation.

The third requirement is that the document has been prepared by or for the party or by or for that party's representative. This broad definition of a representative includes insurers and others. Rule 26(b)(3) thereby expands the privilege beyond its origins in *Hickman* as solely a protection for material prepared by the party's attorney. This sensible expansion of the privilege recognizes that parties and their attorneys often call on others to help in the preparation of a case, and the purposes of the privilege are better served by protection of their products as well.

The protection does not prevent a client from obtaining access to documents prepared for litigation by his *own* attorney. Also, a party has an unqualified right to obtain a copy of a statement he gave to another party concerning the action. This right becomes understandable when a plaintiff has been interviewed by the defendant's insurer shortly after an accident and before the plaintiff hired an attorney. Even when the plaintiff can remember the accident and can give that information to his attorney, the statement itself stands as a critical piece of evidence that the plaintiff's attorney must have to properly evaluate and prepare his case.

Rule 26(b)(3) gives the same unqualified right to any person who has given a statement concerning the action to obtain a copy. Because of these provisions, a lawyer can obtain statements taken by his opponent from his own client, and of any potential witnesses who are sufficiently obliging to obtain their own statements and surrender them to him. We might note here that an attorney can never obtain the statements made by the opposing party to his own attorney because these would be protected by the attorney-client privilege rather than by the qualified work product privilege.

If the work product privilege does apply, the discovering attorney can still obtain the protected documents and tangible things by showing (1) a substantial need for the materials in the preparation of his case and (2) that he is unable, without undue hardship, to obtain a substantial equivalent by other means. This exception requires a court to decide that the policy reasons for the immunity are outweighed by the special need shown in a particular case. The court must, therefore, balance the need to protect the ability of attorneys to prepare their cases in private against the likelihood that serious damage could be done the opposing party by withholding the information from him.

"Substantial need" refers to the importance of the document in the litigation. A special need exists for surrender of documents when they contain information relevant to an essential issue. However, even critical evidence found within a statement does not justify its discovery if the discovering attorney could obtain that information by taking a deposition or through other means. Most frequently, therefore, the exception turns on the ability of the discovering party to obtain a substantial equivalent by other means.

The qualified work product privilege works in the following manner. If, for example, the only eyewitness to an accident has given a written statement to the defendant's lawyer, the plaintiff cannot force the defendant to surrender the statement merely to avoid the cost of taking the witness's deposition. But if that witness's memory faltered or he became uncooperative during his deposition by the plaintiff, the plaintiff's own efforts at preparation could not provide information equivalent to that contained in the written statement. In this situation, the plaintiff can overcome the privilege because these circumstances, rather than his lack of diligence, prevent him from obtaining the information. In addition, he would have a substantial and legitimate need for the eyewitness's account of the events giving rise to his client's case.

4. Opinion Work Product Immunity

Even where a party shows a need sufficient to overcome the qualified work product privilege, and thus obtains a document or an item, the court remains bound by the absolute strictures of Rule 26(b)(3) which protect against disclosure of the "mental impressions, conclusions, opinions, or legal theories of an attorney or other representative of a party concerning the litigation." In addition, courts have even held that an attorney's decisions in selecting or compiling the documents he has prepared represents his mental theories or strategy and is protected under this immunity. Courts protect opinion work product because such matters would rarely contain relevant factual material which could not be gained by other means. In addition, even the value of having those facts available in the judicial process is clearly outweighed by the interest in allowing an attorney to engage in unhindered preparation, especially as he attempts to understand the case in light of the applicable law and design a strategy for presenting that case at trial.

5. Experts

a. Overview

Modern litigation often concerns matters which require the assistance of experts in medicine, technology, or other scientific fields. In preparing cases, therefore, lawyers need to consult experts in order to understand technical issues and to present relevant evidence in an understandable and persuasive form. Lawyers employ experts to prepare reports, to do original research, or to give advice. These consultations thus become a crucial part of one's preparation for litigation and for trial. Unrestricted discovery of this preparation would allow an opponent to uncover the process of thought by which a diligent lawyer prepared his case.

The discovering party typically acquires information from deponents without paying them for their time. However, the party who hires an expert typically pays her for the time she spends in reviewing the case, in reaching conclusions, and in preparing reports. Therefore, the ordinary operation of the discovery rules would allow the other side to acquire, for free, information created at the expense of the other side. Unlimited discovery would also deter experts from participating in litigation because they would risk being called to respond, without compensation, to the deposition requests of all parties.

A lawyer's thorough preparation may also include consultation with multiple experts. Some of these experts will have unfavorable opinions. These opinions, if readily available to the opposing side, could prove very troublesome to a party, and the availability of such information would punish the most thorough and diligent while rewarding the less vigorous. Furthermore, even if the array of experts consulted by an attorney does not contain one with unfavorable opinions, his choice of experts to consult discloses his impressions of a case and elements of his plan for presenting it.

On the other hand, expert testimony can be extremely influential with a jury. Jurors naturally defer to a highly qualified expert on complex technical matters. To prevent a persuasive expert from overpowering a jury, a lawyer must have sufficient prior knowledge of her testimony to prepare an adequate cross-examination. Such preparation is all the more important because the expert may be discussing material beyond the lawyer's knowledge. Therefore, he must be warned of the substance of an opposing expert's direct testimony in order first to understand its effect and basis, and to formulate questions which challenge that expert's opinions. In addition, a lawyer must have information about an expert's credentials in order to place that person's abilities in a realistic context. Before such a cross-examination can be prepared, one must have complete and detailed information about the expert, her credentials, her opinions, and the grounds for those opinions.

Rule 26(b)(4) controls discovery of experts according to their function in a particular litigation. It requires surrender of a detailed report by, and allows free discovery of, an expert who will be called to testify at trial. However, the Rule severely restricts discovery of experts who were hired as consultants for preparation of a suit but who will not be witnesses at trial. In making this distinction, the Rule strikes a balance between the need to protect the privacy of an attorney's preparation through the use of consultants and the need for effective cross-examination of experts who will present evidence at trial.

b. Summary

i. Testifying Experts

(1) **Disclosures**—Rule 26(a)(2) requires the disclosure of the identity of any expert a party intends to call at trial. If that expert is "retained or specially employed to provide expert testimony" at trial, she must prepare a written report containing the information outlined in Rule 26(a)(2)(B). [Note: A treating physician might be called to give her expert testimony about the plaintiff's condition, but she need not prepare a report because she was retained for medical treatment not for purposes of being a trial expert. She would be called as a fact witness even though she is an expert in her field.]

(2) **Discovery:** A party can depose any specially retained testifying expert after receiving the report required by Rule 26(a)(2)(B). In general, neither the qualified nor the unqualified work product privilege applies to this report.

ii. Nontestifying Experts

A party generally cannot depose those specially retained experts that another party does not intend to call for testimony at trial. The two exceptions to this rule are:

- the request for a report prepared pursuant to Rule 35(b) (having to do with the exchange of reports by those who examine the mental or physical conditions of parties), or
- upon a showing of "exceptional circumstances under which it is impracticable for the party seeking discovery to obtain facts or opinions on the same subject by other means."

a. Testifying Experts

Rule 26(a)(2) requires disclosure, without express demand, of the identify of all testifying experts. An expert who is specially employed to testify or who is an employee of a party who regularly gives expert testimony must submit a report stating her expert opinions and the reasons therefor. One who is qualified to be an expert but who derived her information because she was an actor or viewer of the events giving rise to the lawsuit does not have to provide a report under this section.

The report required of specially or generally employed testifying experts must provide an elaboration of the expert's expected testimony and the reasons for the opinions she has reached. The report also must include the expert's qualifications and a list of the cases in which she has been a witness or a deponent within the previous four years. One benefit of the expert's detailed report is that it may allow an opposing party to avoid taking that expert's deposition. An opposing party can rely on the detailed nature of the report because Rule 37(c)(1) prevents the use at trial of evidence which has been omitted from the report. Under Rule 26(b)(4)(C), a party seeking discovery from an expert must pay her a reasonable fee for her time spent in responding, and these fees may be considerable. If a report contains information sufficient to allow the preparation of cross-examination, the opposing party can forego a deposition and avoid this expense. In order to allow lawyers to make this choice, Rule 26 requires service of the original report no later than 90 days before trial.

Rule 26(b)(4)(A) states that a party may depose any testifying expert, and that this deposition shall not be conducted until after delivery of a report required by Rule 26(a)(2)(B). The Rule speaks only of depositions because these (oral or written) are the only discovery devices ordinarily available for use against non-party witnesses. In taking a testifying expert's deposition, the qualified work product privilege and attorney opinion work product immunity would not be a barrier. Rule 26(b)(3) states that the work product protection described therein is "[s]ubject to the provisions" regulating the discovery of experts [subdivision (b)(4)]. This language prevents the use of the qualified work product privilege to block discovery of testifying experts. Most of the recent decisions have also refused to protect the impressions and opinions about the case which attorneys have communicated to testifying experts. The Advisory Committee Notes to the 1993 amendments to Rule 26 indicate that such material must be included in the testifying expert's report and, presumably, would be available in that expert's deposition.

b. Nontestifying Experts

Rule 26(b)(4)(B) restricts discovery of facts known or opinions held by an expert who has been retained or specially employed by another party in anticipation of litigation or preparation for trial and who is not expected to be called as a witness at trial. Discovery of these nontestifying experts may be obtained only when allowed under Rule 35(b) (having to do with the exchange of reports by those who examine the mental or physical conditions of parties) or where *exceptional circumstances* are shown. Courts have extended this shield against discovery to informally consulted experts. For example, if after learning of litigation or its prospect a party consults an expert but does not retain her, the same policies against disclosure would apply. Furthermore, courts have held that a party may not even discover the identity of a specially employed, nontestifying expert absent a showing of exceptional circumstances.

Courts impose a heavy burden on a discovering party seeking to show exceptional circumstances sufficient to obtain discovery of a nontestifying expert. To make the requisite showing, a discovering party must prove that the information he seeks is not only relevant but important to the case and that he would otherwise be unable to obtain a substantial equivalent. Courts require the discovering party to show that the object or condition observed or investigated by the nontestifying expert can no longer be observed because of significant changes or alterations. Assume the defendant's nontestifying expert had, shortly after an accident, observed the area in which an injury occurred. By the time the plaintiff's expert could views the site, weather conditions have substantially changed it. Under these circumstances, critical information about the site can no longer be obtained by the plaintiff regardless of his effort, and that information would rest solely in the hands of the defendant.

However, even in the absence of exceptional circumstances, a party can obtain a nontestifying expert's report if it is to be used as the basis for a testifying expert's opinion. In this situation, the policies favoring full disclosure of information necessary for cross-examination, rather than those supporting attorney privacy, require disclosure.

If an academic engages in research independent of anticipated litigation and on her own initiative but in areas of interest to parties in a suit, she can be deposed. Rule 26(b)(4)(B) does not restrict discovery except of those experts who are retained or specially employed by a party in anticipation of litigation or in preparation for trial. Ordinarily, this academic could be deposed without payment of compensation for her time. In recognition that discovery requests may cause serious burdens for independent researchers, Rule 45 gives a court power to quash or modify any subpoena that requires disclosure of an unretained expert's opinions when those were not developed in respect to the events giving rise to the claim. If the discovering party shows a substantial need and inability to obtain the unretained expert's information, the court may allow a deposition when the discovering party agrees to pay the expert for her time.

Rule 26(b)(4)(C) states that, unless manifest injustice would result, the discovering party must pay any retained expert a reasonable fee for the time spent in responding to discovery. When discovery is obtained from a nontestifying expert, the court shall order the discovering party to pay an additional fee representing a fair portion of the expenses incurred by an opponent in obtaining the expert's facts and opinions. It should be noted that these requirements for compensation apply only to testifying experts and to specially employed, nontestifying experts.

Persons who are experts in their field but who have not been retained in anticipation of litigation have no right to demand compensation for their time. And, Rule 45 provides protection only for unretained experts whose opinions do not arise from the specific events in dispute and which result from a study not made at any party's request. Therefore, the physician who treated the plaintiff shortly after his accident could not demand payment for her time in responding to discovery. As a practical matter, however, such experts tend to be more forthcoming if compensated.

6. Other Privileges

Rule 26(b)(1) of the Federal Rules of Civil Procedure makes clear that discovery may be had only of matter "not privileged." Laws other than the Federal Rules of Civil Procedure provide privileges which allow a party to object to requests for otherwise discoverable material. In describing the applicable rules of privilege, Federal Rule of Evidence 501 states:

> Except as otherwise required by the Constitution of the United States or provided by Act of Congress or in rules prescribed by the Supreme Court pursuant to statutory authority, the privilege of a witness, person, government, State, or political subdivision thereof shall be governed by the principles of the common law as they may be interpreted by the courts of the United States in the light of reason and experience. However, in civil actions and proceedings, with respect to an element of a claim or defense as to which State law supplies the rule of decision, the privilege of a witness, person, government, State, or political subdivision thereof shall be determined in accordance with State law.

In addition, Rule 1101 of the Federal Rules of Evidence states that the "rule with respect to privileges applies at all stages of all actions, cases, and proceedings."

Rule 501 begins by providing for the application in federal court of any privilege established by the United States Constitution, regardless of whether state law otherwise supplies the rule of decision. The best known constitutional privilege is that provided by the Fifth Amendment protecting one from self-incrimination. This privilege, though most significant in criminal prosecutions, is also applicable in civil cases. If testimony would provide the "link in the chain" establishing a person's guilt of a crime, that person may refuse to provide testimony when requested in the discovery stage of a civil action. When interrogatories are sent to a corporation, however, the corporation must designate someone to answer them who does not fear self-incrimination. In a civil case, unlike a criminal case, an adverse inference may be drawn against one who asserts the privilege.

When the parties have asserted state law claims for relief in federal court, the privileges recognized by the law of the forum state may also be asserted with respect to any element of that claim or its state law defenses. Most frequently this means that state law determines the existence of a privilege in a diversity case. In nondiversity cases, where the information sought is relevant both to a federal claim and to a supplemental state claim, the courts have generally held that Rule 501 does not require the application of state privilege law. In some instances, the law of a state, other than the one in which the federal court is located, may supply the claim for relief. Federal courts decide which state supplies the claim, and therefore the available privileges, by applying the choice of law rules of the forum state.

E. ORAL DEPOSITIONS

An oral deposition is often the most important discovery device an attorney will use in the preparation of a case. Depositions also play a major role in the settlement of cases. Although in federal court depositions generally may not be used at trial for the presentation of one's case in chief, they will often prove invaluable in determining what the opposing side will say at trial and what the opposing legal contentions are. They also provide a means whereby an attorney can observe the demeanor of a witness, and through the trial-like examination in a deposition one can also press an equivocating adverse witness to take a definite position.

1. Procedure

Rule 30 of the Federal Rules of Civil Procedure allows an oral deposition to be taken of any party or of a person who is not a party. A deposition may be taken without permission of the court unless the proposed deposition results in more than 10 oral or written depositions by that side or is the second deposition of the proposed deponent. A party formally calls a deposition by serving notice of the deposition on all other parties. The notice must precede, by a reasonable period, the time called for the deposition and include information about the location and the person or persons to be deposed. Notice must be given to all parties even though the deposition is of a nonparty, and all parties may be present at a deposition. As an alternative, the parties may arrange depositions by agreement as is allowed under Rule 29.

If the notice calls for the deposition of a party, service of the notice requires that party's attendance because Rule 37 imposes sanctions on a party who, having received a notice of his deposition, fails to attend. In addition, a party taking the deposition of another party can require that party to bring documents and tangible things to the deposition for review and copying by including in the notice a demand pursuant to Rule 34. If the proposed deponent is not a party to the action, the deposing party must serve that deponent with a subpoena pursuant to Rule 45. "Subpoena" is a Latin word which means under (sub) punishment (poena), and is a document issued by the court of the district in which the person is required to attend a trial or a deposition. A person must attend as required or risk being held in contempt of court. A subpoena duces tecum is a court order requiring the person to bring documents or tangible things with him.

A subpoena can be quashed if it requires a non-party deponent to travel to a place more than 100 miles from his residence or place of business. Also, Rule 45 states that a person commanded to appear by subpoena must be given the fees for one day's attendance and the mileage allowed by law. If the deposition of a non-party deponent cannot be held in the district in which the action is pending—because the deponent cannot be served with a subpoena there— the deposition can be held in the district where he resides. Rule 45 authorizes the issuance of a subpoena by the court of that district. Another procedure which might prove helpful under these circumstances is a telephonic deposition allowed by Rule 30 if the parties agree in writing or the court so orders.

Typically, depositions are taken by stenographic means. This usually means that a court reporter or other stenographer must be hired to sit in on the deposition, to administer the oath to the deponent, and then to transcribe in verbatim form what is said. The use of a court reporter accounts for a substantial portion of the expense of oral depositions. Rule 30 authorizes the deposing party to specify in his notice that the deposition will be taken by tape recording or videotaping. Any other party can, with prior notice and at his expense, use another method for recording the deponent's testimony in addition to the method chosen by the deposing party.

During an oral deposition, the parties engage in examination and cross-examination as they would at trial. All objections made during the examination should be noted, but the testimony of the deponent is to be taken even though there are objections to its admissibility under the Federal Rules of Evidence. Rule 32 provides that objections to the competency of a witness or to the competency, relevancy, or materiality of testimony need not be asserted, and are not waived, if not made during a deposition unless the ground for the objection could have been removed with a timely objection.

A privilege or an immunity from discovery must be asserted or it is waived by disclosure during a deposition. Therefore, a lawyer representing the deponent must object on the basis of privilege during a deposition and instruct the party not to answer those questions which would elicit privileged information. If a deposition is being conducted in bad faith or for the purpose of harassment, a lawyer may halt it in order to make a motion to terminate or limit the examination. On the other hand, if the deponent fails or refuses to answer the questions presented, the deposing party may either adjourn or complete the deposition and then move for an order compelling an answer under Rule 37.

2. Use at Trial

In federal practice the use of oral depositions at trial is limited, reflecting the preference of federal courts for live testimony. There are two tests to be applied in determining whether a deposition may be used at trial. First, the provisions of Rule 32(a) of the Federal Rules of Civil procedure must be consulted. Second, any deposition testimony allowed to be used by Rule 32 must be admissible under the Federal Rules of Evidence applied as though the deponent were then present and testifying.

Rule 32 allows a deposition to be used only against a party who was present or represented at its taking or who had reasonable notice thereof. A deposition of a party may be used at trial by an adverse party for any purpose. If the deposition is of a non-party deponent, the deposition can be used at trial for purposes of contradicting or impeaching the testimony of that deponent. Otherwise, that person's deposition may be used only if, in accordance with Rule 32(a)(3), the deponent is truly unavailable to attend the trial.

The presentation of testimony by deposition is not excludable hearsay simply because of the absence of the deponent, but if the deponent presented hearsay testimony in his answers, the admissibility of this evidence must be judged according to the Federal Rules of Evidence "as though the [deponent] were then present and testifying."

F. Discovery by Written Questions

1. Deposition upon Written Questions

Rule 31 authorizes a deposition upon written questions of a party or of a person who is not a party. A deposition upon written questions can be taken without first seeking leave of court unless that deposition results in more than 10 oral or written depositions by one side. In addition, leave of court must be obtained if the deposition is to be taken of a person who has already been deposed. The attendance of non-party witnesses can be compelled by the use of a subpoena as provided in Rule 45.

To begin the process, the discovering party must serve all parties with the written questions to be propounded and a notice stating the name and address of the person to be deposed and the name and address of the court reporter who will take the answers. Within 14 days after this service, an opposing party must serve all parties with the written cross questions he wishes the court reporter to ask. The deposing party may, within 7 days after receiving those questions, serve further written questions on all parties. Within 7 days of being served with these questions the opposing party may serve re-cross questions. Once this procedure is completed, the court reporter takes the questions to the place for the deposition and records the responses of the deponent.

Elaboration of this laborious procedure may indicate why a deposition upon written questions is not one of the more popular discovery devices. Another disadvantage arises because redirect questions must be formulated before the discovering party hears the deponent's answers. The procedure provides no effective means of addressing evasive or nonresponsive answers. Depositions upon written questions do, however, provide a less expensive means of deposing witnesses located in distant places, and they are adequate for obtaining specific facts.

2. Interrogatories to Parties

Interrogatories (written questions) provide a much simpler method for seeking information about a case. However, interrogatories can only be sent to a party in the suit; only oral and written depositions can be used to obtain discovery from persons who are not parties. Rule 33 allows a party to send up to 25 interrogatories to any other party without leave of court. They may be sent with service of process or served on the plaintiff at any time. The party on whom they are served must respond within 30 days, and the responses must include either answers under oath, or objections, accompanied by an explanation of the grounds therefor.

The major advantage of interrogatories is that they provide an inexpensive means of seeking information from other parties. The answers to interrogatories may also narrow the issues or add detail to generalized allegations in the pleadings. An interrogatory, therefore, is not objectionable merely because it calls for an "opinion or contention that relates to fact or the application of law to fact." As a result, a party cannot object to interrogatories merely because they call for factual responses fraught with legal significance.

Interrogatories are answered by the party to whom they are addressed and not by an attorney, but objections are to be signed by the attorney making them. A party answering the interrogatories should not be required to perform extensive research or to obtain information from documents not within his control. If an answer may be derived from business records and the burden of deriving that answer is substantially the same for the discovering and the interrogated party, the interrogated party can specify the records and provide the discovering party a reasonable opportunity to inspect and copy them. This specification must, however, be sufficiently detailed.

3. Requests for Admissions

Requests seeking admissions of the truth of discoverable matter, or of the genuineness of any document, may be sent to any party. Rule 36 allows requests to be directed without leave of court to the plaintiff at any time or to any defending party with or after service of process on him. A party must respond to a request for admissions within 30 days. The responses need not be under oath but must be signed by either the responding party or his attorney. Form 25 of the forms appended to the Federal Rules of Civil Procedure indicates that the requests may be simple and straightforward. They may, for example, ask whether each of the documents attached, named by number or other designation, is genuine and whether each statement listed is true. Thus, the requests can leave little room for evasion or ambiguity (although little room may be all some responding attorneys need).

Rule 36 only allows requests in regard to matters within the scope of Rule 26(b) (discovery of any matter relevant to the subject matter that is not privileged). The admissions obtained in response to the requests can be used only in the pending action and not in any other proceeding. This restriction prevents using the privilege against self-incrimination as an objection to a request for admission, although the courts have allowed this objection anyway.

A response to a request for admissions may contain objections to the requests. In addition to objecting, the responding party may admit, deny, or state why he cannot admit or deny a request. Any matter admitted is conclusively established for the pending action, but the court may permit amendment or withdrawal of an admission when such serves the presentation of the merits and does not prejudice the requesting party. A denial must fairly and specifically meet the substance of a request or of that part which is denied. The responding party may claim an inability to admit or deny a request if he also states that he has made a reasonable inquiry and that the information known or readily available to him is insufficient.

If a party fails to respond within 30 days and does not request an extension, a request is deemed admitted. The requesting party has no obligation to file a motion to cause this effect. If, on the other hand, a party responds with objections or insufficient answers, the requesting party is authorized by the last paragraph of Rule 36(a) to move to determine the sufficiency of these responses and, if the responses are found to be unjustified, may receive an award for the expenses incurred in bringing that motion. A court may either order an answer or that the matter be deemed admitted. Should a party deny a request for admission and the requesting party successfully prove that matter at trial, the court may, upon motion pursuant to Rule 37(c)(2), require the answering party to pay the requesting party the reasonable expenses incurred in making this proof.

G. REQUESTS FOR INSPECTION OF LAND OR DOCUMENTS

Rule 34 of the Federal Rules of Civil Procedure allows any party, without leave of court, to serve on any other party a request for the production of documentary material, or for entry upon designated land or other property for the purpose of inspection. The request may be served upon the plaintiff after commencement of an action and upon any defending party with or after service of process. Proper requests need only be in accordance with the scope of discovery set out in Rule 26(b).

The documents requested for inspection and copying may include data compilations, such as computerized information, which the producing party may be required to translate into reasonably usable form. The requested document must be in the "possession, custody or control of the party upon whom the request is served." A party ordinarily has sufficient control if, under the circumstances, it is reasonable to expect that he could obtain the document if he wished to do so. For example, a corporation can be required to obtain documents in the possession of former employees who are receiving compensation from the corporation. The fact that documents are in a foreign country is not an excuse for failing to produce them, and the court may even require a party to seek release of documents whose confidentiality is protected by the criminal laws of a foreign country.

A request made pursuant to Rule 34 must describe each item with reasonable particularity. Courts typically require the designation be such that the producing party can reasonably identify the documents by their description. The party upon whom a request is served must, within 30 days, serve a written response including as to each item either a statement that inspection will be permitted or an objection.

If no written response is timely served, the requesting party may seek the imposition of the sanctions available under Rule 37, along with expenses for bringing the motion. In this fashion, the more flagrant disobedience of Rule 34 — the failure even to respond — is punished quickly. A requesting party who receives a response but one he believes is inadequate must first seek a court order demanding an adequate response. If that order is disobeyed, the more severe sanctions of Rule 37 can be imposed.

H. Physical or Mental Examinations

Rule 35 of the Federal Rules of Civil Procedure gives a federal court power to order a physical or mental examination, including a blood test, of a party or of a person in the custody or control of a party. This Rule is valid and controlling in federal court even when the action is based on diversity jurisdiction and is inconsistent with state law. It applies to examinations of defendants as well as of plaintiffs, and a party may seek another's examination even if the two are not opposing parties.

Rule 35 is the only discovery rule which requires an order of court. A party seeking to compel another party to submit to an examination must file and serve a motion showing, with reasonable particularity, that the mental or physical condition of that party is "in controversy" and that there is "good cause" for the examination. Parties can avoid being ordered by the court by entering written stipulations, as authorized by Rule 29, to provide their clients for examination. In addition to avoiding the trouble and cost of responding to the motion, they can secure the opposing party's agreement to furnish his party for examination.

If decision of a substantive issue in the action may be directly affected by the physical or mental condition of a party, that condition would be in controversy. Often this determination can be made from the pleadings. If the plaintiff in a negligence case seeks damages for a continuing injury, for example, that condition is in controversy. A defendant who asserts his mental or physical condition as a defense thereby places that condition in controversy. When the pleadings do not suffice, there must be an affirmative and specific showing in the motion that the condition is in controversy. If a plaintiff sued a bus company and its driver for her injuries incurred in a bus accident, she might have some evidence that the driver had a history of vision problems. She would need something specific to justify this examination because the bus driver's condition would not be in controversy because of the pleadings.

The in-controversy and good-cause requirements are closely related in that they both refer to the legitimate need, in a particular case, for the examination requested. However, good cause may not be shown, even though the condition is in controversy, if adequate alternate means are available for obtaining the same information. If a party has access to a recent examination of the opposing party's condition, a court might view a request for another examination as harassment.

When the condition of a non-party is in controversy, a court for good cause shown may order the examination of that person if he is in the custody or under the legal control of a party. Examination of non-parties has been permitted where a parent or guardian sues for injuries caused a child, but a family relationship is not sufficient if the party does not have legal control of the person to be examined.

Suppose a plaintiff sues seeking damages for a spinal injury and is ordered to appear for an examination by a physician chosen by the defendant. The plaintiff will ordinarily want a copy of the report that physician subsequently provides the defendant. And Rule 35(b)(1) gives her the right to obtain copies of the reports, test results, diagnoses, or conclusions made from the examination. However, if the plaintiff requests and obtains a report of the defendant's examination of her spinal injury, she must supply the defendant any reports she possesses which were made from examinations of the same condition. Furthermore, by obtaining the report from the defendant, the plaintiff waives any privilege she might have to the testimony of doctors who have examined or will examine her in respect to the same condition. Rule 35(b)(3) provides for the application of these provisions even when the examination is taken according to an agreement rather than by court order, *unless* the agreement expressly provides otherwise.

I. Sanctions

1. Summary

a. Requesting and Responding Attorneys

Rule 26(g) requires the certificate of an attorney in regard to all discovery and disclosure documents delivered to other parties. This requirement substitutes for the Rule 11 certificate, which does not apply to discovery documents. (1) Certificate: An attorney of record must sign every disclosure, request, response, or objection made in regard to a discovery or disclosure document. This signature certifies that a disclosure is complete and correct or that any request, response, or objection is:

- consistent with the Rules and existing law, or a good faith argument for modification;
- not interposed for an improper purpose; and
- not unreasonably expensive or burdensome given the
  — needs of the case,
  — discovery already done,
  — amount in controversy, or
  — importance of the issues.

(2) Sanctions: If the certificate is made without sufficient justification, a court by motion of a party or on its own initiative,

- shall impose
- an appropriate sanction, which may include
  —reasonable expenses caused by violation
  —including attorney's fees.

b. Responding Attorneys

Rule 37 generally provides a two-step process for those who fail to respond as required under the discovery rules. (1) The discovering party must move for an order to compel an adequate response. (2) If that order is violated, the court may impose the sanctions listed in Rule 37(b)(2)(A)–(E). A lawyer who could respond to a court's order but fails to do so deliberately makes his case vulnerable to dismissal or the entry of judgment. See Creative Gifts, Inc. v. UFO, 235 F.3d 540, 549 (10th Cir. 2000). In three instances, the blatant refusal to comply with the Rules can lead to the immediate imposition of sanctions [Rule 37(d)] such as when a party:

- fails to appear for his own deposition after service of notice,
- fails to respond to interrogatories (answers or objections), or
- fails to respond after proper service of a request for inspection.

Also, the failure to respond to a request for admissions means that the requests have been admitted. See Rule 36(a).

c. Disclosures, Responses, or Supplements

Rule 37(c) punishes one who makes an incomplete or incorrect disclosure or response by preventing the use of that evidence or witness. If a party is hiding negative information that he wouldn't use at trial, the court may, upon motion, impose other reasonable sanctions including those listed in Rule 37(b)(2)(A)–(C).

2. Procedure

Rule 37 of the Federal Rules of Civil Procedure is the exclusive authority in the Rules for the imposition of sanctions for violation of the discovery rules. Because all but one of the discovery methods can be used without seeking leave of court, the first step in curing a violation of the discovery rules ordinarily is to seek an order of the court compelling compliance. Even at this point, the discovering party can recover his expenses, including attorney's fees, incurred in obtaining the order. Should the recalcitrant party fail to obey an order of the court, the discovering party must then bring a motion for the imposition of the sanctions authorized by Rule 37(b)(2).

If a non-party deponent fails to answer a question at his deposition, the procedure is essentially the same except only the sanction of contempt is appropriate. These motions would ordinarily be made to the court in which the action is pending. However, if a deposition is taken in a district other than where the action is pending, the motions in regard to a non-party deponent must be made to that district court. If the deponent is a party, the motion may also be to the court of the district in which the action is pending.

There are, however, important exceptions to the general scheme for imposing sanctions. Rule 35 requires an order of the court before a physical or mental examination. Rule 37(b)(2) therefore allows the court to impose sanctions for a violation of that order. Rule 37(d) also allows the court to impose sanctions for especially egregious violations of the discovery rules without waiting for the disobedience of an order. These consist of the failure of a party or a person designated by a corporate party to appear for his deposition after being properly served with notice, failure to respond to interrogatories, or failure to serve a written response to a request for production of documents or inspection of land. Under these circumstances, the court may decide to impose one or more of the sanctions listed in Rule 37(b)(2) as may be appropriate. In addition to or in lieu of these sanctions, the court may order the payment by the recalcitrant party or his attorney of any expenses, including attorney's fees, incurred by the discovering party in bringing the motion to impose sanctions.

The sanctions listed in Rule 37(b)(2) include an order striking the pleadings or entering a dismissal or default thereby ending the case, an order that certain designated matters or facts shall be deemed established as claimed by the discovering party, or an order refusing to allow the recalcitrant to support or oppose designated claims or defenses. In addition to or in lieu of these sanctions, the court may hold the recalcitrant party in contempt. Rule 37(b)(2)(D) states, however, that a party or person who fails to submit to an ordered physical or mental examination may not be held in contempt. Any of the other sanctions may, however, be imposed if justified.

Appellate courts will reverse a trial judge's imposition of Rule 37 sanctions only for an abuse of discretion. The general policy of Rule 37 supports the imposition of a sanction as needed to deter similar action in other cases, and this in-terrorem effect operates to justify penalties imposed by a court. In some circumstances, however, a sanction which effectively terminated the action would violate the Due Process Clause. That would be the case when, for example, that severe sanction is imposed on one whose noncompliance with a discovery order was caused by his inability and not by willfulness, bad faith, or fault. For example, a party prevented by the government of another country from delivering papers in accordance with a court's order should not be punished by dismissal if he, in good faith, tried to comply.

J. Hypotheticals and Explanations

1. After a river ferry sank killing dozens of people in Minnesota, the estates of those killed brought a wrongful death action in federal court against the owner of the ferry, Ferry Boat, Inc., a Delaware corporation with its principal place of business in Florida. Ferry Boat's lawyer, Jack Diamond, claims that bad weather caused the sinking, and he has hired Harry Bosch to investigate the accident. At a cost of $12,000 in investigation fees, Bosch discovered that a retired sea captain, who lives near the river, witnessed the accident. However, the captain told Diamond an explo-

sion caused the ferry to sink and that the explosion most likely resulted from poor maintenance of the ferry's engine. The captain gave Diamond a written and signed statement that included his observations and his opinions. Ferry Boat has also turned over to Diamond the maintenance records of the ferry for the year immediately prior to the sinking. **Does the work-product privilege allow Diamond to refuse to divulge the sea captain's name or to surrender his statement or the maintenance records?**

Explanation

The work-product privilege protects the captain's statement but not his identity or the maintenance records.

Rule

(1) The qualified work product privilege covers documents and tangible things that were prepared in anticipation of litigation or for trial by or for a party or by or for a party's agent. (2) Even work product can be obtained if the discovering party has a substantial need for the materials and cannot by other means obtain a substantial equivalent without undue hardship, or the person who gave the statement is requesting a copy of it.

Application

The privilege covers the captain's statement because it is a document prepared for trial by the defendant's attorney. The plaintiffs have no substantial need for or inability to acquire a substantial equivalent of the statement because they can depose the captain and obtain the information given to Diamond. The identity of the captain is not work product because, though the defendant's attorney and his investigator had to expend energy and money to discover the captain, his identity is not their creation—it is not either a document or a tangible thing that they produced. The work product privilege protects that which an attorney creates in preparing his case; it does not protect facts that he learns. Please note that under the 2000 amendment, the defendant is not required to disclose the name of the captain if it does not plan to use him as a witness in any manner. Because his opinion seems unfavorable to the defendant, it would not plan to use him for any reason. Nevertheless, the plaintiffs can demand through interrogatories the name and address of any eyewitnesses to the accident, and the captain's identity would not be privileged.

The maintenance records of the ferry may well be contained on documents that were created by the defendant, but they were not created in anticipation of this litigation. These records were created in the regular course of business, and are therefore not work product. They represent evidence that, in this case, could well prove the negligence of the defendant. And the facts contained in these records may not be available from any other source.

2. Immediately after a serious train accident, Howard Pratt and his assistant rushed to the scene and took written statements from all six railroad employees on the train. His assistant wrote these statements while Mr. Pratt interviewed the six in a group and in the presence of several uninjured passengers. Mr. Pratt was acting as the lawyer for Union Pacific, the owner of the train, and was gathering evidence to be used in any litigation that might arise from the accident. Almost two years later, one of the injured passengers, Jack Snow, sued Union Pacific in federal court. Mr. Snow has taken the deposition of the six railroad employees who were on the train at the time of the accident, but each appears to have forgotten the details surrounding the accident. As a result of his frustration, Mr. Snow has formally requested surrender of the written statements of these six employees that were taken by Mr. Pratt immediately after the accident. **Must the defendant surrender the six statements?**

Explanation

The six statements must be surrendered because, under these circumstances, Mr. Snow can get this eyewitness testimony before trial in no other way.

Rule

(1) Statements taken by the defendant's lawyer in anticipation of litigation are work product and therefore covered by the qualified work product privilege. (2) The plaintiff can overcome the privilege by showing that he has a substantial need and an inability to obtain a substantial equivalent without under hardship. (3) An attorney-client privilege might apply to protect the statements of these employees under the Supreme Court's reasoning in *Upjohn*, but these communications lacked confidentiality and cannot be protected by the privilege.

Application

Snow cannot obtain the equivalent of these statements by taking their depositions because either the passage of time or a concern for their employment has dulled their memories. Under these circumstances, no reason exists to prevent Mr. Snow from obtaining copies of the statements in order to prepare his case for trial. He has a substantial need for eyewitness testimony and he has shown that he cannot without undue hardship obtain a substantial equivalent of the testimony these eyewitnesses gave at the scene of the accident.

3. Harvey Blank works as an automotive engineer at an independent laboratory, and his primary expertise lies in determining the crashworthiness of automobiles and trucks. In January 2006, he witnessed an automobile accident that involved a city bus and minivan carrying six members of a family. The mother and father have sued the manufacturer of their minivan seeking damages in federal court, and they have named Mr. Blank as their expert witness to testify about the lack of crashworthiness of the minivan. The defendant has demanded Mr. Blank's deposition, but the plaintiffs have responded with a request that the defendant pay Mr. Blank $500 per hour for attending the deposition. **Does the defendant have the obligation to pay for Mr. Blank's time in the deposition?**

Explanation

No, Mr. Blank is a fact witness rather than an expert, and his deposition can be taken pursuant to Rule 30, which does not require payment for the deponent's time.

Rule

Rule 26(b)(4)(C) requires the discovering party to pay an expert a reasonable fee for time spent in responding to discovery under this subdivision if the expert was retained or specially employed for purposes of this litigation.

Application

As an eyewitness, Mr. Blank's knowledge is derived primarily from his direct observation of the accident. Although he may give his opinion about the defects of the minivan, he is being deposed as a fact witness and need not be paid.

Part IV

Adjudication

CHAPTER 11

Resolution by the Court

A. Terminology

Challenge for cause—During the voir dire examination of prospective jurors, a lawyer can cause the removal of anyone who provides evidence of bias or partiality.

Default judgment—This is a judgment on the merits of a claim that a judge enters because the defendant has failed to respond in a timely fashion after service of the summons. See Rule 55. In some instances, a judge can enter default against a party who fails to obey his order.

Directed verdict—Upon motion, a judge can grant judgment to the defendant at trial before submitting the case to a jury and after the plaintiff has presented her evidence. The judge must find that the plaintiff has failed to satisfy her burdens of proof in regard to the cause of action. Federal Rule 50 refers to this as a motion for judgment as a matter of law.

Judgment as a matter of law—If it becomes clear that the plaintiff cannot carry her burdens of producing evidence or of persuasion as to any material fact, the judge can grant the defendant a judgment based on the legal conclusion that the plaintiff cannot prevail. Although the plaintiff can move for a judgment as a matter of law, she will have more difficulty showing that the defendant cannot prevail.

Judgment notwithstanding the verdict—In federal practice, this is a renewed motion for judgment as a matter of law. A party who makes a motion for judgment as a matter of law at the close of all of the evidence can renew that motion after the verdict is returned. Under earlier practice, this was referred to as a motion for judgment notwithstanding the verdict or as a motion for judgment *non obstante veredicto*, which has the same meaning but sounds more mystical.

Material fact—A plaintiff must plead and prove a cause of action in order to justify granting her a judicial remedy. Each cause of action consists of a set of elements. The elements of a cause of action are separate requirements, each of which the plaintiff must satisfy. Instead of proving an element of her cause of action, the plaintiff actually must prove facts that satisfy that requirement.

Preemptory challenges—Each party has a set number of challenges that he or she can use to strike prospective jurors at the close of the voir dire examination. Under the common law, these challenges could be used for any reason and were not subject to review by the court. The Supreme Court has applied the Constitution to restrict the use of preemptory challenges because of either the race or gender of the prospective juror.

Standards of proof—The plaintiff's burden of persuasion in a civil jury trial requires her to prove the existence of the material facts by a preponderance of the evidence. The preponderance-standard is the plaintiff's burden in that if the evidence seems of equal weight the jury must find for the defendant. Some issues in civil actions may be subject to a heightened burden so that the plaintiff would be required, for example, to prove actual malice in a public-figure libel suit by clear and convincing evidence. In criminal trials, the prosecution must prove each element of the defendant's guilt beyond a reasonable doubt.

Summary Judgment—This procedure becomes most important in a case set for jury trial, and allows the judge to end the case before trial. The judge must find that no genuine issue of material fact exists and that the moving party is entitled to judgment as a matter of law. If a genuine issue of material fact exists, the case must be presented to a jury for determination of that factual issue.

B. Judicial Resolution of the Case

1. The Plaintiff's Burdens

To understand the entry of a judgment, consider the burdens that the plaintiff must bear in order to justify the grant of judicial relief she seeks. First, she must plead a claim upon which relief can be granted. In other words, she must state a federal or state cause of action that, if proved, would entitle her to recover damages or injunctive relief. Second, since a cause of action consists of a list of requirements, known as elements, the plaintiff must satisfy each of these elements of her cause of action.

A plaintiff satisfies each element through the presentation of evidence that supports the existence of the material facts that establish that element. For example, in a tort cause of action, the plaintiff must show that the negligent act of the defendant proximately caused the plaintiff harm. However, the plaintiff cannot prove negligence in the abstract. She must, for example, prove that the defendant drove his vehicle at an excessive rate of speed into an intersection against a red light and there collided with the car driven by the plaintiff. It is this act that, once proved, establishes the negligence (or lack of due care) element of her tort cause of action. If the plaintiff fails to gather evidence or fails to present sufficient evidence to prove the existence of each material fact supporting her cause of action, she loses on the merits and a judgment can be entered for the defendant as a matter of law.

The plaintiff also can be defeated by affirmative defenses that block her cause of action even if it is proved. For example, the defendant can admit that he breached his agreement with the plaintiff, but claim that their oral contract violated the applicable statute of frauds. If he can prove the applicability of the statute, he obtains a judgment that the plaintiff takes nothing.

2. Judgments as a Matter of Law

In most instances, the defendant will seek a judgment as a matter of law against the plaintiff. Very early in the litigation, the defendant can move for dismissal of the plaintiff's complaint under Rule 12(b)(6) for her failure to state a claim upon which relief can be granted. If the defendant includes in his answer an affirmative defense that appears to defeat the plaintiff's claim, he can seek a motion for judgment on the pleadings under Rule 12(c). The defendant can move at any time for a summary judgment under Rule 56, and the attachment of materials outside the pleadings, such as affidavits, to a Rule 12(b)(6) or Rule 12(c) motion will transform those into motions for summary judgment.

The defendant may assert a motion for summary judgment after the close of pleadings if, for example, he has a limitations defense upon which the court can rule. He can also seek summary judgment after discovery and have that motion adjudicated at the pretrial conference prior to trial. After discovery, the defendant has the opportunity to contend that the plaintiff has gathered no evidence to produce in respect to some material fact. Such "no-evidence" summary judgments can be entered against the plaintiff at this time because she has the burden of producing evidence at trial on each material fact needed to support the elements of her cause of action. If she fails to produce any evidence to prove a material fact, she fails to carry her burden of production. In the absence of such evidence, the judge must rule against the plaintiff and prevent her from going before the jury.

If the plaintiff produces some evidence on the disputed material facts, she can make it past summary judgment. At the trial, the plaintiff presents her evidence on those disputed issues to the jury. Again, if the plaintiff closes her case but fails to present any evidence on a disputed fact, the defendant can move for a judgment as a matter of law. See Rule 50(a). If the judge agrees with the defendant and finds that the plaintiff has not produced any evidence on that disputed issue, he must take the case away from the jury and give the defendant judgment.

If the plaintiff presents some evidence on each disputed material fact, the defendant would then be required to present his evidence on those issues. At the close of the evidence, defendants routinely move for judgment as a matter of law because, they contend, their evidence clearly outweighs that of the plaintiff. Judges typically refuse to grant such motions, and send the case to the jury. If the jury finds in favor of the plaintiff on all disputed issues of material fact, the defendant can renew his motion for judgment as a matter of law. The judge can then decide that, as a matter of law, no reasonable jury could hold as it did on the disputed material facts and grant judgment to the defendant.

The problem for the plaintiff, therefore, is that she has both the burden of producing evidence in order to get her case to the jury and the burden of persuading the jury in regard to the facts needed to support her cause of action. If her inability to carry the burden of production becomes clear before trial, the court should grant defendant judgment because the plaintiff cannot prevail. If the judge hesitates to grant the motion for directed verdict and sends the case to the jury, he can overturn any jury verdict entered in favor of the plaintiff if it is clear that her evidence was insufficient.

C. DISMISSAL

1. Without Prejudice

A court's order dismissing a case can have the same effect as a judgment in particular instances. On the other hand, dismissals entered "without prejudice against refiling," do not prevent the plaintiff from refiling the same claim in another court. A dismissal without prejudice can, however, effectively terminate a claim if the applicable statute of limitations bars refiling. Many states have enacted "savings statutes" that suspend the limitations period during the pendency of the first suit. These statutes thus save the plaintiff from the limitations bar when she refiles her case in the proper court.

Under Rule 41 of the Federal Rules of Civil Procedure, the following dismissals do not operate as an adjudication on the merits and cannot bar refiling: (1) the first voluntary dismissal by notice, if it contains no contrary statement; (2) a dismissal by stipulation of the parties, if it contains no contrary statement; (3) a court order which states that it is without prejudice; or (4) a dismissal because of lack of jurisdiction (subject matter or personal), improper venue, or failure to join a party under Rule 19 (indispensable parties). A dismissal by stipulation, which would ordinarily be without prejudice against refiling, can end the life of a claim if a statement is included making that dismissal one with prejudice against refiling. The parties might include such a statement, for instance, as a condition for settlement of the claim.

2. Voluntary Dismissal

Rule 41 provides for voluntary or involuntary dismissal of actions in federal court, whether these actions were filed there originally or removed to federal court. The Rule provides for voluntary dismissal either with or without leave of court. There are two stages at which an action may be voluntarily dismissed. First, a plaintiff, as a matter of right, may end her action by filing a notice of dismissal before the adverse party either serves an answer or moves for summary judgment. Second, after the defendant has responded with an answer or a motion for summary judgment, the plaintiff may dismiss without leave of court if she obtains a stipulation of dismissal signed by all parties who have appeared. These dismissals are without prejudice unless stated otherwise in the notice or stipulation.

Some voluntary dismissals always require court approval. For example, the representative parties must obtain the court's permission in order to dismiss a class action or a derivative action. Rules 23 and 23.1 impose this requirement to protect the unnamed members of the class or the unnamed shareholders. Rule 41 restricts dismissal at the discretion of the plaintiff to the early stages of litigation before a defendant has expended time or expense on the case. However, Rule 41(a) provides that a notice of dismissal operates as an adjudication on the merits when filed by a plaintiff who has once dismissed an action in either federal or state court based on the same claim. This "two-dismissal" rule prevents a plaintiff's abuse of her unilateral right and prevents harassment of a defendant through multiple dismissals. Rule 41's two-dismissal rule applies if the first voluntary dismissal occurred in state court and the second in federal court, but it does not apply when the second dismissal occurs in state court because the Rule applies only in federal court. If one of the two dismissals occurred through an order of court or by stipulation, the second dismissal will not bar a third refiling.

Even when the plaintiff cannot dismiss by notice or stipulation, Rule 41(a)(2) permits her to obtain a court order for dismissal without prejudice. The court has discretion to deny the plaintiff's motion if such a dismissal would harm the defendant, and it may dismiss only upon conditions which will alleviate that harm. The court might, for example, condition its order upon payment of the defendant's costs or condition any further filing in federal court upon payment of those costs. The defendant also might ask the court to enter a judgment for those costs in case the second filing occurs in state court.

Rule 41(a)(2) limits the power of a court to enter an order of dismissal on plaintiff's motion if a counterclaim has been filed. A court cannot grant the plaintiff's motion over the defendant's objection unless the counterclaim "can remain pending for independent adjudication by the court." This limitation does not apply when the plaintiff's motion is served prior to service of the answer containing the counterclaim.

3. Involuntary Dismissal

Rule 41(b) governs involuntary dismissals—that is, dismissals at the motion of the defendant. An involuntary dismissal does not bar refiling when dismissal was ordered because of lack of jurisdiction, improper venue, or failure to join a party under Rule 19. In addition to these grounds, other jurisdictional reasons for dismissal will overcome the with-prejudice presumption which attaches to a nonspecifying order. One should investigate the specific circumstances of a dismissal, preferably before it is entered.

In Semtek International Inc. v. Lockheed Martin Corp., 531 U.S. 497 (2001), the Supreme Court held that the language of Federal Rule 41(b)—describing a dismissal as one that "operates as an adjudication on the merits"—only means that the case cannot be refiled in the federal court that dismisses it. The Court thus concluded that Rule 41(b) does not purport to determine the res judicata effect of a federal judgment, and could not be given such effect without violating the Rules Enabling Act's ban on affecting substantive rights.

The Court concluded that "with prejudice" against refiling was "an acceptable form of shorthand" for the "adjudication upon the merits" language of Rule 41(b). Therefore, a Rule 41(b) dismissal that "operates as an adjudication upon the merits" merely bars refiling the same claim in the federal court that dismissed it. Even though the Federal Rule did not have res judicata effect, the Court held that special federal common law governs the effect to be given diversity judgments. However, the Court decided that this common law should adopt state res judicata rules to determine the effect of diversity judgments. Therefore, a federal court's judgment in a diversity case will be enforced to the extent of the res judicata law of the state in which that federal court is located.

D. DEFAULT JUDGMENT

Once the plaintiff serves the defendant with process or obtains from the defendant a waiver of service, the defendant has the legal obligation to respond to the complaint. The process served on the defendant includes a copy of the complaint and a summons, which informs the defendant of the obligation to respond or suffer entry of default judgment. The defendant typically has 20 days in which to serve his response to the complaint on the plaintiff's attorney [see Rule 5(b)(1)], as named in the complaint, and, within a reasonable time thereafter, on the court. See Rule 12(a)(1)(A).

The defendant's response can be through a preanswer motion that seeks, for example, dismissal of the complaint for jurisdictional deficiencies or for improper venue. If the defendant serves a preanswer motion on the plaintiff's attorney within the 20-day period, he has satisfied his immediate obligation to respond to the complaint. If his motion is granted, the complaint will be dismissed and no further action in that cause will be required of the defendant. If the court denies his preanswer motion, he will have 10 days after notice of the court's action within which to serve his answer on the plaintiff's attorney. See Rule 12(a)(4)(A). If the defendant fails to serve a timely response, Rule 55 makes him subject to the entry of a default judgment in favor of the plaintiff. Unless a default judgment is set aside pursuant to Rule 60(b), it will stand as a final judgment, generally protected by the rules of claim preclusion.

1. Default

The entry of a default judgment under Rule 55 occurs in two steps — the entry of the default and the entry of the judgment. The entry of a default is a prerequisite to the entry of the judgment. Rule 55(a) permits a district clerk to enter a default, and, not surprisingly, a judge may do so as well. Entry of default is not automatic; the claimant must apply for it. In doing so, the claimant must show that subject matter jurisdiction exists over her claim for relief. She must prove that the defaulting party was amenable to service and was served properly. And she must show that the defendant has failed to respond within the time required by law. These allegations should be supported by affidavit or other competent proof.

A plaintiff can cause the entry of a default against one who fails to respond within the time allowed by the Rules. A plaintiff, as well as a defendant, may default. For example, an answer that includes a counterclaim labeled as such requires a reply by the plaintiff. Rule 12(a)(2) requires the plaintiff to serve a reply within 20 days after the service of the answer. A defendant can also suffer default by failing to respond to a claim asserted by a party other than the plaintiff. For example, a defendant might default by failing to respond in a timely manner to a cross-claim. A third-party defendant can default by failing to respond in a timely manner to a third-party complaint, and for egregious violations of discovery orders, Rule 37(b)(2)(C) authorizes a court to render a default judgment against the disobedient party.

If a default has been entered, it precludes the defaulting party from challenging the well-pleaded factual allegations of the complaint other than those relating to damages. Rule 55(c) authorizes a court to set aside the entry of default for good cause. A court will excuse a defending party who defaults because of excusable neglect if he also has a meritorious defense to the claim. A client's legitimate claim should not easily fall victim to his attorney's tardiness, especially if the attorney's delay was inadvertent. Even if a formal default has not been entered, a defendant answering beyond the time allowed should explain that tardiness to the court.

2. Default Judgment

The clerk may enter a default judgment if (1) someone who is not a minor or incompetent (2) has been defaulted for failing to make an appearance and (3) the claim is for a "sum certain or for a sum which can by computation be made certain." Unlike other judgments, Rule 54(c) restricts a default judgment to the relief sought in the pleading in which the claim was asserted, and it cannot exceed the amount prayed for therein. As noted above, a default judgment enjoys claim-preclusive (res judicata) effect in the absence of fraud, collusion, or lack of jurisdiction.

A court also can enter a default judgment under Rule 55(b)(2). Because courts prefer disposition upon the merits, they enter default judgments only when the evidence indicates the adversary process has been thwarted because of an essentially unresponsive party. Upon application, the judge may enter a default judgment either upon affidavits and the pleadings or after requiring the presentation of evidence. Even if sufficient evidence is presented, Rule 55(b)(2) prohibits the entry of default judgment against a minor or incompetent unless he is represented by a guardian or by some other person appointed by the court under Rule 17(c). If the defaulting party has made some sort of appearance in the action, he must be given notice of the application for judgment at least three days before the hearing. If he fails to overturn the default, however, he can challenge only the allegations of damages or the sufficiency of the complaint. In any case, no right to jury trial exists at a hearing for a default judgment unless mandated by a federal statute.

The party seeking a judgment upon a default for failure to appear should support her application with an affidavit stating that the defaulting party is not in the military service. This requirement comes from the Soldiers' and Sailors' Relief Act, Title 50 U.S.C. App. § 520(1). If the applicant either knows that the defaulting party is in military service or does not know whether he is or not, she must file an affidavit admitting as much. Thereafter, a judge can enter default judgment only after appointing an attorney to represent the defaulting party. The Act restricts entry of default judgment; it does not prevent service of process on persons in the military or hinder entry of the default alone.

A defaulting party can move to set aside a default judgment pursuant to Rule 60(b)(1) by alleging that the default occurred because of excusable neglect. A district court begins with the presumption that default judgments are disfavored and that any doubt should be resolved in favor of setting it aside. The party seeking to set aside the default judgment does, however, bear the burden of showing that he timely sought relief, that his reason for default is excusable and does not reflect culpable conduct, that reopening the case will not prejudice the claimant, and that he has a meritorious defense. In addition, a defaulting party can set aside the judgment under Rule 60(b)(3) if the judgment was entered through fraud, misrepresentation, or other misconduct.

Rule 60(b)(4) requires a court to set aside a default judgment entered without jurisdiction. The Due Process Clause requires the court that enters a default judgment to set it aside if the court did not have personal jurisdiction over the defendant. In some instances, a nonresident defendant may choose to suffer a default in the court of a distant state if he claims that court has no jurisdiction over him. He might choose to run this risk because he has no meritorious defenses to the plaintiff's claim and wishes to avoid litigating even the jurisdictional issue in a distant state. That tactic appears reasonable only when the defendant has no property in the forum state. If he has property there, the plaintiff will seek to execute her judgment in that distant state, and he will have no choice but to challenge the judgment in that state. If the defendant has property only in his home state, the plaintiff must bring her judgment to that state and invoke the jurisdiction of a court of that state in order to execute the judgment. When the plaintiff brings the default judgment to the defendant's home state, claim preclusion rules prevent him from challenging the judgment on the merits. He can, however, contend that the judgment is void because entered by a court that had no jurisdiction over him. If successful, the plaintiff must begin again. If that tactic fails, the defendant must pay the judgment.

E. Summary Judgment

1. Overview

Federal Rule 56(c) allows the grant of summary judgment if the movant shows: "that there is no genuine issue as to any material fact and that the moving party is entitled to a judgment as a matter of law." A material fact is one that must be established to show that the plaintiff has satisfied an element of her cause of action. If no issue exists, that fact should be found as the evidence requires. If all material facts have been established before trial, the court should give her judgment as a matter of law. If the plaintiff has failed to produce evidence on one of the material facts underlying her cause of action, she must lose as a matter of law. A genuine issue of material fact exists only when a reasonable jury could find for either party on the evidence presented.

Summary judgment procedure, as prescribed in Rule 56, allows the early termination of claims where there exists no reason to burden the parties, the court, or the taxpayers with the expense of a full trial. Although summary judgments serve the purpose of making litigation less expensive, burdensome, or wasteful, they necessarily prevent the losing litigant from obtaining a full trial on the issues. And a summary judgment raises much more serious concern when entered in an action intended for jury trial. If a judge enters summary judgment in a jury case, he deprives the parties of their right to have a jury decide the factual issues. However, especially in jury cases, one cannot overlook the need for courts to decide cases summarily when further, expensive litigation will accomplish nothing different.

A properly granted summary judgment does not violate a party's Seventh Amendment right to a jury trial. However, in a jury case, the judge must deny a motion for summary judgment if he finds that a material fact is genuinely in dispute. A dispute exists when the summary judgment evidence allows inferences on either side of the issue. In deciding that such permissible inferences exist, a judge views the evidence in the light most favorable to the party opposing the motion and resolves all doubts in that party's favor. If, in this light, no rational jury could find in favor of the non-moving party, the judge can conclude that no genuine issue exists and enter judgment as a matter of law.

In cases where the plaintiff properly alleges a straightforward claim for liability based on clear principles of law, she has realistic opportunity of obtaining summary judgment. However, summary judgment procedure favors defendants largely because the plaintiff bears the burden of establishing her claim. The plaintiff has the burden of pleading and proving all elements of her claim and must, as a matter of law, lose if she cannot carry both burdens.

2. Burden of Pleading

A plaintiff must include factual allegations in her complaint which, if proved, will establish each element of the claim. The substantive law establishes the elements of a claim as its legal requirements, and the plaintiff must satisfy each requirement in order to have a legal right to a judicial remedy. If she fails to prove factual matters sufficient to support one of the requirements (elements) of the claim (after being given a chance to cure the omission), the plaintiff loses. She loses because the substantive law does not allow her to win by proving only some of the elements. The defendant can raise the issue of such legal insufficiency by asserting a motion to dismiss for failure to state a claim upon which relief can be granted pursuant to Rule 12(b)(6). If the court needs to consider materials outside the complaint, the Rule 12(b)(6) motion becomes a motion for summary judgment subject to the procedural protections of Rule 56.

The plaintiff can also lose as a matter of law when the defendant asserts an affirmative defense. If the defendant can prove his affirmative defense, he prevails as a matter of law even though the plaintiff can prove her claim. For example, a defendant might allege that the plaintiff commenced her action after the statute of limitations had expired. If the defendant can prove this defense, the plaintiff loses. The defendant might obtain a ruling on the defense by filing a motion for judgment on the pleadings under Rule 12(c), but if the court considers materials outside the pleadings this too becomes a motion for summary judgment.

3. Burden of Proof

If the plaintiff pleads her case sufficiently, a judge can enter summary judgment only if he concludes that the plaintiff cannot prove one of the elements of her claim. The plaintiff's burden of proof includes the burden of producing some evidence on each material fact and the burden of persuading the trier of fact in accordance with the applicable standard of proof. The defendant can again prevail by moving for summary judgment on the basis of an affirmative defense. For example, state officials sued under § 1983 have qualified immunity from suits for damages if they can prove that when they acted the constitutional rights of the plaintiff were not clearly established. A confession and avoidance defense defeats even an otherwise valid cause of action, and therefore proof of that defense justifies a judgment as a matter of law.

The plaintiff has the dual burden of pleading her claim for relief and also the burden of proof in regard to the elements of her claim. The Supreme Court, in Schaffer v. Weast, 126 S.Ct. 528 (2005), noted that much confusion arises from the historical meaning of the "burden of proof" because it:

> encompassed two distinct burdens: the "burden of persuasion," *i.e.*, which party loses if the evidence is closely balanced, and the "burden

of production," *i.e.*, which party bears the obligation to come forward with the evidence at different points in the proceeding.

Id. at 533–534, citing Director, Office of Workers' Compensation Programs v. Greenwich Collieries, 512 U.S. 267, 272 (1994).

The burden of proof thus consists of two independent requirements: (a) the burden of producing or going forward with the evidence, and (b) the burden of persuading the fact-finder of the facts needed to sustain a claim or defense. The party bearing either of these burdens is at risk of losing if she fails to carry them adequately. It is said that these burdens can best be described by the risks they imply. For example, the plaintiff has the burden of producing evidence at trial to prove each disputed material fact and thus carries the risk of losing if she fails to provide any evidence.

The burden of proof usually follows the burden of pleading. Therefore, parties often litigate the issue of who bears the burden of pleading when their basic concern is with the burden of proof. In a few instances, the burden of proof will not follow the burden of pleading. For example, Federal Rule 8(c) requires the defendant to plead contributory negligence as an affirmative defense. However, in a diversity case, state law may place the burden on the plaintiff to disprove her own contributory negligence. In adjudicating a state law cause of action, a federal court will follow Rule 8 and place the burden of pleading contributory negligence on the defendant but will follow state law in placing the burden of proof on the plaintiff.

The plaintiff runs the risk of nonproduction in regard to each disputed material fact needed to establish the elements of her claim. A fact that the plaintiff must prove is material because in law it must be proved in order for the plaintiff to establish one of the elements of her claim. If she has no evidence to present to the fact-finder, she has failed to carry his burden and thus loses on the merits. For example, a plaintiff who asserts a tort claim based on the defendant's negligence must prove some factual basis to support the conclusion of negligence. Suppose the plaintiff's only allegation of negligence depends on her contention that immediately before striking the plaintiff's car the defendant was driving 40 miles over the speed limit. If the plaintiff introduces no testimony or other evidence to prove that fact, she has failed to carry her burden of production and will suffer entry of a judgment as a matter of law for the defendant.

4. Burden of Persuasion

The burden of persuasion refers to the standard of proof that tells the jury how to decide close cases. As noted, the burden of persuasion in civil cases generally requires a party to provide credible evidence that, when considered against the contradicting evidence, leads the trier of fact to find that the existence of a contested fact is more probable than not.

In more abstract terms, the party having the burden of persuasion must prove a fact by the greater weight or preponderance of the evidence. If a jury is the trier of fact but has been left in a quandary because the evidence is too evenly balanced, the party having the burden loses. That party loses because her burden places upon her the risk of nonpersuasion. In some civil cases, a party bearing this burden is required to prove matters by clear and convincing evidence. This higher standard enhances the risk that a party's evidence will not persuade the fact-finder and thus increases the burden of persuasion.

5. Summary Judgment Evidence

Rule 56(c) of the Federal Rules of Civil Procedure authorizes the entry of a summary judgment when:

> the pleadings, depositions, answers to interrogatories and admissions on file, together with the affidavits, if any, show that there is no genuine issue as to any material fact and that the moving party is entitled to a judgment as a matter of law.

The evidence submitted in regard to a motion for summary judgment therefore consists of affidavits, depositions, answers to interrogatories, and other sworn documentary materials. The evidence supplied thereby must be at least reducible to admissible evidence under the Federal Rules of Evidence. Rule 43(e) permits the use of oral testimony at hearings and, presumably, at hearings on summary judgment motions. However, if live witnesses are allowed, the hearing on a summary judgment motion takes on the attributes of a trial—and of a trial in which the jury is excluded. Because the judge would necessarily engage in some aspect of fact-finding by judging credibility or weighing any opposing oral testimony, consideration of such evidence appears inconsistent with the Seventh Amendment.

Rule 56 does not mandate the use of sworn documentary evidence by a movant, at least where the defendant is pointing out the absence of evidence to support the plaintiff's case. Indeed, the party opposing the motion for summary judgment need not respond with affidavits or other materials if the movant has not carried his initial burden of showing the absence of any genuine issue of material fact. When the motion is sufficiently supported, however, Rule 56(e) states that the party opposing the motion may not rest on allegations in her pleadings. As a practical matter, the nonmoving party must respond to a motion for summary judgment with sworn documentary evidence to raise a genuine issue of material fact. In some instances, this documentary evidence may not be available when the motion is filed. Rule 56(f) allows the court under these circumstances to order a continuance to permit the nonmoving party to obtain affidavits or depositions.

In Celotex Corporation v. Catrett, 477 U.S. 317 (1986), the Supreme Court cleared the way for no-evidence summary judgments entered after the end of the discovery period. Although the defendant in that case had not presented documentary evidence to negate the existence of the material fact in question, the Court held that Celotex did not have this obligation. In moving for a no-evidence summary judgment, the defendant need not affirmatively negate the existence of a genuine issue when, though requested to do so, the plaintiff has failed to come forward with any proof to satisfy her burden of production. The defendant, Celotex, moved for summary judgment after discovery had been completed and did so based on the absence of any evidence to prove that the plaintiff's decedent had been exposed to an asbestos product manufactured by Celotex. See *id.* at 322. Ms. Catrett had the burden of producing some evidence to prove the material fact of exposure, but during the discovery period had not identified in response to the defendant's interrogatories any witness who could testify on the issue of exposure.

Ms. Catrett responded to Celotex's motion for summary judgment with three documents. One document was a letter from an official of one of Mr. Catrett's former employers who would testify in support of his exposure to asbestos manufactured by Celotex. The Court noted that the plaintiff did not have the obligation to present "evidence in a form that would be admissible at trial in order to avoid summary judgment." *Id.* at 324. The plaintiff did not have the obligation to depose her own witness but she did have the obligation to show that, if reduced to admissible evidence, this witness's testimony would be sufficient to carry her burden of production. The Court did not hold her evidence insufficient but, instead, remanded the case to the court of appeals for reconsideration of this issue.

In rare instances, a judge can find that the evidence produced after discovery is so weak that, though it satisfies the plaintiff's burden of production, it cannot satisfy her burden of persuasion. If so, the judge can decide that no rational jury could find for the plaintiff on this trivial evidence and, therefore, that no genuine issue exists as to that material fact. The judge can more easily make this sort of decision when the law requires a plaintiff to prove a material fact with clear and convincing evidence. This higher burden of persuasion allows the judge more certainty in applying the rational-jury test for the existence of a genuine issue.

F. Entering Judgment at Trial

1. Trial Without a Jury

In federal court, a larger proportion of cases are tried before a judge than in many state court systems. This is because the Seventh Amendment to the Constitution preserves the right to a jury trial only in common law actions. In cases that do not fall within that category, such as admiralty actions or actions in equity (for injunctive relief), the parties will not have a constitutional right to demand a jury trial.

The Federal Rules of Evidence apply to actions tried without a jury, but they are of diminished importance in such cases. Evidentiary rules are drawn primarily to protect the accuracy and fairness of fact-finding by lay persons who might otherwise give determinative weight to inherently unreliable information or who might be diverted from the truth by highly prejudicial material. When the trier of fact is a judge, these dangers presumably do not exist. Therefore, except in regard to privileged matter, the appellate courts generally indulge in the presumption that a trial judge would not rely on inadmissible evidence even though it was admitted.

In nonjury trials, Rule 52(c) allows a defendant to move for judgment as a matter of law on partial findings after the plaintiff has completed the presentation of her evidence. Although this procedure is similar to the motion for judgment in a jury trial, the judge is not required in a nonjury trial to view the evidence in the light most favorable to the plaintiff. Rule 52(a) requires the judge in all cases tried on the facts without a jury, or with an advisory jury, to make findings of fact specially, and to state separately his conclusions of law. Findings of fact and conclusions of law are unnecessary when the court decides Rule 12 motions, summary judgment motions, or any other motion except the motion to dismiss for insufficiency of the evidence.

A party may, within 10 days after the entry of judgment in a nonjury trial, make a motion for amendment of the trial court's findings and may join this with a motion for new trial. Rule 52(b) allows a party to challenge the sufficiency of evidence supporting the findings on appeal, even though he did not make an objection to the findings on that basis or move to amend or for new trial. This is an express exception to the general requirement of contemporaneous objections established in Rule 46, but it would always be advisable to make one's objections in the proper form and at the earliest time.

On appeal, Rule 52(a) provides that findings of fact, whether based on oral or documentary evidence, are not to be set aside unless they are clearly erroneous. The Rule also states that due regard is to be given the trial judge's ability to have considered the credibility of the witnesses. Although an appellate court might be in a better position to make its own determinations as to facts drawn from documentary evidence, the clearly erroneous rule will still apply. The appellate court will give even greater deference where the trial court's fact-finding is based on the credibility of witnesses.

The clearly erroneous rule requires an appellate court to affirm if the trial court's finding is plausible in light of the record in its entirety. If there are two permissible views of the record, a choice of one of these by the trial court cannot be clearly erroneous. The clearly erroneous rule does not apply to conclusions of law, but it does apply to all categories of factual findings whether they involve inferences from facts or mixed questions of law or fact.

2. Right to Jury Trial

The Seventh Amendment to the United States Constitution reads, as follows:

> In Suits at common law ... the right of trial by jury shall be preserved, and no fact tried by a jury, shall be otherwise re-examined in any Court of the United States, than according to the rules of the common law.

This provision does not create a right to jury trial; it preserves the right as it existed, presumably when the first Congress to meet under the Constitution drafted the Bill of Rights that included the provision that is now the Seventh Amendment. Because the Seventh Amendment preserves rather than creates, the Supreme Court uses historical approaches to determine how the right to jury trial should be construed. Looking back into history is never easy, even for historians, and judges must apply what they find in the past to a substantially changed system of procedural and substantive law.

By its own terms, the Seventh Amendment preserves the right to jury trial only in civil actions that are tried in a federal court. The Sixth Amendment imposes a constitutional requirement of jury trial for serious criminal offenses and, therefore, applies to those trials in state court. State courts do not, however, follow the Seventh Amendment in adjudicating civil actions because it does not apply to them. A state may therefore provide for jury trial in state courts when it would not be available in a federal court, and the state can restrict the right even in cases where the Seventh Amendment preserves it.

a. Suits at Common Law

To apply the Seventh Amendment, a federal court must determine whether a current civil action is a suit at common law. In order to do so, the court must find that the civil action was one that would have been a common law action under the law as it existed prior to 1791 (the date of the amendment's ratification). Neither modern judges nor attorneys have the training for such historical examinations. Nevertheless, a court faced with the question must first compare the *claim* in question with 18th-century actions. If the claim is sufficiently similar to one of the then-existing common law actions—a breach of contract cause, for example—the parties will have a right to jury trial.

Doubt arises when the claim also appears similar to an equity action seen in that period—breach of fiduciary duty by a trustee, for example. If the claim being asserted in the case does not closely resemble either an 18th century equitable or common cause of action, the court will turn to a consideration of the nature of the *remedy* sought. Common law actions traditionally provided a damages remedy, and equity actions allowed the plaintiff to obtain injunctive relief. If the claim in the present case demands monetary relief, this characteristic provides strong evidence, through this indirect historical test, that it is a common law claim.

This historical test is complicated by the liberal joinder and new procedural forms allowed under the Federal Rules of Civil Procedure. An initial problem occurred when the plaintiff asserted a claim for injunctive relief (an equity claim), and the defendant asserted a compulsory counterclaim for damages (a common law claim). By following the normal sequence at trial, the court would first decide issues underlying the plaintiff's (equity) claim and would do so without a jury. However, if the court proceeded in this order, it would itself determine issues raised by the common law counterclaim before they could be presented to the jury. The Supreme Court ruled that because a constitutional right to jury trial existed for the legal issues and no constitutional right exists for trial to the judge, the common law issues must be tried first by a jury. See Beacon Theatres, Inc. v. Westover, 359 U.S. 500 (1959).

The second problem was caused when the plaintiff sued for both legal and equitable relief. If the court concluded that the legal issues were only incidental to what is predominantly an equity claim, it would decide the common issues itself, leaving only the question of damages for the jury. The Supreme Court held that Seventh Amendment right to a jury trial requires the court to try those common issues before a jury, and that result cannot be changed by a finding that the legal issues were incidental to the equitable ones. See Dairy Queen, Inc. v. Wood, 369 U.S. 469 (1962).

The third problem arose when the plaintiff used a procedural device historically seen only in the courts of equity, such as a derivative action, to assert a common law claim for damages. Because both legal and equitable remedies can be sought now in a post-merger "civil action," the Seventh Amendment right must be preserved for the legal claim even though in 1791 that claim would have been asserted in a court of equity. See Ross v. Bernhard, 396 U.S. 531 (1970).

A claim for declaratory relief also appears similar to some of the equity procedural devices, but the courts have generally held that declaratory actions can present common law claims. To make this determination, a court must ask what kind of suit would have been brought if the declaratory judgment action had been unavailable. If the declaratory action is only an inverted action at law, and does not clearly appear to be an action in equity, a right to jury trial can be found. For example, if a party brings suit to have a court declare that the defendant's patent is invalid, this suit could only have been prompted by a threat of a patent infringement suit for the common law remedy of damages.

The Seventh Amendment does not preclude the creation by statute of a right to jury trial in other cases because the Amendment does not establish any right to be free of jury trial. Furthermore, no one has a right to jury trial for issues that call for conclusions of law. It is important to realize that judicial decisions that grant judgments as a matter of law do not deny the right to jury trial. The judge grants a judgment as a matter of law by making a decision on a purely legal issue, but only factual issues must be submitted to the jury. Legal history shows that juries were always limited in their power to determine questions of law. A jury does decide mixed factual and legal questions (for example, whether driving at an excessive rate of speed was negligent), but the Seventh Amendment does not prevent a court from applying even the developing legal principles of res judicata to prevent the submission of precluded claims or issues to the jury. This distinction between legal and factual issues also makes possible the use of a judgment as a matter of law to correct an erroneous jury verdict.

b. Demand

A right to jury trial can be lost if a party fails to demand that right in accordance with Rule 38 of the Federal Rules of Civil Procedure. Rule 38(b) requires a party to make the demand in writing not later than 10 days after the last pleading addressed to an issue for which a jury trial is sought. A party must serve the demand on all parties in accordance with Rule 5(d). A party can include the demand in her pleading in order to satisfy these requirements, but, once the demand has been made, it may not be withdrawn except with the consent of all parties.

In a case removed to federal court after all pleadings have been filed in state court, Rule 81(c) authorizes a demand for jury trial by the defendant within 10 days after filing the notice for removal, or by the other parties within 10 days after the notice has been served on them. If the parties have made a demand in state court, or if the forum state law does not require a demand, they need not make a further demand after removal unless the court directs them to do so. If all original pleadings have not been filed in state court before removal to federal court, Rule 38 applies to require a demand within 10 days after the last pleading directed to the issues to be tried by a jury is served.

Rule 39(b) allows the court to try a case with a jury even though a proper demand has not been made if it is one in which such a right would have otherwise existed. Rule 39(c) also authorizes the court, with the consent of the parties, to order trial before a jury even though no right to a jury trial exists. This provision does not apply in actions against the United States or where a federal statute requires that a trial be without a jury.

3. Choosing the Jury

The qualifications of jurors and the selection of jury panels are governed by the Jury Selection and Service Act of 1968, 28 U.S.C. §§ 1861–69. The Act supplies jurors from a fair cross-section of the community and provides all citizens the opportunity to be considered for service. Each district court must establish a plan in accordance with the Act for the random selection of grand and petit jurors from within that district.

One matter considered significant by many attorneys in choosing between federal and state court is the geographic area from which jurors may be drawn in those courts. A state court located in a metropolitan area may draw jurors only from that area, while a federal court in that same metropolitan area may draw jurors from the more rural surrounding areas. Whether it is mythology or accumulated wisdom, some attorneys believe that jurors from rural areas are less prone to award large verdicts than are urban jurors and may forum shop accordingly.

Rule 49 allows the parties to stipulate to a jury of less than twelve or to a less than unanimous verdict. It is still the rule that a unanimous verdict is required in federal court unless the parties stipulate otherwise, but the other implication of Rule 49—that a jury consist of 12 persons—is no longer the law. Local rules may provide for six-person juries in civil cases, and this practice does not violate the Seventh Amendment or Rule 48.

Rule 47(a) gives the federal court wide discretion in conducting the examination of prospective jurors. To expedite the process of choosing a jury panel, federal judges tend to question prospective jurors themselves and do not allow the parties to do so. If the federal judge conducts the examination, the attorneys will be allowed to suggest questions. The parties may, during the voir dire examination (questioning of prospective jurors) or shortly thereafter, make challenges to the individual jurors (polls) or to the whole of the jury panel (array) because of failure to select them properly. Challenges to individual jurors may be by a challenge for cause (failure to satisfy the statutory qualification), a challenge for favor (bias or prejudice), or by a peremptory challenge.

Today, lawyers often refer to challenges made because of bias or prejudice as ones for cause rather than for favor. However, the challenge for cause is more appropriately brought against a potential juror who does not satisfy the statutory qualifications required of jurors in federal court. For example, a juror must be a citizen, be over 18 years of age, be able to read and write English, be mentally competent, and not be a convicted felon. A challenge for favor lies whenever evidence surfaces during the voir dire examination which supports a presumption of partiality on the part of any potential juror. This challenge would be sustained, for instance, whenever a potential juror openly declares his bias or prejudice. But, the challenge can also succeed when based on evidence of a juror's relationship with one of the parties or on evidence of other interests in the case. For example, one who has a financial interest in the outcome of a trial cannot be reasonably expected to be an impartial juror in the case. The law places no limit on the number of challenges for cause or favor because these are provided to assure the parties of a right to trial by a competent and reasonably impartial jury.

Section 1870 of Title 28, United States Code, entitles each party to three peremptory challenges in a civil case. Several parties on the same side may be treated as a single party for the purpose of peremptory challenges and should be so treated when they have identical interests. Peremptory challenges were traditionally allowed without any condition. Lawyers might use their three strikes for any reason which appealed to them. In criminal cases, these challenges have been restricted when shown to be racially motivated. That same rule has now been applied in civil cases between private parties. To show racial motivation, the complaining party must establish a prima facie case by showing a pattern of striking prospective jurors of one race. The opposing side then must provide some legitimate reason for the strikes—one not tainted by a racial motive—to rebut the prima facie case. A similar challenge can be made when the state, or any governmental entity, is a party to a civil case and strikes prospective jurors because of their sex. The sex-discrimination challenge has not been applied in civil cases when only private parties are involved.

4. Presenting the Case

One should consult the local rules of the district court in which a case is pending for any special rules affecting the general proceedings at trial. These rules may, for example, govern the use of experiments or exhibits during trial or the manner in which argument may be made. Proceedings tend to be more formal in federal court than in state court. Attorneys, for instance, are required in federal court to remain behind the podium when examining a witness or when arguing to the jury. These restrictions may unsettle attorneys who prefer to present a case while pacing or standing closer to the jurors.

After choosing a jury, the parties make opening statements and begin the presentation of their direct evidence. The plaintiff presents his direct evidence, followed by the defendant's presentation of evidence. Quite frequently, a defendant will make a motion for judgment as a matter of law—once known as a motion for directed verdict—after the plaintiff has rested. This motion resembles a no-evidence summary judgment motion in that the defendant contends that the plaintiff has failed to carry her burden of production. If the judge concludes that the plaintiff has come forward with some evidence—thereby satisfying this first burden of proof—she will deny the motion.

After the close of the evidence, the parties make final arguments. In most cases, the plaintiff begins the final argument, using only a portion of the time she is allowed. The defendant then makes his complete final argument, and the plaintiff closes by using her remaining time. When the final arguments have been made, the judge instructs the jurors on the law and on the questions presented for their decision. The judge then directs the jury to retire and consider its verdict. The sequence of these events may vary or be modified depending on the nature of the case, the burden of proof, or the number and types of parties.

5. State Law and Federal Trials

The Federal Rules of Evidence were enacted by Congress and became effective on July 1, 1975. These Rules apply in all cases in federal court, including diversity cases, without regard to conflicting state law. Since they were enacted by Congress within its constitutional power over the federal court system, they effectively preempt the area of evidence in federal court and are not to be displaced by the *Erie* doctrine's requirements. However, even though they control in federal court, the Federal Rules of Evidence may themselves require the application of state law, especially with respect to state law governing privileges as these bear on the issues of a state law claim.

State law will, however, affect the burden of proof in diversity cases. Although the Federal Rules of Civil Procedure control pleadings and procedure in federal diversity cases, it has been held that Rule 8(c), providing for the pleading of affirmative defenses, does not govern the placement of the burden of proof on such defenses. A defendant thus has the burden of pleading a defense such as contributory negligence, but state law may require the plaintiff to disprove contributory negligence. In diversity cases, state law governs the substantive elements of the claims and defenses, and thereby influences the legal instructions a federal judge gives the jury.

Even in diversity cases, the form of the judge's instructions to the jury are matters governed by federal not state law. Unlike most state judges, a federal judge may comment on the evidence when instructing the jury so long as she does not act in a manner which effectively prevents the jury from making its own decision on the issues of fact. Rule 51 of the Federal Rules of Civil Procedure provides for the submission by the parties to the court of requests for instructions. The judge must inform the parties of her decision on these requests prior to their jury arguments so the parties can prepare to speak to the law as it will be explained to the jury. A party may not on appeal complain of the court's instructions or of its refusal to give an instruction unless he objects before the jury retires and states the grounds for that objection.

The general practice in federal court is to present the case to the jury for a general verdict. In simple terms, the general verdict asks the jury if the defendant is liable and, if so, for how much. The court has discretion to accompany the general verdict form with written interrogatories upon one or more issues or to present the case to the jury for a special verdict. If the judge asks the jury for a special verdict—to answer only a list of specific questions— some legally required fact question may be omitted. This danger is alleviated by Rule 49(a). It provides for a waiver of a party's right to jury trial on any issue omitted from a special verdict unless that party had demanded its submission before the jury retired. The judge may make a finding on the omitted issue or may deem it to have been decided in accordance with the judgment entered on the special verdict.

On occasion, the instructions may confuse the jury, or the jurors may make mistakes about the law in determining their verdict. If an error is not discovered before the jury is released, the judge has limited power to alter the verdict to correct the jury's error. Some cases have allowed the trial judge to alter or modify a verdict when the mistake was little more than an obvious clerical error. If, on the other hand, jury confusion becomes an issue after the jury is released, Rule 606(b) of the Federal Rules of Evidence prevents the judge from using either the testimony or affidavits of jurors to resolve the problem. Jurors cannot testify about their deliberations unless extraneous prejudicial information was improperly given the jury during those deliberations.

6. Post Verdict Motions

The party who loses before the jury will frequently seek to challenge the verdict by arguing that he should be given a judgment as a matter of law— once known as the motion for judgment notwithstanding the verdict or judgment n.o.v. (an abbreviation of the Latin phrase *non obstante verdicto*). He also will join a motion for a new trial. The motion for judgment as a matter of law is a challenge to the sufficiency of the evidence supporting the verdict. A motion for new trial contends that, even though sufficient evidence may have been presented, the verdict was entered against the great weight of the evidence or because of some unfairness or other serious defect. Both of these motions must be made not later than 10 days after entry of the judgment.

A motion for judgment as a matter of law made after the verdict raises the same legal issue as one made before the verdict, and both are governed by Rule 50 of the Federal Rules of Civil Procedure. Rule 50(b) contains the following statement:

> If ... the court does not grant a motion for a judgment as a matter of law made at the close of all the evidence, the court is considered to have submitted the action to the jury subject to the court's later deciding the legal questions raised by the motion. The movant may renew its request for judgment as a matter of law by filing a motion no later than 10 days after entry of judgment.

Under Rule 50(b), a party must make a motion for judgment as a matter of law at the close of all the evidence (before the jury retires to deliberate), in order to *renew* (or assert) that motion after the verdict goes against him. In simple terms, one must make a motion for judgment as a matter of law at the close of all the evidence in order to make the same motion after the verdict. If the judge denies the motion made at the close of the evidence, she is presumed to have reserved decision on the *legal* questions raised in the motion. The Rule thus indicates that a later decision on the renewed motion is a judicial decision of legal rather than factual issues. The judge's decision after the verdict might otherwise appear to be a reexamination of the jury's fact findings. Requiring a motion at the close of the evidence also gives the opposing party an opportunity to cure the deficiency on which the motion is based. See Freund v. Nycomed Amersham, 347 F.3d 752, 761 (9th Cir. 2003)

Judges use the same standard for deciding the motion for judgment as a matter of law, whether made before or renewed after the verdict, because they both raise the legal question of whether sufficient evidence existed to raise an issue for the jury. The standard is known as the "reasonable (or rational) jury" test. The judge should grant the motion only when a reasonable jury could not find in favor of the party opposing it. The judge may not weigh the evidence or determine the credibility of witnesses, and should give all reasonable inferences to the party opposing the motion. Some trivial amount (a scintilla) of evidence favoring the opposing party is not enough to defeat the motion for judgment; there must be a conflict in substantial evidence to create a jury question.

A motion for new trial may be joined with a motion for judgment, or asserted alone. It can be asserted by any party in either a jury or a nonjury trial. In a nonjury trial, it may be granted for any of the reasons for which rehearings were granted in suits in equity brought in federal court. If asserted in a jury case, Rule 59(a) allows a judge to grant the motion for any of the reasons new trials were granted in actions at law brought in federal court. A new trial can be granted because of errors in the admission or exclusion of evidence in a jury trial, for other errors in regard to the jury charge, because the damages are excessive, or because the verdict is against the great weight of the evidence. New trials should be granted on evidentiary grounds only when the verdict is against the great weight of the evidence and not merely because the judge believes the evidence favors the movant. When different conclusions could have been reached which would have been supported by sufficient evidence, the jury's choice of one of these conclusions cannot be against the great weight of evidence.

A motion for new trial also can be used to raise a challenge to the excessiveness of the jury's damages award. Although the Seventh Amendment has been held to prevent a federal court's addition of damages to a verdict, it does not bar the reduction of an excessive award by the judge. The judge can offer the plaintiff the option to accept the "remittitur"—that is, a reduction of the award—or face a new trial. If the excessive award is the result of passion or prejudice, however, a remittitur is not appropriate because the whole of the award is in question, and a new trial is the only appropriate remedy.

Only final judgments are ordinarily appealable. Therefore, the *grant* of a new trial is not immediately appealable because that ruling shows that the trial court's proceedings are not final. However, upon appeal of the judgment entered in that new trial, the grant of the motion can be raised as error. The trial court leaves in place a final judgment when it *denies* a new trial, and that ruling may be raised as error in the appeal taken from the judgment. Both the grant and the denial of a motion for judgment as a matter of law may be the subject of an immediate appeal because neither ruling requires further proceedings in the trial court.

Suppose a party loses before the jury. In challenging the verdict, he files both a renewed motion for judgment as a matter of law and a motion for new trial. If the trial court grants his motion for judgment as a matter of law, thereby giving him final judgment, his motion for new trial seems moot. However, in the absence of a trial court ruling on the new trial motion, an appellate court could not consider that motion if it decided to reverse the judgment entered as a matter of law. Rule 50(c) solves the problem by requiring the trial court to rule on his motion for new trial. Because the trial court has already given him a judgment as a matter of law, it will either grant or deny the motion for new trial conditioned on the reversal of that judgment. If the trial court conditionally grants the new trial motion and the other party obtains a reversal of the judgment on appeal, the case will be remanded for a new trial. If the motion for new trial was conditionally denied by the trial court, the movant may raise this denial as error during the appeal so that the appellate court can rule on this issue as well as on his judgment as a matter of law.

As noted above, a party's failure to move for judgment as a matter of law at the close of the evidence prevents him from renewing that motion after the verdict has been returned against him. In Unitherm Food Systems, Inc. v. Swift-Eckrich, Inc., 126 S.Ct. 980 (2006), the Supreme Court considered an appellate court's grant of a new trial based solely on the appellant's preverdict Rule 50(a) motion for judgment as a matter of law. The Court held that the appellate court had no power to grant a new trial to a party who failed to file a post-verdict motion for new trial. The Court also concluded that the party's preverdict motion for judgment as a matter of law was alone insufficient to authorize the grant of a new trial by the appellate court.

The Court in *Unitherm* noted with approval its earlier holdings that an appellate court also has no power to grant a judgment as a matter of law to a party that did not renew its preverdict motion for judgment. The Court reasoned that both post-verdict motions were necessary because they allowed the trial judge to make a determination on these legal issues after seeing and hearing the witnesses. Only if the trial judge had this opportunity should the appellate court have power to grant either a judgment as a matter of law or a new trial. A party therefore must assert the post-verdict motions for judgment and new trial before seeking either remedy from an appellate court.

G. Hypotheticals and Explanations

1. In a diversity case in federal court, Clarine Weathers filed a wrongful death claim for damages against American Paint, Inc., and demanded a jury trial. She contends that her husband died of lead poisoning caused by exposure to lead-based paint produced by American Paint. After both parties completed discovery in the case, American Paint filed a motion for summary judgment, contending that Mrs. Weathers had been unable to discover any witness or other evidence to support her contention that Mr. Weathers had been exposed to a lead-based paint produced by American Paint. American Paint concedes that Mr. Weathers worked for more than two decades as a house painter; that it sold lead-based paint during this period; and that he died of lead poisoning. It argues, however, that she cannot satisfy the element of causation without proving the material fact of exposure. Mrs. Weathers contends the motion should be denied because American Paint has produced no affidavit to negate the possibility of her husband's exposure to its paint and because exposure is a fact issue for the jury to decide. **Should the court grant or deny the motion?**

Explanation

American Paint's no-evidence motion for summary judgment should be granted because the plaintiff's failure to carry her burden of production means that she must lose as a matter of law.

Rules

(1) The plaintiff has the burden of proof, which includes the burden of production, and she therefore must produce some evidence to prove the material facts necessary to support each element of her cause of action. (2) After *Celotex*, federal courts grant a summary judgment if, after the plaintiff has had the opportunity to seek discovery, the defendant "points out" (rather than proves) that the plaintiff has no evidence to support a material fact necessary to prove her cause of action.

Application

The plaintiff must carry her burdens in regard to each material fact necessary to support her cause of action in order to prevail. If she fails to carry her burden as to any element, she must lose her case as a matter of law. American Paint has no obligation to prove the absence of exposure; proof of exposure is the plaintiff's burden. Because Mrs. Weathers cannot carry her burden of coming forward with some evidence of the material fact of exposure, she cannot sustain the element of causation. Failing to have any evidence to prove this fact also means that the court will not send her case to the jury.

2. Suppose that in response to American Paint's motion for summary judgment, Mrs. Weathers submitted an affidavit from John Jones, who had employed Mr. Weathers as a house painter for the five years immediately preceding his death. Mr. Jones swore in his affidavit that he had purchased lead-based paint from American Paint during that period and that from personal knowledge he knew Mr. Weathers had used these products on different jobs as his employee. American Paint responded to the Jones affidavit by filing the affidavit of its long-time office manager, Elaine Picket. She swore that she retained complete records of any sale of lead-based paints and that no lead-based paint had been sold by American Paint to John Jones during the time he had employed Mr. Weathers. **Should the court grant or deny the motion?**

Explanation

The court must deny the motion because a genuine issue of material fact exists, and this issue must be decided by the jury.

Rules

(1) In a jury case, the judge must deny a motion for summary judgment if he finds that a material fact is genuinely in dispute. (2) A genuine issue exists when the summary judgment evidence allows inferences on either side of the issue. (3) In deciding that such permissible inferences exist, a judge views the evidence in the light most favorable to the party opposing the motion and resolves all doubts in that party's favor. (4) A judge cannot weigh the evidence or consider the credibility of the persons giving that evidence because these are functions of the jury. (5) Only when no rational jury could find in favor of the non-moving party, can the judge conclude that no genuine issue exists.

Application

In this hypothetical, we face the problem frequently seen in summary judgment practice—the clash of affidavits. One must read affidavits closely to be assured that the sworn statements bear directly upon the material fact in issue and that the affidavit was made on personal knowledge. Assuming these two affidavits were in proper form, they appear to clash directly in that Mr. Jones swears that he bought lead-based paints from the defendant and Mrs. Picket swears that her complete records show no such purchase. This factual dispute requires denial of the motion for summary judgment. A reasonable jury might well find the facts as Mr. Jones would state them and thus conclude that Mr. Weathers had been exposed to lead-based paints sold by American Paint. Because a genuine issue exists, the moving party is not entitled to a judgment as a matter of law.

3. Suppose that at the trial of Mrs. Weathers wrongful-death claim against American Paint, the plaintiff presented all of her evidence and then rested. However, she finished the presentation of her case without calling Mr. Jones to testify and without offering any other evidence to prove that Mr. Weathers had been exposed to lead-based paints sold by American Paint. Although Mr. Jones was available to testify, he no longer believed that he had bought lead-based paint from American Paint. **What should the defendant do, and will it succeed?**

Explanation

The defendant should assert a motion for judgment as a matter of law (once referred to as the motion for directed verdict), and that motion should be granted under these circumstances because the plaintiff has failed to produce any evidence to support the material fact of exposure.

Rules

(1) The motion for judgment as a matter of law raises the same issue as the motion for summary judgment but does so after the plaintiff has had the opportunity to present evidence. (2) Courts often think of this motion as raising the purely *legal* question of whether sufficient evidence exists to raise an issue for the jury. (3) The judge should grant the motion only when a reasonable jury could not find in favor of the party opposing it. (4) The judge may not weigh the evidence or determine the credibility of witnesses, and should give all reasonable inferences to the party opposing the motion, but some trivial amount (a scintilla) of evidence favoring the opposing party is not enough to defeat the motion for judgment.

Application

Having been given the opportunity to present all of her evidence, the plaintiff has failed to carry her burden of production by coming forward with some evidence to prove the material fact of exposure. Failing to carry that burden means that the plaintiff must lose as a matter of law. A claimant who does not carry her burdens as to every element of her cause of action must lose. That is a legal conclusion based on the fundamental notion that plaintiffs can obtain the benefits of a judicial remedy only when they fulfill all of the legal requirements of a cause of action.

CHAPTER 12

Res Judicata

A. Terminology

Claim Preclusion—Claim preclusion alludes to the broad effect of res judicata, while issue preclusion characterizes the narrow result of collateral estoppel. Claim preclusion prevents relitigation of all matters that were or should have been litigated in the first suit.

Collateral Estoppel—Collateral estoppel prevents the relitigation of a particular issue, and courts more often today refer to this concept as issue preclusion.

Issue Preclusion—Issue preclusion prevents relitigation of an issue of law or fact that was actually litigated and decided in the first suit. Since the issue must be actually decided in the first suit, issue preclusion does not bind any party unless he had the full opportunity to litigate that issue.

Judicial Estoppel—If a party makes a sworn factual statement in one suit and obtains a benefit from that court because of this statement, he will be estopped from taking an inconsistent position on the same factual issue in a second suit.
Law of the Case—An appellate court's determination of a party's legal contentions binds that party throughout the remainder of that litigation. The appellate court's decision is said to establish the law of the case in regard to that legal issue.
Privity—A person can be bound by res judicata if, though not a party to the first suit, he was in privity with a party to the first suit.
Res Judicata—Res judicata literally means the thing adjudicated, but this phrase refers to the body of largely common law rules that protect a final decision from relitigation in a second trial court. Res judicata has two strands or effects—claim preclusion (res judicata proper) and issue preclusion (collateral estoppel).

B. Overview of Chapter

The general topic of res judicata includes rules that prohibit the relitigation in a second trial court of a claim or of an issue. To understand res judicata, one must begin by recognizing that the rules of res judicata have been created by courts; they are therefore common law—that is, judge-made—rules of state or federal courts. In addition, this discussion focuses on the *general* rules of res judicata—that is, those that prevail in most jurisdictions. If a state's common law rules of res judicata differ from those generally applicable in other states, those rules nevertheless control the validity of judgments issued and enforced in that state. And those rules have interstate effect because sister states must enforce that first state's judgments according to its res judicata rules. Each state must enforce sister-state judgments as a result of the requirement imposed by federal statute, 28 U.S.C. §1738, enacted under Congress's authority found in Article IV, §1, of the Constitution to require full faith and credit.

Res judicata and the requirement of full faith and credit serve the broad policies favoring the finality of judgments. An unlimited ability to relitigate cases undermines the rule of law because no legal right or responsibility would be settled. Under such a system, litigation would become a never-ending game in which the financial resources of a litigant would be more important than the merits of his legal contentions. By requiring finality, res judicata imposes a rule of respect for the legal efforts of courts and restricts the use of litigation as a means to oppress or harass. A judgment gains this finality even when the court makes errors of law in deciding the case. If the first adjudication of a case was not perfectly performed, a direct challenge through appeal offers an opportunity to correct harmful errors. If that direct challenge fails or if the losing party fails to attempt a direct challenge, res judicata represents the policy that holds that having an end to the dispute is preferable to a continuing attempt to cure every error.

Bringing an end to litigation does not operate to terminate the legal rights of one who has not had a full and fair opportunity to protect those rights. The Due Process Clauses of the Fifth (limiting federal courts) and Fourteenth (limiting state courts) Amendments influence the rules of res judicata and prevent them from depriving anyone of the *opportunity to litigate* legal claims or defenses. No one who was not a party to a suit may be precluded from litigating his legal claims or defenses by the decision in that suit. One must, therefore, find that the party *against whom* preclusion is used had a full and fair opportunity to litigate in the first suit.

In rare instances, persons not named as parties in the first suit may be bound by a court's decision if they had such a close and relevant relationship with a named party that allowing relitigation would be unfair. Courts refer to these persons as being in privity with the named party. For example, the shareholders of a corporation cannot relitigate a case decided against that corporation. After reaching majority, a ward should not, barring fraud or collusion, be free to reopen a case decided against her guardian. Privity thus often refers to a recognized legal power of the named party to bind through litigation the rights and obligations of those they represent but who are not named parties. Privity does not bind a nonparty merely because he has a close relationship of some sort with a named party. For instance, a judgment entered against a husband does not ordinarily bind his wife when she was not a party to the suit but both were injured in an accident.

1. Enforcing the Judgment

One or the other branch of res judicata can become relevant depending on whether the winning party in the first suit is the plaintiff or the defendant. If the defendant prevails by recovering a favorable judgment, that judgment becomes his affirmative defense to an attempt by the plaintiff to reassert the same claim. However, if the plaintiff obtained a judgment on the merits, a defendant's attempt to relitigate will likely occur when the plaintiff seeks to execute—that is, collect on—her judgment. If the plaintiff must execute her judgment in a state other than the one in which it was issued, she must institute a second suit asking a court of the second state to recognize and enforce her judgment If, in this enforcement proceeding, the defendant argues that the judgment is erroneous, the plaintiff must assert claim preclusion, contending that the final judgment precludes the defendant from relitigating the merits of the claim.

Claim preclusion does not, however, prevent a defendant from challenging the jurisdiction of the court which entered it. If successful, a challenge to the first court's jurisdiction invalidates the judgment. However, if the defendant made the same jurisdictional challenge in the first proceeding, he cannot challenge jurisdiction a second time when the plaintiff seeks to execute the judgment. In this instance, the plaintiff would assert issue preclusion to bar the defendant from relitigating the jurisdictional issue a second time. In the older terminology, she would argue that the defendant is collaterally estopped from having a second opportunity to challenge the issue of personal jurisdiction.

2. Choosing the Applicable Rules of Res Judicata

Our federal system, featuring independent state court systems and the federal court system, makes these applications somewhat more complicated. However, as a general rule, when a losing party seeks in one jurisdiction to relitigate a matter decided in another, the res judicata rules of the jurisdiction that issued the judgment control. For instance, assume that the plaintiff brings her Colorado state court judgment to Arizona for enforcement. The federal full-faith-and-credit statute, 28 U.S.C. § 1738, requires Arizona to enforce that judgment, if valid, to the extent it would be enforced in Colorado. In other words, Arizona must apply Colorado's res judicata rules to determine whether a party can relitigate the claim or any issue.

The res judicata rules of the jurisdiction (state or federal) which issued the first judgment guide the preclusion decision of the court (either state or federal) in the second proceeding. The court faced with the issue refers to the common law rules of the jurisdiction in which the claim or issue was adjudicated. If the plaintiff brought her Colorado state court judgment for enforcement in a federal court, that federal court would also decide the scope of enforcement by reference to the res judicata rules of Colorado because federal courts are bound by the policies of § 1738. A federal court judgment registered in another federal district court will be protected by that second federal court's application of federal res judicata rules.

By analogy to § 1738, a federal court judgment entered on the basis of a ground of subject matter jurisdiction other than diversity must be enforced in a state court to the extent required by the federal common law of res judicata. The Supreme Court has altered this requirement when a federal court judgment entered in a diversity case is to be enforced. A judgment entered by a federal court in a case brought solely on the basis of diversity must be enforced by other courts according to the res judicata rules of the state in which the federal court sat when it entered the judgment. In Semtek International Inc. v. Lockheed Martin Corp., 531 U.S. 497 (2001), the Court held that though federal courts have common law power to enforce a federal diversity judgment according to federal rather than state rules, that power should be exercised by applying the forum state's res judicata rules. This decision was justified in part as a means to enforce the policies of *Erie*. Those policies support the conclusion that a federal diversity judgment, which necessarily adjudicates a state cause of action under state substantive law, should not have a significantly different effect from what it would have had if issued by a court of that state. Therefore, the res judicata rules of the forum state will control the scope and effect of a federal judgment entered in a diversity case. See *id.* at 508–509.

Assume a federal court sitting in California in a diversity case dismisses the complaint for failure of the plaintiff to satisfy the California statute of limitations. If the plaintiff refiled the same suit in Maryland to take advantage of that state's more lenient limitations period, the defendant would assert an affirmative defense using the res judicata rules of California.

C. Claim Preclusion

In general, the rules of claim preclusion apply only when three requirements have been satisfied. (1) A final judgment must have been entered on the merits. (2) The second trial court proceeding must be between the same parties who litigated in the first proceeding. (3) The second proceeding has been brought to adjudicate the same claim that was adjudicated in the first proceeding. Furthermore, claim preclusion prevents relitigation of matters which could have been litigated by a party even though not actually raised or decided.

1. Final Judgment on the Merits

Before the second suit can be barred by claim preclusion, the first suit must have been ended by a final decision on the merits. A summary or default judgment satisfies the requirement of a judgment on the merits. And the requirement is obviously satisfied when the first suit ended after a full trial with the entry of a judgment. Confusion can arise, however, when the court enters what it calls a dismissal. That order will be given claim preclusive effect only if the rules of the issuing jurisdiction say so.

Rule 41(b) of the Federal Rules of Civil Procedure authorizes a federal court to dismiss an action, but provides that in three exceptional cases—a dismissal for lack of jurisdiction, for improper venue, or for failure to join an "indispensable" party under Rule 19—this dismissal cannot operate as an adjudication upon the merits. However, when the ground for dismissal does not fit within one of these categories, Rule 41(b) imposes a default rule so that the dismissal operates as an adjudication upon the merits, unless the court in its order otherwise specifies. This provision of Rule 41(b) necessarily supports the conclusion that a court has power expressly to make an involuntary dismissal an adjudication upon the merits if the ground for the dismissal does not fit into one of the three exceptions.

Therefore, if a federal district court enters a dismissal for reasons other than jurisdiction, venue, or Rule 19 and does not specify otherwise, Rule 41(b) makes that dismissal an adjudication upon the merits. If the court or the default rule makes a dismissal an adjudication upon the merits, the dismissal would seem to operate as a judgment on the merits and receive claim-preclusive effect. However, the Supreme Court, through its recent decision in Semtek International, Inc. v. Lockheed Martin Corp., 531 U.S. 497, 506 (2001) held that Rule 41(b) did not authorize a federal court to give a dismissal claim-preclusive effect.

The Court concluded that the "adjudication upon the merits" language of Rule 41(b) had the effect only of prohibiting the plaintiff from refiling his case in the same federal court. In this sense, the better language was to specify that the dismissal was "with prejudice against refiling" in the federal court that dismissed the case. See id. A dismissal "without prejudice against refiling" means that the plaintiff can even refile in the same federal court that entered the dismissal. A federal court might, for instance, dismiss a complaint without prejudice against refiling because the plaintiff seemed unable to properly plead a claim for relief. With a new lawyer, perhaps, the plaintiff would be able to refile in the same federal court.

In Semtek, the plaintiff had filed in a state court in California, but the defendant had removed the case to federal court in that state. That federal court dismissed the action for failure of the plaintiff to comply with the two-year California statute of limitations. The federal court not only dismissed the case in accordance with Rule 41(b), but also stated that the dismissal should be considered an adjudication upon the merits. The Supreme Court noted that, as a general rule, a dismissal for failure to satisfy a statute of limitations does not bar the plaintiff from going to a state with a longer limitations period and filing there. In this case, the plaintiff did just that; it refiled in Maryland state court because that state had a three-year limitation period. However, the

Maryland court held that the federal judgment operated as a decision on the merits and had to be given claim-preclusive effect. The Supreme Court reversed this decision, holding that Rule 41(b)'s language was not intended to have such effect.

2. Mutuality of Parties

The rules of claim preclusion require that both suits involve the same parties—that mutuality of parties exist between the two suits. Neither the Constitution nor the policies of res judicata would allow use of preclusion doctrine against one who was not either a party or in privity with a party to the first suit. Due process prevents the use of res judicata against someone who has not had a full and fair opportunity to present his claim in court. As a result, a court cannot preclude the assertion of similar claims by someone who did not participate in the first suit, even when that someone is a spouse.

For instance, a plaintiff who sued one defendant and lost cannot be barred from suing a second defendant on the same claim. The requirement of mutuality of parties prevents this new defendant from using claim preclusion even though the plaintiff has had her day in court on her claim. The claim being asserted in that suit may not be precisely the same as the one asserted in the first suit because of this different defendant. The reason for insisting on identity between the defending parties seems to derive from the broad effect of claim preclusion. In addition, the different nature of the two defendants may have affected the plaintiff's strategy and chance of success in the first suit, and this difference perhaps justifies preventing a new party from precluding the plaintiff's second suit. As noted below, however, this new defending party might benefit from the narrow effect of issue preclusion.

3. Same Claim

A party cannot be precluded from asserting a claim simply because she had sued the same party for a different reason once before. Before claim preclusion can be applied, therefore, the claims asserted in both suits must be the same. However, a court can give either a broad or narrow interpretation to the requirement that the claims be the same. If a plaintiff injured by the explosion of a hot-water heater sues the manufacturer for negligent construction and loses, she cannot replead the same negligence claim in a second trial court. Or, to be more precise, the manufacturer can successfully assert a res judicata affirmative defense in that second suit. Both claims have been pled under the same theory of liability—in the sense that the common law rule prohibits harm caused by negligence. In addition, both suits would require use of the same evidence because the material facts of both suits are the same.

Suppose, instead, the plaintiff brought a products liability claim for defective design against the manufacturer in the second suit. By narrowly defining the causes of action one could note that the different nature of the illegal action calls for proof of different material facts and thus depends on the use of different evidence. Therefore, if the sameness required for claim preclusion demands identity between the legal theories or the evidence used in both suits, plaintiffs would be able to reformulate their claims and try again. However, under the influence of the *Restatement (Second) of Judgments*, most courts today preclude the assertion in a second suit of any claim that arises from the transaction that gave rise to the first claim. A transaction is defined for these purposes much as the term is defined for purposes of Rule 13(a) to include logically related events or occurrences.

The *Restatement* is drafted by the members of the American Law Institute, and has no direct legal authority. It has, however, been influential in persuading many jurisdictions to take this broader approach to claim preclusion. The transaction test requires plaintiffs to engage in legal research before completing their pleading decisions and to discover all claims which can be alleged in their dispute. By treating such related claims as the same for preclusion purposes, the courts thus further the policies of res judicata without causing unfairness to claimants.

D. ISSUE PRECLUSION

1. Four Requirements

Issue preclusion bars a party from having a second opportunity to contest an issue that he had a full and fair opportunity to litigate in the first suit. It thereby protects other parties "from the expense and vexation attending multiple lawsuits, conserves judicial resources, and fosters reliance on judicial action by minimizing the possibility of inconsistent decisions." Montana v. U.S., 440 U.S. 147, 153–154 (1979). These values clearly outweigh any interest of a party who seeks a second chance to litigate the issue he was able to contest in the first suit.

Assume a plaintiff obtains a federal court default judgment in New York, awarding her $100,000 for personal injuries. The sole defendant, a California domiciliary, failed to answer or respond in any way to the suit. If the defendant has no assets in New York to pay the New York judgment, the plaintiff will have to register the judgment in a court in California in order to execute it against the defendant's property in that state. In some states, the judgment-creditor must file suit in the second state to make her New York judgment a judgment of California. Once that it accomplished, the plaintiff can execute what is now a California judgment against the property of the defendant.

When notified of the enforcement procedure in California, the defendant can appear in the California court, but he cannot assert defenses to the claim underlying the judgment. In the common law terminology of res judicata, the claim has merged into the judgment. It does not matter that the merits of that claim have not been actually litigated because the defendant had the opportunity to do so in New York. However, neither the res judicata rules nor the full-faith-and-credit statute, §1738, requires the answering state to enforce a judgment entered without jurisdiction. As a result, the defendant/judgment-debtor can attack the validity of the New York by contending that the New York court entered its judgment without personal jurisdiction.

Assume instead that the defendant actually contested the New York court's jurisdiction in that court. Having lost on that issue, he refused to litigate the case on the merits. As a result, the New York court entered a default judgment in favor of the plaintiff. When the plaintiff brings this judgment to California for enforcement, the defendant will be precluded (collaterally estopped) from contesting the issue of the New York court's jurisdiction in California. Having had his day in court on that issue, he cannot make a collateral challenge to the New York court's judgment in a second trial court. In modern terms, we would say that issue preclusion stops the defendant from being able to relitigate an issue he had actually litigated in the first court.

Precluding relitigation by the California defendant is justified because the four requirements of issue preclusion would be satisfied. (1) Before precluding relitigation, a court must find that the issue before it is the same as the issue in the first suit. In the California court, the only issue that the defendant could raise was the personal jurisdiction of the New York court. However, he had previously raised this issue before the New York court. (2) The issue must have been actually litigated in the first suit. The defendant took advantage of his opportunity when he appeared before the New York court to contest its jurisdiction. No reason exists to allow him a second chance when the plaintiff brings the judgment for enforcement in California. (3) The issue must be actually decided. Issue preclusion requires a decision on the litigated issue to ensure that both the parties and the court considered the matter seriously. (4) As a related requirement, the issue must be essential to the court's decision. A party might only half-heartedly contest a peripheral issue, but the law can be assured that vigorous advocacy would be called for in respect to an issue that was critical to the court's decision. Furthermore, a party is less likely to seek appellate review of an issue on which the judgment does not depend.

The Second Restatement of Judgments describes the requirements for issue preclusion in the following manner:

> When an issue of fact or law is actually litigated and determined by a valid and final judgment, and the determination is essential to the judgment, the determination is conclusive in a subsequent action between the parties, whether on the same or a different claim

Restatement (Second) of Judgments § 27 (1982).

The Third Circuit has identified the four requirements for issue preclusion in a slightly different form: "(1) the identical issue was previously adjudicated; (2) the issue was actually litigated; (3) the previous determination was necessary to the decision; and (4) the party being precluded from relitigating the issue was fully represented in the prior action." Henglein v. Colt Industries Operating Corp., 260 F.3d 201, 209 (3d Cir.2001), *quoting* Raytech Corp. v. White, 54 F.3d 187, 190 (3d Cir.1995). The court's concern for the protection of the party being estopped also appears in the evaluation of the four Restatement requirements as well.

2. Same Issue

The party asserting issue preclusion must identify the issue of fact, mixed fact and law, or law in the first litigation that will be litigated in the second trial. Of course, one has that problem only when the second suit is somehow different from the first. If the same claim is being asserted and the other requirements of claim preclusion are satisfied, res judicata applies to prevent relitigation of the second claim, including any issue that was or might have been decided in the first suit.

The discussion above of issue preclusion as applied to the relitigation of a jurisdictional issue assumes that the first and second suits are different. In that hypothetical, assume the first suit on the merits of the plaintiff's cause action ends in a judgment for the plaintiff that is not overturned on appeal. If the defendant has no assets located in the forum state, the plaintiff must bring the judgment for enforcement in the state where the defendant's assets are located. The plaintiff there sues upon the judgment, not upon the original cause of action. The objection to personal jurisdiction lies outside the judgment and, therefore, escapes claim preclusion. However, a defendant who appeared and lost his challenge to the first court's personal jurisdiction cannot assert that defense a second time when the plaintiff brings the judgment for enforcement.

a. Issues of Fact

An issue can be defined on different levels. Almost every legal issue turns on the finding of historical facts. To begin with, therefore, an issue can be described as one of fact. Those issues of fact, however, have a close relation with legal issues or conclusions. Suppose in her first suit, Jane Smith contended that Bob James negligently caused an auto accident in which both were injured, but she specifically alleged only that Bob ran a red light. If the jury finds that Bob was not negligent, that finding would clearly bar relitigation between the two parties on the issue of whether Bob caused the accident by running a red light. If the procedural rules applicable in the first action do not require Bob to assert any counterclaim he has arising from that accident, he could bring a second action claiming that Jane was liable for his injuries because she negligently caused the accident. Assume Jane defended herself by claiming that Bob was contributorily negligent by driving at an excessive rate of speed. Bob would contend that the issue of his negligence was decided in the first trial and cannot be relitigated. Jane might respond by contending that the jury ruled on negligence but only based on the evidence she introduced about him running a red light. The general rule, however, is that the issue decided in the first trial was Bob's negligence in causing the accident and, therefore, that legal issue cannot be relitigated. Restatement (Second) Judgments § 27 (1982).

b. Issues of Law

The Supreme Court has recognized that the decision of an "unmixed question of law" may not preclude relitigation in a second suit involving unrelated subject matter. See U.S. v. Stauffer Chemical Company, 464 U.S. 165, 171 (1984). In *Stauffer*, the company challenged the statutory authority of the Environmental Protection Agency to use private contractors to inspect the company's plants in Tennessee to check for violations of the Clean Air Act. The company sought to use issue preclusion on this statutory issue because it had obtained a ruling on that same issue in an earlier suit when the United States attempted to use private contractors to inspect its plant in Wyoming. The Supreme Court upheld the application of issue preclusion against the Government in respect to this unmixed question of law and concluded that the two suits were based on "virtually identical facts." *Id.* at 172.

The Government argued that issue preclusion should not be used against it on unmixed issues of law because that would tend to freeze the law of the land. The Court concluded that the concern for freezing legal rights applied only when issue preclusion on legal issues was sought in the absence of mutuality. In the *Stauffer* case, the Government had engaged in the same litigation twice against the same private party. Applying issue preclusion under these circumstances furthered the res judicata purposes of "protecting litigants from burdensome litigation and of promoting judicial economy." See *id.*

The *Stauffer* holding does not however support the use of issue preclusion to bind the Government to a previous decision on a legal issue that concerns a recurring issue of importance to the general public.

In Commissioner of Internal Revenue v. Sunnen, 333 U.S. 591 (1948), the Supreme Court refused to apply issue preclusion against the IRS even though the facts of the two legal challenges were identical. The taxpayer had licensed a corporation, which he controlled, to use his patent in exchange for a 10% royalty. He had a practice of assigning his royalty rights to his wife for no consideration. In a 1935 proceeding, the Board of Tax Appeals held that the taxpayer was not liable for the income paid to his wife under a 1928 license agreement covering the years 1929 through 1931. However, in the second litigation the question concerned the 1937 tax year, and the taxpayer contended that the earlier decision prevented relitigation of the issue of his liability for royalties paid to his wife. In the period between those two suits, a series of cases had reversed the law as it had stood at the time of the first suit. The Court found that issue preclusion under these circumstances had to give way to the change in legal rules about a taxpayer's liability. Two reasons justified barring issue preclusion. First, applying preclusion would hinder the change in law. Furthermore, using issue preclusion to freeze the tax law for only one taxpayer would allow him to benefit even though the change in law denied that same benefit to other taxpayers.

3. Actually Litigated and Decided

Ordinarily, neither a default nor a consent judgment should be given issue-preclusive effect. Issue preclusion differs from claim preclusion in this important requirement that the issue must have been actually litigated by the parties and decided by the court. Assume a manufacturer sued a patent holder claiming that the defendant's patent was invalid and not infringed by the plaintiff's new product. The patent holder concludes that no reason exists for an appearance in the suit, and the plaintiff takes judgment. A second manufacturer now sues the same patent holder and contends that its product is identical to the first plaintiff's product. The second plaintiff also argues for the application of offensive nonmutual issue preclusion because the default judgment has already established that the patent holder's patent is invalid and not infringed. Even if both suits were brought in the same forum state, issue preclusion could not be used because the patent holder did not actually litigate the patent-validity issue. Issue preclusion has a narrow and focused effect because it depends on the fact that the party to be bound recognized the significance of the issue and had a full and fair opportunity to present his side. These two requirements cannot be satisfied by a default judgment because no actual litigation occurs in that case.

4. Essential to a Valid, Final Judgment

Notice however that the decision does not have to be on the merits. The court's ruling on a motion to dismiss for lack of personal jurisdiction can support issue preclusion even though it is not a final judgment on the merits. If the first court ruled against the party to be bound by issue preclusion after he had presented his written arguments against personal jurisdiction, he will be barred from having a second chance to litigate this issue when the plaintiff tries to enforce the judgment. See R. Casad and K. Clermont, Res Judicata: A Handbook on its Theory, Doctrine, and Practice 124 (2001).

Even if the issue was actually litigated and decided, it must be essential (or necessary) to the judgment in the case. This requirement prevents the application of issue preclusion to incidental issues that the parties may not have taken seriously. Furthermore, the court is unlikely to give thorough treatment to an issue on which its ruling did not depend. Under these circumstances, a second court cannot rely on the trustworthiness of the first court's decision, and the party to be bound may not have had a full and fair opportunity to present his arguments on that issue. If the issue was not critical to the judgment, the party to be bound would have little reason to correct the court's decision through appeal. With little incentive to make a direct challenge to the first court's ruling, the party to be bound by issue preclusion should not be barred from a collateral challenge as well. See Jean Alexander Cosmetics, Inc. v. L'Oreal USA, Inc., 458 F.3d 244, 250 (3d Cir. 2006).

The major unresolved problem among the different jurisdictions concerns how the requirement of essentiality applies when a trial court enters the judgment based on alternative holdings. Suppose a plaintiff asserts a negligence claim against the defendant. After trial, the judge enters judgment for the plaintiff based on two holdings: (1) the defendant was not negligent and (2) the plaintiff's negligence caused the accident. The first Restatement of Judgments took the position that the plaintiff should be bound by the decision on both issues if they had been both actually litigated and decided. However, the Restatement (Second) Judgments § 27, Comment i, concluded that neither determination should be binding on the plaintiff because the alternative holding deters appeal. The plaintiff must challenge two holdings of the trial court in order to prevail upon appeal. Also, the plaintiff may have been distracted by one issue and thus have failed to concentrate sufficiently on the other. Federal courts of appeals have reached inconsistent results. See *Jean Alexander Cosmetics, Inc.*, 458 F.3d at 251.

Some courts apply the first Restatement's approach so long as the alternative holdings have been litigated and decided, and would be essential to the judgment if standing alone. Other courts give issue preclusive effect to both issues only after an appellate court has ruled on both. Still other courts refuse to give either holding issue-preclusive effect because alternative rulings cannot, by definition, be essential to the judgment. One may have difficulty concluding that the first court gave its full attention to both issues if it decided that both support a judgment. The dual basis for a judgment may well discourage the losing party from taking an appeal. A litigant can deal with this problem by identifying and applying whatever rule has been adopted by the jurisdiction that issued the judgment.

5. Non-Mutual Issue Preclusion

Under traditional common law rules, collateral estoppel (or issue preclusion) could be applied only when the parties were the same in both suits—that is, where there existed mutuality of parties. Today, federal law, and the law of many states, no longer requires mutuality of parties as a requirement for the application of issue preclusion. What remains, however, is the absolute requirement that the party being precluded from relitigating an issue was a party to the first suit. In other words, the party against whom a court enforces issue preclusion must have enjoyed a full and fair opportunity to litigate the issue in the first suit.

Non-mutual issue preclusion can be used both defensively and offensively. It can operate defensively to protect a new defendant against a plaintiff who has litigated the same issue against a different defendant and lost. A new plaintiff can assert issue preclusion offensively to preclude a defendant from relitigating the issue of his liability after he lost on that issue in a suit with a different plaintiff.

Remember, the four requirements mentioned above must be satisfied before one can use nonmutual (or any form of) issue preclusion. If the four requirements have been satisfied, its defensive use in the absence of mutuality of parties causes few dangers. For example, suppose a patentee sues defendant-1 in federal court claiming patent infringement. After full litigation, the court decides that the plaintiff's patent is invalid. In a second suit, the plaintiff sues defendant-2 for infringement of the same patent. Defendant-2 can use the first court's decision that the patent is invalid as a defense to bar the plaintiff from relitigating that issue. Even though defendant-2 did not partic-ipate in the first suit, no strong reason exists for denying him the benefit of the previous decision on that issue. Furthermore, the defensive use of issue preclusion encourages plaintiffs to join all possible defendants in one suit. It thus reduces the waste of judicial resources which results from multiple suits on the same issue.

Suppose, however, that a defendant was accused of causing a fire that burned the buildings owned by numerous other persons. The first victim brings suit against the defendant, contending that he negligently injured that plaintiff's property. In this suit, the defendant prevails based on the court's decision that he was not negligent. A second plaintiff sues the same defendant to recover for property damage suffered in the fire and again contends that the defendant was negligent. The defendant cannot use issue preclusion defen-sively against this plaintiff because the second plaintiff was not a party to the first suit and, therefore, has not had his day in court on the issue of negli-gence.

Suppose, after full litigation of the issue, the second trial court decides that the defendant was negligent and awards judgment to the second plaintiff. This suit is then followed, eagerly, by a third suit by yet another plaintiff. The third plaintiff seeks to use issue preclusion offensively against the defendant based on the decision in the second suit. Under these circumstances, courts have hes-itated to allow non-mutual issue preclusion even though the defendant has had its day (or two) in court. This situation calls for the exercise of judicial discre-tion in deciding whether preclusion would cause a fair result. A court should hesitate to allow preclusion whenever, as in this hypothetical, there exist in-consistent decisions on the same issue. Because the defendant won once on the issue of its negligence, he might continue to win. If that is likely, a court should not prevent him from having the opportunity to do so. It would be especially unfair to the defendant if the case in which he lost involved such a small claim that he was not prompted to litigate vigorously. In addition, any special diffi-culty for the defendant in the litigation that is used for preclusion, such as the absence of a key witness, would weigh against issue preclusion as well.

Unlimited use of offensive, nonmutual issue preclusion can generate, rather than deter, multiple lawsuits. In the hypothetical, a single suit was possible and would have conserved judicial resources, but the parties may have chosen to multiply litigation to gain an advantage. To prevent this possibility, a court should ask whether the plaintiff was prevented by any difficulty from joining the first suit. If not, the court can conclude that the plaintiff sat back and waited to see how the other suits would come out. Under these circumstances, it might rule against allowing issue preclusion to deter such wasteful practices.

E. Hypotheticals and Explanations

1. Jane Doe, a citizen of New York sued the City of New York in state court for the return of her car. The city towed her car because she routinely parked it near her apartment in a space reserved by city ordinance for official vehicles. In her suit, Ms. Doe asserted a state cause of action for conversion against the city. After trial, the state court held the city had complied with the provisions of its ordinance and had not converted Ms. Doe's property. Thoroughly disgusted with her treatment in New York state court, Ms. Doe refused to appeal to yet another New York court. She thereafter brought a civil rights lawsuit in federal court in New York. In this federal suit, Ms. Doe asserted a claim for relief against the city under Title 42 U.S.C. §1983 alleging that the towing of her car pursuant to the city ordinance deprived her of property without due process of law and thus violated her constitutional rights. **What defense should the city assert?**

Explanation

The city should assert the defense of res judicata or claim preclusion in that this §1983 claim should have been asserted in the first suit against the city, and that defense should be successful.

Rule

(1) In order to determine the city's res judicata defense, the federal court will apply New York res judicata rules. (2) Claim preclusion rules require enforcement of (a) a final and valid judgments on the merits, (b) entered on the same claim, and (c) between the same parties. (3) Under modern doctrine, courts generally consider as part of the "same claim" all claims that arise from the same transaction or occurrence.

Application

This would be a fairly easy case under the modern res judicata rules. That doctrine forces the plaintiff to join in one suit all claims that she has against the defendant that arise from the same transaction or occurrence. Res judicata policy protects the finality of the first judgment and prevents the plaintiff from filing numerous suits to assert related claims in an attempt to torment or exhaust the defendant. The conversion and civil rights claims both arise from the same incident or transaction—that is, the towing of her car by the city. No law prevented her from asserting the civil rights claim in state court, and she should therefore be barred from forcing the city to litigate yet again about the same conflict.

2. When she became an executive of Flush Drug Co., Inc., Susan Farino signed a contract in which Flush promised her over $100,000 in benefits if it should ever fire her. She had to agree in the contract to an anti-competition clause that prohibited her from engaging in a competing business within two years after leaving Flush's employ. Flush is a Texas corporation, but Ms. Farino is a citizen of New Mexico who works as a Flush representative in that state. After only one year of employment, Flush terminated Ms. Farino and refused to pay the benefits promised under the contract. She sued Flush for breach of contract in a Texas state court seeking the $100,000 in benefits, but that suit ended when Flush was given a summary judgment holding that it did not owe such benefits to Ms. Farino. Ms. Farino did not appeal the Texas judgment, but instead brought a suit in a New Mexico state court seeking $100,000 in damages, challenging the anti-competition clause of her contract with Flush as a violation of Texas anti-trust law. **What should be Flush's defense in the New Mexico court?**

Explanation

Flush should interpose its Texas judgment and assert res judicata or claim preclusion as its defense in the suit in New Mexico.

Rule

(1) Under the Full-Faith-and-Credit statute, 28 U.S.C. § 1738, the New Mexico court is bound to give the same effect to the Texas judgment that a Texas court would. (2) Under modern doctrine, courts generally find that all claims that arise from the same transaction or occurrence are barred from re-litigation as the same claim. (3) A minority rule holds that causes of action that do not depend on the same evidence are not the same claim, and the adjudication of one does not bar the other.

Application

Since a court in one state is asked to enforce the judgment entered by a court of another state, we must remember that the res judicata rules applicable in the state that issued the judgment determine its enforcement in the second state. The Texas lawsuit was a judgment on the merits, and that judgment is final. Mutuality of parties is satisfied because both suits involve the same opposing parties. The only question is whether Texas uses the modern transactional test for determining whether the same claim is being asserted in both suits. Under that rule, Texas law could hold that the breach of contract and anti-trust claims both arose from the contractual relationship that gave rise to the challenges in both of these courts. More to the point, the transactional test is a way of insisting that a party bring forward all claims that should have been adjudicated in the first court.

3. When she became an executive of Flush Drug Co., Inc., Susan Farino signed an anti-competition clause that prohibited her from engaging in a competing business within two years after leaving Flush's employ. Ms. Farino left Flush for a job with Barger Pharmaceuticals, Inc., and Flush sued her for breach of her agreement in Texas state court. Before responding to Flush's complaint in this suit, she agreed to a consent judgment entered by the Texas court. The Texas court accompanied the consent judgment with findings of fact and conclusions of law, holding that the anti-competition agreement was valid and binding. Ms. Farino did not appeal the consent judgment, but later sued Flush in federal court claiming that the anti-competition clause violated federal antitrust laws. **What is Flush's defense in federal court, and should it prevail?**

Explanation

Flush would assert the Texas judgment as a bar to the anti-trust claim asserted in federal court. If Texas follows the common law counterclaim rule, it will succeed.

Rule

(1) First, the res judicata law of Texas will determine the preclusive effect of the Texas consent judgment. (2) Texas may enforce a compulsory counterclaim rule that bars the assertion of a claim that could have been asserted as a counterclaim in the first suit.

Application

If Texas follows the general rule, it will give preclusive effect to a consent judgment entered under these circumstances. Since Ms. Farino did not answer the plaintiff's complaint, she had no opportunity to comply with a pleading requirement that she allege a compulsory counterclaim. Therefore, Flush would assert the *common law* compulsory counterclaim rule, arguing that Ms. Farino cannot be allowed to turn her counterclaim into a second suit that would undermine the consent judgment. If such a rule did not apply, Ms. Farino would be able to reopen the very issue that was determined by judgment in the first suit, and allowing her second suit would directly undermine that judgment. See Martino v. McDonald's System, Inc., 598 F.2d 1079 (7th Cir. 1979).

4. Assume James Fontaine was accused, but later acquitted, of the criminal charge that he knowingly disclosed the name of a secret agent working for the Central Intelligence Agency. In his criminal trial, the U.S. Government presented evidence that Mr. Fontaine violated the federal statute that prevents disclosure, but the jury concluded that this evidence did not prove beyond a reasonable doubt that he had committed the offense. Two suits follow the end of this criminal trial. First, the U.S. Government now sues in a civil suit seeking damages for Mr. Fontaine's disclosure of the CIA agent's identity. That agent, Becky Davis, has also sued Fontaine for the tort of disclosing her identity and seeks damages from him in her own civil action. In both suits, Mr. Fontaine interposes the defense of issue preclusion. In support of this defense, he contends that the judgment of acquittal in the criminal prosecution was based on a jury finding that he did not disclose Ms. Davis's identity as a CIA agent. **(a) Can Mr. Fontaine use issue preclusion to defeat the Government's civil suit? (b) (a) Can Mr. Fontaine use issue preclusion to defeat Ms. Davis's civil suit?**

Explanation

(a) Mr. Fontaine cannot use issue preclusion against the Government in its civil suit.

Rule

Issue preclusion does not apply when the party against whom preclusion is sought had a significantly heavier burden of persuasion with respect to the issue in the initial action than in the subsequent action. See Restatement (Second) Judgments §28(4) (1982).

Application

The Government had the highest burden of persuasion in regard to the issue of disclosure in the criminal trial. There, the Government had to prove beyond a reasonable doubt that Mr. Fontaine disclosed Ms. Davis's identity as a CIA agent. In the second suit, the Government will need only to prove the fact of his disclosure by a preponderance of the evidence, the least burdensome civil standard of persuasion. Therefore, the jury in the criminal trial held only that the Government had not satisfied the onerous criminal burden. A jury in the civil trial could well find in favor of the Government under the lower preponderance burden of persuasion.

Explanation

(b) Mr. Fontaine cannot use issue preclusion to defeat Ms. Davis's suit.

Rule

No res judicata rule can be used to foreclose litigation by someone who was not a party or in privity with a party to the first suit.

Application

Since Ms. Davis was not a party to the criminal trial, she cannot be bound in any way by the determination in that case. Res judicata only prevents a person from having a *second* chance to litigate a claim or issue: It does not prevent courts from adjudicating the same issue more than once. Ms. Davis could not have participated in the criminal trial and has, therefore, had no opportunity to prove that Mr. Fontaine disclosed her CIA status. If a court precluded her from litigating Mr. Fontaine's responsibility for her injury, it would deprive her of the opportunity to assert her rights and would thereby deprive her of due process.

5. Henry Stern was driving his car with his wife, Lilly Young, as his passenger when it collided with two other cars in an intersection. Young sued one of the other drivers, Dan Strong, for her injuries, and Stern joined a claim for his damages for loss of consortium. The jury returned a general verdict finding damages for Young but none for Stern. [Assume the jury was asked only whether Strong should be held liable in damages to Stern.] Stern later brought a suit against Toby Lang, the third driver for the personal injuries he suffered in the accident. Lang claims that the jury in the first suit concluded that Stern was contributorily negligent, and he contends that this finding precludes Stern's second suit. **Should this defense prevail apply?**

Explanation

Lang cannot use claim preclusion to bar Stern's suit because mutuality of parties does not exist between the first and second suits. Lang could assert defensive nonmutual issue preclusion if the requirements for issue preclusion were satisfied.

Rule

The requirements for the successful assertion of issue preclusion are the following: (a) preclusion must be of the same issue of law or fact; (b) that issue must be actually litigated and determined; (c) by a valid and final judgment; and (d) the issue must be essential to that judgment.

Application

Lang's contention is that the jury in the first suit determined that Stern could not recover because his negligence contributed to the accident. One might argue that the issue of Stern's contributory negligence in causing the collision with Strong might well not be the same as the issue of Stern's contributory negligence in colliding with Lang. The answer to that question is mooted by the fact that the jury's decision in the first suit was too inconclusive to establish issue preclusion. The jury's general verdict could represent a decision that Stern was negligent in causing the accident. However, it could just as well represent a conclusion that Strong was liable to both Stern and Young, but that Stern had suffered no actual damages through loss of consortium. The court in the second suit cannot be certain that the issue of Stern's contributory negligence was actually decided, and that means that relitigation of the issue cannot be precluded.

6. The plaintiff from Texas brought suit against a California defendant in federal court in Texas. The defendant filed a motion to dismiss on two grounds; it claimed that the court had no subject matter jurisdiction because this claim was for an amount less than $75,000 and that the court had no personal jurisdiction over the defendant in Texas. The federal district court dismissed the action in a written opinion in which it stated: "This court has neither subject-matter nor personal jurisdiction in this case. The claim asserted by the plaintiff cannot, to a legal certainty, satisfy the amount-in-controversy requirement for general diversity jurisdiction. Furthermore, the nonresident defendant in this case has no minimum contacts with Texas sufficient to make it amenable to the issuance of the court's process." Instead of appealing this decision, the plaintiff immediately brought the same claim in a federal court in California. The defendant filed a motion to dismiss for lack of subject matter jurisdiction, and in this motion contended that the decision of the federal court in

Texas precludes relitigation of that subject matter jurisdictional issue. **Does issue preclusion apply to preclude that federal court from considering the issue of its subject matter jurisdiction? Would your answer change if the plaintiff had appealed the dismissal, and the court of appeals had upheld dismissal on both grounds?**

Explanation

In the absence of a final judgment on the merits, claim preclusion cannot apply. The problem with issue preclusion arises because we cannot determine with certainty that the first court's decision on subject matter jurisdiction was essential to its judgment (or dismissal).

Rule

(1) The Restatement (Second) of Judgments supports the conclusion that a decision that rests on alternative grounds cannot be the basis for issue preclusion as to either. Under older rules, courts barred relitigation of either ground based on the conclusion that both were essential to the court's decision. (2) If the plaintiff had appealed the dismissal, and the court of appeals upheld the dismissal on both grounds, courts would preclude relitigation of both issues.

Application

The defendant cannot use the first court's decision on personal jurisdiction because the issues are not the same: the personal jurisdiction of the court in Texas is different from the personal jurisdiction of the court in California. In this case, the defendant seeks to use the first court's dismissal for lack of subject matter jurisdiction to preclude more litigation of that issue. The defendant's problem arises in trying to satisfy the essential-to-the-judgment requirement for issue preclusion. The plaintiff might argue that the alternative grounds for the first court's decision provides less assurance that that court carefully considered the subject matter jurisdiction issue. Furthermore, because the court stated two grounds for its dismissal a plaintiff is deterred from appealing the case even though it might have thought the court erred in dismissing. For these reasons, many courts refuse to use issue preclusion when the issue to be precluded was not alone the basis for the first court's judgment.

7. A Texas car dealer, Motor Sports, Inc., sold a new BMW automobile to a visiting country music star, Georgia Peach. Ms. Peach thereafter drove her new car home to Tennessee. Two months after the purchase, the BMW's steering system malfunctioned causing Peach to be involved in a serious

accident in California. After recovering from her injuries, Peach filed suit in federal court in California against Motor Sports. After being served in Texas, Motor Sports and its attorney decided that it had no obligation to participate in any way in that suit. Peach took a default judgment against the car dealer for $4 million. She then initiated proceedings in a federal court in Texas to execute the California judgment, but Motor Sports now challenges that judgment as being invalid for lack of personal jurisdiction. **Does res judicata bar Motor Sports from challenging this judgment? Would the answer be different if Motor Sports had appeared in the California proceedings solely to challenge that court's personal jurisdiction?**

Explanation

Claim preclusion bars Motor Sports from challenging the merits of the judgment even though it was a default judgment. However, claim preclusion applies only if this was a valid and final judgment. A court cannot enter a valid judgment unless it has constitutionally sufficient personal jurisdiction over the defendant.

Rule

(1) Even under the full-faith-and-credit requirement of 28 U.S.C. § 1738, the defendant can challenge the judgment if the issuing court lacked personal jurisdiction. (2) However, if Motor Sports had litigated that issue before the federal court in California, it could not now relitigate before the federal court in Texas. Issue preclusion prevents the defendant from having a second challenge to the jurisdiction of the court.

Application

The issue of a court's jurisdiction is critical to the enforceability of the judgment that it enters. Claim preclusion does not prevent Motor Sports from having one opportunity to challenge the jurisdiction of the federal court in California. It can have that opportunity in California, or it can await the plaintiff's attempt to enforce her default judgment in Texas to make its challenge. However, Motor Sports cannot have two chances at the issue: It cannot challenge jurisdiction in California and then attempt to litigate the same issue again in Texas.

8. Acme Medical Inventions, Inc., holds a patent on a stent used for surgical correction of heart problems. Acme brought suit in federal court asserting a federal law claim for infringement of its patent by Bolden Stents, Inc. After a full trial that primarily concerned the validity of Acme's

patent, the federal judge explicitly held that the patent was invalid. On that ground, the court entered a final judgment on the merits in favor of Bolden. Acme did not appeal this judgment but, instead, brought a second suit in federal court against Clark Medical Equipment, Inc., for infringement of its stent patent. Clark contends that Acme's patent is invalid and that the first patent infringement suit precludes Acme from relitigating that issue. **Can Clark use issue preclusion?**

Explanation

Clark cannot use claim preclusion to bar the patent infringement suit because claim preclusion requires mutuality of parties, and Clark was not a party to the first suit. However, most jurisdictions allow issue preclusion when mutuality of parties between the two suits does not exist.

Rule

(1) The usual requirements for issue preclusion must be satisfied before nonmutual issue preclusion can occur. (2) One can assert nonmutual issue preclusion only against someone who was a party to the first suit and had a fair and full opportunity to litigate the issue.

Application

In this instance, the party asserting issue preclusion was not a party to the first suit, but Acme was a party to the first suit and had a full and fair opportunity to defend its patent in that litigation. Under these circumstances, issue preclusion furthers the ends of preventing multiple suits about the same issue and thus saves judicial resources and unnecessary costs to litigants. In this case, Clark has defensively asserted issue preclusion to prevent Acme from relitigating the validity of its patent. No unfairness will be caused Acme, even though it would prefer to relitigate in order to have a different result.

9. A passenger bus owned by Interstate Bus Lines, Inc., (IBL) ran off the road in rainy weather and struck a building. The accident caused serious injuries to ten passengers. While the other nine were recovering from their injuries, Jack Hill sued IBL for $2 million in damages in Arizona, claiming that IBL was negligent in various particulars and that this negligence caused his injuries. After a full trial, the jury held IBL liable for its negligence and awarded Hill $250,000 in damages. The judgment for Hill was upheld on appeal. Immediately after the appellate decision, Sue Lee brought suit in state court in Nevada for her injuries in the bus accident and claimed that IBL was negli-

gent for the same reasons given by the jury in the first suit. Lee seeks a partial summary judgment on the issue of IBL's negligence, which will make IBL liable for any damages she can prove. **Can she use issue preclusion?**

Explanation

Lee apparently can satisfy the four requirements for issue preclusion, but she would be asserting nonmutual issue preclusion offensively. The offensive assertion of nonmutual issue preclusion raises questions about fairness that a court should consider before preventing relitigation.

Rule

(1) If Arizona allows the offensive use of nonmutual issue preclusion, Ms Lee can use it in Nevada. (2) Courts refuse on equitable grounds to allow this brand of issue preclusion when the new plaintiff could easily have joined in the first suit but did not. (3) Further unfairness can result when subsequent plaintiffs seek to use issue preclusion but inconsistent prior judgments exist.

Application

The Nevada court might well allow Lee to assert issue preclusion based on the Arizona judgment if Arizona law allows the offensive use of nonmutual issue preclusion. One concern under Arizona law would be whether Lee could have joined in Hill's suit. This concern arises from the fact that the offensive assertion of issue preclusion can waste rather than save judicial resources. In an accident with multiple injured parties, the benefits of issue preclusion might cause potential plaintiffs not to join together but sue individually and then take advantage of any favorable judgment. In this case, a court would understand that an individual plaintiff from another state would sue in that state. An Arizona court would also consider other factors, such as the reliability of the first judgment. If the Hill suit had been for a negligible amount of money, IBL might not have litigated its rights vigorously. That does not seem to be the case here.

10. Suppose Lena Baker had sued IBL for her injuries in the accident, and the case went to judgment before the Hill case did. In the suit by Baker, the jury found that IBL was not negligent and should not be liable. Hill's judgment is entered later. Under these circumstances, should Lee be able to make offensive use of nonmutual issue preclusion using the finding of negligence in the Hill case rather than in the Baker case?

Explanation

Rule

When inconsistent judgments exist, courts will not allow a subsequent plaintiff to use nonmutual issue preclusion.

Application

Plaintiffs can unfairly wait for favorable judgments before seeking to use issue preclusion offensively. Allowing Lee to choose the Hill judgment under these circumstances is unfair to IBL because the court in Lee's suit cannot with any assurance conclude that this issue has been authoritatively determined. The inconsistent judgments show that IBL could well prevail in the third suit as well as in the first. IBL cannot assert issue preclusion defensively against Lee based on the Baker judgment because Lee was not a party to the Baker suit. Given the different rights of the two parties, inconsistent judgments should prevent plaintiffs from using issue preclusion.

INDEX